NELSON·GCSE
MATHS

INTERMEDIATE 2

BARBARA BALL·DEREK BALL — SERIES EDITORS
CHRISTINE ATKINSON·WENDY FISHER·MARGARET POSTON
JEREMY RICHARDSON·ADRIAN SMITH

Thomas Nelson & Sons Ltd
Nelson House
Mayfield Road
Walton-on-Thames
Surrey KT12 5PL

© Barbara Ball, Derek Ball, Christine Atkinson, Wendy Fisher, Margaret Poston, Jeremy Richardson, Adrian Smith 1999

The right of Barbara Ball, Derek Ball, Christine Atkinson, Wendy Fisher, Margaret Poston, Jeremy Richardson and Adrian Smith to be identified as authors of this work has been asserted by them in accordance with the Copyright, Design and Patents Act 1988.

First published by Thomas Nelson & Sons Ltd 1999
ISBN 0-17-431484-1
9 8 7 6 5 4 3 2
03 02 01 00

All rights reserved. No part of this publication may be reproduced, copied or transmitted in any form or by any means, electronic or mechanical, including photocopy, recording, or any information storage retrieval system, without permission in writing from the publisher or under licence from the Copyright Licensing Authority Ltd, 90 Tottenham Court Road, London W1P 9HE.

Printed by Zrinski Printing and Publishing House, Čakovec, Croatia

Acquisition: Jean Carnall
Editorial: Jenny Lawson, First Class Publishing
Production: Liz Carr
Design & Illustration: Ian Foulis & Associates
Cover design: R&B Creative Services

The authors and publishers are grateful to the following schools involved in trials of material from this series:

Worle School, Avon; Holte School, Birmingham; The Woodrush School, Birmingham; Hayle Community College, Cornwall; Ash Green School, Coventry; Stainburn School, Cumbria; The Deanes School, Essex; Cirencester Kingshill School, Glos.; Pontllanfraith High School, Gwent; The Hayling School, Hants; Swakeleys School, Hillingdon; Crown Hills Community College, Leicester; Hampstead School, London; St Martin's in the Fields High School, London; Kenton School, Newcastle upon Tyne; Walbottle High School, Newcastle upon Tyne; Belfast Royal Academy, Northern Ireland; The Bluecoat School, Nottingham; Bretton Woods School, Peterborough; Eccles C of E School, Salford; Our Lady of Mount Carmel High, Salford; Ludlow C of E School, Salop; St Richard Gwyn R.C. School, South Glam; Headlands School, Wilts.

Some of the revision questions on pages 155–301 have been reproduced from past examination papers, as cited in the text. Copyright in these questions is held by the examintion boards, and the publishers would like to thank the Midland Examining Group (MEG), Northern Examinations and Assessment Board (NEAB), Northern Ireland Council for the Curriculum, Examinations and Assessment (CCEA), Southern Examining Group (SEG), London Examinations, a division of Edexcel Foundation, and the Welsh Joint Education Committee (WJEC) for permission to reproduce this material. The answers supplied to these questions are, however, the responsibility of the authors.

The map on p.241 is based on Ordnance Survey mapping with the permission of The Controller of Her Majesty's Stationery Office, © Crown copyright (399752).

While every effort has been made to trace copyright holders, if any acknowledgements have been inadvertently omitted, the publishers will be pleased to make the necessary arrangements at the earliest opportunity.

CONTENTS

1 Further methods of computation   1

Values of numbers • Without a calculator • Estimation, and the efficient use of a calculator • Four rules of fractions • Fractions and recurring decimals • Reciprocals • Powers and roots • Standard form • Direct proportion • Inverse proportion

2 Transformations   21

Reflecting shapes • Rotating shapes • Translations • Enlargement

3 Algebraic manipulation   41

Changing the subject of a formula • Multiplying out brackets and factorising • Multiplying out two brackets • Factorising into two brackets

4 Statistics and probability   50

Collecting data • Two-way tables • Measuring the average • Interquartile range • Cumulative frequency • Scatter diagrams and correlation • Probability revisited

5 Equations   73

Always, sometimes, never • More linear equations • Simultaneous equations • Quadratic equations

6 Measures revisited   84

Formulae for finding perimeter, area, volume and surface area • Relationships between units • Volume, capacity and density • Upper and lower bounds of measures • Area of a trapezium • Bearings and trigonometry

7 Using graphs to solve problems   102

Using graphs to solve equations • Using graphs to solve simultaneous equations • Graphs of equations with x^2: quadratic graphs • Graphs of equations with x^3: cubic graphs • Graphs of equations with $\frac{1}{x}$: reciprocal graphs • Identifying graphs • Solving quadratic and cubic equations using graphs and trial and improvement • Inequalities • Solving inequalities • Regions • Interpreting graphs of real-life situations

8 Properties of shapes   132

Ruler and compass constructions: perpendiculars • Symmetry in triangles and quadrilaterals • Similarity • Isosceles triangles and right-angled triangles • Regular and irregular polygons • Chords, arcs and tangents • Angle in a semicircle

Revision Exercises   155

REVISION GUIDE   166

Revision Topic Guide   168

Revision Notes and Exercises

NUMBER   169
ALGEBRA   192
SHAPE, SPACE and MEASURES   223
HANDLING DATA   257
COURSE REVISION EXERCISES   281

Answers

Selected Exercises for Chapters 1–8   287
Revision Guide Exercises   289

Index   313

1

FURTHER METHODS OF COMPUTATION

This chapter is about:

- place value in whole numbers and decimals
- equivalence between fractions, decimals and percentages
- arithmetic of whole numbers and decimals without a calculator
- calculating with fractions
- estimating and rounding
- using a calculator efficiently
- recurring decimals
- powers, roots and indices
- reciprocals
- standard form with and without a calculator
- direct and inverse proportion.

Values of numbers

In our place value system, digits stand for different numbers depending on their position.

9 stands for: 90 in 894 9000 in 359 500 $\frac{9}{10}$ in 56.98

DISCUSSION POINT

What does the digit 7 stand for in the number 0.275?

What is 0.275 as a fraction in its simplest form?

What is $\frac{23}{100}$ as a decimal and as a percentage?

What is 24% as a decimal and as a fraction?

EXERCISE 1

1 (a) What does the digit 3 stand for in each of these numbers?

    (i) 0.032   (ii) 3.17   (iii) 7.382   (iv) 11.153

(b) Each of the numbers in part (a) is multiplied by 100. What does the digit 3 stand for in each of the new numbers?

2 **(a)** What does the digit 8 stand for in each of these numbers?

    (i) 382 076   **(ii)** 7.118   **(iii)** 807 156   **(iv)** 17.481

    (b) Each of the numbers in part (a) is divided by 10. What does the digit 8 stand for in each of the new numbers?

3 Write these fractions as decimals, and as percentages.

    (a) $\frac{3}{100}$ **(b)** $\frac{7}{10}$ **(c)** $\frac{21}{100}$ **(d)** $\frac{345}{1000}$ **(e)** $\frac{24}{1000}$

    (f) $\frac{80}{1000}$ **(g)** $\frac{6}{1000}$ **(h)** $\frac{15}{10}$ **(i)** $\frac{204}{100}$ **(j)** $\frac{4}{100}$

4 Write these fractions as decimals, and as percentages.

    (a) $\frac{1}{5}$ **(b)** $\frac{4}{5}$ **(c)** $\frac{3}{50}$ **(d)** $\frac{7}{20}$ **(e)** $\frac{11}{20}$ **(f)** $\frac{2}{25}$ **(g)** $\frac{18}{25}$

5 Write these decimals as percentages, and as fractions, in their simplest form.

    (a) 0.8   **(b)** 0.3   **(c)** 0.64   **(d)** 0.35   **(e)** 0.09

    (f) 0.005   **(g)** 0.104   **(h)** 0.975   **(i)** 0.045   **(j)** 0.1875

6 Write these percentages as decimals, and as fractions, in their simplest form.

    (a) 80%   **(b)** 55%   **(c)** 4%   **(d)** 12.5%   **(e)** 67.5%

    (f) 0.1%   **(g)** 30.5%   **(h)** $7\frac{1}{2}$%   **(i)** $6\frac{1}{4}$%   **(j)** $66\frac{2}{3}$%

Without a calculator

DISCUSSION POINT

How can you work out 0.275×100, without a calculator?

How can you work out $0.275 \div 10$, without a calculator?

How can you work out these, without a calculator?

    0.0815×300 $7.47 \div 90$

How do you calculate these?

    45% of £80   17.5% of £28 $33\frac{1}{3}$% of £75

EXERCISE 2

1 Find the answers to these.

    (a) 7.43×10 **(b)** 0.056×10 **(c)** 4.003×100 **(d)** $0.059\,02 \times 1000$

    (e) 23.06×1000 **(f)** 34.125×100 **(g)** $21 \div 100$ **(h)** $3.15 \div 100$

    (i) $0.4 \div 10$ **(j)** $75 \div 1000$ **(k)** $0.05 \div 100$ **(l)** $0.072 \div 10$

2 Find the answers to these.

    (**a**) 2.7×20 (**b**) $27 \div 300$ (**c**) $8.64 \div 200$ (**d**) 0.41×4000

    (**e**) 23×600 (**f**) $6.3 \div 900$ (**g**) 5.35×80 (**h**) $720 \div 600$

    (**i**) $0.087 \div 30$ (**j**) 0.0045×8000

3 Find these amounts.

    (**a**) 25% of 32   (**b**) 75% of 56   (**c**) 35% of 60   (**d**) 56% of 50

    (**e**) 60% of £3.10   (**f**) 15% of £72.60   (**g**) 2% of 650   (**h**) 10% of 345

    (**i**) 5% of 568   (**j**) 95% of 444

4 Find these amounts.

    (**a**) 12.5% of 56   (**b**) 55% of 136   (**c**) 62.5% of 540

    (**d**) 40% of 1.6   (**e**) 17.5% of £3.48   (**f**) 17.5% of £422.40

    (**g**) $33\frac{1}{3}$% of 429   (**h**) $66\frac{2}{3}$% of 375   (**i**) $3\frac{1}{3}$% of 666

    (**j**) $96\frac{2}{3}$% of 666

DISCUSSION POINT

How would you calculate 347×58, without a calculator?

How would you calculate $567 \div 39$, without a calculator?

There are two ways of giving the answer to the second question.

- If you have 567 matches and want to fill boxes with 39 matches in each box, you will give the answer one way (with a 'remainder').
- If you have 39 objects which weigh a total of 567 g and want to find their mean weight you will give the answer another way (with decimals).

EXERCISE 3

1 Calculate these multiplications.

    (**a**) 24×23 (**b**) 34×46 (**c**) 47×53 (**d**) 83×19

    (**e**) 57×58 (**f**) 69×96 (**g**) 33×72 (**h**) 47×78

2 Calculate these multiplications.

    (**a**) 123×12 (**b**) 237×23 (**c**) 388×39 (**d**) 409×53

    (**e**) 807×67 (**f**) 422×247 (**g**) 336×663 (**h**) 509×708

3 Calculate these divisions.

    (**a**) $682 \div 22$ (**b**) $918 \div 27$ (**c**) $663 \div 39$ (**d**) $943 \div 41$

    (**e**) $1184 \div 37$ (**f**) $2898 \div 46$ (**g**) $5226 \div 78$ (**h**) $1914 \div 66$

4 Calculate these divisions. Give each answer as a whole number and a remainder.

(a) $78 \div 14$ (b) $90 \div 17$ (c) $300 \div 13$ (d) $550 \div 29$

(e) $700 \div 63$ (f) $683 \div 38$ (g) $729 \div 26$ (h) $1000 \div 91$

5 Calculate these divisions. Give each answer as a decimal, correct to 2 decimal places.

(a) $20 \div 17$ (b) $40 \div 19$ (c) $78 \div 45$ (d) $300 \div 23$

(e) $437 \div 73$ (f) $1000 \div 13$ (g) $897 \div 79$ (h) $603 \div 38$

Estimation, and the efficient use of a calculator

DISCUSSION POINT

How can you make an estimate for the answers to these calculations?

$$5.88 \times 312 \qquad (9.85)^2 \times 15.6 \qquad 0.248 \times 8.41$$

How can you work out these, using a calculator?

$$9.04 \div (12.3 - 3.1^2) \qquad \frac{4.78 - 1.94}{5.63 + 0.42} \qquad \frac{6.21^2 + 1.79^2}{3.02^2 - 1.88^2}$$

EXERCISE 4

1 Estimate the answer for each of these. Do *not* use a calculator.

(a) 3.15×1.84 (b) 52.1×0.248

(c) $7958 \div 39.5$ (d) $593.8 \div 0.0314$

(e) 34.7×0.0612 (f) $0.744 \times 2.52 \times 39.7$

(g) $(9.69 \times 0.103) \div 2.13$ (h) $(2.05 \times 0.475) \div 10.3$

(i) $41.24 \div (4.88 \times 2.30)$

2 Estimate the answer for each of these. Do *not* use a calculator.

(a) $\sqrt{103} \div (4.78)^2$ (b) $\dfrac{7.84 \times 2.81}{3.28 - 1.04}$

(c) $\dfrac{8.23 \div 2.17^2}{0.985}$ (d) $15.195 - (3.08 - 0.878)$

(e) $\dfrac{17.72 + 2.55}{8.38 - 3.51}$ (f) $\dfrac{23.76 - 8.19}{3.859 + 0.263}$

3 Use a calculator to work out the answer to each of the calculations in Questions 1 and 2. Give your answers correct to 3 significant figures.

Four rules of fractions

DISCUSSION POINT

The number $\frac{7}{2}$ means 7 halves. $\frac{7}{2}$ is called a **top-heavy fraction**.

This picture might help explain why $\frac{7}{2} = 3\frac{1}{2}$.

$3\frac{1}{2}$ is called a **mixed number**.

• How would these be written as mixed numbers?

$\quad \frac{5}{3} \qquad\qquad \frac{5}{2} \qquad\qquad \frac{8}{3} \qquad\qquad \frac{7}{4}$

• How would these be written as top-heavy fractions?

$\quad 2\frac{1}{4} \qquad\qquad 1\frac{1}{5} \qquad\qquad 3\frac{3}{4} \qquad\qquad 5\frac{2}{3}$

EXERCISE 5

1 Convert these to mixed numbers.

(a) $\frac{7}{3}$ (b) $\frac{11}{2}$ (c) $\frac{21}{4}$ (d) $\frac{12}{5}$ (e) $\frac{13}{7}$ (f) $\frac{21}{8}$

2 Convert these to top-heavy fractions.

(a) $1\frac{1}{6}$ (b) $3\frac{1}{5}$ (c) $4\frac{3}{4}$ (d) $5\frac{5}{8}$ (e) $1\frac{2}{7}$ (f) $8\frac{1}{3}$

DISCUSSION POINT

How can you work out these, without a calculator?

$\quad 3\frac{3}{4} + \frac{7}{8} \qquad\qquad 5\frac{1}{2} - 2\frac{2}{3} \qquad\qquad 4\frac{1}{4} \times 3\frac{1}{2} \qquad\qquad 9 \div \frac{3}{4}$

EXERCISE 6

1 (a) $\frac{3}{4} + \frac{1}{2}$ (b) $\frac{1}{4} + \frac{1}{8}$ (c) $\frac{1}{3} + \frac{1}{6}$ (d) $\frac{4}{5} + \frac{7}{10}$

(e) $\frac{3}{4} + \frac{1}{3}$ (f) $2\frac{5}{8} + 1\frac{3}{4}$ (g) $5\frac{2}{3} + 12\frac{2}{3}$ (h) $7\frac{1}{2} + 6\frac{3}{5}$

(i) $23\frac{5}{6} + 6\frac{2}{3}$ (j) $4\frac{2}{5} + 2\frac{3}{4}$

2 (a) $1 - \frac{2}{5}$ **(b)** $2\frac{1}{4} - 1\frac{3}{4}$ **(c)** $\frac{3}{5} - \frac{1}{10}$ **(d)** $\frac{7}{8} - \frac{3}{4}$

    (e) $\frac{5}{6} - \frac{2}{9}$ **(f)** $8\frac{3}{8} - 3\frac{3}{4}$ **(g)** $8\frac{1}{5} - 2\frac{1}{2}$ **(h)** $6\frac{2}{3} - 4\frac{1}{2}$

    (i) $11\frac{1}{3} - \frac{3}{5}$ **(j)** $3\frac{1}{4} - 2\frac{3}{5}$

3 (a) $\frac{3}{8} \times \frac{2}{3}$ **(b)** $\frac{1}{5} \times \frac{3}{4}$ **(c)** $\frac{1}{2} \times \frac{5}{8}$ **(d)** $\frac{1}{3} \times \frac{9}{10}$

    (e) $6 \times \frac{3}{4}$ **(f)** $7\frac{1}{2} \times 3\frac{1}{3}$ **(g)** $2\frac{1}{4} \times 3\frac{1}{5}$ **(h)** $12\frac{1}{4} \times 2\frac{2}{7}$

    (i) $6\frac{2}{5} \times \frac{5}{8}$ **(j)** $1\frac{4}{5} \times 3\frac{1}{3}$

4 (a) $\frac{5}{8} \div 5$ **(b)** $\frac{3}{4} \div 6$ **(c)** $4 \div \frac{1}{3}$ **(d)** $2\frac{1}{2} \div \frac{1}{2}$

    (e) $\frac{1}{2} \div \frac{1}{4}$ **(f)** $\frac{1}{10} \div \frac{1}{5}$ **(g)** $1\frac{3}{5} \div 1\frac{1}{3}$ **(h)** $6\frac{2}{5} \div 1\frac{3}{5}$

    (i) $1\frac{3}{4} \div 4\frac{3}{8}$ **(j)** $4\frac{1}{2} \div 7\frac{1}{2}$ **(k)** $8\frac{1}{3} \div 1\frac{2}{3}$ **(l)** $2\frac{1}{4} \div \frac{1}{5}$

> Work out Questions 5 and 6 just as if the letters were numbers.

5 (a) $\frac{a}{2} + \frac{a}{4}$ **(b)** $\frac{x}{2} + \frac{y}{3}$ **(c)** $\frac{b}{3} - \frac{c}{6}$ **(d)** $\frac{p}{4} - \frac{p}{6}$

    (e) $\frac{e}{3} \times \frac{f}{4}$ **(f)** $\frac{x}{2} \times \frac{x}{6}$

6 (a) $\dfrac{(x + 1)}{2} + \dfrac{x}{3}$ **(b)** $\dfrac{(a - 2)}{3} + \dfrac{(3a + 2)}{9}$

    (c) $\dfrac{(c + 3)}{3} - \dfrac{(c + 2)}{6}$ **(d)** $\dfrac{(2y - 3)}{3} - \dfrac{(3y - 2)}{5}$

7 A student walks for $\frac{1}{3}$ mile to the bus stop, and then travels $5\frac{3}{4}$ miles by bus to school.

    (a) What is the total distance travelled to school by this student?

    (b) A second student is driven to school for a distance of $7\frac{1}{2}$ miles. How much further does this student travel to school?

8 To change gallons to litres, you can work out an approximate answer by multiplying the number of gallons by $4\frac{1}{2}$.
Use this approximation to change $7\frac{1}{2}$ gallons into litres.

9 It takes $2\frac{1}{2}$ minutes to swim $3\frac{3}{4}$ lengths of a swimming pool at a constant speed.

    (a) How long does it take to swim one length of the pool?

    (b) If the pool is 50 m long, how far does the swimmer travel in one minute?

10 A 1-litre carton of milk contains the equivalent of $1\frac{3}{4}$ pints.

    (a) How many pints are the same as $5\frac{1}{2}$ litres?

    (b) What fraction of a litre is 1 pint?

Fractions and recurring decimals

DISCUSSION POINT

$\frac{1}{3} = 0.333\,33...$

The digit 3 is repeated forever! This can be written as $0.\dot{3}$. The dot above the 3 means that the digit recurs.

$\frac{5}{12} = 0.416\,666... = 0.416\dot{6}$.

The dot is just above the 6 because this is the digit that recurs.

$\frac{2}{7} = 0.285\,714\,285\,714\,285\,714\,28... = 0.\dot{2}85\,71\dot{4}$.

This time the whole pattern between the two dots recurs.

How can these be written as recurring decimals?

$\frac{2}{3}$ $\qquad$ $\frac{5}{9}$ $\qquad$ $\frac{5}{7}$ $\qquad$ $\frac{1}{6}$

EXERCISE 7

1 (a) Write down all the fractions you can make using two of the digits 3, 4 and 6.

(b) Change each fraction to a decimal, correct to 3 significant figures. Use recurring decimals if necessary.

(c) Write the fractions in order of size.

2 (a) Write down all the fractions you can make with two of the digits 1, 7 and 9.

(b) Change each fraction to a decimal.

(c) Write the fractions in order of size.

(d) What is the connection between the smallest and largest fraction?

3 Choose your own set of three digits. Answer Question 2 for your three digits.

COURSEWORK OPPORTUNITY

Spreadsheet

Recurring decimals

The period of a recurring decimal is the number of digits in the repeating pattern.

$\frac{1}{7} = 0.\dot{1}42\,85\dot{7}$ has a period of 6

$\frac{1}{13} = 0.\dot{0}76\,92\dot{3}$ has a period of 6

$\frac{1}{11} = 0.\dot{0}\dot{9}$ has a period of 2.

♦ Explore the periods of different decimals.
   You could explore decimals where the number on the bottom is prime
   ($\frac{1}{7}$, $\frac{1}{11}$, $\frac{1}{13}$, etc.) separately from others ($\frac{1}{12}$, $\frac{1}{14}$, $\frac{1}{15}$, $\frac{1}{18}$ etc.).
♦ Families of decimals can be explored: e.g. $\frac{1}{7}$, $\frac{2}{7}$, $\frac{3}{7}$, $\frac{4}{7}$, $\frac{5}{7}$, $\frac{6}{7}$. A wheel can be
   used to summarise the results for a family.
   This wheel is for sevenths.
♦ Look for patterns in wheels.
   Some families need two or more wheels.

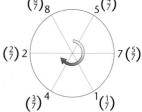

Reciprocals

DISCUSSION POINT

The reciprocal of 4 is $1 \div 4 = \frac{1}{4}$.   The reciprocal of $\frac{1}{2}$ is $1 \div \frac{1}{2} = 2$.

The reciprocal of $\frac{3}{4}$ is $1 \div \frac{3}{4} = \frac{4}{3}$.   The reciprocal of 0.4 is $1 \div 0.4 = 2.5$.

• What does the word **reciprocal** mean?
• What are the reciprocals of these numbers?

   $\frac{3}{8}$ $3\frac{1}{2}$ 8   1   0.9

EXERCISE 8

1 Write down the reciprocals of these numbers.

   (a) 5   (b) 10   (c) 9   (d) 27

2 Find the reciprocals of these numbers.
   Give your answers as mixed numbers.

   (a) $\frac{1}{100}$ (b) $\frac{2}{3}$ (c) $\frac{5}{8}$ (d) $\frac{1}{6}$

3 Find the reciprocals of these numbers.

   (a) $3\frac{1}{4}$ (b) $4\frac{1}{2}$ (c) $1\frac{1}{3}$ (d) $2\frac{2}{7}$

4 Find the reciprocals of these numbers. Give your answers as decimals.
   (a) 0.8   (b) 0.25   (c) 2.5   (d) 0.75

5 (a) What is the reciprocal of $\frac{2}{5}$?
   (b) What is the reciprocal of your answer to part (a)?
   (c) What do you notice?

6 Choose any number. Write down its reciprocal. Write down the reciprocal of your answer. What do you notice?

7 (a) What is the reciprocal of $\frac{3}{7}$?

(b) Multiply $\frac{3}{7}$ by its reciprocal.

(c) Repeat this with several other numbers.

(d) What do you notice about your results?

Powers and roots

Five squared is twenty-five and, so, the **square root** of twenty-five is five.
$$5^2 = 25 \Rightarrow \sqrt{25} = 5$$
Four cubed is sixty-four and, so, the **cube root** of sixty-four is 4.
$$4^3 = 64 \Rightarrow \sqrt[3]{64} = 4$$
Three to the power of four is eighty-one and, so, the **fourth root** of eighty-one is three.
$$3^4 = 81 \Rightarrow \sqrt[4]{81} = 3$$

EXERCISE 9

1 Find the value of each of these.

(a) 2^4 (b) 3^5 (c) 10^4 (d) 5^4 (e) 6^3

(f) $\sqrt[4]{16}$ (g) $\sqrt[3]{1000}$ (h) $\sqrt[3]{125}$ (i) $\sqrt[3]{64}$ (j) $\sqrt[4]{81}$

2 For most of these, the value is a whole number. If the value is a whole number, find it.

(a) 5^4 (b) 2^7 (c) 6^4 (d) 4^5

(e) 7^4 (f) 5^1 (g) $\sqrt{169}$ (h) $\sqrt{56}$

(i) $\sqrt[3]{27}$ (j) $\sqrt[7]{128}$ (k) $\sqrt[5]{120}$ (l) $\sqrt[4]{100}$

DISCUSSION POINT

This table shows powers of 2. How should it be completed?

			2^{-1}	2^0	2^1	2^2		
					2	4	8	

- What does this tell you about the value of 2^0?
- What does this tell you about the values of 2^{-2} and 2^{-3}?
- What is the value of 2^{-5}? What is the value of 5^{-2}?
- What is the connection between negative indices and reciprocals?

The power is sometimes called the **index**.
$$2^3 \quad 2^{-4}$$
      index

The plural of index is **indices**.

EXERCISE 10

1 Produce a table, like the one in the DISCUSSION POINT on page 9, using 5 instead of 2. Use indices from –4 to 4.

2 Produce another table, like the one in the DISCUSSION POINT, using the number 9.

3 Produce another table, using the number 10.

4 Write down the value of each of these.

(a) 5^0 (b) 7^0 (c) 8^0 (d) x^0 (e) $(2a)^0$

(f) $(a + b)^0$ (g) 5×4^0 (h) 3×6^0 (i) $2a^0$ (j) $7y^0$

5 What is the connection between

(a) 2^2 and 2^{-2}?   (b) 9^1 and 9^{-1}?

(c) 5^3 and 5^{-3}?   (d) y^4 and y^{-4}?

(e) y^n and y^{-n}?

6 Write each of these as a fraction.

(a) 7^{-2} (b) 6^{-3} (c) 2^{-5} (d) 9^{-3} (e) $(\frac{1}{2})^{-1}$ (f) $(\frac{2}{3})^{-2}$

DISCUSSION POINT

In these, each * stands for a digit. Find the digits. Discuss the methods you use to find the digits.

$2^2 \times 2^3 \times 2^4 = 2^*$ $3^8 \div 3^5 = 3^*$ $10^{-4} \times 10^2 = 10^{-*}$ $5^{-3} \times 5^{-4} = 5^{-*}$

$10^2 \div 10^{-5} = 10^*$ $(10^2)^3 = 10^*$ $4^3 \times 3^4 = 2^* \times 3^*$ $a^5 \times a^3 = a^*$

$p^{-2} \div p^{-5} = p^*$ $5a^3 \times 6a^2 = {**}a^*$

- Now simplify each of these.

  $16a^3 \div 8a^2$ $18n \div 3n^2$ $12c^3 \div 4c^3$ $4e \times 5f^2$ $(y^3)^2$ $(2d^4)^3$

- Is $2a^3$ the same as $(2a)^3$? Explain.

EXERCISE 11

1 In these, some digits have been replaced by stars.
Copy each of them, putting back the digits.

(a) $3 \times 3^2 \times 3^3 = 3^*$ (b) $2^5 \div 2^3 = 2^*$

(c) $5^4 \times 5^3 \div 5 = 5^*$ (d) $7^5 \times 7^* \div 7^6 = 7^8$

Nelson GCSE Maths   FURTHER METHODS OF COMPUTATION (INTERMEDIATE)

2 Answer Question 1 for these.

    (a) $6^{-2} \times 6^4 = 6\star$

    (b) $8^{-2} \div 8^{-1} = 8^{-\star}$

    (c) $10^{\star} \times 10^{-3} \times 10^{-4} = 10^{-2}$

    (d) $7^{-1} \div 7^{-3} = 7\star$

    (e) $4 \div 4^{\star} = 4^{-2}$

    (f) $12^{-2} \div 12^{-5} = 12\star$

3 Simplify each of these.

    (a) $d^4 \times d^5$ **(b)** $e^8 \div e^3$ **(c)** $a^6 \div a^7$ **(d)** $5b^3 \times 3b$

    (e) $12c^2 \div 12c$ **(f)** $18e^4 \div 12e^6$ **(g)** $4f^2 \times 16g^3$ **(h)** $(h^4)^6$

    (i) $(3j^2)^5$ **(j)** $(k^2)^{-4}$ **(k)** $15d^{-1} \div 5d^{-4}$ **(l)** $(10m^{-4})^{-3}$

4 Simplify each of these.

    (a) $a^3b \times b^4$ **(b)** $x^3y \times xy^2$ **(c)** $3e^2f^2 \times 4ef^3$ **(d)** $6p^3q^2 \div 3pq$

    (e) $(2ab)^3$ **(f)** $(4c^2d^3)^2$

5 Find the value of p in each of these.

    (a) $3^p = 27$ **(b)** $p^3 = 125$ **(c)** $5 \times 2^p = 80$ **(d)** $4^p \times \frac{5}{32} = 160$

6 Find the value of x in each of these.

    (a) $25 \times 125 = 5^x$ **(b)** $9 \times 3^2 = 3^x$ **(c)** $4^3 \times 16 = 4^x$ **(d)** $25 \div 5^x = 5^{-1}$

    (e) $(2^3)^x = 2^{12}$ **(f)** $(5^x)^{-2} = 5^{-8}$

7 Find the value of x, y and z in each of these.

    (a) $6^5 = 2^x \times 3^y$

    (b) $3^3 \times 6^4 = 2^x \times 3^y$

    (c) $35 \times 49 = 5^x \times 7^y$

    (d) $4^2 \times 9^3 \times 6^4 = 2^x \times 3^y$

    (e) $6^5 \div 6^2 = 2^x \times 3^y$

    (f) $35 \times 49 \times 14 \times 10 = 2^x \times 5^y \times 7^z$

    (g) $10^5 \div 6^5 = 2^x \times 3^y \times 5^z$

    (h) $2^5 \times 3^3 = 12^x \times 6^y$

8 Find the value of x, y and z in each of these.

    (a) $2^3 + 2^4 = 2^x \times 3^y$

    (b) $2^7 \times 3^8 - 2^6 \times 3^8 = 2^x \times 3^y$

    (c) $2^5 \times 3^9 - 2^5 \times 3^8 = 2^x \times 3^y$

    (d) $2^5 \times 3^7 + 2^6 \times 3^7 = 2^x \times 3^y$

    (e) $2^6 \times 3^3 + 2^5 \times 3^4 = 2^x \times 3^y \times 5^z$

Standard form

35 000 can be written as 3.5×10^4.

0.0641 can be written as 6.41×10^{-2}.

In general, a number is written in standard form as:

A is a number, between   → $A \times 10^n$ ← n is a whole number,

1 and 10.   positive or negative.

EXERCISE 12

1 Write each of these in standard form.

(a) 53   (b) 761.8   (c) 0.014   (d) 0.000 045 601

(e) 2 000 000

2 Write each of these so they are *not* in standard form.

(a) 2.65×10^3 (b) 1.06×10^7 (c) 3×10^{-1} (d) $2.007\,006 \times 10^{-3}$

(e) 9.03×10^{-3}

DISCUSSION POINT

How can you work out these, without a calculator, leaving your answers in standard form?

$$(1.2 \times 10^4) \times 3 \qquad (1.5 \times 10^3) \times (4 \times 10^4) \qquad (4 \times 10^3)^2$$

$$(8.4 \times 10^6) \div (2 \times 10^4) \qquad (2 \times 10^3) \div 4 \qquad \sqrt{9 \times 10^6}$$

$$(5 \times 10^3) \times (3 \times 10^4) \qquad (6 \times 10^4) + (7 \times 10^3) \qquad (3 \times 10^7) - (9 \times 10^6)$$

EXERCISE 13

1 Write the answer to each of these calculations in standard form.

(a) $(1.4 \times 10^3) \times (3 \times 10^2)$ (b) $(5 \times 10^5) \times (1.2 \times 10^3)$

(c) $(2.1 \times 10^3) \times 4$ (d) $(3 \times 10^5) \times 4$

(e) $(6 \times 10^2) \times 5$ (f) $(5 \times 10^4) \times (3 \times 10^2)$

2 Write the answer to each of these calculations in standard form.

(a) $(2 \times 10^3)^2$ (b) $(3 \times 10^4)^2$

(c) $(8.1 \times 10^4) \div 3$ (d) $(4.2 \times 10^3) \div 2.1$

(e) $(4 \times 10^6) \div 8$ (f) $(7.5 \times 10^5) \div (2.5 \times 10^2)$

3 Write the answer to each of these calculations in standard form.

(a) $(9.3 \times 10^7) \div (3 \times 10^4)$ (b) $(4.8 \times 10^6) \div (6 \times 10^3)$

(c) $\sqrt{4 \times 10^2}$ (d) $(2 \times 10^7) \div (5 \times 10^2)$

(e) $5 \times 10^3 \times (3 \times 10^2)$ (f) $(2 \times 10^6) \div (8 \times 10^2)$

4 Write the answer to each of these calculations in standard form.

(a) $(2.3 \times 10^5) + (7 \times 10^4)$ (b) $(8.4 \times 10^3) + (9.2 \times 10^4)$

(c) $(5.9 \times 10^7) - (8 \times 10^6)$ (d) $(6 \times 10^4) - (7 \times 10^2)$

DISCUSSION POINT

How can you work out these, without a calculator, leaving your answers in standard form?

$(1.4 \times 10^{-3}) \times 3$	$(1.3 \times 10^3) \times (5 \times 10^{-5})$	$\sqrt{4 \times 10^{-6}}$
$(3.6 \times 10^{-6}) \div (3 \times 10^4)$	$(2 \times 10^4)^{-2}$	
$(4 \times 10^{-3}) \times (3 \times 10^{-4})$	$(6 \times 10^{-4}) + (7 \times 10^{-3})$	$(4 \times 10^{-5}) - (8 \times 10^{-6})$

EXERCISE 14

1 Write the answer to each of these calculations in standard form.

   (a) $(1.6 \times 10^4) \times (4 \times 10^{-1})$ **(b)** $(2.5 \times 10^{-3}) \times (3 \times 10^{-1})$

   (c) $(4 \times 10^{-2}) \times 7.5$ **(d)** $(7 \times 10^8) \times (8 \times 10^{-2})$

   (e) $(2.4 \times 10^{-2}) \times (5 \times 10^4)$ **(f)** $(8 \times 10^3) \times (3.5 \times 10^{-5})$

2 Write the answer to each of these calculations in standard form.

   (a) $(6 \times 10^{-2}) \times (9 \times 10^{-3})$ **(b)** $(1.2 \times 10^{-2})^2$

   (c) $(6.3 \times 10^{-3}) \div 9$ **(d)** $(3.6 \times 10^1) \div (9 \times 10^{-3})$

   (e) $(2.4 \times 10^{-3}) \div (8 \times 10^{-5})$ **(f)** $\sqrt{9 \times 10^{-4}}$

3 Write the answer to each of these calculations in standard form.

   (a) $(7 \times 10^{-5}) + (5 \times 10^{-5})$ **(b)** $(8 \times 10^{-3}) - (5.1 \times 10^{-4})$

   (c) $\sqrt{8.1 \times 10^{-5}}$

DISCUSSION POINT

How can you use a calculator to work out the answers to questions like those in the last two exercises? Use a calculator to check your answers to the last two exercises.

EXERCISE 15

1 This table shows the sizes of some of the oceans and seas of the world.

   (a) How many times is the area of the Arctic Ocean greater than the area of the Black Sea?

   (b) What is the difference in the areas of the Mediterranean Sea and the Black Sea?

   (c) What is the combined area of the Atlantic Ocean and the Caribbean Sea?

Ocean/sea	Approx. area (in sq. miles)
Pacific	6.4×10^7
Atlantic	3.2×10^7
Indian	2.8×10^7
Arctic	5.1×10^6
Mediterranean	1.0×10^6
Caribbean	7.5×10^5
Black	1.7×10^5

Nelson GCSE Maths   FURTHER METHODS OF COMPUTATION (INTERMEDIATE)

Population density is the average number of people living in each square kilometre of a country.
Population density = population ÷ area

2 (a) France has a population of 5.5×10^7 and an area of 5.5×10^5 square kilometres. What is the population density of France?

(b) Japan has a population of 1.2×10^9 and an area of 3.7×10^5 square kilometres. What is the population density of Japan?

(c) The area of the UK is approximately 2.4×10^5 square kilometres. The population density is estimated as 240 people per square kilometre. Estimate the population of the UK.

3 This diagram shows the main stars that make up Orion and the distance of each star from Earth.

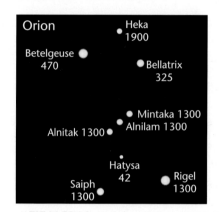

Orion is the name given to a group of stars. This group can be regularly seen on a clear night. The distance to a star is measured in light years.

(a) Which of the stars in Orion is furthest from Earth?

(b) How many times is the distance to Rigel greater than the distance to Bellatrix?

(c) How many light years further is Heka than Betelgeuse?

(d) One light year is 9.5×10^{12} km.
How far from Earth, in kilometres, is the nearest star in Orion?

4 The nearest star to Earth is the Sun, at a distance of 1.5×10^8 km. The next nearest star is called Alpha Centauri, which is 2.6×10^5 times further away than the Sun. How far is Alpha Centauri from Earth?

5 (a) The total mass of all the oceans is estimated as 1.35×10^{18} tons. The total mass of the planet Earth is 4.4×10^3 times greater than the mass of the oceans. Estimate the mass of Earth.

(b) The mass of the planet Pluto is about 0.004 times the mass of Earth. Estimate the mass of Pluto.

6 The common wasp has an average length of 1.4×10^{-2} m. Wasps' nests can contain as many as 2×10^4 wasps. If all the wasps in the nest flew in one long line, nose-to-tail, how long would the line of wasps be?

Direct proportion

DISCUSSION POINT

This table shows the cost of different numbers of chocolate bars.

Number of bars (n)	2	5	8	10
Cost (C)	50p	£1.25	£2	£2.50

- How can you work out the cost of 20 bars of chocolate?
- If you *treble* the number of bars of chocolate, what happens to the cost?
- If you *halve* the number of bars of chocolate, what happens to the cost?

The values of C and n in the DISCUSSION POINT above are said to be **directly proportional**.
This graph shows the relationship between C and n.

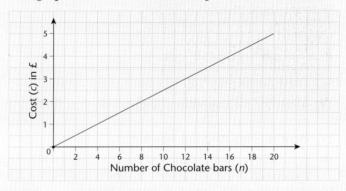

When two quantities are directly proportional, the graph is a straight line through the origin.

EXERCISE 16

1 The table shows how many French francs you can buy at a particular bank for different amounts of money.

Pounds (£)	2	3	5	10	20	50
Francs (fr)	18.4	27.6	46	92	184	414

(a) Is the number of pounds directly proportional to the number of francs?

(b) What is the exchange rate (in other words, how many francs do you get for a pound)?

(c) How many francs would you get for £50?

(d) What is 414 francs worth in pounds?

2 Another bank offers 9.5 francs for every £1, but always charges a fee of £3 for changing the money.

   (a) How much will it cost to buy 19 francs?

   (b) How much will it cost to buy 95 francs?

   (c) Is the number of pounds directly proportional to the number of francs at this bank?
Explain your answer.

3 A woman is allowed to earn £5000 before she has to pay any income tax.
She then pays 25% of anything more than £5000 that she earns.
Is the amount of tax she pays proportional to her earnings?
Give reasons for your answer.

4 Monsieur Ohm, a French scientist, carried out experiments measuring voltage (V) and current (I) in an electrical circuit.
Here are some results.

Voltage (V)	50	60	80	120	200
Current (I)	124	154	200	295	510

   (a) Draw a line graph to represent these results.

   (b) Allowing for experimental error, do you think V is directly proportional to I?
Give reasons for your answer.

5 When paying for your electricity, there is always a fixed standing charge that you pay every time you have a bill.
You then pay money for every unit of electricity used.
Is the amount of your bill proportional to the quantity of electricity used?

6 If two coaches can seat 88 people, how many people can be seated on five similar coaches?

7 If five books cost £38, how much would seven books cost?

8 Eight video tapes cost £36. How much will five video tapes cost?

9 A train travelling at a constant speed covers 25 miles in half an hour.
How far will it travel in 45 minutes?

10 Four CDs cost £51.96. How much will ten CDs cost?

DISCUSSION POINT

This table shows the radii of some circles and their corresponding areas.

Radius (r)	1	2	3	4	5	6
Area (A)	3.14	12.57	28.27	50.27	78.54	113.10

- Is the area of the circle proportional to its radius?

Draw a graph of area against (radius)^2.

- Is A directly proportional to r^2?
- What is the value of $A \div r^2$?

Inverse proportion

DISCUSSION POINT

In a lottery game, the main prize of £6000 is shared equally between any winners. How can you complete this table?

Number of winners (n)	1	2		8	10		25
Prize money each person gets (P)	6000	3000	1200	750		300	

- If you *double* the number of winners, what happens to the prize money each person gets?
- If you *halve* the number of winners, what happens to the prize money each person gets?

In the DISCUSSION POINT above, the prize money is **inversely proportional** to the number of winners. If P and n are inversely proportional then P multiplied by n is constant. In this case, $P \times n = 6000$.

The graph showing the relationship between P and n is a **hyperbola**.

If, instead, P is plotted against $\frac{1}{n}$, the graph is a straight line.

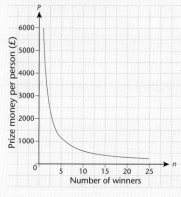

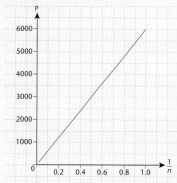

EXERCISE 17

1 A train is travelling on a journey of 120 miles.

(a) Copy and complete this table showing the time taken for the journey at different average speeds.

Average speed (m.p.h.)	30	40	60		100	
Time taken (hours)	4	3		1.5		1

(b) Draw a graph to represent the information in this table.

(c) Explain why the time taken for the journey is inversely proportional to the average speed.

2 The time taken to complete a job is inversely proportional to the number of people working.
It takes 6 people 18 hours to complete the job.

(a) How long would it take with 3 people working?

(b) How long would it take with 9 people working?

3 A teacher has £120 to spend on books.

(a) Copy and complete this table which shows information about the number of books that can be bought and the cost of the books.

Cost of each book (£c)				4	5	6		11
Number of books that can be bought (n)							10	

(b) Is *n* inversely proportional to *c*?
Explain your answer.

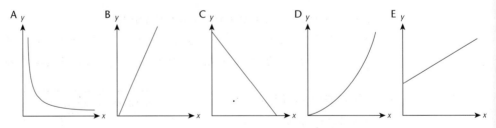

4 (a) Which of these graphs suggests *y* is directly proportional to *x*?

(b) Which of the graphs suggests *y* is inversely proportional to *x*?

Nelson GCSE Maths FURTHER METHODS OF COMPUTATION (INTERMEDIATE)

Estimation

Make an estimate of the answer to a calculation to check that your answer is correct.

	Roughly	Using a calculator
4.15×9.89	$4 \times 10 = 40$	41.0 to 3 s.f.
$\dfrac{4.96^2 + 3.11^2}{16.89}$	$\dfrac{25 + 9}{17} = 2$	2.03 to 3 s.f.

Fractions

Adding and subtracting

Example 1
Work out $2\frac{3}{4} + 1\frac{5}{8}$.

Either

$$2\frac{3}{4} + 1\frac{5}{8}$$
$$= 3 + \frac{3}{4} + \frac{5}{8}$$
$$= 3 + \frac{6}{8} + \frac{5}{8}$$
$$= 3 + \frac{11}{8}$$
$$= 4\frac{3}{8}$$

Or

$$2\frac{3}{4} + 1\frac{5}{8}$$
$$= \frac{11}{4} + \frac{13}{8}$$
$$= \frac{22}{8} + \frac{13}{8}$$
$$= \frac{35}{8}$$
$$= 4\frac{3}{8}$$

Example 2
Work out $5\frac{2}{5} - 3\frac{1}{2}$.

Either

$$5\frac{2}{5} - 3\frac{1}{2}$$
$$= 2 + \frac{2}{5} - \frac{1}{2}$$
$$= 2 + \frac{4}{10} - \frac{5}{10}$$
$$= 2 - \frac{1}{10}$$
$$= 1\frac{9}{10}$$

Or

$$5\frac{2}{5} - 3\frac{1}{2}$$
$$= \frac{27}{5} - \frac{7}{2}$$
$$= \frac{54}{10} - \frac{35}{10}$$
$$= \frac{19}{10}$$
$$= 1\frac{9}{10}$$

Multiplying

$$2\frac{2}{3} \times 4\frac{1}{2} = \frac{8}{3} \times \frac{9}{2} = \frac{8 \times 9}{3 \times 2} = 12$$

Dividing

$$1\frac{3}{4} \div 2\frac{1}{3} = \frac{7}{4} \div \frac{7}{3} = \frac{7}{4} \times \frac{3}{7} = \frac{3}{4}$$

Recurring decimals

Remember that $\frac{a}{b}$ is the same as $a \div b$. So
$$\frac{7}{8} = 7 \div 8 = 0.875$$

Some fractions produce recurring decimals

$$\frac{1}{3} = 0.333... = 0.\dot{3} \qquad \frac{2}{3} = 0.666... = 0.\dot{6} \quad \frac{1}{6} = 0.1666... = 0.1\dot{6}$$

$$\frac{1}{7} = 0.142\,857\,142\,857... = 0.\dot{1}4285\dot{7} \qquad \frac{8}{13} = 0.615\,384\,615\,384... = 0.\dot{6}1538\dot{4}$$

Reciprocals

The **reciprocal** of n is $\dfrac{1}{n}$.

Number	Reciprocal
3	$\frac{1}{3}$
$\frac{1}{3}$	3
$\frac{2}{5}$	2.5
$\frac{a}{b}$	$\frac{b}{a}$

Powers, roots and indices

$5^3 = 125$ means $\sqrt[3]{125} = 5$

$2^5 = 32$ means $\sqrt[5]{32} = 2$

Any number raised to the power of zero is equal to 1.

$5^0 = 1$ $\qquad$ $27^0 = 1$ $\qquad$ $16.5^0 = 1$ $\qquad$ $x^0 = 1$ $\qquad$ $(a + b)^0 = 1$ $\qquad$ $(x^2 + y)^0 = 1$

A negative power means '$1 \div \ldots$'

$7^{-1} = \frac{1}{7}$ $\qquad$ $18^{-1} = \frac{1}{18}$ $\qquad$ $5^{-2} = \frac{1}{5^2} = \frac{1}{25}$ $\qquad\qquad$ $n^{-3} = \frac{1}{n^3}$

Rules for indices

$a^m \times a^n = a^{m+n}$	$3a^4 \times 4a^5 = 12a^9$
$a^m \div a^n = a^{m-n}$	$15b^7 \div 5b^2 = 3b^5$
$a^0 = 1$	$37^0 = 1$
$a^{-m} = \frac{1}{a^m}$	$(0.25)^{-1} = \frac{1}{0.25} = 4$

Standard form

$1.083 \times 10^5 = 1.083 \times 10 \times 10 \times 10 \times 10 \times 10 = 108\,300$

$2.2 \times 10^{-4} = 2.2 \div 10^4 = 2.2 \div 10\,000 = 0.000\,22$

Direct proportion

Suppose A is **directly proportional** to B.

If A is trebled, then B is trebled. If A is halved, then B is halved, etc.

Direct proportion can be represented by a straight-line graph passing through the origin.

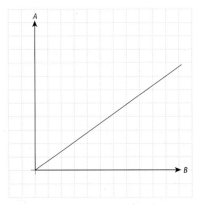

Inverse proportion

Suppose C is **inversely proportional** to D.

If C is trebled, then D is divided by 3. If C is halved, then D is doubled, etc.

The answer to 'C multiplied by D' is always the same.

2 TRANSFORMATIONS

- transformations: reflection, rotation, translation and enlargement
- using transformations to investigate patterns and shapes
- combinations of transformations.

Reflecting shapes

DISCUSSION POINT

In this diagram, the blue shape has been reflected to produce the red shape.

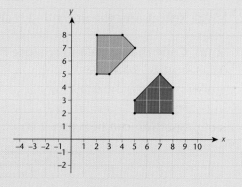

- Where is the mirror line?
- What is the equation of the mirror line?

Transforming shapes means changing them in some way. The shape you start with is called the **object**; the result of changing the shape is called the **image**.

One way to transform shapes is to **reflect** them. To reflect a shape you need a **mirror line** to reflect it in. The mirror line becomes a line of symmetry for the completed diagram.

EXERCISE 1

1 (a) Copy these axes and quadrilateral A on to squared paper.

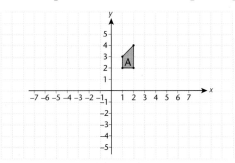

(b) Reflect A in the *x*-axis. Label the image B.

(c) Reflect A in the *y*-axis. Label the image C.

(d) Reflect A in the line *y* = *x*. Label the image D.

(e) Reflect A in the line *y* = –*x*. Label the image E.

(f) Reflect A in the line *x* = 3. Label the image F.

(g) Reflect A in the line *y* = –1. Label the image G.

2 (a) Copy these axes and triangle P on to squared paper.

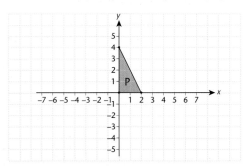

(b) What type of triangle is triangle P?

(c) Reflect triangle P in the *x*-axis. Label the image Q.

(d) What shape is produced by triangles P and Q together? Describe the symmetry of this shape.

(e) Reflect triangles P and Q in the *y*-axis.

(f) What shape has been made by the complete picture? Describe the symmetry of this shape.

3 (a) Copy shape W and the lines *a*, *b* and *c* on to isometric paper.

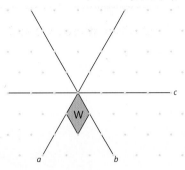

(b) What is the name given to shape W?

(c) Reflect W in line *a*. Label the image X.

(d) What shape do W and X make together?
Describe the symmetry of the shape.

(e) Reflect W in line *b*. Label the image Y.

(f) What shape do W, X and Y make together?
Describe the symmetry of this shape.

(g) Reflect W, X and Y together in line *c*.

(h) What is the shape of the finished diagram?
Describe its symmetry.

4 The transformation Δ1 → Δ2 is produced by a reflection in the line *y = x*.

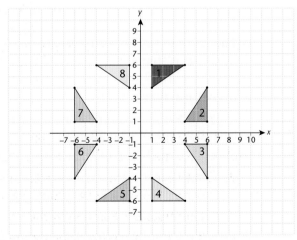

Each of these is produced by a reflection.
Give the equation of the mirror line for each one.

(a) Δ1 → Δ8	**(b)** Δ1 → Δ4	**(c)** Δ2 → Δ7	**(d)** Δ6 → Δ3
(e) Δ5 → Δ6	**(f)** Δ7 → Δ8	**(g)** Δ3 → Δ4	**(h)** Δ1 → Δ6
(i) Δ8 → Δ3	**(j)** Δ7 → Δ4		

Nelson GCSE Maths   TRANSFORMATIONS (INTERMEDIATE)

5 (**a**) Copy these axes, shape A and the lines $y = x$ and $y = -x$ on to squared paper.

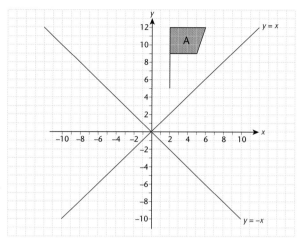

(**b**) Reflect A in the line $y = x$. Label the image B.

(**c**) Reflect B in the x-axis. Label the image C.

(**d**) Reflect C in the line $y = -x$. Label the image D.

(**e**) What single transformation reflects A on to D?

(**f**) Reflect D in the y-axis. Label the image E.

(**g**) Reflect E in the line $y = x$. Label the image F.

(**h**) What single transformation reflects C on to F?

(**i**) What single transformation reflects A on to F?

6 The triangle FGH has coordinates F(5, 10), G(2, 6) and H(2, 10). Reflect this triangle in the line $y = x + 3$.

Rangoli patterns

To create a Rangoli pattern draw a few lines on square dotty paper.

Reflect what you have drawn in a vertical line.

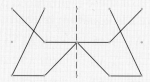

Now reflect the result in a horizontal line.

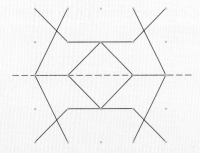

Reflect the whole shape in a diagonal line.

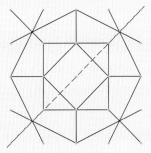

Finally, join several of these patterns together, and add colour.

EXERCISE 2

1 Copy these lines on to square dot paper, and use them to make a Rangoli pattern.

2 Repeat Question 1, starting with these lines.

3 Repeat Question 1, starting with these lines.

You could choose your favourite Rangoli pattern and use it to make a poster.

4 Make up some Rangoli patterns of your own.

Rotating shapes

DISCUSSION POINT

This transformation is not a reflection but a **rotation**.

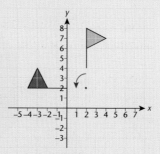

- How would you describe this rotation?
- What stays the same about a shape when it is rotated?
- What stays the same about a shape when it is reflected?

To rotate a shape, you need a **centre of rotation**, an **angle of rotation**, and to know if you are rotating the shape **clockwise** or **anticlockwise**.

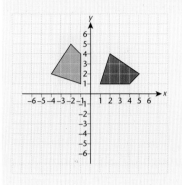

In this diagram, the blue object has been rotated 90° clockwise about the origin, (0, 0) to give the red image.

▷ Resource Sheet A:
Isometric dot
▷ Resource Sheet C:
Rotations
▷ Compasses
▷ Protractor

You may find
tracing paper
useful for some of
the questions in
this exercise.

EXERCISE 3

1 (a) Copy these axes and shape A.

(b) Rotate A through a quarter turn clockwise about the origin. Label the image B.

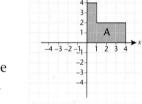

(c) Rotate A through half a turn about the origin. Does it matter which direction you rotate A? Label the image C.

(d) Rotate A, 90° anticlockwise about the origin. Label the image D.

(e) Describe the symmetry of the completed picture.

2 (a) Copy shape P on to isometric dot paper and mark point C.

(b) Rotate P, 60° clockwise about point C.
Label the image Q.

(c) Rotate Q, 60°clockwise about point C.
Label the image R.

(d) Rotate R, 60° clockwise about point C.
Label the image S.

(e) Keep rotating your image through 60° until there is no room to draw any more images. Describe the symmetry of your completed picture.

3 (a) Copy shape W and points A, B and C on to isometric dot paper.

(b) Rotate W, clockwise through 60° about point A. Label the image X.

(c) Rotate W, anticlockwise through 120° about point B. Label the image Y.

(d) Rotate W, anticlockwise through 240° about point C. Label the image Z.

4 Copy each of these diagrams, and carry out the rotation described.

A: 90° clockwise about the point (3,3)

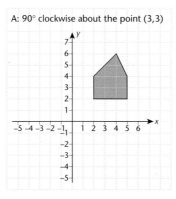

B: 90° anticlockwise about the point (1,1)

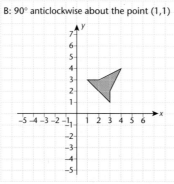

C: 270° clockwise about the point (–3,0)

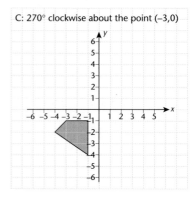

For Question 5, you need a copy of Resource Sheet C: Rotations.

5 In each of the diagrams A–H on the Resource Sheet, shape Q is an image of shape P after a rotation. For each diagram,

(a) find and mark the centre of rotation

(b) write down the angle and direction of the rotation

6 Copy this on to centimetre-squared paper.

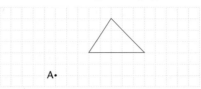

A•

Use a compass and a protractor to construct the image of the triangle when it is rotated clockwise by 120° about the point A.

Translations

DISCUSSION POINT

- What has been done to transform the blue triangle on to the red triangle?
- What stays the same about the triangle?

The transformation in the Discussion Point above is called a **translation**. When a shape is translated, *every* point on the shape moves the *same distance*, and in the *same direction*. A **vector** can be used to describe this movement.

These diagrams show some translations and their respective vectors.

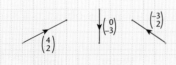

EXERCISE 4

1 Write down the vectors which describe each of these translations.

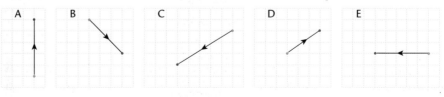

2 Write down the vectors which describe each of these translations.

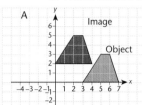 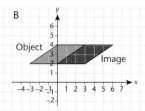 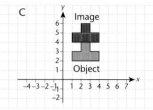

3 (a) Copy this set of axes and shape F.

(b) Translate F using the vector $\begin{pmatrix} 6 \\ -3 \end{pmatrix}$.
Label the image G.

(c) Translate F using the vector $\begin{pmatrix} 0 \\ -5 \end{pmatrix}$.
Label the image H.

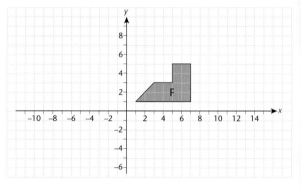

(d) Translate F using the vector $\begin{pmatrix} -10 \\ 4 \end{pmatrix}$.
Label the image I.

(e) Translate F using the vector $\begin{pmatrix} -5 \\ -4 \end{pmatrix}$. Label the image J.

4 Imagine translating a shape by the column vector $\begin{pmatrix} -2 \\ 5 \end{pmatrix}$. What is the column vector which maps the image back on to the object?

5 In each translation in this question, the object is a single point. Copy and complete this table.

Object	Vector	Image
(2, 3)	$\begin{pmatrix} 2 \\ 2 \end{pmatrix}$	
(4, 0)	$\begin{pmatrix} 0 \\ 1 \end{pmatrix}$	
(6, −2)	$\begin{pmatrix} 2 \\ 4 \end{pmatrix}$	
(−2, −4)	$\begin{pmatrix} 3 \\ -5 \end{pmatrix}$	
(2, 1)		(4, 3)
(−3, −5)		(−3, 0)
(5, −4)		(−1, 5)
	$\begin{pmatrix} 4 \\ 3 \end{pmatrix}$	(5, 4)
	$\begin{pmatrix} -2 \\ 0 \end{pmatrix}$	(0, −3)
	$\begin{pmatrix} 2 \\ -5 \end{pmatrix}$	(−2, −2)

6 The blue triangle can be translated in many different ways to another triangle on the grid.

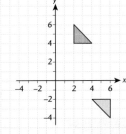

What translation is needed if the resulting triangle forms

(a) a square with the green triangle?

(b) a parallelogram with the green triangle?

Resource Sheet D: *Transformation game*
Resource Sheet E: *Transformation cards*

DISCUSSION POINT
Transformation game

This is a game for two or three players. To play this game, you need a copy of Resource Sheet D: *Transformation game* and a set of cards made from Resource Sheet E. This includes a triangular marker as the playing piece.

- Shuffle the cards and place them face down in the middle of the table.
- Deal three cards to each player.
- Place the marker on the starting position on the grid.
- Choose any of the three cards you are holding that will transform the marker on to one of the other positions indicated on the grid.
- Place the card face up on the table so the other players can see it, and then carry out the transformation described on the card. *The marker must land on one of the other positions shaded on the grid.*
- You score the number of points indicated by the new position of the marker on the grid.
- Take the next card from the top of the pile to replace the one you have used.
- The other player(s) then take turns to make their moves, starting from the new position of the marker.
- If you cannot play a card which will transform the marker on to one of the other triangles on the grid, you miss a turn, but you can swap one or more of your cards with those on the pile.
- If the other players do not think you have carried out the transformation correctly, they can challenge you. If they are correct, you lose a turn.

The winner is the player who has the highest total score within the time agreed.

Enlargement

Look at these diagrams.

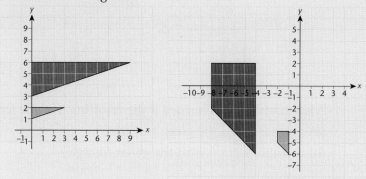

- What has to be done to transform the blue triangle on to the red triangle?
- What is the same about the blue triangle and the red triangle? What is different?
- What is needed to map the red triangle back on to the blue triangle?
- How many times bigger than the blue triangle is the red triangle?
- Imagine drawing lines through corresponding vertices of the blue triangle and the red triangle. Where do these line meet?

Now answer similar questions about the transformation which maps the blue quadrilateral on to the red quadrilateral.

The transformation in the DISCUSSION POINT above is called an **enlargement**. To enlarge a shape you need to know the **centre of the enlargement** and the **scale factor**. In both these diagrams, the red shape is the image of the blue shape.

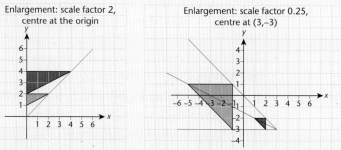

Enlargement: scale factor 2, centre at the origin

Enlargement: scale factor 0.25, centre at (3,−3)

Even if the object becomes *smaller*, the transformation is *still* called an enlargement. When this happens, the scale factor of the enlargement is a number less than 1.

EXERCISE 5

1 (a) Copy these axes and shape A on to squared paper.

   (b) Enlarge A by scale factor 2 with the origin as the centre. Label the image B.

   (c) Enlarge A by scale factor 3 with the point (4, 4) as the centre. Label the image C.

   (d) Enlarge A by scale factor 0.5 with the point (–6, 4) as centre. Label the image D.

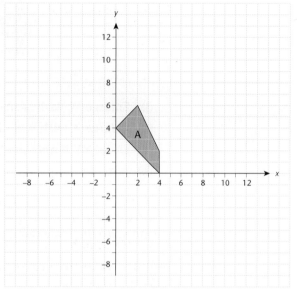

2 (a) Copy these axes and shape P on to squared paper.

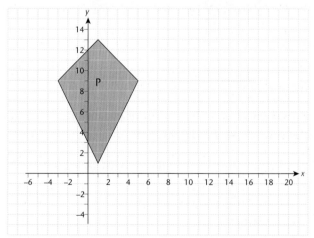

   (b) Enlarge P by scale factor 0.5, centre (20, 9). Label the image Q.

   (c) Enlarge P by scale factor 0.25, centre (20, 9). Label the image R.

   (d) Enlarge P by scale factor 0.75, centre (20, 9). Label the image S.

   (e) Describe the enlargement which maps R on to Q.

   (f) Describe the enlargement which maps R on to S.

   (g) Describe the enlargement which maps Q on to S.

   (h) Describe the enlargement which maps S on to Q.

Nelson GCSE Maths   TRANSFORMATIONS (INTERMEDIATE)

3 (a) Copy shape W and points A, B and C on to isometric paper.

W

•B

•A

•C

(b) Enlarge W with scale factor 2 about point A. Label the image X.

(c) Enlarge X with scale factor 1.5 about point B. Label the image Y.

(d) Enlarge Y with scale factor $\frac{2}{3}$ about point C. Label the image Z.

(e) Why are X and Z the same size?

4 In each of these diagrams, the red shape is the image of the blue shape after enlargement. Copy each diagram, find the centre of enlargement and state the scale factor.

A
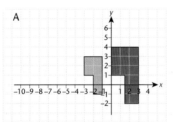

B
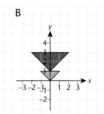

C
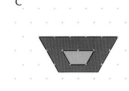

For Question 5, you need a copy of Resource Sheet F: Enlargements.

5 In each of the diagrams A–D on the Resource Sheet, shape Q is the image of shape P after enlargement. For each diagram

(a) find and mark the centre of enlargement

(b) write down the scale factor

6 This diagram shows an enlargement in which the blue shape is mapped on to the red shape.

(a) What is the scale factor of the enlargement?

(b) What are the coordinates of the centre of the enlargement?

(c) What is the ratio of the perimeter of the blue shape to the perimeter of the red shape?

(d) What is the ratio of the area of the blue shape to the area of the red shape?

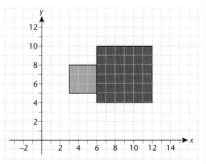

7 (a) Copy this picture on to isometric dot paper.

(b) What is the scale factor of the enlargement?

(c) Mark the centre of the enlargement. Label this point C.

(d) What is the ratio of the perimeter of the object to the perimeter of the image?

(e) What is the ratio of the area of the object to the area of the image?

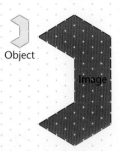

Object

Image

Making generalisations

8 (a) Draw some more shapes on grid paper. Enlarge your shapes by different scale factors. For each enlargement, write down the ratio of the area of the objects to the area of the image.

(b) What is the connection between the scale factor of the enlargement, and the ratio of the areas?

9 Copy and complete this table.

Object		Scale factor	Image	
Perimeter	Area		Perimeter	Area
12 cm	8 cm²	5		
20 cm	24 cm²		40 cm	
	6 cm²	3	15 cm	
15 cm		3		72 cm²
20 cm	16 cm²			64 cm²
30 cm		0.5		10 cm²

DISCUSSION POINT

If two shapes are exactly the same shape and size, they are said to be **congruent**.

If they are the *same shape* but *different sizes*, they are said to be **similar**.

Consider the transformations: reflection, rotation, translation, enlargement.

- In which transformations are the object and image congruent?
- In which transformations are the object and image similar?

EXERCISE 6

1 Copy this design on to squared paper.

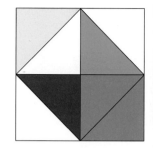

(a) The red triangle can be transformed on to the blue triangle by a reflection.
Draw the line of reflection and label it *a*.

(b) The red triangle can be transformed on to the yellow triangle by a rotation.
Mark the centre of the rotation and label it B.
What is the angle of rotation?

(c) The green square can be transformed on to the whole square by an enlargement. Mark the centre of the enlargement and label it C.
What is the scale factor?

2 Copy this design on to isometric paper.

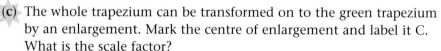

(a) The red trapezium can be transformed on to the blue trapezium by a reflection.
Draw the line of reflection and label it *a*.

(b) The red trapezium can be transformed on to the yellow trapezium by a rotation. Mark the centre of rotation and label it B.
What is the angle of rotation?

(c) The whole trapezium can be transformed on to the green trapezium by an enlargement. Mark the centre of enlargement and label it C.
What is the scale factor?

(d) The black trapezium can be transformed on to the whole trapezium by an enlargement. Mark the centre of enlargement and label it D.
What is the scale factor?

3 Copy this design on to isometric paper.

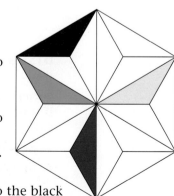

(a) The red triangle can be transformed on to the blue triangle by a reflection.
Draw the line of reflection and label it *a*.

(b) The red triangle can be transformed on to the yellow triangle by a rotation.
Mark the centre of rotation and label it B.
What is the angle of rotation?

(c) The red triangle can be transformed on to the black triangle by a rotation.
Mark the centre of rotation and label it C.
What is the angle of rotation?

4 (a) Copy these axes and shape P on to squared paper.

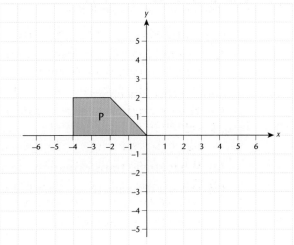

(b) Carry out the transformations as directed by this flow chart.

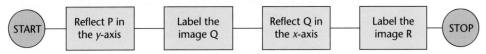

START → Reflect P in the y-axis → Label the image Q → Reflect Q in the x-axis → Label the image R → STOP

(c) What single transformation maps P directly on to R?
Describe this transformation fully.

5 (a) Copy these axes and triangle P on to squared paper.

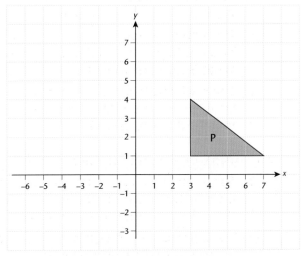

(b) Carry out the transformations as directed by this flowchart.

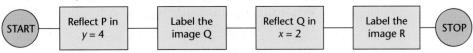

START → Reflect P in y = 4 → Label the image Q → Reflect Q in x = 2 → Label the image R → STOP

(c) What single transformation maps P directly on to R?
Describe this transformation fully.

6 Repeat Question 5 for this flowchart. Use the same axes, and the same triangle P.

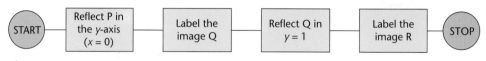

7 Look at this flowchart.

Making and testing a generalisation

(a) What single transformation, do you think, maps P directly on to R?

(b) Draw a diagram to see whether your answer to part (a) is correct.

8 (a) Copy these axes and shape P on to squared paper.

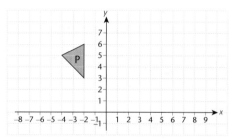

(b) Carry out the transformations as directed by this flowchart.

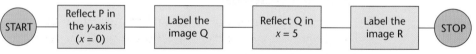

(c) What single transformation maps P directly on to R? Describe this transformation fully.

9 (a) Repeat Question 8 for this flowchart. Use the same axes, and the same shape P.

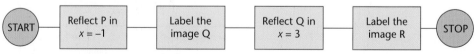

(b) Look at this flowchart.

Making and testing a generalisation

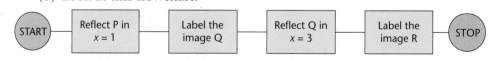

What single transformation, do you think, maps P directly on to R? Check your prediction.

Dynamic geometry

10 (a) Copy these axes and shape P on to squared paper.

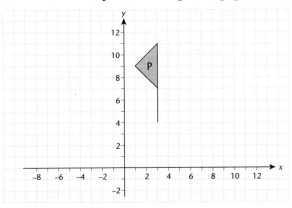

(b) Start with shape P and carry out the instructions in this flowchart.

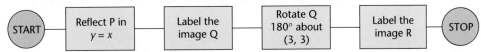

START → Reflect P in $y = x$ → Label the image Q → Rotate Q 180° about (3, 3) → Label the image R → STOP

(c) Describe fully the single transformation which maps shape P on to shape R.

CHAPTER SUMMARY

Transformations

Transforming shapes means changing them in some way.
The shape you start with is called the **object**; the result of changing the shape is called the **image.**

Reflections need a mirror line. Every point on the object is the same distance from the mirror as the corresponding point on the image.

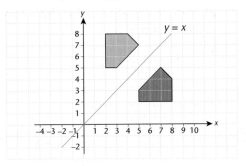

This is a reflection in the line $y = x$.

Rotations need a centre, an angle of rotation and a direction of rotation.

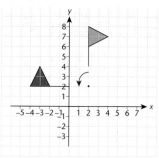

This is an anticlockwise rotation of 90° about the point (2, 2).

Translation is a sliding movement. **Vectors** are used to describe translations.

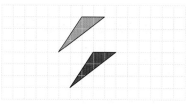

This is a translation by the vector $\begin{pmatrix} 1 \\ -3 \end{pmatrix}$.

Enlargements need a scale factor and a centre of the enlargement. Even if the object becomes smaller we still call it an enlargement.

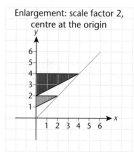

Enlargement: scale factor 2, centre at the origin

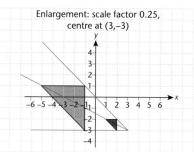

Enlargement: scale factor 0.25, centre at (3,–3)

ALGEBRAIC MANIPULATION

This chapter is about:

- changing the subject of a formula
- multiplying out brackets
- factorising.

Changing the subject of a formula

EXERCISE 1

1 Find the value of $\frac{1}{2}st^2$ when $s = 10$ and $t = 12$.

2 The cost of gas is given by the formula $C = 0.06n + 15$ where n is the number of units used.
What is the cost if 150 units are used?

3 If $v = u - at$, find v when $a = -2$, $t = 5$ and $u = 17$.

4 If $v = \sqrt{a - 3b}$, find the value of v when
   (a) $a = 27$ and $b = 4$ (b) $a = -1.5$ and $b = -2.6$

5 If $\frac{1}{f} = \frac{1}{u} + \frac{1}{v}$, find the value of f when
   (a) $u = 16$ and $v = 25$ (b) $u = -1.25$ and $v = 0.97$

6 If $y = mx + c$, find
   (a) x when $y = 3$, $m = 2$ and $c = 1$ (b) c when $y = 4$, $x = 2$ and $m = 1$

7 If $a = \frac{1}{2}(x + y + z)$, find
   (a) x when $a = 3$, $y = 1$ and $z = 2$ (b) z when $a = 17$, $x = -4$ and $y = 20$

8 If $p = \frac{q}{2} + \frac{r}{3}$, find
   (a) q when $p = 5$ and $r = 9$ (b) r when $p = 0.5$ and $q = 2$

9 If $T = \frac{\lambda x}{a}$ find

    (a) x when $T = 10$, $\lambda = 5$ and $a = 8$ **(b)** λ when $T = 6$, $x = 3$ and $a = 7$

10 If $E = \frac{\lambda x^2}{2a}$ find

    (a) λ when $E = 3$, $x = 6$ and $a = 4$ **(b)** a when $E = 15$, $x = 5$ and $\lambda = 4$

11 If $I = \frac{PRT}{100}$ to find

    (a) T when $I = 9$, $P = 30$ and $R = 3$ **(b)** P when $I = 6$, $R = \frac{1}{2}$ and $T = 30$

12 If $A = \frac{ma}{M + m}$, find

    (a) a when $m = 2$, $M = 7$ and $A = 3$ **(b)** M when $m = 4$, $a = 9$ and $A = 6$

DISCUSSION POINT

$$y = \frac{7x^2 - 8}{3}$$

How can you change the subject so that it becomes $x = ...$?
You can check your result by substituting in some numbers.

EXERCISE 2

1 Make x the subject in each of these equations.

    (a) $a = c + x$ **(b)** $a = x + c$ **(c)** $a = xb$ **(d)** $a = bx$

    (e) $a = bx + c$ **(f)** $a = bc + x$ **(g)** $a = bx + c$ **(h)** $a = b^2 x$

    (i) $a = bx^2$ **(j)** $a = \frac{x}{b}$ **(k)** $a = \frac{b}{x}$

2 Change the subject in each of these equations.

    (a) Make R the subject in $v = iR$.   **(b)** Make r the subject in $C = 2\pi r$.

    (c) Make g the subject in $E = mgh$.   **(d)** Make b the subject in $V = lbh$.

    (e) Make a the subject in $v = u + at$.   **(f)** Make C the subject in $F = 1.4C + 32$.

    (g) Make V the subject in $D = \frac{M}{V}$.   **(h)** Make v the subject in $A = kv^2$.

    (i) Make l the subject in $t = 2\pi \sqrt{\frac{l}{g}}$.   **(j)** Make u the subject in $v^2 = u^2 + 2as$.

Multiplying out brackets and factorising

DISCUSSION POINT

In *Book 1*, Chapter 13, you did some work on multiplying out brackets. Here is a reminder. Make sure you understand each of these.

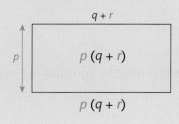

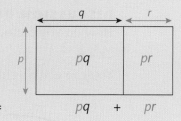

$$p\,(q + r) \qquad = \qquad pq \quad + \quad pr$$

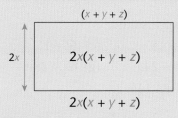

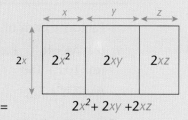

$$2x(x + y + z) \qquad = \qquad 2x^2 + 2xy + 2xz$$

Multiplying out brackets is sometimes called **expanding**.

Exercise 3

1 Multiply out the brackets in these expressions.

(a) $4(c + d)$ (b) $6(s + t + u)$

(c) $f(f + g + h)$ (d) $2k(k + l + m)$

(e) $r(1 + 2r)$ (f) $3d(d - 2)$

(g) $2x(3x + 4)$ (h) $5c(2f - c)$

(i) $5a(b + a)$ (j) $-2y(3 - y)$

(k) $-6b(b + 4a)$ (l) $-4y(3x - 2)$

2 Expand and simplify each of these expressions.

(a) $3t + t(2 + t)$ (b) $x(x + y) + y(x - y)$

(c) $a(a - 3) - a(2a - 6)$ (d) $b^2 - 2b(5 - b)$

(e) $a - a(1 - a)$ (f) $x(y - z) - y(x - z)$

(g) $d(d - 3) - 2(d - 3)$ (h) $5a(b + c) - 3a(b - c)$

Instead of removing brackets, sometimes, brackets are put into an expression. This is called **factorising**. The number which goes outside the bracket is called the **common factor**.

DISCUSSION POINT

How do you factorise these?

$2x + 8$ $\qquad\qquad$ $3ab + 6a$ $\qquad\qquad$ $4a^2 - 2a$

You can always check the factorising by multiplying out the bracket.

EXERCISE 4

1 Factorise each of these expressions.

(a) $3a + 9$ $\qquad$ (b) $9b + 15$ $\qquad$ (c) $6f - 15$ $\qquad$ (d) $6c + 4d$

(e) $10a + 15b$ $\qquad$ (f) $18p - 24q$ $\qquad$ (g) $8x - 28y$ $\qquad$ (h) $24a - 40b$

(i) $27f + 72g$ $\qquad$ (j) $-21a - 14b$

2 Factorise each of these expressions.

(a) $2x - 6$ $\qquad$ (b) $3a + 15$ $\qquad$ (c) $5xy - 7x$ $\qquad$ (d) $7a + 7b$

(e) $ab - 6a$ $\qquad$ (f) $xy + 5x$ $\qquad$ (g) $3ab - 5a$ $\qquad$ (h) $3xy - 6x$

(i) $5de + 20e$ $\qquad$ (j) $4yz + 12z$ $\qquad$ (k) $8d^2 + 10d$ $\qquad$ (l) $9x^2 - 12x$

(m) $9xz + 6x^2$ $\qquad$ (n) $24a^2 - 3ab$ $\qquad$ (o) $4a^2 - 24a$ $\qquad$ (p) $7xy - 6x^2y^2$

(q) $10xy + 2x^2y^2$ $\qquad$ (r) $2x^3 - 5x$ $\qquad$ (s) $3x^3 + 15x^2$ $\qquad$ (t) $7x^2y + 3xy^2$

COURSEWORK OPPORTUNITY

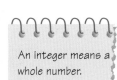

An integer means a whole number.

Consecutive integers

The number 21 can be written as the sum of three consecutive integers.

$21 = 6 + 7 + 8$

♦ Which numbers can be written as the sum of three consecutive integers?

♦ Which numbers can be written as the sum of two, four, five ... consecutive integers?

♦ Prove some of your results using algebra.

♦ Given a number, work out a method of finding *all* the ways it can be written as the sum of consecutive integers.
For example, $21 = 10 + 11 = 6 + 7 + 8 = \dots.$

♦ Extend your exploration to include integers which are not consecutive.

Multiplying out two brackets

DISCUSSION POINT

One way of multiplying 2-digit numbers together is like this:

	20	6
30	600	180
4	80	24

$$26 \times 34 = (20 + 6) \times (30 + 4)$$

So

$$26 \times 34 = 600 + 180 + 80 + 24 = 884$$

Try this method on other numbers.

A similar method can be used to multiply out brackets with algebra. For example, this is how $(x + 3)(x + 5)$ can be multiplied out:

	x	3
x	x^2	$3x$
5	$5x$	15

So

$$(x + 3)(x + 5) = x^2 + 3x + 5x + 15$$
$$= x^2 + 8x + 15$$

Multiply out these brackets.

$$(3m - 4n)(m + 5n) \qquad (x + 5)^2$$

Use whatever non-calculator method you like to do the multiplications in this exercise.

EXERCISE 5

1 (a) 32×13 (b) 24×43 (c) 57×71 (d) 97×25
    (e) 101×68

2 (a) 32^2 (b) 45^2 (c) 87×78 (d) 232×12
    (e) 457×68

EXERCISE 6

1 Expand these brackets.

(a) $(a + 2)(b + 3)$ (b) $(x + 3)(y + 7)$ (c) $(p + 5)(q + 8)$ (d) $(f + 8)(g - 3)$

2 Expand and simplify these expressions.

(a) $(m + 2)(m + 1)$ (b) $(m + 3)(m + 4)$ (c) $(m + 5)(m + 6)$

(d) $(m + 4)(m + 7)$ (e) $(x - 4)(x + 2)$ (f) $(x - 10)(x + 3)$

(g) $(x + 7)(x - 9)$ (h) $(x - 2)(x + 4)$ (i) $(x - 8)(x - 7)$

(j) $(x - 2)(x - 5)$ (k) $(x - 1)(x - 5)$ (l) $(x - 4)(x - 6)$

(m) $(a - 2)(a + 6)$ (n) $(y - 4)(y + 3)$ (o) $(x + 6)(x - 8)$

(p) $(x - 1)(x + 2)$ (q) $(x + 7)(x - 3)$ (r) $(a - 2)(a + 9)$

3 Expand and simplify these expressions.

(a) $(2x + 3)(3x + 5)$ (b) $(7x - 5)(3x + 2)$ (c) $(5x - 1)(7x + 2)$

(d) $(2x + 3)(2x - 5)$ (e) $(8x + 1)(2x - 5)$ (f) $(4x + 3)(2x - 7)$

(g) $(3x + 1)(x + 3)$ (h) $(2x - 5)(5x - 2)$ (i) $(4x - 7)(7x + 4)$

(j) $(2x + 3y)(x + y)$ (k) $(3x + 4y)(x + 2y)$ (l) $(4x - y)(2x - 5y)$

(m) $(3x - 4y)(4x - 3y)$ (n) $(2x - 3y)(x + 2y)$ (o) $(6x - 5y)(5x + 6y)$

$$(x + 5)^2 = (x + 5)(x + 5) = x^2 + 10x + 25$$
$$(2x - 3)^2 = (2x - 3)(2x - 3) = 4x^2 - 12x + 9$$

EXERCISE 7

1 Expand and simplify these expressions.

(a) $(x + 1)^2$ (b) $(x + 2)^2$

(c) $(x - 3)^2$ (d) $(x + 4)^2$

(e) $(x - 5)^2$ (f) $(x + 7)^2$

(g) $(x + 10)^2$ (h) $(x - 20)^2$

2 Expand and simplify these expressions.

(a) $(2x + 1)^2$ (b) $(3x + 2)^2$

(c) $(4x - 3)^2$ (d) $(5x - 4)^2$

(e) $(x + 2y)^2$ (f) $(3x - 2y)^2$

(g) $(4x + 5y)^2$ (h) $(x - 10y)^2$

3 Expand and simplify these expressions.

(a) $(x + 1)(x - 1)$ (b) $(x + 2)(x - 2)$

(c) $(x + 3)(x - 3)$ (d) $(x + 4)(x - 4)$

(e) $(x + 5)(x - 5)$ (f) $(x + 8)(x - 8)$

(g) $(x + 10)(x - 10)$ (h) $(x + a)(x - a)$

Factorising into two brackets

This special relationship
$$(x + a)(x - a) = x^2 - a^2$$

is called **the difference of two squares**. It can be used to **factorise** the difference of two squares.

Example
$$x^2 - 9 = x^2 - 3^2 = (x + 3)(x - 3)$$

DISCUSSION POINT
Discuss how the difference of two squares can be used to help you to do these.
- Factorise $a^2 - 36b^2$.
- Find the value of 19×21.
- Find the value of $66^2 - 34^2$.
- Find the value of 49^2.

EXERCISE 8

1 Factorise these expressions.

(a) $x^2 - 64$ (b) $x^2 - 36$ (c) $x^2 - 100$ (d) $9 - x^2$

(e) $16x^2 - 9$ (f) $25x^2 - y^2$ (g) $49x^2 - 81y^2$ (h) $\frac{1}{4}x^2 - \frac{1}{9}y^2$

(i) $\frac{1}{16}a^2 - \frac{1}{36}b^2$

2 Calculate

(a) $98^2 - 2^2$ (b) $88^2 - 12^2$ (c) $46^2 - 44^2$ (d) $37^2 - 27^2$

(e) $251^2 - 249^2$ (f) $786^2 - 214^2$ (g) 29×31 (h) 99×101

(i) 998×1002 (j) 62×58 (k) 49×51 (l) 71×69

(m) 49^2 (n) 29^2 (o) 99^2

3 Factorise these expressions.

In Question 3, take out a common factor first.

(a) $2x^2 - 8$ (b) $3y^2 - 48$ (c) $5x^2 - 45$ (d) $3x^2 - 12y^2$

(e) $36y^2 - 4x^2$ (f) $28x^2 - 63y^2$

DISCUSSION POINT
Discuss these to make sure you understand how to factorise expressions into two brackets.

$x^2 + 4x + 3 = (x + 3)(x + 1)$ $x^2 - 11x + 18 = (x - 9)(x - 2)$
$x^2 - 2x - 63 = (x - 9)(x + 7)$ $2x^2 + 7x + 3 = (x + 3)(2x + 1)$
$3x^2 + 5x - 2 = (3x - 1)(x + 2)$ $x^2 + 6xy + 8y^2 = (x + 4y)(x + 2y)$

EXERCISE 9

1 Factorise these expressions (into two brackets).

(a) $x^2 + 8x + 15$ (b) $x^2 - 8x + 15$ (c) $x^2 + 16x + 15$ (d) $x^2 + 9x + 20$

(e) $x^2 - 9x + 20$ (f) $x^2 + 12x + 20$ (g) $x^2 - 12x + 20$ (h) $x^2 + 21x + 20$

(i) $x^2 - 21x + 20$ (j) $x^2 + 13x + 12$ (k) $x^2 - 13x + 12$ (l) $x^2 + 8x + 12$

(m) $x^2 - 8x + 12$ (n) $x^2 + 7x + 12$ (o) $x^2 - 7x + 12$

2 Factorise these expressions.

(a) $x^2 + x - 2$ (b) $x^2 + 7x - 18$ (c) $x^2 + 3x - 18$ (d) $x^2 - 3x - 18$

(e) $x^2 - x - 12$ (f) $x^2 + 6x - 16$ (g) $x^2 + 2x - 48$ (h) $x^2 - 13x - 48$

(i) $x^2 + 5x - 24$ (j) $x^2 - 4x - 21$ (k) $x^2 - 2x - 15$ (l) $x^2 + 4x - 32$

3 Factorise each of these.

(a) $3x^2 + 4x + 1$ (b) $2a^2 + 3a + 1$ (c) $2b^2 + 5b + 2$

(d) $3c^2 + 10c + 3$ (e) $2a^2 - 3a + 1$ (f) $2b^2 - 5b + 2$

(g) $3c^2 - 10c + 3$ (h) $4x^2 + 5xy + y^2$ (i) $2x^2 + 5xy + 2y^2$

(j) $2a^2 + 7ab + 3b^2$ (k) $2a^2 + 5ab + 3b^2$ (l) $4m^2 + 12mn + 9n^2$

4 Factorise each of these.

(a) $2x^2 + 3x - 2$ (b) $3x^2 + x - 2$ (c) $6x^2 + 11x - 10$

(d) $4x^2 - 4xy - 3y^2$ (e) $4x^2 - 12x + 9$ (f) $16y^2 - 40y + 25$

(g) $4a^2 + 9ab - 9b^2$ (h) $3x^2 - 8xy - 3y^2$

You can factorise an expression in three ways.

- Finding a common factor $4xy + 2x^2 = 2x(2y + x)$
- Using the difference of two squares
  $x^2 - 9 = (x + 3)(x - 3)$ $5x^2 - 20 = 5(x^2 - 4) = 5(x + 2)(x - 2)$
- Using two brackets
  $x^2 + 5x - 6 = (x - 1)(x + 6)$ $2x^2 + 7x + 3 = (2x + 1)(x + 3)$

You can check your results by multiplying out the brackets.
You often have to decide which technique is required.

EXERCISE 10

1 Factorise these expressions.

(a) $4a - 8b$ (b) $x^2 - 36$ (c) $x^2 + 8x + 7$ (d) $ab + 5a$

(e) $4a^2 - 49b^2$ (f) $x^2 - 13x + 42$ (g) $x^2 - 8x + 15$ (h) $x^2 - 4x - 45$

2 Factorise these expressions.

(a) $x^2 - 2x - 15$ (b) $x^2 + 5x - 36$ (c) $9 - 100x^2$ (d) $x^2 - 11x + 24$

(e) $x^2 + 6x$ (f) $x^2 - 13x + 40$ (g) $12x^2 - 8x$ (h) $x^3 - 7x^2$

 3 Factorise these expressions.

(a) $x^3 + 5x^2 + 6x$ (b) $2x^2 + 9x - 5$ (c) $4y^2 - 4y + 1$ (d) $2z^2 + 5z + 2$

(e) $2x^2 + 3xy + y^2$ (f) $4x^2 + 12xy + 9y^2$ (g) $a^3 + 6a^2 + 5a$ (h) $9z^2 - 81p^2$

CHAPTER SUMMARY

Changing the subject of a formula

Example: Make L the subject of the equation $s = \frac{1}{2}n(A + L)$.

Double both sides: $\qquad\qquad\qquad\qquad\qquad 2s = n(A + L)$

Divide by n: $\qquad\qquad\qquad\qquad\qquad\quad \frac{2s}{n} = A + L$

Subtract A: $\qquad\qquad\qquad\qquad\qquad\quad L = \frac{2s}{n} - A$

Multiplying out brackets

$n(a + b) = na + nb$

$a(na + b) = na^2 + ab$

	x	2
x	x^2	$2x$
3	$3x$	6

$(x + 2)(x + 3)$
$= x^2 + 2x + 3x + 6$
$= x^2 + 5x + 6$

	x	-5
x	x^2	$-5x$
-5	$-5x$	25

$(x - 5)^2$
$= (x - 5)(x - 5)$
$= x^2 - 10x + 25$

	a	b
a	a^2	ab
$-b$	$-ab$	$-b^2$

$(a + b)(a - b)$,
$= a^2 + ab - ab - b^2$
$= a^2 - b^2$

Factorising

Common factors
$4a^2 + 12a = 4a(a + 3)$
$10ab - 6b^2 = 2b(5a - 3b)$

Quadratic factors
$a^2 + 4a + 3 = (a + 3)(a + 1)$

$n^2 - 5n + 6 = (n - 2)(n - 3)$

$x^2 - x - 6 = (x - 3)(x + 2)$

$2x^2 + 5x + 2 = (2x + 1)(x + 2)$

Difference of two squares
$a^2 - b^2 = (a + b)(a - b)$
$25y^2 - 9z^2 = (5y + 3z)(5y - 3z)$

4 STATISTICS AND PROBABILITY

This chapter is about:

- designing and criticising questionnaires
- bias in questions
- selecting a suitable sample
- interpreting two-way tables
- calculating mean, median and modal class for grouped frequency distributions
- cumulative frequency diagrams: median and interquartile range
- drawing scatter diagrams and lines of best fit
- probabilities involving more than one event.

Collecting data

DISCUSSION POINT

Usually you start a statistical investigation with an idea about something and you try to demonstrate that your idea is either right or wrong.
This idea is called a **hypothesis.**
To demonstrate your idea is either right or wrong, you collect data to provide evidence.

- What data would you collect to test this hypothesis?

  The older you are, the more television you watch.

- What questions do you need to ask?

- How would you design an observation sheet or questionnaire to record the data?

- Why is it *not* a good idea to ask questions like these?

  You don't have to go to bed by 9 o'clock, do you?
  Surely you like watching *Friends*, don't you?

EXERCISE 1

1 A student is conducting a survey into which school subjects students think are important, and which they enjoy most. She intends using a questionnaire.

   (**a**) What is wrong with the wording of these questions?

   Do you find History boring, like most students?

   Do you agree that Maths is important for getting a job?

   Do you like games as a break from dull classroom subjects?

   (**b**) Suggest some better worded questions to use instead of these.

2 Sometimes, it is convenient to have questions on your questionnaire which can be answered either *yes* or *no*.
Reword each of these questions so that they can be answered *yes* or *no*. You might need to use several questions in place of one of these questions.

   What sports do you like?

   What do you do on Saturdays?

   What are your views about smoking?

3 Sometimes it is useful to have a definite number as the answer to a question. Reword each of these questions so that the answer is a number.

   Do you take a lot of subjects at school?

   Is your science class a big group?

   Do you come from a large family?

   Do you often go for a bike ride?

You could choose your own hypothesis instead of these.

4 Design an observation sheet or questionnaire to test some of these hypotheses.

Older students spend more money on food during the day than younger students

PAGE 22

TEACHERS OWN NEW CARS

Broadsheet newspapers use longer words than tabloids

Older students do more homework than younger students

Females spend more time shopping than males

Most students live within one mile of their school

HABITS

DISCUSSION POINT

Suppose you want to test this hypothesis:

The older you are, the more television you watch.

- *Who* would you include in your survey? Why would you choose these people?

The people you choose to ask are called a **sample**.

- Are there any people you would deliberately exclude from your survey? Why?

- *Where* would you go to ask your questions?

One student suggests that her sample will consist of her twenty-five class mates, her mother and her baby sister.

- How reliable are her results likely to be?

Another student says that his sample will consist of fifty other students in Y11 and fifty adults at his local sports club.

- What might be wrong with choosing a sample like this?

▷ Resource Sheet G: *Fish*

EXERCISE 2

1 A student is interested in finding out whether traditionally popular sports are still as popular as they used to be. He decides to ask people at his football club.

   (a) Why is this not a good sample?   (b) Suggest a better sample.

2 A journalist is interested in finding out whether more of the food shopping nowadays is done by men. She decides to sample people in the local supermarket between 10 a.m. and 10.30 a.m. on a particular Thursday.

   (a) Why is this not a good sample?   (b) Suggest a better sample.

3 The librarian is interested in finding out how often students use the school library. She decides to leave a questionnaire at the book issue desk in the library during lunchtime one Friday.

   (a) Why is this not a good sample?   (b) Suggest a better sample.

4 A student is interested in how many people take sea-side holidays in different months of the year. He decides to ask all the people in his class.

   (a) Why is this not a good sample?   (b) Suggest a better sample.

5 (a) Think of a hypothesis about all the students in your school.

   (b) Describe how you might choose an appropriate sample of students in your school to test your hypothesis.

For Question 6 you need a copy of Resource Sheet G: Fish

6 (a) Choose an appropriate sample of fish from the Resource Sheet. Write about how you chose your sample.

(b) Estimate the mean length of the fish on the sheet by finding the mean length of fish in your sample.

(c) How can you improve the accuracy of your estimate?

Two-way tables

Data from questionnaires and from other sources is sometimes conveniently displayed in tables.

EXERCISE 3

1 The number of students in each year of a school are shown in this table.

(a) What percentage of the students are in Y7?

(b) When a celebrity visits the school a student is chosen at random to welcome the celebrity. What is the probability that this student will be from Y10?

Year	No. of pupils
7	180
8	160
9	120
10	115
11	125

2 The members of a sports club are described in this table.

(a) What percentage of the members are children?

(b) Someone from the sports club is chosen at random. Find the probability that this person is

	Children	Adults
Male	30	60
Female	20	90

(i) an adult female **(ii)** not an adult female

3 This table describes the age and gender of the audience at a cinema.

(a) What percentage of the audience was
(i) under 16? **(ii)** female?
(iii) 30 or over?

(b) Of the whole audience, which is the greater percentage: males under 20 *or* females aged 30 and over?

Age (y)	Males	Females
$y < 16$	16	24
$16 \leq y < 20$	26	33
$20 \leq y < 30$	37	68
$30 \leq y < 50$	47	42
$y \geq 50$	2	5

(c) Someone from the audience is selected at random.
What is the probability that this person is

(i) male? **(ii)** under 20? **(iii)** a female under 30?

(iv) *not* a female under 30?

(v) *either* a male under 30 *or* a female under 20?

Measuring the average

A reminder
- To find the **mean**, you add up all the results and divide the answer by the number of results.
- To find the **median**, put the results in order and choose the middle result.
- The **mode** is the result which occurs most frequently.

EXERCISE 4

1 This table shows information about the number of people absent from work during one week.

Day	No. of people absent
Monday	15
Tuesday	12
Wednesday	14
Thursday	10
Friday	2

    (a) Calculate the mean number of people absent per day.

    (b) Find the median number of people absent.

    (c) Which, out of the mean or the median, best describes the average number of people absent from work each day?

2 The distribution of homework marks for a class of students is shown in this table.

Mark	Frequency
0	1
1	0
2	1
3	3
4	2
5	4
6	4
7	6
8	8
9	0
10	1

    (a) Calculate the mean homework mark for this class of students.

    (b) Find the median homework mark for the class.

    (c) What is the modal homework mark?

3 The number of pages devoted to sport in some newspapers is recorded.

8, 4, 6, 32, 20, 8, 28, 8, 16, 32, 6, 12

    (a) What is the modal number of pages?

    (b) What is the median number of pages?

    (c) What is the mean number of pages?

    (d) Copy and complete these sentences about these newspapers.

        A: Half of the newspapers have ____ or more pages devoted to sport.

        B: ___ newspapers have more than the mean number of pages devoted to sport.

        C: None of the measures of average is a good representation of the number of pages devoted to sport. This is because _____.

4 A class of 30 people were asked how many brothers and sisters they had. The results are shown in this pie chart.

Measure the angles on the pie chart with a protractor.

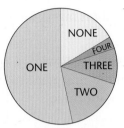

No. of brothers and sisters	Frequency
0	5
1	
2	
3	
4	

(a) Copy the table and use the pie chart to complete it.

(b) What is the mode for the number of brothers and sisters?

(c) What is the median number?

(d) What is the mean number, correct to one decimal place?

(e) What percentage of the people asked had two brothers and sisters?

(f) Someone from the class is chosen at random. What is the probability that they have three brothers and sisters?

DISCUSSION POINT

This table shows the distribution of books borrowed from the school library by a group of Y11 students.

No. of books borrowed during the year	No. of students (frequency)
0–4	23
5–9	48
10–14	15
15–19	5
20–24	7
25–29	2

- What is the modal group?
- Why is it not possible to calculate the exact median for this data from the table?
- How can you find an estimate for the median of this data?
- Why is it not possible to calculate the exact mean for this data from the table?
- How can you calculate an estimate for the mean number of books borrowed per student?

1 This is the distribution of examination marks for a group of Y11 students.

(a) What is the modal class?

(b) Estimate the median exam mark for these students.

(c) Estimate the mean exam mark for these students.

Exam mark	Frequency
30–34	1
35–39	0
40–44	2
45–49	2
50–54	5
55–59	8
60–64	10
65–69	1
70–74	1

2 This table shows the number of days absent from work over the last year for employees at a factory.

(a) What is the modal class?

(b) Estimate the median number of days absent.

(c) Estimate the mean number of days absent.

No. of days absent	No. of employees
0–14	86
15–29	30
30–44	5
45–59	0
60–74	1
75–89	2

3 The distribution of ages of people attending a gym on one day are recorded in this table.

Calculate the mean age of the people attending the gym.

Age (years)	Frequency
$10 \leq y < 20$	12
$20 \leq y < 30$	35
$30 \leq y < 40$	28
$40 \leq y < 50$	16
$50 \leq y < 60$	4

4 The waiting time for patients in the casualty department of a hospital, before being seen by a doctor, are recorded.

Estimate the mean waiting time for a patient at this hospital.

Waiting time (t minutes)	No. of patients (f)
$0 \leq t < 60$	15
$60 \leq t < 120$	21
$120 \leq t < 180$	5
$180 \leq t < 240$	4
$240 \leq t < 300$	2

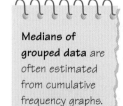

Medians of grouped data are often estimated from cumulative frequency graphs. This is explained on page 59.

Interquartile range

Mean, median and mode measure the *average* result. We can also compare the *consistency* of the results by seeing how spread out they are. To measure this, we can either find the **range** or the **interquartile range**. This is how you work out interquartile range.

Here are the marks obtained by 17 students in a test marked out of 70.

14, 12, 22, 34, 23, 33, 61, 49, 27, 31, 54, 43, 19, 27, 24, 33, 62

List the marks in order of size.

12, 14, 19, 22, 23, 24, 27, 27, 31, 33, 33, 34, 43, 49, 54, 61, 62

           ↑   ↑   ↑

lower quartile   median   upper quartile

The median is the middle number: 31.

The lower quartile is the median of the data which is below the median. For this data, the lower quartile lies midway between the values 22 and 23, so a value of 22.5 is used.

The upper quartile lies midway between the values 43 and 49, i.e. at 46.

The interquartile range is the difference between the upper and lower quartiles.

In this example, the interquartile range is

46 − 22.5 = 23.5

> The range is the difference between the largest and smallest results.

DISCUSSION POINT

Here are the recent test results of three students.

Student 1	78	25	43	57	23	48	62	73	80	91
Student 2	64	67	62	67	66	63	65	65	68	68
Student 3	65	absent	14	75	69	62	64	96	66	65

- What does the mean tell us about these students?
  Who has the highest mean mark?
- What does the range for each set of results tell us about these students?
- Work out the median and the interquartile range for each set.
  What do these results show?
- What are the advantages and disadvantages of using the interquartile range rather than range?

Nelson GCSE Maths   STATISTICS AND PROBABILITY (INTERMEDIATE)

1 So far this season, Rovers have played 15 matches, scoring 1, 3, 0, 2, 1, 5, 2, 3, 4, 1, 3, 0, 3, 1 and 4 goals.
United have played 12 games, scoring 4, 2, 3, 4, 1, 0, 0, 2, 1, 6, 3 and 5 goals.

(a) Find the medians and interquartile ranges of both teams' results.

(b) Compare the performance of the two teams in terms of the goals they have scored in their matches so far.

> A constellation is a group of stars which form a pattern in the sky.

2 These diagrams show the main stars in the constellations of Orion and Pegasus. The numbers on the diagram are the distances of each star from Earth, measured in light years.

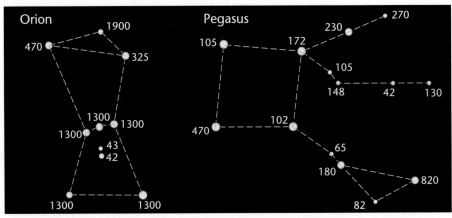

(a) Find the mean distance from Earth of the stars in each constellation.

(b) Find the range of the distances from Earth of the stars in each constellation.

> For (e), your answer may include any of the calculations you made in parts (a) to (d).

(c) Find the median distance from Earth of the stars in each constellation.

(d) Find the interquartile range of the distances from Earth of the stars in each constellation.

(e) Compare the distances to the stars in each constellation in terms of their average and spread.

3 A student asks the ages of her teachers. This is what she recorded.

25   37   42   28   23   45   51   46   26

(a) For the teacher's ages, find
  (i)   the mean age   (ii) the range
  (iii) the median age   (iv) the interquartile range

(b) Two years later, the same teachers are again asked about their ages. How will the values of the mean, median, range and interquartile range have changed?

4 Here are the weekly wages of eleven employees working in a shop.

£75　£68　£102　£45　£90　£7　£124　£110　£45　£45　£66

(a) Calculate the mean wage.

(b) Find the median wage.

(c) Work out the interquartile range.

(d) Suppose all employees are given a £20 pay rise.
How does this affect the mean, median and interquartile range.

(e) Instead of the £20, all employees are given a 10% pay rise.
How does this affect the mean, median and interquartile range?

Cumulative frequency

DISCUSSION POINT

During the months of March, April and May, the outside temperature was recorded each day.

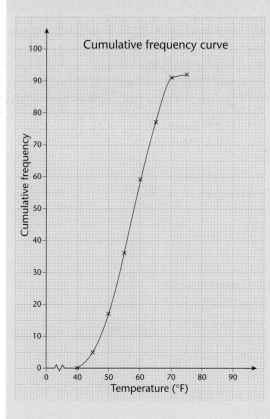

Temperature (°F)	Number of days
41–45	5
46–50	12
51–55	19
56–60	23
61–65	18
66–70	14
71–75	1

This graph, produced from the result, is called a **cumulative frequency curve**.

- How has it been produced?
- How can we use the graph to estimate the median and the interquartile range of the data?
- What is the minimum temperature recorded for the 5% of warmest days?
- A day is picked at random from these three months. How can you find the probability that the temperature on this day is higher than 60° F?

Straight lines can be used instead of a curve to join the points on a cumulative frequency diagram. This produces a **cumulative frequency polygon**.

1 This cumulative frequency polygon shows the temperatures, measured daily, for 90 days during the Summer.

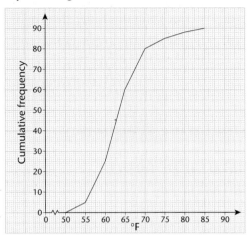

From the graph, estimate the median and the interquartile range.

2 At a secondary school of 1000 students, a survey is carried out to see how far students live away from the school.
This cumulative frequency curve summarises the results.

(a) Estimate the median distance between school and home.

(b) Estimate the range and the interquartile range for this data.

(c) One student is picked at random. What is the probability that this student lives within one mile of the school?

(d) Students who live more than two miles from school are provided with transport. How many students are provided with transport?

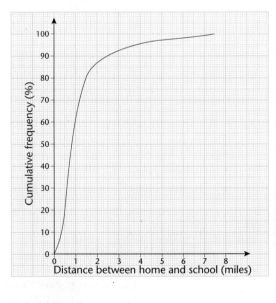

(e) For most students, the transport is free, but for those living more than 3 miles away there is a charge of £5 per week.
How many students have to pay £5 towards their transport?

3 This cumulative frequency curve shows the examination results of 240 Y11 students in their mock GCSE Intermediate Mathematics.

The top 15% students were awarded a grade B.
The next 25% were awarded a grade C.
The next 30% were awarded a D.
The next 25% were awarded an E, and the rest were ungraded.

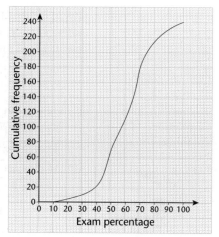

(a) What is the lowest mark a student could have achieved if she was told that she was in the top half of the year?

(b) A student received a mark of 54%. What grade should this student be given?

(c) A student was given a grade C. Between what range of values must this student's mark have been?

(d) A student is chosen at random. What is the probability that this student achieved at least 70% in the exam?

4 A number of batteries of two different types, A and B, were tested to see how long they lasted in continuous use.
These cumulative frequency graphs show the results.

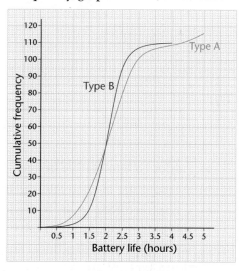

(a) Use the graphs to estimate the median for each type of battery.

(b) Use the graphs to estimate the interquartile range for each type of battery.

(c) Comment on the differences between the performance of type A and type B batteries.

5 Patients in a hospital were asked how long they had waited before having their operation. These are the results.

Time (t months)	Frequency	Cumulative frequency
$0 \leq t < 2$	37	37
$2 \leq t < 4$	20	57
$4 \leq t < 6$	35	
$6 \leq t < 8$	40	
$8 \leq t < 10$	41	
$10 \leq t < 12$	24	
$12 \leq t < 14$	15	
$14 \leq t < 16$	9	
$16 \leq t < 18$	3	

In Question 5, use the upper bound of the class interval to plot the points. For example, the first point should be plotted at (2, 37).

(a) Copy and complete the cumulative frequency table.

(b) Draw a cumulative frequency polygon to represent these results.

(c) Estimate the median waiting time.

(d) Estimate the interquartile range for these results.

(e) What is the probability that a patient has to wait more than a year for an operation?

6 This table shows the sizes of Cornish primary schools.

Number of students	Number of schools
1–50	4
51–100	22
101–150	48
151–200	32
201–250	17
251–300	5
301–350	1

(a) Produce a cumulative frequency curve for these results.

(b) Estimate the median and the interquartile range.

(c) Schools with less than 70 students are given extra money for equipment. About how many schools receive this extra money?

(d) The biggest 10% of schools are put on a building programme for extra classrooms. About how many students must a school have, before it is put on the building programme?

In Question 7, draw both cumulative frequency curves on the same set of axes.

7 This table shows the distribution of salaries of male and female employees in an office block.

Salary (£ w per year)	Frequency of males	Frequency of females
$w \leq 5000$	0	12
$5000 \leq w < 10\,000$	18	35
$10\,000 \leq w < 15\,000$	37	24
$15\,000 \leq w < 20\,000$	23	8
$20\,000 \leq w < 25\,000$	5	3
$25\,000 \leq w < 30\,000$	1	1
$30\,000 \leq w < 35\,000$	1	0

Compare the distributions of salaries for men and women, using the median and interquartile range.

Scatter diagrams and correlation

DISCUSSION POINT

What do these scatter diagrams tell you?

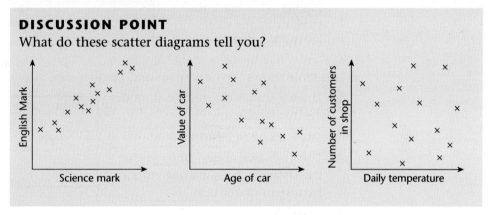

On a scatter diagram, a straight line is sometimes drawn which goes as to close to the points as possible. This line is called a **line of best fit**. It can be useful for relating two sets of data and predicting results .

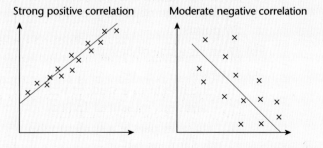

EXERCISE 8

1 This table shows the exam marks of twelve students in Science and
English tests.

(a) Draw a scatter diagram for
the English and Science
marks. Draw in a line of
best fit.

(b) Describe the relationship
between the performance
of a student in Science and
in English.

(c) Another student scored 65
in the Science test but
missed the English test.
Predict what mark this
student might score
on the English test.

Student	Science mark	English mark
1	59	69
2	45	50
3	60	75
4	38	40
5	44	51
6	71	95
7	34	37
8	59	69
9	57	72
10	53	68
11	56	69
12	80	78

2 This table shows the handspans and English shoe sizes of 20 Y10 students.

(a) Draw a scatter diagram of shoe size
against handspan.

(b) Draw a line of best fit.

(c) Use your line of best fit to predict
the shoe size for someone with a
handspan of 260 mm.

(d) Use your line of best fit to predict
the handspan for someone with a
shoe size of 2.

Handspan (mm)	English shoe size
170	4
180	6
210	6
205	7
180	$4\frac{1}{2}$
235	10
230	9
235	8
205	$8\frac{1}{2}$
200	7
195	6
200	6
230	10
215	9
170	$5\frac{1}{2}$
210	7
225	8
230	$8\frac{1}{2}$
190	$5\frac{1}{2}$
215	$8\frac{1}{2}$

For Question 3,
you need a copy of
Resource Sheet H:
Y10 Data.

3 (a) Draw a scatter diagram representing
the heights and armspans of the
students. You need only plot about
20 points.

(b) Draw in a line of best fit.

(c) Estimate
   (i) the height of a student whose
       armspan measured 155 cm
   (ii) the armspan of a student who
       is 5 ft 6 ins tall

4 For each of these, sketch a scatter diagram which could represent the relationship between the sets of data.

(a) Ice-cream sales and daily temperature

(b) The heights of adults and their ages

(c) The weights of pieces of cheddar cheese and their prices

(d) The number of potatoes in a kilogram and the size of the potatoes

(e) The number of sweaters sold and the daily temperature

5 Explore any possible correlations between the age, height and value of the trees listed in this table.

Tree	Age (years)	Height (m)	Value (£)
1	120	7	165
2	21	3	10
3	80	7	85
4	80	7	20
5	102	8	130
6	55	6	75
7	19	3	15
8	17	3	10
9	83	7	85
10	85	7	160
11	124	8	210
12	38	6	40
13	80	7	35
14	80	7	110
15	21	2	10
16	116	8	90
17	55	5	70
18	110	8	190
19	112	9	200
20	28	4	30

COURSEWORK OPPORTUNITY

Database

Testing a hypothesis

♦ Choose a hypothesis to test. It could be one of those you have worked on earlier in the chapter.

♦ Design a suitable questionnaire or data observation sheet to collect the data you need to prove or disprove your hypothesis.

♦ Choose a suitable sample for your survey.
Remember to explain how you chose your sample.

♦ Use some of the statistics you have met in this chapter to analyse your data.

♦ Finally, decide whether or not your hypothesis appears to be true.

Probability revisited

Exercise 9

1 Matthew and Anne often play snooker against each other. So far, Matthew
has won 15 games and Anne has won 21 games. Use this evidence to
estimate the probability that Anne wins the next game.

2 A weather forecaster says that there is a 20% chance of rain tomorrow.
What is the chance that it will not rain tomorrow?

3 (a) A 10p coin and a 5p coin are tossed together.
  List all the possible ways in which they can land.

  (b) (i)   What is the probability of obtaining two heads?
  (ii) What is the probability of obtaining at least one tail?
  (iii) If you repeated the experiment 100 times, on how many
      occasions would you expect to get a head and a tail?

4 (a) List all the possible outcomes when you toss three coins.

  (b) What is the probability that you end up with three tails?

  (c) What is the probability that you end up with at least one head?

5 (a) Copy and complete this table, showing the possible outcomes when
  two ordinary fair dice are thrown and their scores added.

  (b) Why are 'scoring a 2' and 'scoring an
    8' not equally likely?

  (c) Use your completed table to answer
    these questions.

    (i)   What is the probability of
        scoring 1?

    (ii) What is the probability of
        scoring 5?

    (iii) What is the probability of
        scoring an even number?

  (iv) What is the probability of scoring a prime number?

	1	2	3	4	5	6
1						
2		4				
3						9
4	5					
5						
6						

6 This table shows the numbers of students in a class who are male and
female and who are left- or right-handed.

If one person is chosen at random from
this class what is the probability that this
person is

(a) left-handed?   (b) female?   (c) a right-handed male?

	Male	Female
Left-handed	3	1
Right-handed	12	9

7 In a normal set of dominoes each piece has two 'numbers' on it, represented by spots. Each number is between 0 (blank) and 6. All the dominoes in the set are different. Here are four examples.

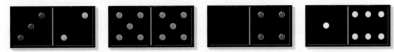

It may help you to list all the dominoes

How many dominoes are there in a complete set?

8 What is the probability that if I pick a single domino, without looking, from a normal set, the total number of spots is 12?

9 What is the probability that a domino, picked at random from a normal set, has

(a) less than 12 spots on it?   (b) a total of 9 spots on it?

10 (a) What is the modal number of spots on a single domino from a normal set?

(b) What is the probability that a domino with this number of spots is chosen?

11 A domino is chosen at random from a normal set.

(a) What is the probability that a domino with an even number of spots is chosen?

(b) What is the probability that the number of spots on the chosen domino is a square number?

(c) What is the probability that the chosen domino has at least one 'six' on it'?

(d) What is the probability that both numbers on the domino are odd?

(e) What is the probability neither of the numbers on the domino is a prime number?

12 One domino is chosen and noted. It is then replaced and the dominoes shuffled. Another domino is chosen.

(a) What is the probability that the 'double blank' is chosen both times?

(b) What is the probability that the total number of spots on both dominoes is less than 22?

(c) What is the probability that at least one of the dominoes contains at least one 'six'.

(d) What is the probability that neither of the dominoes contains a prime number?

(e) What is the probability that both of the dominoes contain at least one 'three'?

Nelson GCSE Maths STATISTICS AND PROBABILITY (INTERMEDIATE)

DISCUSSION POINT

Mary is running in the school sports. The probability that Mary wins the 100 metres race is 0.85. The probability that she wins the 200 metres is 0.6. Her performance in the 100 metres does not affect her performance in the 200 metres.

- What is the probability that she wins both races?
- What is the probability that she wins just one of the races?

This tree diagram may help you answer these questions.

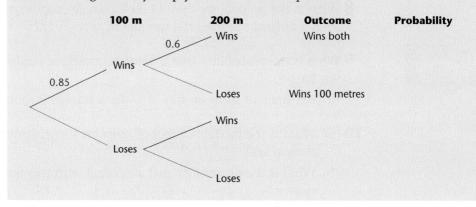

EXERCISE 10

1 I have just bought a computer and a video.
The probability that my computer goes wrong in the first two years is 0.15.
The probability that my video goes wrong in the first two years is 0.2.
What is the probability that in the first two years

(a) my computer does *not* go wrong?

(b) *neither* my computer *nor* my video goes wrong?

(c) either my computer or my video goes wrong, *but not both*?

2 These spinners are numbered as shown.

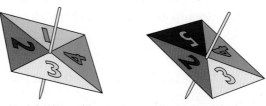

What is the probability that when both spinners are spun together

(a) at least one of the numbers is 2?

(b) the numbers are the same?

(c) the sum of the numbers is more than 4?

3 A shop sells red windmills and blue windmills to children.
The shop keeper picks a windmill at random and gives it to the child.
The probability of picking a red windmill is 0.6.
Some of the windmills do not work. The probability that a red windmill
does not work is 0.2. The probability that a blue windmill does not work
is 0.3. A child buys a windmill. What is the probability that it is

(a) blue?   (b) a blue windmill that works?

(c) a windmill that does not work?

4 Two normal dice are thrown and their scores are multiplied together.
What is the probability that the number obtained is

(a) greater than 20?   (b) even?

(c) a square number?   (d) a prime number?

5 Two normal packs of playing cards are shuffled together.
One pack has blue backs and the other pack has yellow backs.
A card is picked at random. What is the probability that it is

(a) a heart?

(b) a black card (spades or clubs) with a blue back?

(c) a spade with a yellow back?

(d) not a diamond and does not have a blue back?

(e) either a diamond or has a blue back but not both?

6 The chance of a type of drawing pin landing point up is 0.35. If it does
not land point up, it lands on its side.

(a) Two of these drawing pins are thrown. What is the probability that
    (i) both land on their sides?
    (ii) exactly one of them lands point up?

(b) Three of these drawing pins are thrown. What is the probability that

    (i) all three land point up?   (ii) at least one lands point up?

7 Donna and Wayne each write each of the letters of their own name on a
different card. So each of them has five cards.
Both sets of cards are placed face down on a table.
Wayne and Donna each pick up one of their own cards.
What is the probability that they both pick up a card containing

(a) an N?   (b) the same letter?

8 Peanuts are sold in blue bags and red bags. Some of the bags have tokens
to win prizes. The probability of a red bag having a token is $\frac{1}{24}$.
The probability of a blue bag having a token is $\frac{1}{12}$.
In a particular shop, the chance of being sold a red bag of peanuts is $\frac{3}{4}$.
If you buy one bag of peanuts, what is the probability of winning a prize?

Statistics for small data sets

For these numbers: 5, 6, 2, 4, 7, 7, 7, 2

To find the **mean,** add all the items and divide by 8, because there are 8 items.

Mean = 40 ÷ 8

= 5

The **mode** is 7 (because there are more 7s than any other number).

Put the results in order

| 2 | 2 | 4 | 5 | 6 | 7 | 7 | 7 |

lower quartile   median   upper quartile

The median is $5\frac{1}{2}$. It splits the results into two equal halves.

The lower quartile is 3. One quarter of the results are below it.

The upper quartile is 7. Three quarters of the results are below it.

Interquartile range = upper quartile – lower quartile

= 7 – 3

= 4

Range = highest result – lowest result

= 7 – 2

= 5

The mean, median and mode measure the *average* value of the data. The range and interquartile range give some indication of how *spread out* the data is.

Mean, median and modal class for grouped frequency distributions

This is a frequency distribution of ages of people in a social club.

To work out the mean, assume everyone in a class is the middle age of that class.

The **modal class** is 30 to 40 years (i.e. the class with the highest frequency).

Age (years)	Frequency (f)	Middle value	Frequency × middle value
$10 \leq y < 20$	4	15	60
$20 \leq y < 30$	33	25	825
$30 \leq y < 40$	60	35	2100
$40 \leq y < 50$	41	45	1845
$50 \leq y < 60$	22	55	1210
Total frequency	160	Estimated total of ages	6040

$$\textbf{Estimated mean} = \frac{\text{Estimated total of ages}}{\text{Total frequency}} = \frac{6040}{160}$$

This gives a mean of 38 years.
The median is the age of the 80th person, who is the 43rd person out of the 60 people in 30-40 years class (because 4 + 33 + 43 = 80).
So, 37 years is a reasonable *estimate* for the **median age**.

Cumulative frequency diagrams

Another way of estimating the median and interquartile range is to use cumulative frequency diagrams. This example uses the same data about ages of people in a social club.

Use the upper bound of the class interval for plotting points.

Age (years)	Frequency	Cumulative frequency
$10 \leq y < 20$	4	4
$20 \leq y < 30$	33	37
$30 \leq y < 40$	60	97
$40 \leq y < 50$	41	138
$50 \leq y < 60$	22	160
Total	160	

To work out the numbers in this column: add up the frequencies as you go along.

These should be the same.

From the table, the points (20, 4), (30, 37), (40, 97), (50, 138) and (60, 160) are plotted, and joined up with a smooth curve or with straight lines.

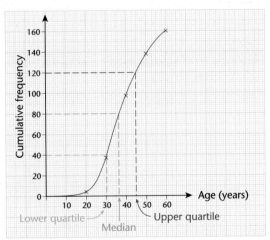

From the graph the median is 37 years and the interquartile range is 45 − 31 = 14 years.

Scatter diagrams

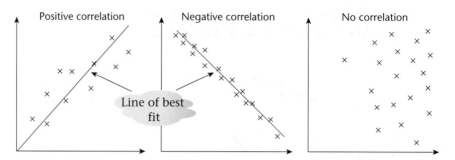

Probabilities involving more than one event

Example: In a bag, there are 4 blue balls and 3 red balls. One ball is chosen, replaced and then another chosen.

You can count all the 49 possibilities in this table to answer questions.

Probability of throwing two red balls $= \frac{9}{49}$

Probability of throwing one red and one blue ball $= \frac{12}{49} + \frac{12}{49} = \frac{24}{29}$

	B	B	B	B	R	R	R
B	BB	BB	BB	BB	BR	BR	BR
B	BB	BB	BB	BB	BR	BR	BR
B	BB	BB	BB	BB	BR	BR	BR
B	BB	BB	BB	BB	BR	BR	BR
R	RB	RB	RB	RB	RR	RR	RR
R	RB	RB	RB	RB	RR	RR	RR
R	RB	RB	RB	RB	RR	RR	RR

You can use a tree diagram to show the probabilities.

First draw	Second draw	Outcome	Probability
	B ($\frac{4}{7}$)	BB	$\frac{4}{7} \times \frac{4}{7} = \frac{16}{49}$
B ($\frac{4}{7}$)	R ($\frac{3}{7}$)	BR	$\frac{4}{7} \times \frac{3}{7} = \frac{12}{49}$
	B ($\frac{4}{7}$)	RB	$\frac{3}{7} \times \frac{4}{7} = \frac{12}{49}$
R ($\frac{3}{7}$)	R ($\frac{3}{7}$)	RR	$\frac{3}{7} \times \frac{3}{7} = \frac{9}{49}$

Probability of throwing one red and one blue ball $= \frac{12}{49} + \frac{12}{49} = \frac{24}{49}$

Probability of throwing two red balls $= \frac{9}{49}$

It is worth checking that all the probabilities in the right-hand column in the tree diagram add to 1.
$\frac{16}{49} + \frac{12}{49} + \frac{12}{49} + \frac{9}{49} = \frac{49}{49} = 1$

5 EQUATIONS

This chapter is about:

- linear equations
- simultaneous equations
- quadratic equations.

Always, sometimes, never

EXERCISE 1

1 For each of these pairs of expressions, try to find a value for the letter which makes the expressions equal. For some, there is more than one answer, for some one answer, and for some no answer at all.

(a) $a + 7$ and $a + 8$ (b) $y + 4$ and $4y$

(c) x^2 and $3x$ (d) $2g$ and $g + 20$

(e) $4(j + 1)$ and $4j + 4$ (f) $5(d + 2)$ and $5d + 2$

(g) $2a$ and $3a$ (h) $w - 3$ and $w + 3$

(i) x^2 and 25   (j) $a(a + 2)$ and $a^2 + 2a$

2 Invent another pair of expressions that are equal for only one value of x.

3 Invent another pair of expressions, that are equal for two values of x.

4 Invent another pair of expressions that are never equal.

5 Invent another pair of expressions that are equal for all values of x.

6 For each of these pairs of expressions, decide which ones are *sometimes equal*, which are *never equal* and which are *always equal*.

(a) $2y$ and y^2 (b) $r + r + r$ and $3r$

(c) $3x$ and $x + 6$ (d) $b + 10b$ and $11b$

(e) $b + 12$ and $b + b$ (f) $6g - g$ and $6(g - 1)$

(g) $4z + 1$ and $5z$ (h) $2(a + b + 1)$ and $2a + 2b + 1$

(i) $3a + 6b$ and $3(a + 2b)$ (j) $7a + b$ and $7(a + b)$

Testing generalisations by checking particular cases

Spreadsheet

7 Which of these expressions are always equal? Explain why.

$$\tfrac{1}{2}x + y \qquad \frac{x}{2} + \frac{y}{2} \qquad \tfrac{1}{2}(x + y) \qquad \frac{x + y}{2} \qquad \frac{x}{2} + y$$

$$x + \tfrac{1}{2}y \qquad \frac{y}{2} + x \qquad \tfrac{1}{2}x + \tfrac{1}{2}y$$

More linear equations

DISCUSSION POINT

You met linear equations in Chapter 13 in *Book 1*. Here are some more difficult linear equations. Can you solve them?

- $\frac{x}{5} - 4 = 3$
- $5x + 2 = \tfrac{3}{2}x + 16$
- $3x - \tfrac{1}{2}(x - 2) = 6$

- $\frac{x + 3}{5} - 1 = \frac{x - 4}{3}$
- $\frac{2x - 5}{6} + \frac{x + 2}{3} = \frac{3}{2}$

Exercise 2

1 Solve these equations.
   (a) $\frac{a}{3} + 4 = 11$ (b) $\frac{b}{9} - 6 = 0$ (c) $10 + \frac{2c}{3} = 2$

   (d) $\frac{17 + d}{3} = 5$ (e) $\frac{12 - e}{4} = 5$ (f) $27 - \frac{2f}{3} = 22$

2 Solve these equations.
   (a) $40 + 5a = 24 + 3a$ (b) $7b - 3 = 6b + 3$ (c) $10c + 60 = 5c + 35$
   (d) $4d - 10 = 2d - 3$ (e) $8e + 2 = 3e - 6$ (f) $10f - 7 = 6f - 4$

3 Solve these equations.
   (a) $3(a + 2) - 14 = 13$ (b) $2(2b - 15) = 6 + b$ (c) $2(c + 20) = 3(5 - c)$
   (d) $5(d + 2) = 2(d - 4)$ (e) $5(e - 2) = 2(e - 3)$ (f) $5(2f + 3) = 2(15 - f)$

4 Solve these equations.
   (a) $\frac{a + 6}{3} - 6 = \frac{2 - a}{2}$ (b) $\frac{2(b + 2)}{3} - 9 = \frac{5 - b}{5}$

   (c) $\frac{c + 4}{3} = 1 + \frac{c - 1}{6}$ (d) $\frac{2d + 21}{4} = 2 + \frac{d + 2}{8}$

   (e) $\frac{4e + 3}{2} + \frac{16e + 7}{4} = 7$ (f) $\frac{3(f + 3)}{2} - 3f = 6 + \frac{2 - f}{2}$

Simultaneous equations

Here are two examples of how to find a pair of numbers which obey two rules at the same time, i.e. *simultaneously*.

Example 1

$$x + y = 7 \quad \Rightarrow \quad x + y = 7$$
$$x + 3y = 11 \qquad x + y + y + y = 11$$

Compare these equations.

There are two extra 'y's in the second one and there is an extra 4 on the 'total'.

So, $2y = 4$ and y must be 2.

If $y = 2$, then x must be 5 for $x + y = 7$ to be true.

Check that when $x = 5$ and $y = 2$, the second rule $x + 3y = 11$ is true too.

Example 2

$$x + y = 8 \quad \Rightarrow \quad x + y = 8$$
$$x + 5y = 0 \qquad x + y + y + y + y + y = 0$$

The four extra 'y's in the second equation have made the 'total' go down by 8.

So, $4y = -8$ and y must be -2.

If $y = -2$, then x must be 10 so that $x + y = 8$.

Check that these values make the second equation true, too.

EXERCISE 3

1 For each pair of simultaneous equations, find the values which make both equations true.

    (a) $a + b = 7$ (b) $2c + d = 10$ (c) $e + f = 6$

          $a + 3b = 11$ $c + d = 7$ $e + 4f = 9$

2 For each pair of simultaneous equations, find the values which make both equations true.

    (a) $g + h = 13$ (b) $4j + k = 43$ (c) $3m + n = 18$

          $3g + h = 25$ $j + k = 13$ $7m + n = 10$

DISCUSSION POINT

This pair is harder to solve.

$$x + y = 5$$
$$3x + 2y = 18$$
$$\Rightarrow$$
$$x + y = 5$$
$$x + x + x + y + y = 18$$

There are extra of both x and y in the second equation, which have added 13 to the total. So, $2x + y = 13$.

This does not give one of the values, so another step is needed.

If $x + y = 5$, can you see that $2x + 2y = 10$, $3x + 3y = 15$, ..., $10x + 10y = 50$? There are many equations like this that are also true.

Choose the $2x + 2y = 10$ version.

$$2x + 2y = 10$$
$$3x + 2y = 18$$
$$\Rightarrow$$
$$x + x + y + y = 10$$
$$x + x + x + y + y = 18$$

The extra x has added 8 to the total, so $x = 8$. If $x + y = 5$, then $y = -3$. Check that these values of x and y make the second equation true, too.

- What would happen if you worked from the $3x + 3y = 15$ version?

- Why is it not sensible to choose the $7x + 7y = 35$ version?

To keep track of how you've solved the equations, it is a good idea to label the equations and record each step, like this.

EXERCISE 4

1 For each pair of equations, find the values which make both equations true.

(a) $a + b = 10$	(b) $2c + 5d = 29$	(c) $e + f = 10$
$2a + 3b = 23$	$c + d = 7$	$3e + 4f = 39$
(d) $g + h = 13$	(e) $4j + 2k = 24$	(f) $5m + 3n = 4$
$3g + 2h = 34$	$j + k = 9$	$m + n = -2$

2 For each pair of equations, find the values which make both equations true.

(a) $4a + 3b = 32$	(b) $2c + 3d = 53$	(c) $3e + 5f = -1$
$5a + 2b = 26$	$3c + 2d = 47$	$4e + 3f = 39$

In Question 2, you will have to multiply both equations to make the coefficients of one letter the same.

What happens when the coefficients have different signs?
In Example 1, if you add the two equations together, the terms in y cancel.
The coefficients must both be the same number, one positive and the other
negative, *before* you add the equations. In Example 2, you need to multiply
$2x - y = -8$ by 3 to make the y terms cancel.

Example 1

$$2x + y = 12 \quad ①$$
$$x - y = 3 \quad ②$$

$①+②$

$$3x = 15$$
$$x = 5$$

In ①

$$2 \times 5 + y = 12$$

$\Rightarrow$

$$y = 2$$

Example 2

$$x + 3y = 10 \quad ①$$
$$2x - y = -8 \quad ②$$

$②\times 3$

$$6x - 3y = -24 \quad ③$$

$①+③$

$$7x = -14$$
$$x = -2$$

In ①

$$-2 + 3y = 10$$

$\Rightarrow$

$$y = 4$$

EXERCISE 5

1 Add these pairs of equations to find the values which make them both true.

(a) $a + b = 13$
     $a - b = 7$

(b) $2c + d = 20$
     $c - d = 4$

(c) $e + f = 11$
     $3e - f = 25$

(d) $g - h = 1$
     $3g + h = 27$

(e) $4j - k = 0$
     $j + k = 10$

In Questions 2 and 3, make the coefficients numerically the same before you add.

2 For each of these pairs of equations, find the values which make them both true.

(a) $a + b = 18$
     $a - 2b = 9$

(b) $2c + d = 22$
     $c - 2d = 1$

(c) $e + 2f = 19$
     $3e - f = 15$

(d) $g - h = 7$
     $3g + 2h = 26$

(e) $4j - k = 75$
     $j + 3k = 35$

3 For each of these pairs of equations, find the values which make both equations true.

(a) $2a - b = 9$
    $3a + 2b = 31$

(b) $2c - d = 3$
    $4c + 3d = 31$

(c) $2e + f = 21$
    $3e - 2f = 14$

(d) $4g + 2h = 32$
    $3g - h = 34$

(e) $4j - 3k = 11$
    $5j + 2k = 8$

(f) $4m + 7n = -5$
    $5m - 6n = -21$

The pairs of equations in Question 4 are different, because there are two negative signs.

4 For each of these pairs of equations, find the values which make both equations true.

(a) $2a - b = 18$
    $3a - b = 28$

(b) $3c - d = 13$
    $c - d = 3$

(c) $5e - f = 24$
    $2e - f = 3$

(d) $3g - h = 21$
    $5g - 2h = 34$

(e) $2j - k = 22$
    $j - 3k = 21$

DISCUSSION POINT
Sometimes a different method of solving pairs of equations in easier.
Look at these equations.

$5x + y = 48$

$y = 3x$

You can solve them by substituting $3x$ for y in the first equation.
Make sure you understand how to do this.

EXERCISE 6

1 Solve these simultaneous equations.
   (a) $2x + y = 36$ (b) $5x - y = 42$ (c) $x + y = 26$
       $y = x$ $y = 3x$ $y = 2x - 1$

2 Solve these simultaneous equations.
   (a) $x + 2y = 48$ (b) $2x + 3y = 38$ (c) $y = 3x + 4$
       $y = x + 3$ $y = 2x - 6$ $y = x + 2$

EXERCISE 7

You can solve
these equations by
whichever method
you find easiest.

1 Solve these simultaneous equations.
   (a) $3s + 2t = 2$ (b) $7s + 2t = 22$ (c) $3s - t = 26$
       $2s + 5t = 16$ $s + t = 1$ $s + t = 2$
   (d) $3s - t = 53$ (e) $3s - 4t = 19$ (f) $3s + 4t = -19$
       $s + 4t = 9$ $t = 9 - 2s$ $2s - t = 4$

2 Solve these simultaneous equations.
   (a) $v + w = 5$ (b) $v = 5 - w$ (c) $v = w + 2$
       $3v + w = 2.6$ $3v + 5w = 22$ $3v + w = 11$
   (d) $v = 5w$ (e) $10v + 3w = 24$ (f) $5v + 3w = 14$
       $v + w = 9$ $3v - 5w = 19$ $3v + 2w = 7$

Simultaneous equations can also be solved by drawing graphs. This is
explained in Chapter 7 (see page 104).

EXERCISE 8

1 Two numbers have a sum of 39 and a difference of 11.
   Find the numbers.

2 A chocolate bar costs x pence and an ice cream costs y pence.

Two chocolate bars and one ice cream cost 50 pence.

Three chocolate bars and one ice cream cost 70 pence.

Find out how much a single chocolate bar costs.

Find out how much a single ice cream costs.

3 A farmer can buy three cows and four sheep for £1120 or she can buy six cows and four sheep for £1840.

Find out how much a cow costs and how much a sheep costs.

4 The cost of four cups and three saucers is £2.70. The cost of three cups and five saucers is £2.85. Find the cost of one cup, and the cost of one saucer.

DISCUSSION POINT

Red Phone offer three different charge bands:

- A: £15 a month line rental plus 40p per minute, or part of a minute, for each call made.

- B: £25 a month line rental plus 20p per minute, or part of a minute, for each call made.

- C: £35 a month line rental plus 10p per minute, or part of a minute, for each call made.

Which is the best charge band to choose?

Quadratic equations

DISCUSSION POINT

If $ab = 0$ what can you say about the value of a or b?

Here is an example of a quadratic equation.

$(x - 3)(x + 1) = 0$

- What are the *two* solutions of this equation?

- What are the solutions of the equation $x(x - 5) = 0$?

EXERCISE 9

1 For each of these quadratic equations, find the two solutions.

    (a) $(x - 3)(x - 6) = 0$ **(b)** $(x + 3)(x - 6) = 0$

    (c) $(x - 3)(x + 6) = 0$ **(d)** $(x + 3)(x + 6) = 0$

2 Solve these equations.

(a) $(x - 2)(x - 4) = 0$

(b) $(x + 2)(x + 9) = 0$

(c) $(x + 3)(x - 7) = 0$

(d) $(x - 2)(x - 24) = 0$

(e) $(x - 8)(x + 4) = 0$

(f) $(x - 6)(x + 3) = 0$

DISCUSSION POINT

- Factorise $x^2 - 5x - 6$.
- What are the two solutions of the quadratic equation $x^2 - 5x - 6 = 0$?
- What are the solutions of the equation $x^2 + 8x = 0$?
- Does the equation $x^2 = 16$ have two solutions?
- What about the equation $x^2 - 6x + 9 = 0$?

EXERCISE 10

1 Factorise these quadratic equations to solve them.

(a) $x^2 + 3x + 2 = 0$

(b) $x^2 + 4x + 3 = 0$

(c) $x^2 + 6x + 8 = 0$

(d) $x^2 + 6x + 5 = 0$

(e) $x^2 + 8x + 12 = 0$

(f) $x^2 + 7x + 12 = 0$

(g) $x^2 + 8x + 15 = 0$

(h) $x^2 + 6x + 9 = 0$

(i) $x^2 + 9x + 20 = 0$

(j) $x^2 + 4x + 4 = 0$

2 Factorise these equations to solve them.

(a) $x^2 + x - 2 = 0$

(b) $x^2 - x - 6 = 0$

(c) $x^2 + 3x - 4 = 0$

(d) $x^2 + 4x - 5 = 0$

(e) $x^2 - x - 12 = 0$

(f) $x^2 + 4x - 12 = 0$

(g) $x^2 - 2x - 8 = 0$

(h) $x^2 + 2x - 15 = 0$

(i) $x^2 - 4x - 12 = 0$

(j) $x^2 + 5x + 4 = 0$

3 Factorise these equations to solve them.

(a) $x^2 - 2x + 1 = 0$

(b) $x^2 - 4x + 3 = 0$

(c) $x^2 - 6x + 8 = 0$

(d) $x^2 - 6x + 5 = 0$

(e) $x^2 - 8x + 16 = 0$

(f) $x^2 - 7x + 10 = 0$

(g) $x^2 - 8x + 15 = 0$

(h) $x^2 - 6x + 9 = 0$

(i) $x^2 - 9x + 20 = 0$

(j) $x^2 - 4x + 4 = 0$

4 Factorise these equations to solve them.

(a) $2x^2 + 3x + 1 = 0$

(b) $3x^2 - 7x + 2 = 0$

(c) $3x^2 + 11x + 6 = 0$

(d) $2x^2 + x - 1 = 0$

(e) $6x^2 - x - 2 = 0$

(f) $6x^2 - 13x - 5 = 0$

(g) $5x^2 - 9x - 2 = 0$

(h) $4x^2 + 5x - 6 = 0$

(i) $2x^2 + 3x - 20 = 0$

(j) $10x^2 + 3x - 4 = 0$

DISCUSSION POINT
How would you solve this equation?

$x^2 + 4x = 21$

For this exercise,
rearrange where
necessary before
trying to solve the
equation.

EXERCISE 11

1 Solve these equations.

(a) $x^2 + 6x = 27$ (b) $x^2 - 6x = 7$

(c) $x^2 - 2x - 35 = 0$ (d) $x^2 + 4x - 45 = 0$

2 Solve these equations.

(a) $x^2 - x = 2$ (b) $x^2 + 36 = 15x$

(c) $x^2 - 12x = 13$ (d) $x^2 = 6x + 27$

3 Solve these equations.

(a) $x^2 + 8 = 9x$ (b) $x^2 - x = 72$

(c) $x^2 - 25 = 0$ (d) $4x^2 - 49 = 0$

4 Solve these equations.

(a) $x^2 + 5x - 36 = 0$ (b) $x^2 - 27x = -72$

(c) $x^2 - 81 = 0$ (d) $x^2 - 8x + 12 = 0$

Graphs can also be used to solve quadratic equations.
This is explained in Chapter 7 (see page 114).

EXERCISE 12

1 A rectangle has a width of x cm and a length 10 cm longer than its width.
Its area is 24 cm².

(a) Find a quadratic equation satisfied by x.

(b) Solve the equation to find the width of the rectangle.

(c) What solution does the equation have which is *not* the width of the
rectangle?

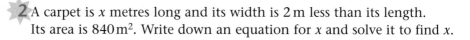 **2** A carpet is x metres long and its width is 2 m less than its length.
Its area is 840 m². Write down an equation for x and solve it to find x.

Nelson GCSE Maths   EQUATIONS (INTERMEDIATE)

3 A rectangle has a perimeter of 30 cm and one side is x cm.
Its area is 50 cm². What are the possible values for x?

4 A rectangular run for a pet rabbit is made by fencing off some grass next to a wall.

The total length of the fencing is 21 m. The width of the rabbit run is x m.
The area of the rabbit run is 55 m².
Write down an equation for x and solve it to find x.
Which of the solutions to the equation is a sensible solution to the problem?

5 A photograph 24 cm by 30 cm is mounted on a rectangular card so that there is a border, b cm wide, all the way around it.
The area of the border is 792 cm².
Write down an equation satisfied by b, and solve it to find the value of b.

6 The hypotenuse of a right-angled triangle is 1 cm longer than one side and 8 cm longer than the other side. Find the length of each side of the triangle.

CHAPTER SUMMARY

Linear equations and fractions

There are several ways of tackling equations with fractions. Sometimes, it is simplest to work with the fractions. At other times, it is easier to multiply through by a suitable number to clear the fractions.
The methods shown here indicate possible approaches.

Working with fractions

Example 1

$$\frac{x}{5} - 4 = 3$$

$$\Rightarrow \qquad \frac{x}{5} = 7$$

$$\Rightarrow \qquad x = 35$$

Example 2

$$5x + 2 = \tfrac{3}{2}x + 16$$

$$\Rightarrow \quad 5x - \tfrac{3}{2}x = 16 - 2$$

$$\Rightarrow \qquad \tfrac{7}{2}x = 14$$

$$\Rightarrow \qquad 7x = 28$$

$$\Rightarrow \qquad x = 4$$

Example 3

$$3x - \tfrac{1}{2}(x - 2) = 6$$
$$\Rightarrow \quad 3x - \tfrac{1}{2}x + 1 = 6$$
$$\Rightarrow \quad \tfrac{5}{2}x + 1 = 6$$
$$\Rightarrow \quad \tfrac{5}{2}x = 5$$
$$\Rightarrow \quad \tfrac{1}{2}x = 1$$
$$\Rightarrow \quad x = 2$$

Multiplying to clear the fractions

Example 1

$$\frac{x + 3}{5} - 1 = \frac{x - 4}{3}$$
$$\Rightarrow \quad 3(x + 3) - 15 = 5(x - 4) \qquad \text{(Multiply by 15)}$$
$$\Rightarrow \quad 3x + 9 - 15 = 5x - 20$$
$$\Rightarrow \quad 14 = 2x$$
$$\Rightarrow \quad x = 7$$

Example 2

$$\frac{2x - 5}{6} + \frac{x + 2}{3} = \frac{3}{2}$$
$$\Rightarrow \quad (2x - 5) + 2(x + 2) = 9 \qquad \text{(Multiply by 6)}$$
$$\Rightarrow \quad 2x - 5 + 2x + 4 = 9$$
$$\Rightarrow \quad 4x = 10$$
$$\Rightarrow \quad x = 2.5$$

Simultaneous equations

Example 1

$$3x + 2y = 8 \quad ①$$
$$5x + 3y = 13 \quad ②$$

$①× 3$ $\quad 9x + 6y = 24 \quad ③$
$②× 2$ $\quad 10x + 6y = 26 \quad ④$
$④-③$ $\quad x = 2$
In① $\quad 6 + 2y = 8$
$$2y = 2$$
$$y = 1$$
Check in② $\quad 5x + 3y = 10 + 3 = 13✓$

Example 2

$$y = x + 8 \quad ①$$
$$x + y = 14 \quad ②$$

Substitute①in② $\quad x + x + 8 = 14$
$$2x = 6$$
$$x = 3$$
In① $\qquad\qquad\quad y = 3 + 8 = 11$
Check in② $\quad x + y = 3 + 11 = 14✓$

Solving quadratic equations by factorisation

To solve $x^2 - 3x - 4 = 0$, first factorise

$x^2 - 3x - 4 = (x - 4)(x + 1)$

So

$(x - 4)(x + 1) = 0$

To make zero, one of the factors must be zero.

So, either $x - 4 = 0$ or $x + 1 = 0$

$$\Rightarrow x = 4 \text{ or } x = -1$$

6 MEASURES REVISITED

This chapter is about:

- identifying formulae for perimeter, area, volume and surface area of shapes
- percentages
- volume, capacity and density
- upper and lower bounds
- area of a trapezium
- bearings
- trigonometry problems.

Formulae for finding perimeter, area, volume and surface area

DISCUSSION POINT

Write down all the formulae you can think of for finding perimeters, areas and volumes of shapes.

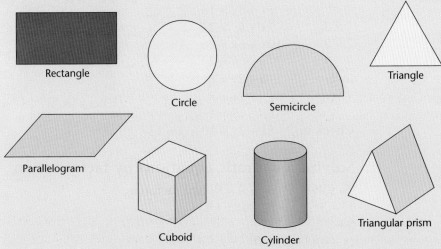

Rectangle

Circle

Semicircle

Triangle

Parallelogram

Cuboid

Cylinder

Triangular prism

How do you remember which formulae are for volumes, which are for areas and which are for lengths?

Suppose the length of one edge of a cube is a. Then the total edge length is $12a$.

The surface area of the cube is $6a^2$. The volume of the cube is a^3.
Area is obtained by multiplying two lengths together.
In the example of the cube:

$6a^2 = 6 \times a \times a$

Volume is obtained by multiplying three lengths together.
In the example of the cube:

$a^3 = a \times a \times a$

Here are some more examples.
- The circumference of a circle (length) is $2\pi r = 2 \times \pi \times r$.
- The area of a circle (area) is $\pi r^2 = \pi \times r \times r$.
- The volume of a cylinder (volume) is $\pi r^2 h = \pi \times r \times r \times h$.

Exercise 1

In this exercise, each small letter stands for a length. The large letter, A, stands for an area.

1 Each of these is a formula for length *or* a formula for area *or* a formula for volume. Which is which?
Which shape is each formula for?

(a) lw (b) $2(l + w)$ (c) $\frac{1}{2}bh$ (d) bh

(e) Ah (f) lwh (g) $2(lw + wh + hw)$ (h) $\frac{1}{2}\pi r^2$

2 Each of these is a formula for length *or* a formula for area *or* a formula for volume. Which is which?

(a) $2\pi r^2 + 2\pi rh$ (b) $\frac{ab}{2}$ (c) $\sqrt{c^2 - a^2}$ (d) $2A + ph$

(e) $\frac{2A}{b}$ (f) $a^2 b$ (g) $2a^2 + 4ab$ (h) $(\pi + 2)r$

3 One of these formulae is for the volume of a sphere.
One is for the surface area.

$$4\pi r^2 \qquad \frac{4}{3}\pi r^3$$

Decide which is which. Explain how you know.

4 If r and h are length measurements on a solid shape, which of these formulae could represent the volume of the shape?

$$\pi^2 rh - \pi r^2 h \qquad \pi r^2 h + 2\pi rh \qquad \pi r^2 h - r^2 h \qquad \pi r^2 h - r^2 h^2$$

5 V is a volume, A is an area and h is a length. Decide whether each of these formulae is for a length, an area or a volume.

(a) $\dfrac{V}{h}$ (b) $\dfrac{A^2}{3h}$ (c) $\dfrac{2V}{h^2}$ (d) $\dfrac{A^2}{V+h^3}$ (e) $\sqrt{3Vh}$ (f) $\dfrac{h(V+2Ah)}{A}$

Relationships between units

Chapter 12 in *Book 1* considered relationships between units. These ideas are revised here in the context of finding one quantity as a percentage of another. There is an example in the CHAPTER SUMMARY on page 100.

EXERCISE 2

1 (a) How many centimetres are there in one metre?

(b) What percentage of a metre is 25 centimetres?

2 (a) How many grams are there in a kilogram?

(b) What is 400 g as a percentage of 2 kg?

3 (a) What is 75p as a percentage of £3?

(b) What is 350 g as a percentage of 5 kg?

(c) What is 800 ml as a percentage of 3.6 litres?

(d) What is eight weeks as a percentage of one year?

4 A car journey takes $2\frac{1}{4}$ hours.
A woman picks up her friend after 35 minutes.
What percentage of the time has passed before she picks her friend up?

5 A room has an area of 14 m².
A rug in the room is a rectangle, 130 cm by 90 cm.
What percentage of the floor of the room does the rug cover?

6 What percentage of a week is Friday?

7 What percentage of a mile is 100 yards?

8 What percentage of a mile is a kilometre?

9 What percentage of a kilogram is 2 lb?

10 What is 15 metres as a percentage of 50 feet?

One mile is 1760 yards.
Five miles is about the same as eight kilometres.
One kilogram is approximately 2.2 lb.
One metre is approximately 3.28 feet.

11 (a) What percentage of a day does the hour hand take to travel once between 3 and 4 on a clock face?

(b) What percentage of a day does the minute hand take to travel once between 3 and 4 on a clock face?

12 (a) What percentage of a litre is a pint?

(b) What percentage of a pint is a litre?

There are approximately $1\frac{3}{4}$ pints in a litre.

Volume, capacity and density

DISCUSSION POINT

Look at these two tins from the kitchen.

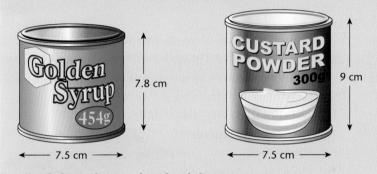

- Find the volume of each of the tins.
- Compare the weights of the contents of the tins.
- What does this tell you about golden syrup and custard powder?

The density of something is its weight (or mass) per given amount of volume.

$$\text{density} = \frac{\text{mass}}{\text{volume}}$$

The contents of a tin of golden syrup weigh 454 g.
The volume of the tin is 345 cm³.
So, the density of the syrup is

454 g ÷ 345 cm³ = 1.3 g/cm³ (correct to 2 significant figures)

The density of water is 1 g/cm³.
So, golden syrup is 1.3 times heavier than water.

Exercise 3

1 Here is a tin of custard powder.

(a) Find the volume of the tin.

(b) Find the density of the custard powder, correct to 2 significant figures.

2 Here is a tin of cocoa.

(a) Find the volume of the tin.

(b) Find the density of the cocoa, correct to 2 significant figures.

1 litre = 1000 cm³

3 A one-litre bottle of olive oil weighs 1590 g when full and 670 g when empty. Find the density of the olive oil, correct to 2 significant figures.

4 This packet of wheat biscuits contains 24 biscuits.

One serving (two biscuits) weighs 37.5 g.

(a) Find the volume of the packet.

(b) Find the density of the biscuits.

5 A 250 g packet of tea is a cuboid, 7 cm by 9 cm by 12 cm. Find the density of the tea.

6 This jar contains 411 g of mincemeat. Find the density of the mincemeat.

7 A packet of beef stock cubes is a cuboid, 6.5 cm by 4.3 cm by 4.3 cm. The stock cubes weigh 71 g. Find the density of the stock cubes.

8 This table contains information about some items of food.

	Capacity of container (ml)	Weight of contents (g)
Custard	900	623
Baked beans	540	538
Golden syrup	345	454
Jam	280	340
Soup	430	425
Lemon curd	350	411
Cocoa	480	226

(a) Show these results on a scattergram. Use a horizontal scale of 1 cm to represent 100 ml, and a vertical scale of 1 cm to represent 100 g.

(b) What does 1000 ml of water weigh? Plot a point on the scattergram to represent water and join this point to the origin.

(c) Which foods are heavier than water?

(d) Which food has the highest density? Which has the lowest?

(e) Join the point representing jam to the origin.
Use this line to estimate the capacity of a 200 g jar of jam.

(f) Use your graph to estimate the weight of 300 ml of cocoa.

9 A jar containing 340 g of jam has a capacity of 280 ml.
What will be the capacity of a jar containing 170 g of the same jam?

10 The capacity of a tin containing 226 g of cocoa is 480 ml.
What will be the capacity of a tin containing 339 g of cocoa?

The density of fresh water is 1 g/cm³.
The density of pure gold is 19 g/cm³.
The density of aluminium is 11 g/cm³.

11 What is the mass of a litre of water?

12 What is the volume of gold which weighs 50 g?

13 What is the weight of an aluminium rod with volume 50 cm?

14 The height of a 400 g can of tomatoes is 10.8 cm.

10.8 cm

A 300 g can of tomatoes has the same diameter. What is its height?

15 The diameter of a 430 g can of soup is 7.2 cm.

←——7.2 cm——→

An 860 g can of soup has the same height. What is its diameter?

Upper and lower bounds of measures

DISCUSSION POINT

It is never possible to measure anything *exactly*. The accuracy depends on the measuring instrument used.

• Suppose you are told that the length of a line is 23 cm.
  How accurate would you assume this measurement is?

• Suppose you are told that the length of a line is 23.0 cm.
  How accurate do you think this measurement is?

• What about these measurements?

| 2.65 m | 4.3 km | 503 km | 60 m |

Upper and lower bounds

Something might be measured as 19 cm to the nearest centimetre.
This means that
• the upper bound for its length is 19.5 cm, and
• the lower bound for its length is 18.5 cm.

Another way of writing this is 19cm ± 0.5 cm.

Something might be measured as 18.3 cm to the nearest millimetre.
This means that
• the upper bound for its length is 18.35 cm, and
• the lower bound for its length is 18.25 cm.

Another way of writing this is 18.3 cm ± 0.05 cm.

Something might be measured as 85 g to the nearest 5 g. This means that
• the upper bound for its mass (weight) is 87.5 g, and
• the lower bound for its mass is 82.5 g.

Another way of writing this is 85 g ± 2.5 g.

1 The weight of a package is measured as 170 g ± 10 g.
What are the upper and lower bounds for the weight of the package?

2 A time is given as 55 seconds ± 2.5 seconds.
What are the upper and lower bounds for the time?

3 A length is 230 cm to the nearest 10 cm. What is the longest it could be?

4 A length is 815 m to the nearest 5 m. What is the shortest it could be?

5 A line is 13.6 cm long to the nearest 0.1 cm.
Which of these could *not* be the length of the line?

| 13.649 | 13.7 | 13.61 | 13.55 | 13.66 |

6 A petrol pump shows the petrol delivered to be 19.82 litres, correct to the nearest 0.01 litres.
What are the greatest and least possible amounts of petrol delivered?

7 What is the difference between saying that the mass of an object is 5 kg and saying that it is 5.0 kg?

8 Give the upper and lower bounds for each of these measurements.
    (**a**) 18 cm   (**b**) 1.9 kg   (**c**) 43.2 s   (**d**) 7.31 kg
    (**e**) 20.0 m   (**f**) 5.04 s   (**g**) 5.40 s   (**h**) 3.700 km

9 A time for a race is given as 10.56 s to the nearest $\frac{1}{100}$ of a second.
What are the upper and lower bounds for the time?

10 The length of a shelf is measured as 1.60 m to the nearest centimetre.
What are the upper and lower bounds?

11 A pizza is being manufactured to sell from the freezer.
The diameter of the pizza is between 23 cm and 24 cm and the thickness is between 2 cm and 3 cm.
When designing a box for the pizzas a clearance of 5 mm is required all around the pizza, and also above it.
    (**a**) Sketch the smallest and largest pizzas.
    (**b**) Sketch the smallest box which would be suitable for *all* pizzas.
    (**c**) Calculate the surface area of this box.

12 A chocolate manufacturer wants to sell a filled bar in a protective card box. The bar of chocolate measures 16 ± 0.5 cm by 8 ± 0.5 cm by 15 ± 2 mm. A clearance of 2 mm is required in all directions for the box.

(a) Sketch the smallest and largest bars of chocolate that might be made.

(b) Sketch the smallest suitable box for any of the bars of chocolate.

(c) Find the area of card needed to make the box.

13 The radius of a cylinder is 4.5 cm correct to the nearest 0.1 cm and its length is 12 cm, correct to the nearest centimetre.

(a) What are the greatest and least possible values for the radius?

(b) What are the greatest and least possible values for the length?

(c) What is the least possible value for the volume of the cylinder?

14 A 100-metre race is measured correct to the nearest metre. The winner's time of 14.8 seconds is correct to the nearest tenth of a second.

(a) What are the maximum and minimum possible distances for the race?

(b) What are the maximum and minimum possible times for the race?

(c) What are the maximum and minimum possible speeds for the race?

Area of a trapezium

DISCUSSION POINT

There are various ways to find the area of a trapezium.

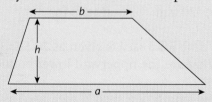

Here are three ways.

- *Method 1:* Put two trapeziums together to form a parallelogram.

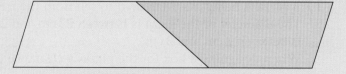

- *Method 2:* Split the trapezium into a rectangle and two triangles.

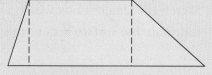

Justifying a generalisation

- *Method 3:* Transform the trapezium into a parallelogram. Do this by constructing a line through the mid-point of one side and parallel to the other side. Then, rotate the triangle obtained through 180°.

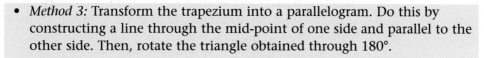

Use each of these ways to show this result:

Area of a trapezium = half the sum of the parallel sides × height

$$= \tfrac{1}{2}(a + b)h$$

EXERCISE 5

1 Find the areas of these trapezia.

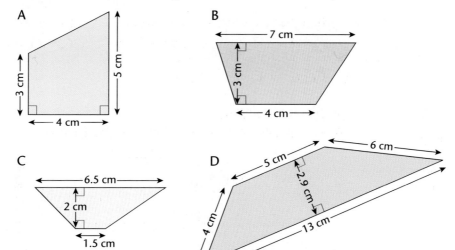

A

3 cm

5 cm

4 cm

B

7 cm

3 cm

4 cm

C

6.5 cm

2 cm

1.5 cm

D

5 cm

6 cm

2.9 cm

4 cm

13 cm

2 This isosceles trapezium has two angles of 45°. Find its area.

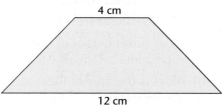

4 cm

12 cm

3 A square has sides of length 7 cm. Points are marked to divide each side in the ratio 3:4, as shown. Find the area of trapezium PQRS.

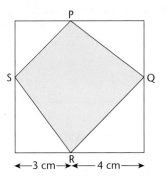

4 Find the volumes of these trapezium prisms.

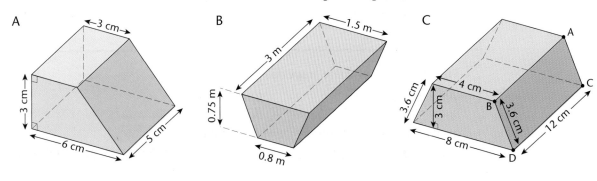

5 Here is a triangular prism.
  (a) Find the volume of the prism.

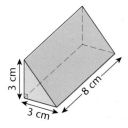

  (b) The triangular prism is cut into two pieces by a plane parallel to the base and half way up. Find the volume of the piece which is a trapezium prism.

You will need to use Pythagoras' theorem for Question 6.

6 An isosceles trapezium is formed by removing an equilateral triangle from a parallelogram, as shown.
  (a) What is the height of the trapezium?
  (b) What is the area of the trapezium?

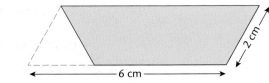

Bearings and trigonometry

Bearings are always given using three digits, e.g. 050°.

A bearing is an angle measured clockwise from North.
A bearing can be any angle between 000° and 360°

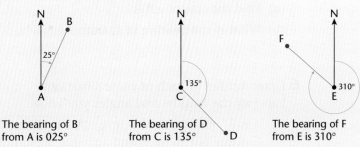

The bearing of B
from A is 025°

The bearing of D
from C is 135°

The bearing of F
from E is 310°

It always helps to make a sketch of a bearings problem before you do it.
Include a North arrow somewhere on your sketch to remind yourself where
North is.

EXERCISE 6

▷ Protractor

1 Write each of these directions as a bearing.

    (a) Due South   **(b)** Due West   **(c)** SE   **(d)** NE   **(e)** SW   **(f)** NW

You can draw
sketches to help you
answer Question 2.
You might find it
helpful to think of
first going from B
to A, and then
turning around to
go from A to B.

2 (a) The bearing of A from B is 055°. What is the bearing of B from A?

    (b) The bearing of P from T is 130°. What is the bearing of T from P?

    (c) The bearing of X from F is 195°. What is the bearing of F from X?

    (d) The bearing of D from L is 030°. What is the bearing of L from D?

    (e) The bearing of A from R is 320°. What is the bearing of R from A?

    (f) The bearing of D from B is 230°. What is the bearing of B from D?

3 A yacht race takes place around an equilateral triangular course ABC.
C is due East of B.

    (a) What is the bearing of B from C?

    (b) What is the bearing of C from A?

    (c) What is the bearing of B from A?

4 P, Q, R and S are marker posts for a square landing site for parachute
jumpers.
The bearing of Q from P is 110°.

Find the bearing of

    (a) S from P   **(b)** R from P

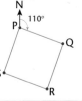

5 A, B and C represent three towns. A and B are both the same distance from C.

The bearing of B from A is 30°.
The bearing of C from B is 140°.

(a) Find the size of ∠ABC.

(b) What is the bearing of C from A?

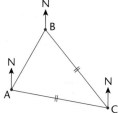

6 Draw *sketches* of each of these situations.
Label all the lengths and angles you know.

A: A is 37 miles, on a bearing of 040°, from B.
C is due North of B, and also due West of A.

B: X is 12 km from Y, on a bearing of 120°.
Z is due East of Y, and also due North of X.

C: P is on a bearing of 030° from Q. R is on a bearing of 300° from Q.

7 U is 4 km due West of H, and R is 3 km due North of U.

(a) Draw an accurate plan to show U, H and R, using a scale of 1 cm to represent 1 km.

(b) Use a protractor to find the bearing of H from R.

8 An aeroplane leaves Plymouth for Birmingham, 250 km away, on a bearing of 030°. It then leaves Birmingham for London, which is 150 km, away on a bearing of 140°.

(a) Draw an accurate plan of the aeroplane's flight, using a scale of 1cm to represent 50 km.

(b) The plane flies directly back to Plymouth.
How far does it have to fly, and on what bearing?

9 A town, T, is five miles North of a coastguard look-out post C.
A ship, S, is on a bearing of 110° from T, and 050° from C.

(a) Draw an accurate plan to show T, C and S.

(b) Use your plan to find out how far the ship is from both T and C.

10 A walker spots a church spire in the distance on a bearing of 290°.
She then walks North East for a distance of 2 miles.
The church spire is now due West of her.
Draw an accurate plan to find out how far East of the church she is.

DISCUSSION POINT

Discuss how you would use trigonometry to answer these questions.
A woman is one mile West and three miles North of a café.
She walks directly towards the cafe.
• On what bearing is she walking?

The woman then leaves the café and walks ten miles on a bearing of 050°
to get back to her car.
• How far is the car to the North of the café?
• How far is the car to the East of the café?

This is a reminder
of the
trigonometric
formulae

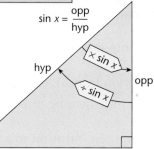

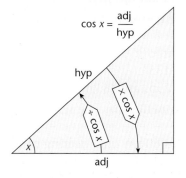

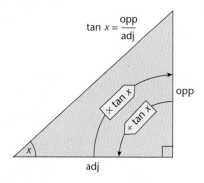

For each question
in Exercise 7, make
a sketch of the
situation and,
then, calculate
your answer
correct to a
sensible degree of
accuracy.

EXERCISE 7

1 A plane flies 150 km on a bearing of 063° from Heathrow airport.
How far North and East is the plane from the airport?

2 A ship sails 65 km on a bearing of 160° from a port.
How far South and East has the ship sailed?

3 A church spire is 1 mile South and 1.5 miles West of where you are
standing. On what bearing does it lie?

4 A fell runner runs 500 m West and then 350 m North. He then heads
straight back to his starting point. On what bearing is he heading?

5 Ambridge, A, is 12 miles from Borchester ,B, on a bearing of 020°.
Penny Hasset, P, is 16 miles from Borchester, B, on a bearing of 110°.
Calculate

(a) the size of ∠ABP   (b) the distance from Ambridge to Penny Hasset

6 Two ships, A and B, leave port P. Ship A sails 8 km on a bearing of 300°,
and ship B sails 5.8 km on a bearing of 210°. Calculate

(a) the size of ∠APB   (b) the distance between the two ships

7 Easby, E, is 16 miles from Farsley, F, on a bearing of 085°.
Garforth, G, is 10 miles from Farsley on a bearing of 175°. Calculate

(a) the size of ∠EFG   (b) the bearing of Easby from Garforth

8 Two walkers leave the café, C, at the same time. A man, M, leaves on a
bearing of 050°. A woman, W, leaves on a bearing of 140°. When the
woman has walked three miles, she can see the man on a bearing of 020°.
Calculate

(a) the size of ∠MCW

(b) the size of ∠CWM

(c) how far the man has gone

(d) the distance between the man and the woman

9 Ship A leaves harbour, H, on a bearing of 045°. Ship B leaves the harbour
on a bearing of 135°.
When the two ships are 48 km apart, ship A is 18 km from H. Calculate

(a) the size of ∠AHB   (b) the size of ∠HAB   (c) the bearing of B from A

10 A helicopter flies 60 km on a bearing of 040° and, then, turns on to a new
bearing of 110°, and flies a further 50 km.

(a) Calculate the total eastward distance it flies.

(b) Calculate the total northward distance it flies.

(c) What is the shortest distance between starting and finishing points?

EXERCISE 8

1 Find the areas of these right-angled triangles.

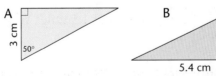

2 Find the areas of these isosceles triangles.

For Questions 2, 3
and 4, draw in and
then calculate the
height of the
triangle or
trapezium.

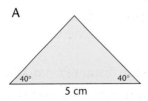 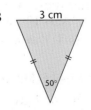 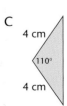

3 Find the areas of these triangles.

A

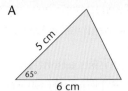

B

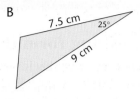

C

4 This an isosceles trapezium. Find the area of the trapezium.

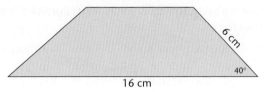

5 Find the areas of these trapezia.

A

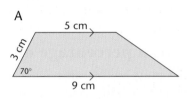

B

C

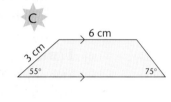

6 The area of this triangle is 5 cm². Find the perimeter of the triangle.

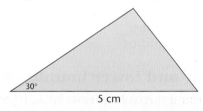

COURSEWORK OPPORTUNITY

Water channels

Spreadsheet

A channel for water is made from a strip of metal 12 cm wide, which is bent into the shape of a trapezium.

In the first instance, the strip is bent so that the width of the base is 6 cm and the trapezium is isosceles.

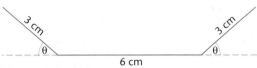

♦ Find the area of the cross section of the channel for different values of θ.

♦ Which value of θ gives the *maximum* cross-sectional area?

♦ Try other lengths for the base and investigate how to get the maximum cross-sectional area for the channel.

Nelson GCSE Maths   MEASURES REVISITED (INTERMEDIATE)

r = radius
h = height
l = length
w = width
A = area
V = volume

Distinguishing formulae

In formulae for length, each term consists essentially of just one length.

- Circumference of a circle = $2\pi r$
- Perimeter of a rectangle = $2(l + w)$
- Base of a triangle = $\dfrac{2A}{h}$

In formulae for area, each term consists essentially of two lengths multiplied together.

- Area of a circle = πr^2
- Surface area of a cylinder = $2\pi rh + 2\pi r^2$
- Cross-section of a prism = $\dfrac{V}{h}$
- Area of rectangle = lw

In formulae for volume, each term consists essentially of three lengths multiplied together.

- Volume of a cuboid = lwh
- Volume of a cylinder = $\pi r^2 h$
- Volume of a prism = Ah

Finding one quantity as a percentage of another

The units of the two quantities must be the same.

For example, to find what percentage 450 g is of 2 kg work out

$$\frac{450\,\text{g}}{2000\,\text{g}} \times 100\% = 22.5\%$$

$$\text{Density} = \frac{\text{mass}}{\text{volume}}$$

Upper and lower bounds of measures

Something might be measured as 19 cm to the nearest centimetre. This means that

- the **upper bound** for its length is 19.5 cm, and
- the **lower bound** for its length is 18.5 cm.

Another way of writing this is 19 cm ± 0.5 cm.

Something might be measured as 18.3 cm to the nearest millimetre. This means that

- the **upper bound** for its length is 18.35 cm, and
- the **lower bound** for its length is 18.25 cm.

Another way of writing this is 18.3 cm ± 0.05 cm.

Something might be measured as 85 g to the nearest 5 g. This means that

- the **upper bound** for its mass (weight) is 87.5 g, and
- the **lower bound** for its mass is 82.5 g.

Another way of writing this is 85 g ± 2.5 g.

Area of a trapezium

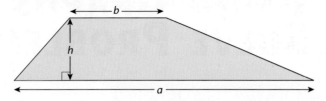

Area of trapezium = half sum of parallel sides × height
$$= \tfrac{1}{2}(a + b)h$$

Bearings

A bearing is an angle measured clockwise from North.
A bearing can be any angle between 000° and 360°.

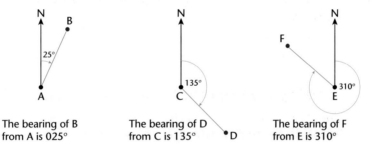

The bearing of B
from A is 025°

The bearing of D
from C is 135°

The bearing of F
from E is 310°

Trigonometry

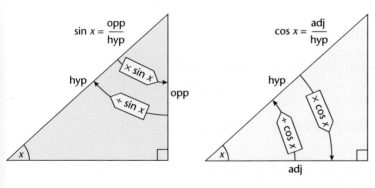

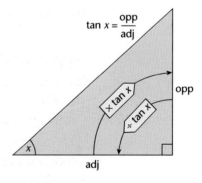

$$\sin x = \frac{\text{opp}}{\text{hyp}}$$

$$\cos x = \frac{\text{adj}}{\text{hyp}}$$

$$\tan x = \frac{\text{opp}}{\text{adj}}$$

7

USING GRAPHS TO SOLVE PROBLEMS

This chapter is about:

- using graphs to solve equations including simultaneous equations
- graphs of quadratic functions, cubic functions and reciprocal functions
- solving equations using trial and improvement
- solving inequalities, and using inequalities to describe regions
- interpreting everyday graphs.

Using graphs to solve equations

DISCUSSION POINT

This is the graph of
$y = 2x + 3$.

You can use this graph to
see what is the value of
x on the graph, when
$y = 14$.

Notice that $x = 5.5$ is the
solution of the equation
$2x + 3 = 14$.

- Use the same graph to
  solve the equation
  $2x + 3 = 8$.

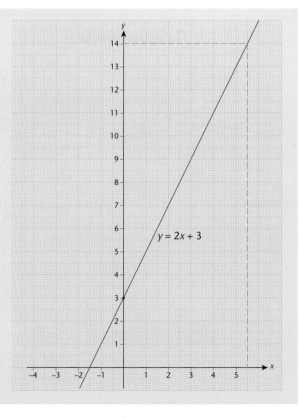

$y = 2x + 3$

This is the graph of $y = x^2$. It can be used to solve the equation $x^2 = 10$, by finding all the values of x for which $y = 10$.

- How many values are there?
- What are these values?

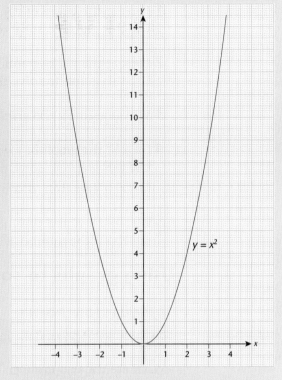

On this scale of graph, it is only possible to be accurate to 1 decimal place. For greater accuracy, the scale of the graph needs to be larger.

This is the graph of $y = x^3 - 4x$.

- Use it to solve the equation $x^3 - 4x = 2$.
- What are the roots of the equation $x^3 - 4x = 0$?

The solutions of an equation are sometimes called the **roots** of the equation.

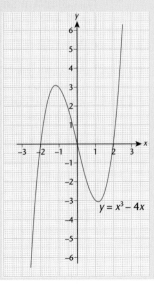

1 Look at the graph of $y = 2x + 3$ in the DISCUSSION POINT on page 102.
Use this graph to solve the equation $2x + 3 = 10$.

2 Look at the $y = x^2$ graph in the DISCUSSION POINT on page 103.
Use this graph to solve the equation $x^2 = 13$.

3 Why does the $y = x^2$ graph show there no solutions to the equation $x^2 = -4$?

4 Look at the graph of $y = x^3 - 4x$ in the DISCUSSION POINT on page 103.
Use this graph to solve these equations.
   (a) $x^3 - 4x = 0$ (b) $x^3 - 4x = 3$ (c) $x^3 - 4x = 5$

5 If $x^3 - 4x = K$ and there is only one positive solution for x, what can you say about the number K?

Using graphs to solve simultaneous equations

DISCUSSION POINT

Two numbers add up to ten, and the second number is three less than the first.

What are the two numbers?

If the pair of numbers are called x and y then the rule 'they add up to 10' can be written in algebra as $x + y = 10$.

The rule 'the second is 3 less than the first' can be written as $y = x - 3$.

This diagram shows the graphs of $x + y = 10$ and $y = x - 3$.

There is one point which is on both lines and, so, obeys both rules.

- What is it?

- Check that the x and y coordinates of this point do add up to 10, and that one coordinate is 3 less than the other.

- Which coordinate, x or y, is the first number? Which is the second number?

- How do you know there is no other pair of numbers which obeys both rules?

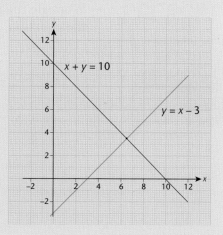

▷ Graph paper

EXERCISE 2

1 Draw the graphs of $x + y = 5$ and $y = x + 4$, and then use your graphs to find this pair of numbers.

In each question in Exercise 2, draw both graphs on the same set of axes.

They add up to 5, and the second is 4 more than the first.

2 Draw the graphs of $x + y = 2$ and $y = x + 5$, and then use your graphs to find this pair of numbers.

They add up to 2, and the second is 5 more than the first.

3 (a) Write down equations for these two rules about a pair of numbers, x and y.

They add up to 8, and the second is 3 more than the first.

(b) Draw the graphs of the equations, and find the pair of numbers.

4 (a) Write down equations for these two rules about a pair of numbers, x and y.

They add up to 2, and the difference between them is 7.

(b) Draw the graphs of the equations and find the pair of numbers.

5 Draw graphs to find this pair of numbers.

They add up to 3, and the difference between them is 8.

6 For each of these, draw graphs to find a pair of numbers, x and y, which obey both rules.

   (a) $y = x + 2$ and $y = 2x - 3$ **(b)** $x + y = 4$ and $y = 3x - 2$

   (c) $y = x + 1$ and $y = 2x + 3$ **(d)** $y = \frac{1}{2}x + 1$ and $y = 3x - 3$

7 For each of these, draw graphs to find a pair of numbers, x and y, which obey both rules. Explain what happens and what it means.

   (a) $y = 4 - x$ and $x + y = 6$ **(b)** $y = 2x - 3$ and $\frac{1}{2}y = x + 1$

For Question 8, you may want to rearrange each equation first.

8 Solve these simultaneous equations by drawing graphs.

   (a) $2x - y = 1$ **(b)** $x + y = 4$

        $x + 2y = 5$ $3x - y = 1$

   (c) $-x + y = 2$ **(d)** $-x + y = 2$

        $3x - y = 5$ $3x - 3y = -6$

Graphs of equations with x^2: quadratic graphs

DISCUSSION POINT

Draw the graph of $y = x^2 + 2x - 1$ for $-4 \leq x \leq 4$.

Use your graph to find the roots of the equation $x^2 + 2x - 1 = 0$.

▷ Graph paper

EXERCISE 3

1 This table shows some (x, y) pairs which may be plotted to draw the graph of $y = x^2 + 3x - 1$.

x	−4	−3.5	−3	−2.5	−2	−1.5	−1	−0.5	0	0.5	1	1.5	2
y	3	0.75	−1	−2.25	−3	−3.25	−3	−2.25	−1	0.75	3	5.75	9

(a) Plot the whole number values, and whichever of the in-between points you need, in order to draw a smooth curve.

(b) Use your graph to find the (approximate) roots of $x^2 + 3x - 1 = 0$.

2 (a) Use this table to draw the graph of $y = \frac{1}{2}x^2 - 2x + 1$.

x	−2	−1.5	−1	−0.5	0	0.5	1	1.5	2	2.5	3	3.5	4	4.5	5
y	7	5.125	3.5	2.125	1	0.125	−0.5	−0.875	−1	−0.875	−0.5	0.125	1	2.125	3.5

(b) Use your graph to solve the equation $y = \frac{1}{2}x^2 - 2x + 1$.

3 (a) Use this table to draw the graph of $y = 5 - 2x^2$.

x	−3	−2.5	−2	−1.5	−1	−0.5	0	0.5	1	1.5	2	2.5	3
y	−13	−7.5	−3	0.5	3	4.5	5	4.5	3	0.5	−3	−7.5	−13

(b) Use your graph to solve the equation $y = 5 - 2x^2$.

4 (a) Draw the graph of $y = x^2 + 3x - 2$, for $-5 \leq x \leq 2$.

(b) Use your graph to solve the equation $x^2 + 3x - 2 = 0$.

5 (a) Draw the graph of $y = x^2 + 2x - 3$, for $-5 \leq x \leq 3$.

(b) Use your graph to solve the equation $x^2 + 2x - 3 = 0$.

(c) What is the minimum value of y on the graph?

6 (a) Draw the graph of $y = x^2 + 5x + 3$, for $-6 \leq x \leq 1$.

(b) Use your graph to solve the equation $x^2 + 5x + 3 = -2$.

7 **(a)** Draw the graph of $y = x^2 - 2x$, for $-2 \le x \le 4$.

(b) Solve the equation $x^2 - 2x = 5$.

(c) What is the minimum value of y on the graph?
For which value of x does this minimum value occur?

8 **(a)** Draw the graph of $y = x^2 - 4x + 2$, for $-2 \le x \le 5$.

(b) On the same axes, draw the graph of $y = 2 - x$.

(c) Solve the equation $x^2 - 4x + 2 = 2 - x$.

9 **(a)** Draw the graph of $y = 2x^2 - 3x - 4$, for $-2 \le x \le 4$.

(b) On the same axes, draw the graph of $y = 2x$.

(c) Solve the equation $2x^2 - 3x - 4 = 2x$.

10 **(a)** Draw the graph of $y = -x^2 + 5x - 2$, for $-1 \le x \le 6$.

(b) Solve the equation $-x^2 + 5x - 2 = 0$.

(c) What is the maximum value of y on the graph?
For which value of x does this maximum value occur?

11 **(a)** Draw the graph of $y = (5 - x)(x + 2)$, for $-3 \le x \le 6$.

(b) Solve the equation $(5 - x)(x + 2) = 0$.

DISCUSSION POINT

This is the graph of $y = x^2 + 4x - 5$.

Factorise $x^2 + 4x - 5$.

- What is the connection between the factors and the points where the graph crosses the x-axis?

- Where does the graph cross the y-axis?
  How does the equation tell you this?

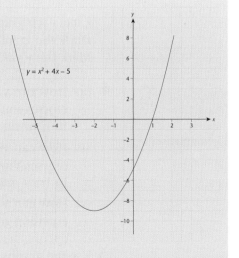

The graph has a line of symmetry.

- What is the equation of this line?
- What are the roots of $x^2 + 4x - 5 = 0$?

EXERCISE 4

1 The quadratic expression $x^2 - 5x - 6$ factorises to $(x - 6)(x + 1)$.

    (a) Which of the graphs on Resource Sheet I: *Quadratic graphs* is
$y = x^2 - 5x - 6$?
On a copy of Resource Sheet I, label this graph with both ways of
writing the equation: $y = x^2 - 5x - 6$ and $y = (x - 6)(x + 1)$.

    (b) Draw the graph's line of symmetry on Resource Sheet I, and write its
equation on the line.

    (c) Mark on the graph the y value of the point where the graph crosses
the y-axis.

2 **(a)** Factorise $x^2 - 6x + 5$.

    (b) Which of the graphs on Resource Sheet I is $y = x^2 - 6x + 5$?
Label this graph with both ways of writing the equation.

    (c) Draw the graph's line of symmetry on Resource Sheet I, and write its
equation on the line.

    (d) Mark on the graph the y value of the point where the graph crosses
the y-axis.

3 For each of these equations, find the graphs on Resource Sheet I.

$$y = x^2 + 4x + 3 \qquad y = 8 + 2x - x^2 \qquad y = x^2 - 5x + 4$$
$$y = 5 - 4x - x^2 \qquad\qquad y = x^2 + 4x$$

Label each graph with both ways of writing the equation.
Draw the graph's line of symmetry and write its equation on the line.
Mark the y value of the point where the graph crosses the y-axis.

4 **(a)** How can you tell from the equation of a quadratic graph where it
crosses the y-axis?
In how many places can it cross the y-axis?

    (b) How can you tell from the equation of a quadratic graph where it
crosses the x-axis?
In how many places can it cross the x-axis?

    (c) How can you tell from the equation of a quadratic graph what the
equation of its line of symmetry is?

5 Use the graphs on Resource Sheet I: *Quadratic graphs* to find the two roots
of each of these equations.

    (a) $y = x^2 + 4x + 3$ **(b)** $y = x^2 - 6x + 5$ **(c)** $y = x^2 - 5x - 6$

    (d) $y = 5 - 4x - x^2$ **(e)** $y = x^2 - 5x + 4$ **(f)** $y = 8 + 2x - x^2$

    (g) $y = x^2 + 4x$

Graphs of equations with x^3: cubic graphs

DISCUSSION POINT
Two examples of equations with x^3 are $y = x^3$ and $y = x^3 - 4x$.
These are their graphs.

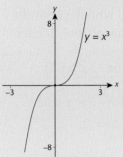

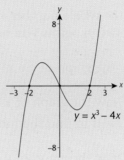

A graph plotter or graphical calculator might be useful.

Here are some more examples of equations with x^3.

$$y = x^3 - 2x^2 \quad y = x^3 - 9x \quad\quad y = x^3 + 3x^2 - 5x - 2 \quad\quad y = x^3 + x^2$$

Here are their graphs. Try to identify which is which.

A
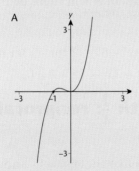

B
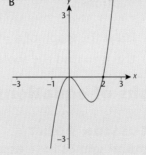

C
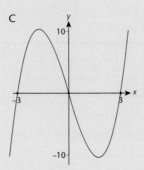

D
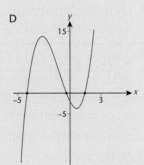

EXERCISE 5

1 This table shows some (x, y) pairs which may be plotted to draw the graph of

$y = \frac{1}{5}x^3 - x^2 + 2.$

Plot the whole number values, and whichever of the in-between points you need, to draw a smooth curve.

x	y
–2	–3.6
–1.5	–0.925
–1	0.8
–0.5	1.725
0	2
0.5	1.775
1	1.2
1.5	0.425
2	–0.4
2.5	–1.125
3	–1.6
3.5	–1.675
4	–1.2
4.5	–0.025
5	2
5.5	5.025
6	9.2

2 Draw the graph of $y = x^3 + 2x - 1$ for $-2 \leq x \leq 2$.

3 (a) Draw the graph of $y = x^3 - 4x$ for $-3 \leq x \leq 3$.

(b) Use it to find the roots of $x^3 - 4x = 0$.

4 (a) Draw the graph of $y = x^3 + 3x^2$ for $-4 \leq x \leq 1$.

(b) Use it to solve these equations.

(i) $x^3 + 3x^2 = 0$

(ii) $x^3 + 3x^2 = 4$

(iii) $x^3 + 3x^2 = 5$

(c) If $x^3 + 3x^2 = K$, for what values of K will there be three solutions?

> In Questions 2 to 5, you may find it helpful to make a table of all the y values you need.

5 (a) Draw the graph of $y = x^3 + 3x^2 - 5x - 2$ for $-5 \leq x \leq 2$.

(b) Use it to find the roots of $x^3 + 3x^2 - 5x - 2 = 0$.

Graphs of equations with $\frac{1}{x}$: reciprocal graphs

DISCUSSION POINT

Reciprocal graphs have equations like these: $y = \frac{10}{x}$ and $y = \frac{100}{x}$.

In this table, the rule connecting x and y is $y = \frac{6}{x}$. Some of the y values are given. Work out the missing y values.

x	–60	–12	–6	–5	–4	–3	–2	–1	0	1	2	3	4	5	6	12	60
y		–0.5		–1.2	–1.5				???	6		2			1		

Why is no value given for $6 \div 0$?

This extra table shows what happens as x draws closer to 0.

Work out the y values.

x	–1	–0.5	–0.3	–0.1	0	0.1	0.3	0.5	1
y					???				

This is the graph of $y = \frac{6}{x}$. The shape of this graph is called a **rectangular hyperbola**.

All reciprocal graphs have two separate branches, and these must *not* be joined.

If the scale on the *x*-and *y*-axes is the same, then the graph is symmetrical.

- What are the lines of symmetry?
- What would the graph of $y = -\frac{6}{x}$ look like?

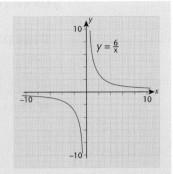

EXERCISE 6

▷ Graph paper

1 Draw the graph of $y = \frac{4}{x}$ for $-5 \le x \le 5$.

2 (a) Draw the graph of $y = \frac{12}{x}$ for $-10 \le x \le 10$.
   (b) On the same axes, draw the graph of $y = \frac{8}{x}$.
   (c) On the same axes, draw the graph of $y = \frac{5}{x}$.
   (d) How does the graph of $y = \frac{a}{x}$ change, as *a* changes?
   (e) What happens if *a* is a negative number?

3 (a) Draw the graph of $y = \frac{3}{x}$ for $-3 \le x \le 3$.
   (b) Find *x* on the graph when
      (i) $y = 2.2$ **(ii)** $y = -1.3$
   (c) For what values of *x* on the graph is *y* positive, but less than 2?
   (d) For what values of *x* on the graph is *y* negative, but greater than -1?
   (e) For what values of *x* on the graph is $-2 \le y \le 2$?

4 (a) Draw the graph of $y = \frac{10}{x}$ for $-10 \le x \le 10$.
   (b) Draw the graph of $y = x$ on the same axes to solve the equation $\frac{10}{x} = x$.
   (c) Compare your answer to part (b) with the value of $\sqrt{10}$.
      Explain why $\sqrt{10}$ is the *exact* solution to the equation $\frac{10}{x} = x$.

5 A rectangle has length *x* and width *y*. Its area is 100 and its perimeter is 50.
   (a) Explain why $y = \frac{100}{x}$ and $y = 25 - x$.
   (b) Draw the graph of $y = \frac{100}{x}$ for $0 \le x \le 40$.
   (c) On the same axes, draw the line $y = 25 - x$.
   (d) Use the graphs to solve the equation $\frac{100}{x} = 25 - x$.
   (e) What is the length and width of the rectangle?

Identifying graphs

▷ Resource Sheet J:
Sorting non-linear
graphs

A graph plotter or
graphical calculator
might be useful.

DISCUSSION POINT

Four families of graphs have been looked at in this chapter: straight lines, quadratic graphs, cubic graphs, and reciprocal graphs.

How do you decide to which family a graph belongs?

For each of these graphs, say which of the four families it belongs to.

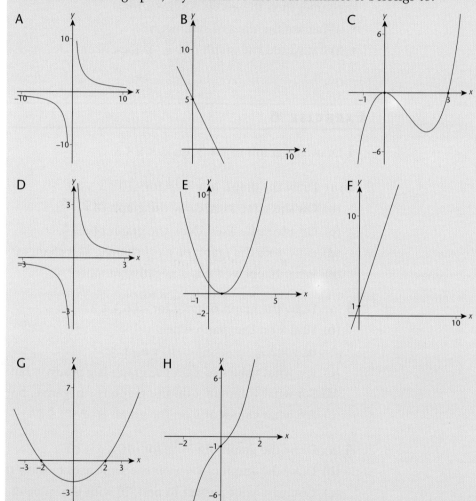

Once you know the family, can you match it to a suitable equation?

What are the important details you need to look for?

These are the equations of the graphs. Match the graphs to the equations.

$$y = 3x + 1 \qquad y = 5 - 2x \qquad y = \tfrac{1}{2}x^2 - 2 \qquad y = x^2 - 2x + 1$$

$$y = x^3 - 3x^2 \qquad y = x^3 + 2x - 1 \qquad y = \frac{8}{x} \qquad y = \frac{1}{x}$$

Now play the game *Sorting non-linear graphs*, using the cards from Resource Sheet J.

Making
generalisations

1 Look at these three graphs.

A

B

C

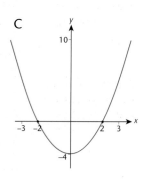

(a) Three of these four equations match the three graphs.

$$y = x^3 - x \qquad y = \frac{10}{x} \qquad y = 3x + 2 \qquad y = x^2 - 4$$

Which equation matches which graph?

(b) Sketch the fourth graph.

2 Look at these three equations.

$$y = x^3 \qquad y = 3 - x^2 \qquad y = \frac{5}{x}$$

(a) Three of these four graphs match the three equations.

A

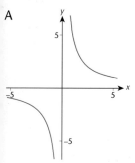

B

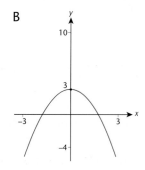

C

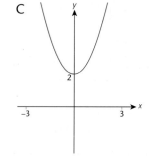

D

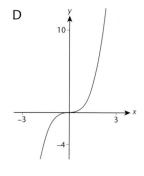

Which graph matches which equation?

(b) Suggest the fourth equation.

3 (a) Look at these three graphs.

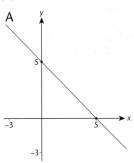
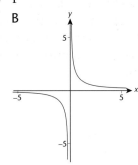
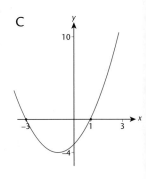

(b) Match the graphs to three of these four equations.

$$y = x^2 + 2x - 3 \qquad y = 5 - x \qquad y = \frac{1}{x} \qquad y = x^3 - 3$$

(c) Sketch the fourth graph.

Solving quadratic and cubic equations using graphs and trial and improvement

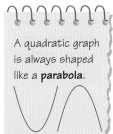

A quadratic graph is always shaped like a **parabola**.

Here are the quadratic graphs for the equations $y = x^2 - 3x + 1$, $y = x^2 + 4x + 4$ and $y = x^2 + 3x + 3$.

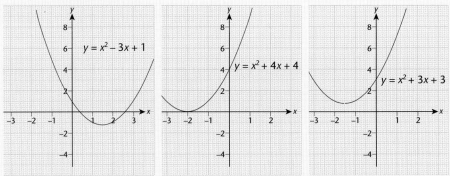

- The graph of $y = x^2 - 3x + 1$ crosses the x-axis at *two* points.
  This means that the equation $x^2 - 3x + 1 = 0$ has *two* solutions.
- The graph of $y = x^2 + 4x + 4$ touches the x-axis at *one* point.
  This means that the equation $x^2 + 4x + 4 = 0$ has *one* solution.
- The graph of $y = x^2 + 3x + 3$ does not meet the x-axis at all.
  This means that the equation $x^2 + 3x + 3 = 0$ has *no* solutions.

So, some quadratic equations have *two* solutions, some have *one* solution and some have *no* solutions.

Spreadsheet

DISCUSSION POINT

Use the graph of $y = x^2 - 3x + 1$ on page 114 to find the approximate values of the two solutions to $x^2 - 3x + 1 = 0$.
Now use trial and improvement to find each of these solutions, correct to 2 decimal places.

EXERCISE 8

1 This is the graph of $y = x^2 - 3x - 3$.

   (a) From the graph, write down approximate values for the two roots of the equation $x^2 - 3x - 3 = 0$.

   (b) Use trial and improvement to find the two roots of the equation, correct to 2 decimal places.

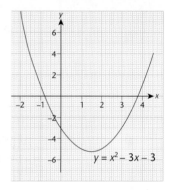

2 For each of these equations, state the number of solutions by looking at its graph. Then, using the graph, write down approximate values for the solutions. Then use trial and improvement to find each solution, correct to 2 decimal places.

   (a) $x^2 + 4x - 4 = 0$

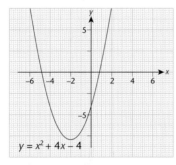

   (b) $x^2 - x + 2 = 0$

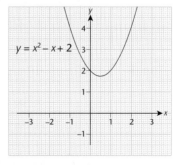

   (c) $5 + 2x - x^2 = 0$

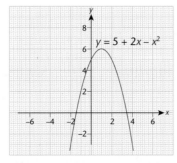

   (d) $x^2 - 5x + 6.25 = 0$

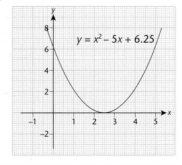

A cubic graph is always shaped like one of these.

Here are the cubic graphs for the equations $y = x^3 + x - 4$, $y = 2x^3 - 3x^2 + 1$ and $y = x^3 - 3x^2 + 1$.

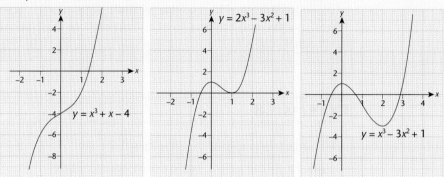

- The graph of $y = x^3 + x - 4$ crosses the x-axis at *one* point.
  This means that the equation $x^3 + x - 4 = 0$ has *one* solution.

- The graph of $y = 2x^3 - 3x^2 + 1$ crosses the x-axis at one point and touches it at another.
  This means that the equation $2x^3 - 3x^2 + 1 = 0$ has *two* solutions.

- The graph of $y = x^3 - 3x^2 + 1$ crosses the x-axis at three points.
  This means that the equation $x^3 - 3x^2 + 1 = 0$ has *three* solutions.

So, some cubic equations have *three* solutions, some have *two* solutions and some have *one* solution.

DISCUSSION POINT

Look at this graph of $y = x^3 - 2x^2 + 2$.

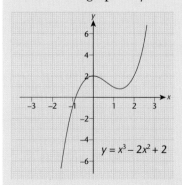

How many solutions are there to the equation $x^3 - 2x^2 + 2 = 0$?

Now use trial and improvement to find the solution, correct to 2 decimal places.

1 This is the graph of $y = x^3 + 2x^2 - 4$.

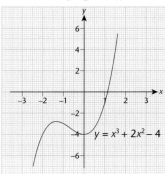

(a) From the graph, write down an approximate value for the root of the equation $x^3 + 2x^2 - 4 = 0$.

(b) Use trial and improvement to find this root, correct to 2 decimal places.

2 For each of these equations, state the number of solutions, by looking at its graph. Then, using the graph, write down approximate values for the solutions. Then, find each solution, correct to 2 decimal places.

(a) $5 - x^3 = 0$

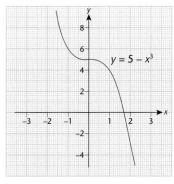

(b) $x^3 - 4x + 5 = 0$

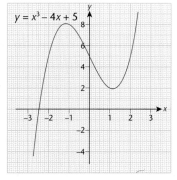

(c) $x^3 - 4x + 2 = 0$

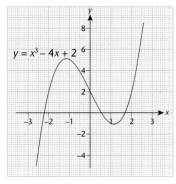

How many solutions?

Some quadratic equations have two solutions, some have one solution and some have no solutions.

♦ Find examples of quadratic equations with different numbers of solutions. You might want to draw graphs using a graphical calculator or graph plotter on a computer. Or you could look at tables of values on a spreadsheet.

♦ Now find cubic equations with different numbers of solutions.

♦ Write about how you go about finding an equation with a given number of solutions.

Inequalities

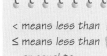

< means less than
≤ means less than or equal to
> means greater than
≥ means greater than or equal to

DISCUSSION POINT

If n is a positive whole number and $n < 6$, then n could be 1 or 2 or 3 or 4 or 5.

• If y is a whole number, and $-5 < y \leq 1$, what could y be?

• If m is a square number, and $10 < m < 30$, what could m be?

• If p is a prime number, and $20 < p < 30$, what could p be?

Inequalities can be shown on a number line

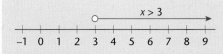

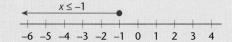

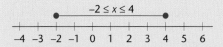

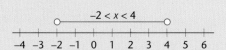

• What do the hollow and filled circles indicate?

If x has been rounded to the nearest whole number and $x = 26$, this is the range of possible values for x.

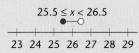

$$25.5 \leq x < 26.5$$

• Draw a diagram to show the possible values for x if $x = 310$ to the nearest ten.

EXERCISE 10

1 Write down all the possible values for these.

  (a) e, if e is a positive even number, and $17 < e < 30$

  (b) n, if n is an integer, and $-4 < n \le 5$

  (c) g, if g is a multiple of 8, and $16 < g \le 40$

  (d) p, if p is a prime number, and $40 < p < 50$

  (e) t, if t is a triangular number, and $10 \le t < 30$

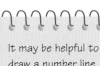

An **integer** is a whole number.

2 There were twenty marks for a test. No one scored full marks.
Everyone scored at least half marks.
If m is a mark obtained for the test, write the range of values for m.

3 Describe the range of values for x shown on these number lines.

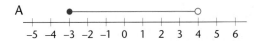
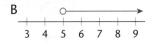

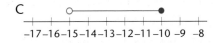

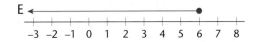

4 Which of these are *true* and which are *false*?

  (a) $15 < x$ and x could be 14   (b) $x \ge -4$ and x could be -2

  (c) $x > -2.8$ and x could be -5 (d) $x \le 12$ and x could be 12

  (e) $-5 > x$ and x could be -3

5 All these numbers have been rounded. Write the range of possible values for each one.

It may be helpful to draw a number line for each part of Question 5.

  (a) $n = 13$, to the nearest whole number

  (b) $x = -5$, to the nearest integer

  (c) $m = 17.2$, to 1 decimal place

  (d) $N = 3000$, to the nearest 1000

  (e) $N = 3000$, to the nearest 100

  (f) $t = 5.84$, to 2 decimal places

  (g) $w = 0.0002$, to 1 significant figure

Nelson GCSE Maths · USING GRAPHS TO SOLVE PROBLEMS (INTERMEDIATE)

Solving inequalities

DISCUSSION POINT

- For what values of x is $2x + 3 \leq 7$?

  Show the range of values on a number line.

- For what values of x is $x^2 > 16$?

  Show the range of values on a number line.

- For what values of x are each of these true?

  $$5 < x + 3 < 10 \qquad\qquad -1 \leq 2x + 3 \leq 15$$

  Show each of the solutions on a number line.

Solving an inequality means saying for what values of x the inequality is true.

Here are some examples.

- If $x + 2 > 5$, the solution is $x > 3$.
- If $9 > x - 6$, the solution is $x < 15$.
- If $x^2 \leq 25$, the solution is $-5 \leq x \leq 5$.

EXERCISE 11

1 Solve these inequalities and show the range of values on a number line.

   (**a**) $x + 3 < 10$ (**b**) $3x \leq -12$

   (**c**) $17 < 3x + 2$ (**d**) $3x - 5 \geq 7$

   (**e**) $-5 < 2x - 3$ (**f**) $10 - 2x \geq 5$

   (**g**) $10 \leq x + 5 \leq 20$ (**h**) $-1 < x - 2 < 5$

   (**i**) $-5 \leq 2x + 1 \leq 15$

2 Solve these inequalities.

   (**a**) $x^2 \leq 36$ (**b**) $x^2 \geq 9$

   (**c**) $1 > x^2$ (**d**) $2x^2 < 50$

   (**e**) $47 \leq 3x^2 - 1$ (**f**) $x^3 > 8$

Regions

Look at this diagram.

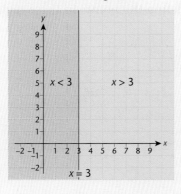

- The line $x = 3$ is a boundary line.
- All the points in the blue region have an x-coordinate which is bigger than 3 so that region is called $x > 3$.
- All the points in the orange region have $x < 3$.

Any line can be thought of as a boundary between two regions.

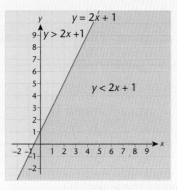

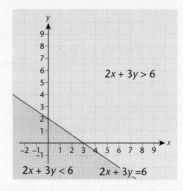

Sometimes the points on the boundary line are included in the region. Notice the difference in these two diagrams.

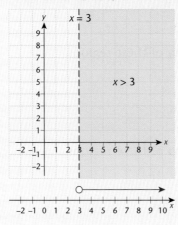

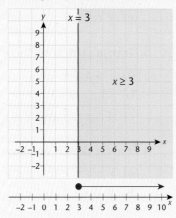

DISCUSSION POINT

Some regions have more than one boundary.

Write down inequalities to define the points in these regions.

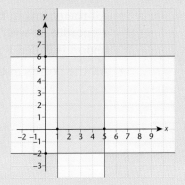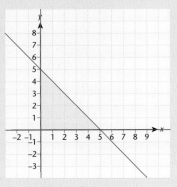

EXERCISE 12

1 Draw a sketch to show each of these regions.

(a) $x < 2$

(b) $y \geq 1$

(c) $x \geq 3$ and $y < 4$

(d) $-1 \leq x \leq 2$

(e) $2 \leq y \leq 3$

(f) $-2 < x \leq 3$ and $-1 < y \leq 5$

2 Draw a sketch to show each of these regions.

(a) $y \geq 2x + 1$

(b) $y < x + 3$

(c) $y > x + 1$

(d) $2y \leq 4x + 3$

(e) $x + y \geq 5$

3 Draw a sketch to show each of these regions.

(a) $1 \leq x \leq 4$

(b) $-3 \leq y \leq -1$

(c) $4 \leq x \leq 5$ and $2 \leq y \leq 4$

4 Draw a sketch to show each of these regions.

(a) $y > x + 1$ and $y < x + 3$

(b) $x + y \geq 2$ and $x + y \leq 5$

5 Identify the shaded regions in each of these diagrams.

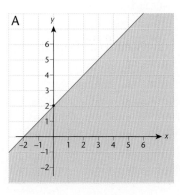

A

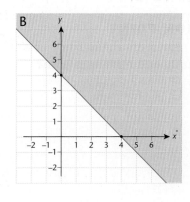

B

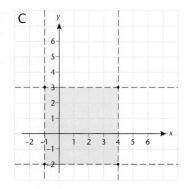

C

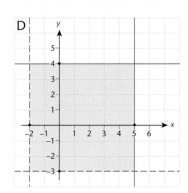

D

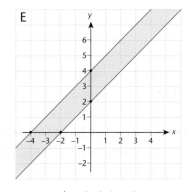

E

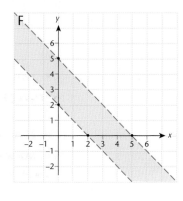

F

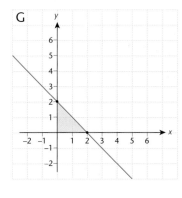

G

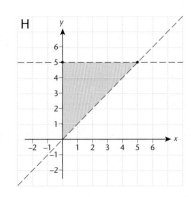

H

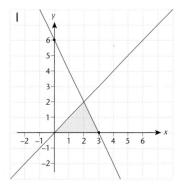

I

6 (a) Draw a sketch to show each of these regions.

    (i) $x < 4,\ y \geq 1,\ y \leq x$

    (ii) $x + y < 5,\ x \geq 0,\ y \geq 1$

    (iii) $y > 2x - 1,\ 2x + y < 7,\ y \leq 5$ and $x \geq 0$

How many points in each region have integer coordinates?
Write down the coordinates of one of these points for each region.

(b) The graph of $y = x^2$ passes through each of the regions in part (a).
For each region, write down the coordinate of one point with integer
coordinates which lies on the graph and also in the region.

Interpreting graphs of real-life situations

DISCUSSION POINT
This graph represents the journey of a cyclist travelling to a shop, doing some shopping and returning home.

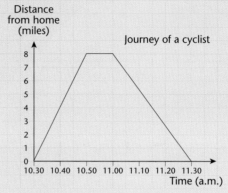

- How far is the shop away from the cyclist's home?
- How can you tell from the graph that the cyclist travelled faster going to the shop than returning home?
- How long did the cyclist take to reach the shop?
- What was the average speed while travelling to the shop?
- How long did the cyclist spend at the shop?
- How long did the return journey take?
- What was the average speed on the return journey?

EXERCISE 13

1 A woman walked to her friend's house, stayed there for a while and returned home.

(a) How far is it to the friend's house?

(b) How long did it take to reach the friend's house?

(c) What was the woman's average speed while walking to the friends house?

(d) How long did the woman spend visiting her friend?

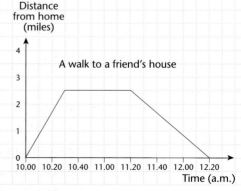

(e) Did the woman walk faster on her way to visit her friend, or on the way back home?

(f) How long was the woman away from home for?

2 A man cycles home from work at a constant speed.
This is the distance–time graph of his journey.

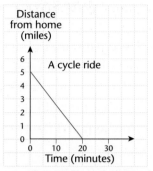

(a) What is the distance between the man's home and work?

(b) How long does it take the man to travel home?

(c) What is his average speed during the journey?

3 While on a walk, a girl stopped for a rest. Her full journey is shown on this distance–time graph.

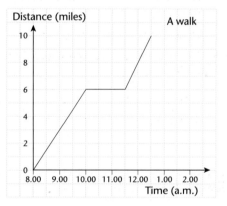

(a) At what time did the girl start her journey?

(b) How far did she walk before resting?

(c) Was she walking or resting at midday?

(d) How long did she rest for?

(e) How far did she walk altogether?

(f) Did she walk faster before having a rest, or after?

4 At 1.00 p.m., a boy starts to walk at a constant speed of 4 m.p.h. from home. He walks until 3.30 p.m. without a break.

(a) Draw a distance-time graph to represent his journey.

(b) Use your graph to estimate how far he had walked by 2.20 p.m.

5 A car travels at an average speed of 30 m.p.h. Draw a distance–time graph to represent its journey over a period of 5 hours.

6 A man drove to a theatre, 30 miles away, watched a concert and then drove home again. He left home at 6.00 p.m. and arrived at the theatre at 7.30 p.m. just in time for the start of the concert. The concert lasted for 2 hours. Afterwards, the man returned home at a speed of 30 m.p.h.

(**a**) Draw a distance-time graph to represent the man's trip to the theatre, including the journey home.

(**b**) What was the average speed on the way to the theatre?

(**c**) At what time did the man arrive home?

(**d**) How long did the journey home take?

DISCUSSION POINT

This vase has different girths, or distances around it, at different heights. Explain the relationship between the shape of the vase and the shape of this graph.

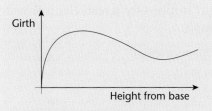

• Suppose you were filling up the vase with water flowing at steady rate of say 150 ml per sec.
What would the graph of depth of water against time look like?

Exercise 14

1 For each of these containers, draw sketch graphs of girth plotted against height from base.

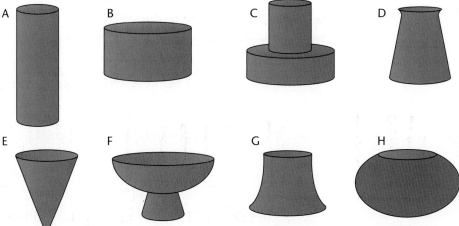

A   B   C   D

E   F   G   H

Nelson GCSE Maths   USING GRAPHS TO SOLVE PROBLEMS (INTERMEDIATE)

2 These sketch graphs show girth plotted against height from base for different containers. Sketch each container.

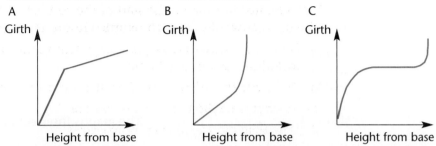

A

Girth

Height from base

B

Girth

Height from base

C

Girth

Height from base

3 Each of the containers in Question 1 is filled with water flowing in at a constant rate. For each container, draw a sketch graph of the depth of water against time.

4 These are graphs for containers being filled with water at a steady rate.

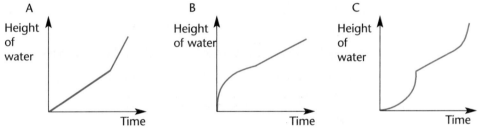

A

Height of water

Time

B

Height of water

Time

C

Height of water

Time

Sketch a possible container for each.

5 These are plans of race tracks.

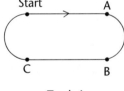

Track A

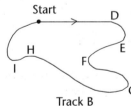

Track B

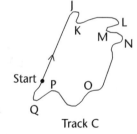

Track C

Sketch a graph of speed against time for each track. Indicate on your graph the places related to the points marked.

6 These are sketch graphs of speed against time for two race tracks.

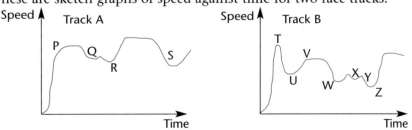

Speed   Track A

Time

Speed   Track B

Time

Draw a possible track for each, labelling the points marked.

Solving simultaneous equations by drawing graphs

Example: Find where the graphs of these equations intersect.

$x + y = 5$

$y = 2x + 1$

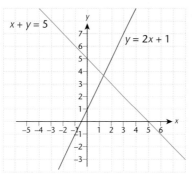

The graphs intersect at $(1\frac{1}{3}, 3\frac{2}{3})$.

So the solution to the equations is
$x = 1\frac{1}{3}$ and $y = 3\frac{2}{3}$.

Graphs involving x^2: quadratic graphs

All quadratic graphs have the shape of a **parabola**. They all have one line of symmetry.

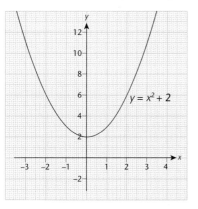

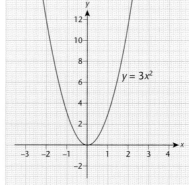

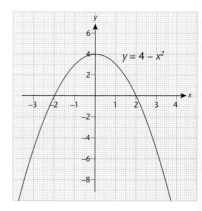

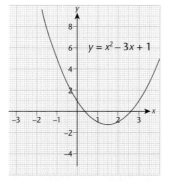

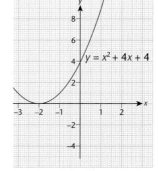

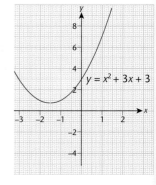

Graphs involving x^3: cubic graphs

A cubic graph is always shaped like one of these.

Here are two examples of cubic graphs

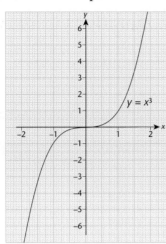

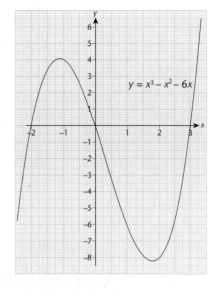

Graphs involving $\frac{1}{x}$: reciprocal graphs

These have equations like $y = \frac{6}{x}$ and $y = \frac{12}{x}$.

This is the graph of $y = \frac{1}{x}$.

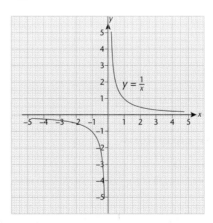

The graph has two separate branches because when $x = 0$, it is impossible to find a value for y.

Using graphs to solve equations

Quadratic equations

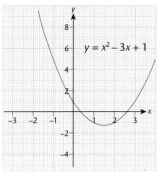

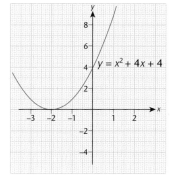

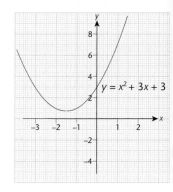

$x^2 - 3x + 1$ has two solutions.

$x^2 + 4x + 4 = 0$ has one solution.

$x^2 + 3x + 3 = 0$ has no solution.

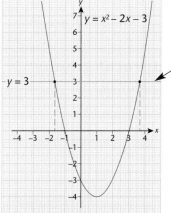

Straight lines can also be drawn on quadratic graphs to solve quadratic equations.

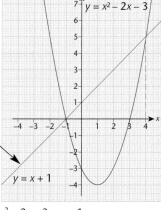

$x^2 - 2x - 3 = 3$ has solutions $x = 3.6$ and $x = -1.6$.

$x^2 - 2x - 3 = x + 1$ has solutions $x = -1$ and $x = 4$.

Cubic equations

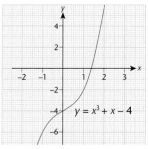

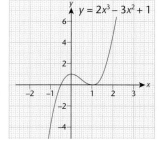

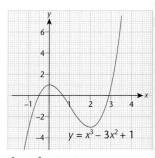

$x^3 + x - 4 = 0$ has one solution.

$2x^3 - 3x^2 + 1 = 0$ has two solutions.

$x^3 - 3x^2 + 1 = 0$ has three solutions.

Trial and improvement can be used to get more accurate answers than can be obtained from a graph.

Inequalities

< means less than
≤ means less than or equal to
> means greater than
≥ means greater than or equal to

Inequalities show the range of values for which a statement is true. They use the symbols $<$ $\leq$ $>$ and $\geq$.

Examples

$$2x - 5 \leq 7$$
$$\Rightarrow \quad 2x \leq 12$$
$$\Rightarrow \quad x \leq 6$$

$$6 - x < 5$$
$$\Rightarrow \quad 6 < 5 + x$$
$$\Rightarrow \quad 1 < x$$

These inequalities can be shown on a number line.

The empty circle means the end point is not included in the range. The filled circle means it is.

Regions

Inequalities are used to describe **regions** on a graph.

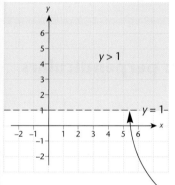

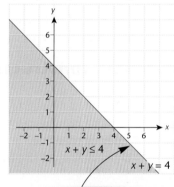

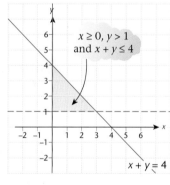

The dotted line means that the points on the boundary line are not included in the region. The solid line means that they are.

Travel graphs

A line going up means the object is moving away.

A line going down means the object is coming back.

A horizontal line means the object is not moving.

The steeper the line, the faster the object is travelling.

PROPERTIES OF SHAPES

- ruler and compass constructions
- classifying triangles and quadrilaterals
- problems about areas of triangles and quadrilaterals
- similarity
- problems using Pythagoras' theorem
- regular and irregular polygons
- chords, arcs and tangents of circles, and the angle in a semicircle.

Ruler and compass constructions: perpendiculars

DISCUSSION POINT

- Draw a line 8cm long. Use compasses and a ruler to draw the **perpendicular bisector** of this line.
- L is a line and P is a point not on the line. How far is P from L?

.P

L ⎯⎯⎯⎯⎯⎯⎯⎯⎯⎯⎯⎯⎯⎯⎯⎯

Discuss how you can use compasses and a ruler to construct a line through P which is perpendicular to L.

This is called **dropping a perpendicular** from point P on to line L.

- Draw triangle ABC accurately and make a suitable construction to find the area of the triangle.

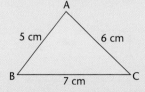

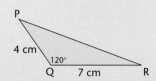

- Draw triangle PQR. How can you drop a perpendicular from point P on to the base QR? What is the area of this triangle?

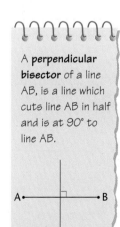

A **perpendicular bisector** of a line AB, is a line which cuts line AB in half and is at 90° to line AB.

▷ Protractor
▷ Compasses
▷ Resource Sheet K:
  Dropping
  perpendiculars

EXERCISE 1

1 In each of the triangles on Resource Sheet K, use compasses to drop a perpendicular from the point labelled P on to the line labelled L. Measure and write down the length of each perpendicular.

2 Work out the area of each of the triangles on Resource Sheet K. You will need to measure the triangles.

3 This diagram shows a triangle with a perpendicular dropped from each vertex to the opposite side of the triangle.

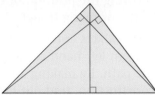

Use compasses to drop perpendiculars from all three vertices on to the opposite sides for each of the triangles on Resource Sheet K. What do you notice?

4 Here is a sketch of a trapezium.

(**a**) Draw the trapezium accurately.

(**b**) Use compasses to drop a perpendicular from one vertex of the trapezium on to a side and, hence, find the area of the trapezium.

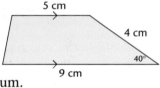

5 Here is a sketch of a parallelogram.

(**a**) Draw the parallelogram accurately.

(**b**) Use compasses to drop a perpendicular from one vertex of the parallelogram on to a side and, hence, find the area of the parallelogram.

(**c**) Check your answer to part (b) by using trigonometry.

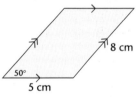

6 ABCD is a rhombus.

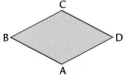

If a perpendicular is dropped from A on to BD, and another perpendicular is dropped from C on to BD, what will happen? Explain why.

Nelson GCSE Maths · PROPERTIES OF SHAPES (INTERMEDIATE)

7 A ship is two miles due North of a lighthouse. It is sailing on a bearing of 140°.

    (a) Make an accurate scale drawing of the path of the ship in relation to the lighthouse.

    (b) By dropping a perpendicular, find how close the ship gets to the lighthouse.

8 This diagram shows a sketch of the path across a rectangular field. The field contains a drinking trough, T, for cattle.

    (a) Make an accurate plan of the field, showing the position of the path and of the drinking trough T.

    (b) Two walkers enter the field from the bottom left-hand corner and walk along the path. By making an accurate construction, find out how near the walkers come to the drinking trough.

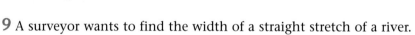

9 A surveyor wants to find the width of a straight stretch of a river.

He starts at A and measures the angle between the bank he is on and the direction of a tree on the opposite bank. He then walks 75 yards along the bank to point B and measures the angle TBA.

    (a) Make an accurate scale drawing to show the positions of the points A, B and T.

    (b) Use an accurate construction to estimate the width of the river.

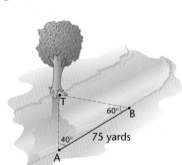

10 Someone wants to work out the height of a church tower. She measures the angle of elevation of the top of the tower as 30°. She walks 20 metres towards the church and measures the angle of elevation again. This time it is 40°.

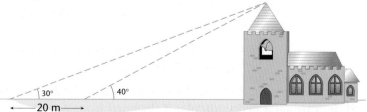

Make an accurate scale drawing and use an accurate construction to estimate the height of the church tower.

Symmetry in triangles and quadrilaterals

EXERCISE 2

1 A square is cut into quarters along both diagonals to give four triangles.

The four triangles are rearranged to make different designs.
Here are two designs.

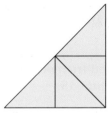 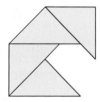

  (**a**) Sketch a design, made from all four triangles, which has

      (**i**)   one line of symmetry

      (**ii**) two lines of symmetry and rotational symmetry of order 2

      (**iii**) rotational symmetry of order 2 but no line symmetry

      (**iv**) rotational symmetry of order 4 but no line symmetry

  (**b**) What other possible types of symmetry could designs have?

2 One of the diagonals of this kite is a line of symmetry. This means that
the blue half of the kite is a reflection of the red half in diagonal AC.
In other words, D is the reflection of B in the mirror line AC.

  (**a**) What does this tell you about the lengths of
AB and AD?

  (**b**) What does this tell you about the lengths of
CB and CD?

  (**c**) What does this tell you about the lengths of
BE and DE?

  (**d**) What does this tell you about the areas of
triangles ABC and ADC?

  (**e**) What does this tell you about the angle between
the diagonals of the kite?

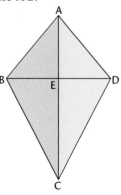

3 A parallelogram has rotational symmetry of order 2.

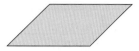

    (**a**) What does the symmetry tell you about the sides of the parallelogram?

    (**b**) What does the symmetry tell you about the angles of the parallelogram?

4 A rhombus has two lines of symmetry and rotational symmetry of order 2.

    (**a**) What does the symmetry tell you about the sides of the rhombus?

    (**b**) What does the symmetry tell you about the angles of the rhombus?

    (**c**) What does the symmetry tell you about the diagonals of the rhombus?

5 ABC is a right-angled triangle. ADBC is the shape made when you reflect the triangle in the line AB.

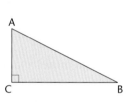
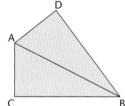

    (**a**) What is shape ADBC called?
        What can you say about the sides and angles of this shape?

    (**b**) What shape is made when you reflect the triangle in the line BC?
        What can you say about the sides and angles of this shape?

    (**c**) What shape is made when you reflect the triangle in the line AC?
        What can you say about the sides and angles of this shape?

6 Copy and complete this table for quadrilaterals. For each entry, put either the name of a special type of quadrilateral, or a sketch of a quadrilateral, or write *Not possible*.

QUADRILATERALS

	Diagonals the same length	Diagonals different lengths
4 lines of symmetry		
3 lines of symmetry		
2 lines of symmetry		
1 lines of symmetry		
0 lines of symmetry		

Similarity

In Mathematics, two shapes are **similar** if they are the same shape.
They can be a different size.

All squares are similar.
Two different rectangles might or might not be similar.

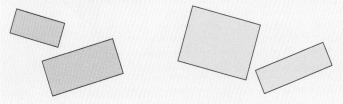

Two different triangles can be similar.

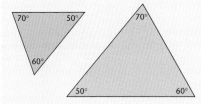

Triangles are similar when the angles of
one triangle are the same as the angles
of the other.

EXERCISE 3

1 (a) Sketch two equilateral triangles of different sizes.

   (b) What size are the angles of each of the triangles?

   (c) Are *all* equilateral triangles similar?

2 This picture shows sketches of two rhombuses.
Are all rhombuses similar?

Explain your answer.

3 Each of these statements is *true* or *false*. If the statement is *false*, give three
examples of the shape: two which are similar and one which is not.

A: All circles are similar.

B: All right-angled triangles are similar.

C: All isosceles triangles are similar.

D: All kites are similar.

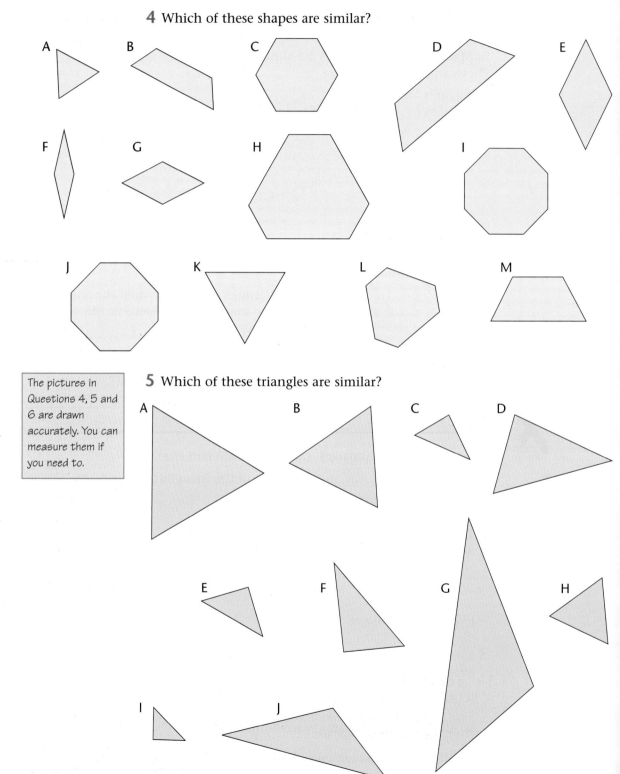

4 Which of these shapes are similar?

A B C D E

F G H I

J K L M

The pictures in Questions 4, 5 and 6 are drawn accurately. You can measure them if you need to.

5 Which of these triangles are similar?

A B C D

E F G H

I J

6 In which of these is the inside triangle similar to the outside triangle?

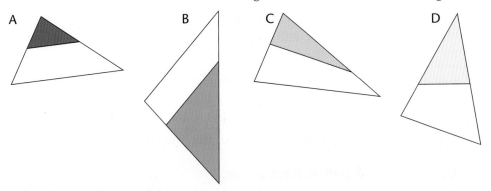

DISCUSSION POINT

Draw these three triangles.

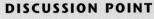

Measure the lengths of the sides of all the triangles. What do you notice?

How does this help you to calculate the value of *x* and *y* in each of these diagrams?

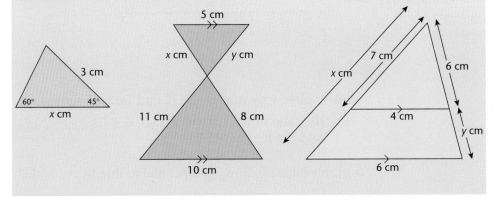

EXERCISE 4

1 These two triangles are similar.
Find the length of the line marked *p*.

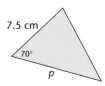

2 Look at this diagram.

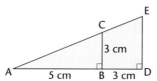

    (a) Explain why triangles ABC and ADE are similar.

    (b) Find the length of the line DE.

3 Look at this diagram.

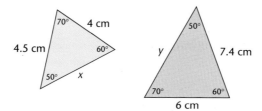

    Find the lengths of the lines marked x and y, correct to 1 decimal place.

4 Look at this diagram.

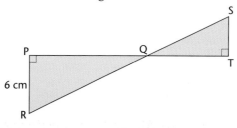

    (a) Explain why triangles PQR and TQS are similar.

    (b) The ratio of the lengths PQ:QT is 4:3.
         Find the length of ST.

5 In this diagram, line DE is parallel to line BC.

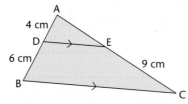

    (a) Explain why triangles ABC and ADE are similar.

    (b) Calculate the length of AE.

6 In this diagram, line GH is parallel to line EF.

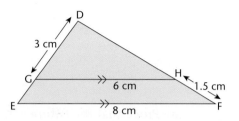

(a) Explain why triangles DGH and DEF are similar.

(b) Find the length of line DE.

(c) Find the length of line DH.

7 In this diagram, line AB is parallel to line CD.

(a) Explain why the triangles are similar.

(b) Find the length of line AE.

(c) Find the length of line BC.

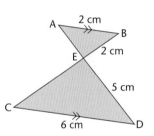

8 In this diagram, AE:ED = 1:4.

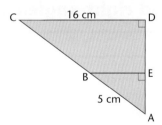

(a) Explain why triangles AEB and ADC are similar.

(b) Find the length of BE.

(c) Find the length of BC.

9 In this diagram, the two angles marked x are equal.

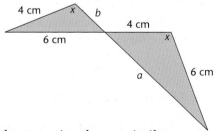

(a) Explain why the two triangles are similar.

(b) Find the length of the line marked a.

(c) Find the length of the line marked b.

10 This right-angled triangle can be dissected into two right-angled triangles.

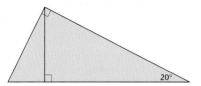

(a) Prove that the two new right-angled triangles are similar to each other and to the original triangle.

(b) Is the same true for *any* right-angled triangle?

11 In this diagram; ABC is a right-angled triangle and line BD is perpendicular to the side AC.

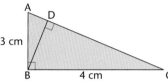

(a) Prove that the triangles ABC, ADB and BDC are similar.

(b) Find the length of AC.

(c) Find the length of BD.

(d) Find the ratio into which side AC is divided by the point D.

Isosceles triangles and right-angled triangles

Remember that the exterior angle of a triangle is equal to the sum of the interior opposite angles.

$r = s + t$

EXERCISE 5

1 Triangle ABC has been divided by the line BD. $\angle ABD = 80°$ and AB = BD.

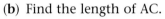

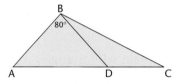

(a) What size are the angles of triangle ABD?

(b) If triangle BDC is isosceles, find the sizes of the three angles of triangle ABC.

2 Triangle EFG has been divided by the line GH. The lines EH, FH and GH are all the same length.

(a) Copy the diagram and mark the sizes of all the angles.

(b) Now do the same thing, but with angle EGH marked as 65° instead of 50°.

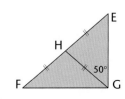

(c) What sort of triangle is triangle EFG in both cases?

(d) Is this *always* true, whatever the size of angle EGH?

3 Triangle ABC has been divided into two triangles by the line BD.
Lines BC and DC are equal in length and lines DB and AD are equal
in length.

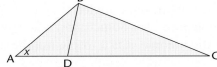

(a) Copy the diagram and label each of the angles on the diagram in
terms of x.

(b) What is the relationship between angle ABC and angle BAC?

(c) If triangle ABC is isosceles, what size are its three angles?
There are two possible answers.

EXERCISE 6

Pythagoras'
theorem:
$a^2 + b^2 = c^2$
for any right-
angled triangle.

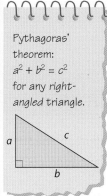

1 Calculate the length of the side marked ? in each of these triangles.

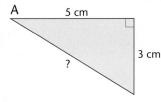
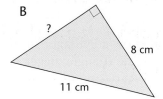
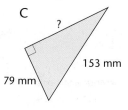

2 Calculate the length of the sides marked ? in each of these triangles.

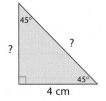
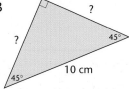
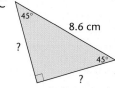

3 The lengths of the sides of a rectangle are 11 cm and 14 cm.
Find the lengths of the diagonals of the rectangle.

4 The lengths of the diagonals of a rhombus are 8 cm and 12 cm.
(a) Find the length of a side of the rhombus.
(b) Find the perimeter and area of the rhombus.

5 The lengths of the diagonals of a square are 15 cm.
Find the area of the square.

DISCUSSION POINT
Pythagorean triads

Think about right-angled triangles where the lengths of two of the sides are whole numbers. Sometimes, when you work out the length of the third side of the triangle, it is a whole number too.

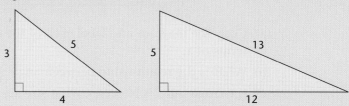

A set of three whole numbers which fit round a right-angled triangle is called a Pythagorean triad. Both (3, 4, 5) and (5, 12, 13) are Pythagorean triads. Find some more Pythagorean triads. These diagrams might help you.

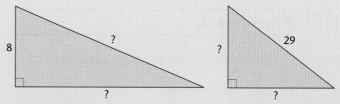

If you know a Pythagorean triad, you can always find another one by making the triangle bigger.

- (3, 4, 5) is a Pythagorean triad. So (6, 8, 10) is also a Pythagorean triad.
- (5, 12, 13) is a Pythagorean triad. So (15, 36, 39) is also a Pythagorean triad.

Write down some more Pythagorean triads by using this method.

Use the triads from the DISCUSSION POINT to answer the questions in Exercise 7.

EXERCISE 7

1 (a) The diagonals of a rectangle are each 13 cm long.
Its length and its width are both a whole number of centimetres.
What are they?

(b) In another rectangle, the length of each diagonal is 25 cm.
The length and the width of the rectangle are both a whole number of centimetres. What are they? (There are two possible answers.)

2 The perimeter of this isosceles trapezium is 58 cm.

(a) Find the distance between the two parallel sides of the trapezium.

(b) Find the area of the trapezium.

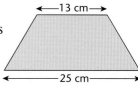

3 The lengths of the diagonals of this rhombus are 16 cm
and 30 cm.

(a) Find the area of the rhombus.

(b) Find the perimeter of the rhombus.

(c) A rectangle has the same area and same perimeter
as the rhombus. Find the lengths of its sides.

(d) Is the total length of the diagonals of the rhombus
more, or less, than the total length of the diagonals of the rectangle?

Regular and irregular polygons

A polygon is regular if all its sides *and* its angles are equal. This was first
discussed in Chapter 2 in *Book 1*. An easy way to find the angles at the
corner of a *regular* polygon is to remember that all
the exterior angles add up to 360°.

An easy way to find the *sum* of the angles of *any*
polygon is to divide it into triangles.

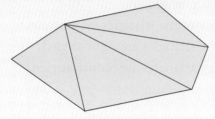

Nelson GCSE Maths PROPERTIES OF SHAPES (INTERMEDIATE)

DISCUSSION POINT
- What is the *angle at each corner* of a regular pentagon?
  A regular hexagon? A regular octagon? A regular nonagon?
  A regular decagon? A regular heptagon?
- What is the *sum of the angles* in a pentagon?
  A hexagon? A heptagon? An octagon? A nonagon? A decagon?

EXERCISE 8

▷ Protractor
▷ Resource Sheet L:
  Regular polygons

1 Which of these shapes is regular?

A 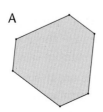 B 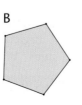 C 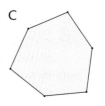 D

2 All the angles of a pentagon are equal, but the pentagon is not regular.

   (**a**) What size must each angle be?

   (**b**) Draw accurately a pentagon which has all its angles equal but which is not regular.

3 Draw accurately a hexagon which has all its *sides* equal, but which is not regular.

4 This pentagon has one line of symmetry.

   (**a**) What does the symmetry tell you about the angles of the pentagon?

   (**b**) What does the symmetry tell you about the sides of the pentagon?

   (**c**) If ∠A = 80° and ∠C = 130°, find the other angles of the pentagon.

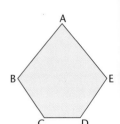

5 A regular hexagon is divided into triangles by drawing all the diagonals from one vertex, as shown.

   (**a**) How many of the triangles are isosceles?

   (**b**) How many triangles are right-angled?

   (**c**) How many triangles are obtuse angled?

For Questions 6, 7 and 8, you will need a copy of Resource Sheet L: Regular polygons.

6 (**a**) Answer Question 5 for polygons with other numbers of sides, by copying and completing this table.

Regular polygon being divided	Number of isosceles triangles	Number of right-angled triangles	Number of acute-angled triangles
Triangle			
Square			
Pentagon			
Hexagon			
Heptagon			
Octagon			
Nonagon			
Decagon			

Keep any drawings you make for Question 6. You may need them for Questions 7 and 8. You may find it helpful to cut them up.

   (**b**) How many isosceles triangles are there in a polygon with 20 sides? With 25 sides? With any number of sides?

   (**c**) How many right-angled triangles are there in a polygon with 20 sides? With 25 sides? With any number of sides?

   (**d**) How many acute-angled triangles are there in a polygon with 20 sides? With 25 sides? With any number of sides?

7 This regular octagon is divided into triangles.

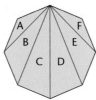

(a) Which *two* triangles could you use to make a kite? A rectangle?
A rhombus? A square? A parallelogram? An isosceles triangle?

For some of these shapes more than one choice is possible.
For other shapes, it is impossible.

(b) This regular nonagon is divided into triangles.

Answer part (a) for this nonagon.

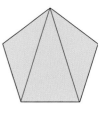

8 This regular pentagon is divided into triangles.

(a) Find the sizes of the angles in each of the triangles.
Try to do this, *without* using a protractor.

(b) Find the sizes of the angles in each of the triangles for
three other regular polygons divided in the same way.

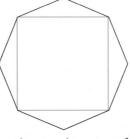

▷Resource Sheet L:
Regular polygons

EXERCISE 9

1 This regular octagon is divided into five pieces.

> You might want to
> use a copy of
> Resource Sheet L:
> *Regular polygons*
> for any of the
> questions in this
> exercise.

(a) Name each of the five pieces using one of these.

> equilateral triangle   isosceles triangle   right-angled triangle
> rhombus   rectangle   square   kite
> parallelogram   trapezium

Two shapes are
congruent if one
fits exactly on to
the other (after
turning over if
necessary).

(b) Which of the five pieces are congruent?

(c) What size are the three angles in one of the triangles?

2 This regular octagon is divided into four pieces.

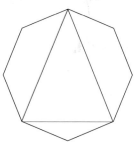

(a) Name each of the four pieces using one of the words in Question 1(a).

(b) Which of the pieces are congruent?

(c) What size are the four angles in one of the four-sided shapes?

(d) What size are the three angles in the larger triangle?

3 This is the same diagram as in Question 2, except that one of the longest diagonals has been added.

(a) Give a reason why the longest diagonal divides the larger triangle of Question 2 into two congruent triangles.

(b) What size are the angles in one of these congruent triangles?

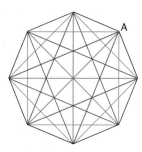

4 Here is a mystic octagon design.

There are six angles which meet at the vertex marked A.
Use your answers to Questions 1, 2 and 3 to find the size of each of these six angles.

5 How many lines are there in a mystic octagon design (including the sides of the octagon itself)?
Count the lines in more than one way, to check that your answer is correct.

Mystic roses

A mystic rose is a regular polygon with all its diagonals drawn.

Here are some mystic roses.

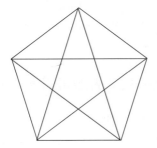
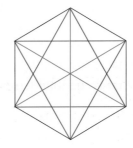
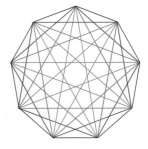

Investigate mystic roses with 4, 5, 6, 7, ... sides. You can use the ideas of Exercise 9 as a starting point.

Chords, arcs and tangents

EXERCISE 10

▷ Compasses
▷ Resource Sheet L:
  Regular polygons

1 Here is a square drawn inside a circle. The blue curve is called an **arc** of the circle. The red side of the square is a **chord** of a circle.

   (**a**) If the circle has a radius of 4 cm, how long is the circumference of the circle?

   (**b**) How long is the blue arc?

   (**c**) Use Pythagoras' theorem to find the length of the red chord.

2 (**a**) Draw a circle with radius 4 cm, and construct this design inside your circle.

   (**b**) The red arc has its centre at A.
      This red arc is a fraction of the circumference of a circle.
      What fraction is it?

   (**c**) What is the length of the red arc on your drawing?

   (**d**) What is the total length of all the curved lines on your drawing?

3 Look at the drawing you made for Question 2. The regular hexagon is made from six chords.

   (a) What is the length of one of the chords?

   (b) What is the perimeter of the regular hexagon?

4 In this regular octagon each side is 3 cm long.

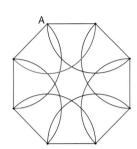

   (a) The red arc has its centre at A. What fraction of a whole circumference is this arc?

   (b) What is the length of this arc?

   (c) What is the total length of the curved lines ?

DISCUSSION POINT

Look at these diagrams

A tangent is a line which touches a circle but does not cross it.

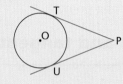
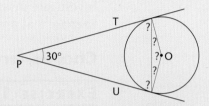

- In the first diagram, the red line is a tangent to the circle. It meets it at the point T. If the line OT is drawn in, what angle will it make with the tangent?

- The second diagram shows two tangents to a circle with centre O.
  They meet the circle at points T and U.
  The distance OP is 13 cm. The radius of the circle is 5 cm.
  How can you find the lengths of the tangents PT and PU?

- Find the angles marked ? in the third diagram.

EXERCISE 11

1 A square has sides of length 10 cm. A circle is drawn so that the sides of the square are tangents to the circle.

   Find the radius of the circle.

←10 cm→

2 Here is a circle of radius 2 cm and a tangent.

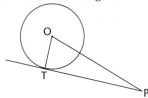

The length of the line TP is 4 cm. Find the distance of P from O.

3 Here is a circle of radius 8 cm and two tangents.

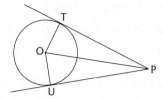

The distance of the point P from O is 17 cm. Find the lengths of PT and PU.

4 Two radii and two tangents to a circle are drawn.
They form the sides of a kite.

Find the other three angles of the kite.

5 PT and PU are tangents to the circle with centre O. ∠TOU is 110°.
Find all the angles.

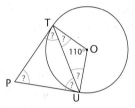

6 PT and PU are tangents to the circle with centre O.
∠PTU is 70°.
Find all the angles marked with a ?.

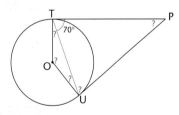

7 A ball of radius 10 cm is dropped into a cone. The ball touches the sides of the cone 25 cm from the vertex of the cone.

(**a**) How far is the centre of the ball above the bottom of the cone?

(**b**) How far is the bottom of the ball above the bottom of the cone?

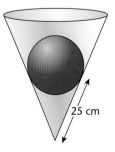

Angle in a semicircle

> Card
> Scissors
> Set squares

Making a generalisation

1 (a) Draw two points A and B, 6 cm apart.

(b) Place your card so that the points A and B lie on the edges of the card, as shown below.

> For Question 1, you need a set square, or a piece of paper or card with an angle of 90°.

Mark the position of the point P at the 90° angle.
Do this for several possible positions of the card.

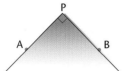 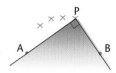

(c) What do you think the locus of point P is?

2 A semicircle has AB as its diameter. P is a point lying on the semicircle. O is the centre of the semicircle.

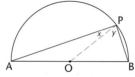

(a) Prove that the triangle APB is divided into two isosceles triangles by the line OP.

(b) The angles at P are labelled x and y, as shown in the diagram. Find the sum of the angles of the triangle APB in terms of x and y.

(c) What does this tell you about $x + y$?

(d) What does this tell you about the angle APB?

(e) What happens to angle APB as P moves round the semicircle?

Justifying a generalisation

The questions in Exercise 13 are about this theorem.

The angle in a semicircle is 90°

EXERCISE 13

1 In this diagram, O is the centre of the circle. Angle ABC is 40°.
Find the size of the other two angles of triangle ABC.

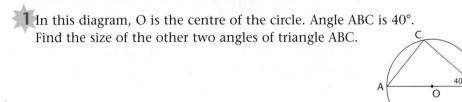

2 Make a sketch of each of these diagrams.
In each diagram, O is the centre of the circle.

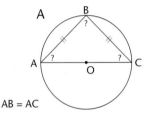

AB = AC

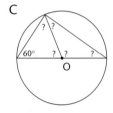

Work out all the angles.

3 In this diagram, a quadrilateral is drawn inside a circle.
The diagonal AC of the quadrilateral goes through the
centre of the circle, O.
∠DAB is 130°.
Find the sizes of the other three angles: ∠ABC, ∠BCD
and ∠CDA.

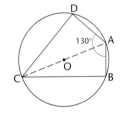

4 A kite is drawn inside a circle.
Prove that two of the angles of the kite are right angles.

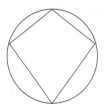

5 This isosceles trapezium is inscribed in a circle.
Make a sketch of this diagram.
Draw in the diagonals of the trapezium.
Find the angles between these diagonals.

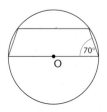

Nelson GCSE Maths PROPERTIES OF SHAPES (INTERMEDIATE)

Similar shapes

In Mathematics, two shapes are **similar** if they are the same shape; they can be a different size.

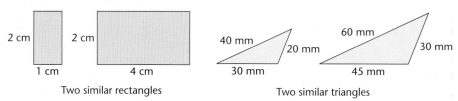

Two similar rectangles   Two similar triangles

If two shapes are similar their sides are in the same ratio. This result can be used to calculate lengths.

The lengths in triangle DEF are $\frac{8}{6}$ times those in triangle DGH.

So, length of DE is $\frac{8}{6} \times 3\,cm = 4\,cm$.

So, GE = 1 cm, $\frac{1}{3}$ of GD.

Hence, FH is $\frac{1}{3}$ of DH. So, DH is $3 \times 1.5\,cm = 4.5\,cm$.

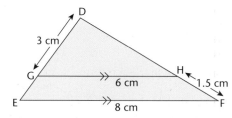

Pythagoras' theorem

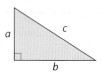

It is useful to remember these **Pythagorean triads**:

3, 4, 5
5, 12, 13
8, 15, 17

$a^2 + b^2 = c^2$

Polygons

A **regular polygon** has all its sides equal *and* all its angles equal.

In a **regular polygon** with n sides, all the **exterior angles** are equal and are found by dividing 360° by n.

The **sum of the angles of a polygon** can be found by dividing the polygon up into triangles.

Circles

Line AB is a **chord**.
Arc AB is coloured red.

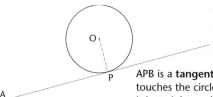

APB is a **tangent**, which touches the circle at P. It is at right angles to the radius OP.

The angle in a semicircle is 90°.

REVISION EXERCISES

1: FURTHER METHODS OF COMPUTATION

Do not use a calculator for this exercise except for Question 5(b).

1 Write in words the value of the digit 6 *after* each of these numbers is multiplied by 100.
  (a) 216   (b) 3641   (c) 34.68   (d) 0.006

2 Work out these.
  (a) 0.8×0.4 (b) 40×0.05
  (c) 12.5×0.04 (d) $20 \div 2.5$
  (e) $0.8 \div 4$ (f) $4.9 \div 0.007$
  (g) $0.0018 \times 3000\,000$ (h) $11 \div 0.125$

3 Write these fractions as decimals.
  (a) $\frac{4}{100}$ (b) $\frac{98}{10\,000}$ (c) $\frac{4}{5}$
  (d) $\frac{1}{8}$ (e) $\frac{7}{20}$ (f) $\frac{2}{3}$

4 Write these percentages as fractions, in their simplest form.
  (a) 40%   (b) 5%   (c) 37.5%
  (d) 2.5%   (e) 465%

5 (a) Calculate these multiplications.
      (i) 456×23 (ii) 508×84
  (b) Calculate these divisions.
      (i) $1378 \div 26$ (ii) $3096 \div 72$
  (c) Calculate these divisions. Give each answer as a whole number with a remainder.
      (i) $700 \div 16$ (ii) $954 \div 34$
  (d) Calculate these divisions. Give each answer as a decimal, correct to 2 decimal places.
      (i) $286 \div 41$ (ii) $1000 \div 29$

6 (a) Estimate the answer to each of these calculations.
      (i) $40.26 \div 7.98$
      (ii) $(9.58)^2 \times (4.78 + 0.311)$
      (iii) $\dfrac{\sqrt{63 \times 3.77}}{1.89}$
      (iv) $\dfrac{21.3 \times 3.065}{7.15 + 7.921}$
  (b) Use a calculator to find answers to each of the calculations in part (a), correct to 3 significant figures.

7 Write down the value of each of these.
  (a) The reciprocal of 4   (b) The reciprocal of 0.5
  (c) The reciprocal of $\frac{2}{3}$ (d) The reciprocal of $1\frac{1}{4}$
  (e) 9^2 (f) 2^5
  (g) 4^3 (h) 6^0
  (i) $\sqrt{121}$ (j) $\sqrt[3]{27}$
  (k) 4^{-1} (l) 27^0
  (m) 2^{-4} (n) 5^{-2}

8 Work out these.
  (a) $\frac{1}{4} + \frac{1}{2}$ (b) $\frac{2}{3} + \frac{1}{6}$ (c) $\frac{3}{4} - \frac{3}{8}$
  (d) $\frac{4}{5} - \frac{3}{10}$ (e) $\frac{5}{8} + \frac{2}{3}$ (f) $3\frac{1}{2} - \frac{2}{3}$
  (g) $5\frac{2}{5} - 3\frac{3}{4}$ (h) $\frac{4}{5} \times \frac{15}{16}$ (i) $\frac{3}{8} \times \frac{5}{6}$
  (j) $2\frac{1}{4} \times \frac{2}{9}$ (k) $5\frac{1}{3} \times 2\frac{3}{8}$ (l) $\frac{5}{8} \div \frac{3}{8}$
  (m) $3\frac{1}{4} \div 5\frac{1}{2}$ (n) $4\frac{1}{6} \div 3\frac{8}{9}$

9 Work out the answers to these, in standard form.
  (a) $(4 \times 10^6) \times (2 \times 10^3)$
  (b) $(8.1 \times 10^5) \times (3 \times 10^4)$
  (c) $(3.2 \times 10^2) \times (4 \times 10^{-3})$
  (d) $\sqrt{9 \times 10^6}$
  (e) $(8 \times 10^5) \div (4 \times 10^3)$
  (f) $(6 \times 10^4) + (9 \times 10^3)$
  (g) $(5 \times 10^8) + (2 \times 10^5)$
  (h) $(7 \times 10^4) - (2 \times 10^2)$

10 Copy and complete each table.
  (a) b is directly proportional to a.

a	24	60	70	
b	36			300

  (b) f is inversely proportional to e.

e	2	6	9	
f	36			4

2: TRANSFORMATIONS

1 Copy this diagram on to squared paper and reflect shape A in the mirror line.

▷ Resource Sheet A:
   Isometric dot

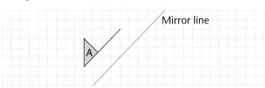

Mirror line

A

2 Copy this diagram and enlarge shape B by scale factor 2, with centre of enlargement point C.

C

B

3 Copy this diagram on to squared paper.
  (**a**) Translate the shape using the vector $\binom{5}{2}$.
  (**b**) Translate the shape using vector $\binom{-3}{-4}$.

4 Copy each of these diagrams.

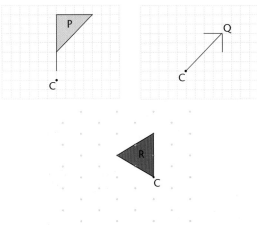

  (**a**) Rotate shape P, 90° clockwise about point C.
  (**b**) Rotate shape Q, 180° clockwise about point C.
  (**c**) Rotate shape R, 120° anticlockwise about
  point C.

> You need isometric dot
> paper for Question 4(c).

5 Triangles A, C and D have been drawn on the
grid below. Make a copy of this diagram.

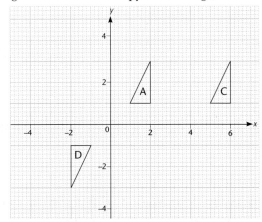

  (**a**) Draw the reflection of triangle A in the
  y-axis. Label the new triangle B.

(**b**) (**i**) Describe the single transformation
  which maps A onto triangle C.
  (**ii**) Describe the single transformation
  which maps triangle C onto triangle B.

(**c**) Describe the single transformation which
  maps triangle A onto triangle D.

MEG 1998

6 Copy this diagram on to squared paper.

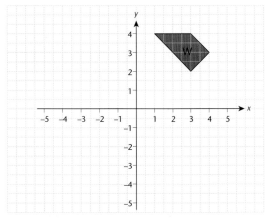

  (**a**) Reflect shape W in the line $x = -1$.
  (**b**) Reflect shape W in the line $x + y = 3$.

7 A shape has perimeter 24 cm and area 20 cm².
It is enlarged by scale factor 3.
  (**a**) What is the perimeter of the enlargement?
  (**b**) What is the area of the enlarged shape?

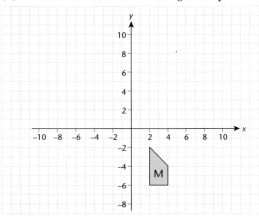

8 (**a**) Copy this diagram on to squared paper.
  (**b**) Translate shape M using vector $\binom{0}{8}$.
  Label the image N.
  (**c**) Rotate N 180° about the point (0, 4).
  Label the image L.
  (**d**) What single transformation maps L directly
  on to M?

9 The parallelogram $ABCD$ has vertices (6, 3), (9, 3), (12, 9) and (9, 9) respectively.

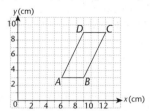

An enlargement scale factor $\frac{1}{3}$ and centre (0, 0) transforms parallelogram $ABCD$ onto parallelogram $A'B'C'D'$.
- **(a) (i)** Draw the parallelogram $A'B'C'D'$.
  - **(ii)** Calculate the area of parallelogram $A'B'C'D'$.
- **(b)** The side AB has length 3 cm. The original shape $ABCD$ is now enlarged with a scale factor of $\frac{2}{5}$ to give $A''B''C''D''$. Calculate the length of side $A''B''$.

SEG 1994

10 Describe fully the transformation which maps shape S on to shape T in each of these diagrams.

A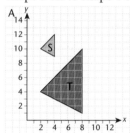

B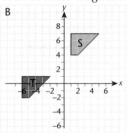

C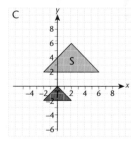

D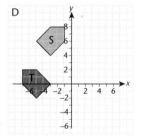

E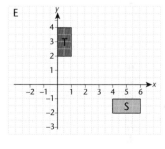

1 $v = u + at$
- **(a)** Calculate v when $a = 4$, $t = 1.5$ and $u = 3$
- **(b)** Rearrange the formula to make a the subject.
- **(c)** Calculate a when $v = 12$, $u = 9$ and $t = 6$.
- **(d)** Rearrange the formula to make u the subject.

2 $V = \pi r^2 h$
- **(a)** Given that $r = 5$ and $h = 3.6$, calculate V to 3 significant figures.
- **(b)** Rearrange the formula to make r the subject.

3 Expand and simplify these.
- **(a)** $3(x + 7)$
- **(b)** $(p + 3)(2p + 1)$
- **(c)** $(y - 2)(4y + 3)$
- **(d)** $(2x - 3)^2$

4 Expand and simplify these.
- **(a)** $(x + 2y)(x + 4y)$
- **(b)** $(a + 2b)(2a + b)$
- **(c)** $(2p - 3q)(4p + q)$
- **(d)** $(3a - 5b)(3a + 5b)$

5 Factorise these.
- **(a)** $10x + 15$
- **(b)** $5r - 20pr + 10qr$
- **(c)** $3xy - 6y^2$
- **(d)** $3r^2t + 9rt^2 - 15rt$

6 Factorise these.
- **(a)** $x^2 + 8x + 7$
- **(b)** $n^2 - 7n + 10$
- **(c)** $a^2 + 4a - 12$
- **(d)** $p^2 - p - 12$

7 Factorise these.
- **(a)** $9x^2 - y^2$
- **(b)** $a^2 - 49b^2$
- **(c)** $36f^2 - 25g^2$
- **(d)** $8m^2 - 18n^2$

8 Work out the answer to these, *without* using a calculator.
- **(a)** $21^2 - 1^2$
- **(b)** $32^2 - 2^2$
- **(c)** $43^2 - 3^2$
- **(d)** 51^2

9 (a) Use the formula
$$S = C(r + H)$$
to calculate the exact value of S when $C = 2\frac{2}{5}$, $r = 1\frac{1}{2}$ and $H = 1\frac{5}{6}$.
- **(b)** $S = C(r + H)$
  - **(i)** Make C the subject of the formula.
  - **(ii)** Make r the subject of the formula.

CCEA 1996

10 (a) Simplify
- **(i)** $3x^2 + 5x^2 - 2x^2$
- **(ii)** $(2x^5)^3$
- **(iii)** $3(a + 2b) + 2(3a + b) + 8(a - b)$

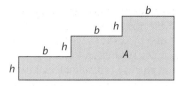

(b) The diagram shows the side view of a set of steps.

  (i) Write down an expression, in its simplest form, for the area, A, of the side of the steps.

  (ii) The area of the side of the steps is 3240 cm² and the breadth, b, of each step is 36 cm. Calculate the height, h, of each step.

(c) Factorise completely: $4xy^2 - 8x^2y$

CCEA 1998

4: STATISTICS AND PROBABILITY

1 Which of these three questions is likely to provide the most useful information about what people watch on television?

A: Most people prefer *Coronation Street* to *EastEnders*. Are you one of these people?

B: Do you prefer BBC programmes because they are not interrupted by advertisements?

C: If you could not watch television for one week, which programmes would you tape on a video recorder?

Explain why you chose your question.

2 An advertising company want to carry out a survey to find out about the usefulness of mobile phones. They ask 100 mobile phone users if they have found their phones useful.

(a) What is wrong with this survey?

(b) How could you carry out a more useful survey?

3 The table shows information about a group of children.

		Boys	Girls
Wears	Yes	5	3
glasses	No	14	10

(a) A boy in the group is chosen at random. What is the probability that he wears glasses?

(b) A child in the group is chosen at random. The probability that the child wears glasses is 0.25. What is the probability that the child does not wear glasses?

SEG 1998

4 The number of runs scored by each batsman in two cricket teams during a match is shown in this table.

Batsman number	Team A	Team B
1	12	85
2	15	42
3	20	0
4	9	0
5	18	8
6	15	16
7	21	7
8	6	5
9	14	5
10	25	2
11	5	0

(a) Compare the runs scored by the two teams, by finding the median and interquartile range.

(b) Compare the two teams, by calculating the mean and the range.

5 (a) For each pair of variables below, state whether you think there would be:

    positive (direct) correlation
or **negative** (inverse) correlation
or **no** correlation.

Give a brief reason for your choice.

  (i) *The amount of rain falling* and *the number of people outdoors*.

  (ii) *The amount of apples a person ate* and *the person's results in mathematics tests*.

This is a scatter diagram showing students' percentage scores in Paper 1 and Paper 2 of a Mathematics examination.

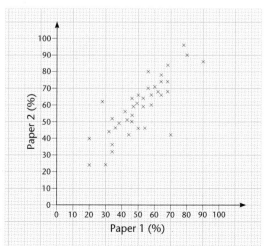

Nelson GCSE Maths Revision

(b) What type of correlation does the diagram show?

Student A scored 43% on Paper 1, but did not take Paper 2.

(c) Use the scatter diagram to estimate the percentage the student might have scored on Paper 2.

Edexcel 1996

6 There are 14 women in a nursing home.
The graph shows the distribution of their ages.

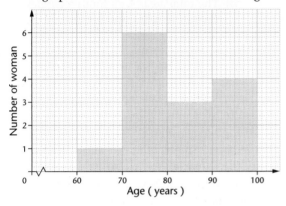

(a) Copy and complete this table for these data.

Age y years	Number of women
$60 \leq y < 70$	
$70 \leq y < 80$	
$80 \leq y < 90$	
$90 \leq y < 100$	

(b) Calculate an estimate of the mean age of these women.

SEG 1996

7 In a mock Mathematics GCSE examination, students took two examination papers.
Their marks are shown in this table.

Student	Paper 1 (%)	Paper 2 (%)
1	76	56
2	54	50
3	60	50
4	55	48
5	48	46
6	81	60
7	65	55
8	85	62
9	61	55
10	70	61

(a) Draw a scatter diagram to represent this information. Mark on a line of best fit.

(b) Another student scored 58% on Paper 1, but was absent for Paper 2.
Use your diagram to estimate what this student would have scored on Paper 2.

8 The table shows the running time of the top 100 selling CDs during one particular week.

Running time (minutes)	Number of CDs (frequency)	Cumulative frequency
$t \leq 40$	0	
$40 \leq t < 45$	2	
$45 \leq t < 50$	18	
$50 \leq t < 55$	37	
$55 \leq t < 60$	30	
$60 \leq t < 65$	11	
$65 \leq t < 70$	2	

(a) Copy and complete the table.
(b) On graph paper, draw the cumulative frequency curve for this information.
(c) Use your graph to estimate the median running time for these CDs.
(d) Estimate the interquartile range for this information.
(e) Somebody buys one of these CDs.
What is the probability that the CD plays for more than one hour?

9 Two fair dice are used in a game.
The first dice is numbered 1, 2, 2, 3, 3, 3.
The second dice is numbered 3, 3, 4, 4, 5, 5.

Both dice are rolled together. The score is the *positive difference* between the numbers shown on the dice.

(a) Copy and complete this table, showing the possible outcomes.

		2nd dice					
		3	3	4	4	5	5
	1	2					
1st	2	1					
dice	2	1					
	3	0					
	3	0					
	3	0	0	1	1	2	2

(b) What is the most likely score?
(c) What is the probability of scoring 0?
(d) What is the probability of scoring more than two?

10 A dice is biased. The probabilities of different scores are shown in this table.

Score	1	2	3	4	5	6
Probability	0.1	0.1	0.15	0.15	0.15	

(a) What is the probability of scoring a 6?

(b) If the dice is thrown 200 times, how many times would you expect to score a 4?

(c) The dice is rolled twice and the scores added together to give a total.
What is the probability of scoring
(i) a total of 12?
(ii) What is the probability of scoring a total of 7?

5: EQUATIONS

1 Solve these equations for n.
(a) $7n + 9 = 44$ (b) $3n + 11 = 5$
(c) $4n - 13 = 17$ (d) $n - 3 = 2n + 5$

2 Solve these equations for x.
(a) $\frac{x}{7} - 2 = 1$ (b) $7x - 5 = 15 - x$
(c) $\frac{2x + 1}{3} = \frac{x - 1}{2}$ (d) $\frac{x + 4}{3} - 1 = \frac{2x + 1}{5}$

3 Solve these simultaneous equations.
(a) $x + 2y = 1$ (b) $5x + y = 17$
    $2x + y = 5$ $4x - 2y = 15$

4 Solve these simultaneous equations.
(a) $7x + 3y = 24$ (b) $3x + 2y = 4$
    $y = 3x$ $3y = 4x + 23$

5 Solve these equations.
(a) $3x^2 = 75$ (b) $x^2 = 9x$
(c) $x^2 + 8x = 0$ (d) $(2x - 1)(x + 3) = 0$

6 (a) Factorise $x^2 - 3x - 10$.
(b) Solve the equation $x^2 - 3x - 10 = 0$.

7 Solve these equations.
(a) $x^2 + 8x + 15 = 0$ (b) $x^2 - 10x + 21 = 0$
(c) $x^2 - 6x - 16 = 0$ (d) $2x^2 - 7x + 3 = 0$

8 *Question*: 'Think of a number. Square it. Add double the number you first thought of. What is your answer?'

Answer: '63'

What numbers could have been thought of?

9 (a) Find, in its simplest form, an expression for
(i) the perimeter, P, of the polygon shown below.

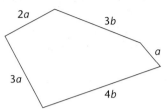

(ii) The total area, A, of four rectangles, each of length c and breadth d.

(b) Darren had n pence.
His mother gave him $(n + 50)$ pence and he got 70 pence for delivering a letter. This made his total £3.
(i) Write down an equation, **in pence**, for n.
(ii) Find the value of n.

CCEA 1996

10 A shop sells chests of drawers in 2 different widths, "**standard**" and "**wide**".

A "**standard**" chest of drawers has d drawers.

The cost, S pounds, may be calculated using the formula

$$S = 29 + 15d$$

(a) Calculate the cost of a "**standard**" chest of drawers with 3 drawers.

Another "**standard**" chest of drawers costs £119.

(b) Calculate the number of drawers this chest has.

The cost, W pounds, of a "**wide**" chest of drawers may be calculated using the formula

$$W = k + md.$$

k and m are constants and d is the number of drawers.

The cost of a "**wide**" chest of drawers with 4 drawers is £117.

The cost of a "**wide**" chest of drawers with 6 drawers is £149.

(c) (i) Use the information to write down two equations in k and m.
(ii) Solve the equations to find the value of m.

Edexcel 1995

1 In the following expressions, a and b both represent lengths.

$$a + b \qquad a^2b^2 \qquad ab \qquad \sqrt{a^2 + b^2}$$
$$\frac{a}{b} \qquad ab^3 \qquad a^2b \qquad a^5b$$

By considering dimensions of each expression, write down
(a) which represents an area,
(b) which represents a volume.

MEG 1996

2 A television programme lasts for $1\frac{1}{4}$ hours. Ann misses the first 35 minutes of the programme. What percentage of the programme does she miss?

3 The lengths of the sides of this triangle are all correct to the nearest centimetre.

(a) What are the upper and lower bounds for the perimeter of this triangle?

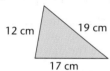

12 cm, 19 cm, 17 cm

(b) Two of these triangles are placed together as shown.

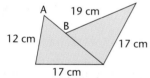

A, 19 cm, B, 12 cm, 17 cm, 17 cm

What are the upper and lower bounds for the length of AB?

4 This rhombus and trapezium have the same area.

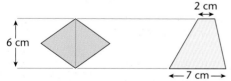

2 cm, 6 cm, 7 cm

Find the length of the other diagonal of the rhombus.

5 In the diagram, ABC is a right-angled triangle and AB is 10 cm. D is the mid-point of AB. ∠ADC is 60°.
(a) Calculate the length of AC.
(b) Calculate the size of ∠ABC.

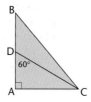

B, D, 60°, A, C

Smunchies

Each pack of Smunchies contains 120 potato crisps, correct to the nearest 10. Each crisp weighs 1.65 grams, correct to the nearest hundredth of a gram.
(a) Copy and complete the table.

	Lower Limit	Upper Limit
Number of crisps		
Weight of each crisp	g	g

Smunchies

4 cm, 24 cm

The pack of Smunchies is in the form of a cylinder of radius 4 cm and length 24 cm.
(b) Calculate the volume of the pack. (You may take π = 3.14)

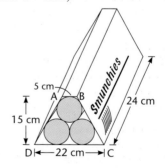

5 cm, A, B, Smunchies, 24 cm, 15 cm, D, 22 cm, C

For a special offer, three packs of Smunchies are put in a container of length 24 cm (CE in the diagram) and constant cross-section (the trapezium ABCD in the diagram). The width of the top of the container (AB) is 5 cm, the width of the base (DC) is 22 cm and the perpendicular height is 15 cm.
(c) Calculate the volume of space wasted in this type of container.

CCEA 1996

7 This is a drawing of a trapezium prism. Face BFGC is a square.

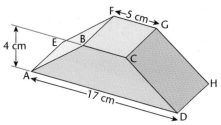

(a) Find the volume of the prism.
(b) An enlargement is made of the prism with scale factor 3.5. The new prism is labelled A'B'C'D'E'F'G'H' so that A' corresponds with A, B' corresponds with B, and so on.
  (i) What is the length of A'D' and B'F'?
  (ii) ∠BAD is 70°. What size is ∠B'A'D'?
  (iii) What size is ∠FCB? What size is ∠F'C'B'?

8 A ship sails on a two stage journey from A to B to C. The first stage of the journey from A to B is shown. A to B is a journey of 90 km on a bearing of 032°.

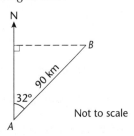

Not to scale

(a) Calculate the distance travelled east during the first stage of this journey.
The second stage of the journey from B to C is a distance of 150 km on a bearing of 090°.

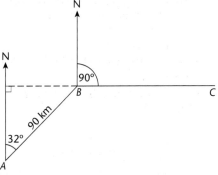

(b) Find the total distance travelled east on the journey from A to C.
Hence calculate the bearing of C from A.

SEG 1996

9 A racing course for yachts is laid out in the shape of a regular nonagon. A is due North of I. What is the bearing
(a) B from A?
(b) B from I?
(c) I from H?
(d) D from C?
(e) E from C?

10 A saucepan made of stainless steel has a height of 11 cm and a diameter of 21 cm. The thickness of the base of the saucepan is 3 mm, and the thickness of the sides of the saucepan is 2 mm.

The density of stainless steel is 11.8 g/cm³.

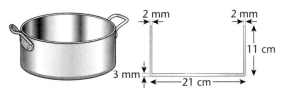

Calculate the mass of the saucepan. Give your answer to an appropriate degree of accuracy. (You may ignore the mass of the handles.)

7: USING GRAPHS TO SOLVE PROBLEMS

1 Which of these statements are true, and which are false?

A: The point $(2, -1)$ is on the line $y = x - 3$.

B: The point $(-3, 4)$ is on the line $y = 7 - x$.

C: The point $(0, 2)$ is on the line $y = \frac{1}{2}x + 2$.

D: The point $(3, 1)$ is on the curve $y = x^2 - 2x - 2$.

2 This is the graph of $3x - y = 2$.

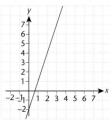

(a) Copy the graph on to squared paper.
(b) On the same axes, draw the graph of $y = x + 3$.
(c) Solve the equations $3x - y = 2$ and $y = x + 3$.

3 (a) Draw the graph of
  $y = x^2 - 3x - 1$ for $-2 \le x \le 5$.
(b) Solve $x^2 - 3x - 1 = 0$.

4 (a) On a copy of the grid, draw the graph of
$y = x^2 - x - 4$.
Use values of x between -2 and $+3$.

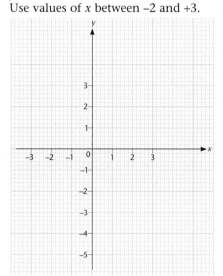

(b) Use your graph to write down an estimate for
  (i) the minimum value of y.
  (ii) the solutions of the equation
    $x^2 - x - 4 = 0$

Edexcel 1998

5 (a) Draw the graph of $y = \frac{5}{x}$ for $-5 \le x \le 5$.
(b) On the same axes, draw the graph of $y = 5 - x$.
(c) What are the solutions to the equation
    $5 - x = \frac{5}{x}$?

6 The equation $x^3 - 3x = 25$ has a solution
between 3 and 4. Use trial and improvement to
find the solution correct to 2 decimal places.

7 Match each equation to one of these graphs.

A 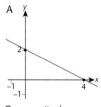   B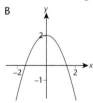

C 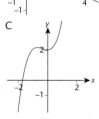   D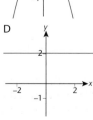

(a) $y = x^3 + 2 + x^2$ (b) $y = 2 - \frac{1}{2}x$
(c) $y = 2$ (d) $y = -x^2 + 2$

8 Joanne has $5x$ pence and Daniel has x pence.
Joanne has at least 30 pence but less than
60 pence.
  (a) Express this information about Joanne's
    money, using inequalities in x.
  (b) Mark all the possible values of pence that
    Daniel could have on the number line.

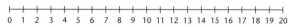

CCEA 1996

9

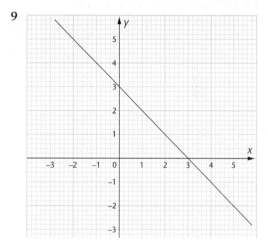

The graph of $y = 3 - x$ is shown on the diagram
above.
  (a) (i) On a copy of the diagram, draw the
    graph of $y = 2x + 1$.
    You may find it helpful to copy and
    complete this table.

x	0	1	2
y			

  (ii) Use the graphs to find the solution of
    the simultaneous equations
    $y = 3 - x$,
    $y = 2x + 1$.
  (b) Find the integer values of x for which
    $0 < 3 - x < 5$.
  (c) On your diagram indicate clearly the region
    for which
    $y \ge 0,$
    $y \le 3 - x$
    and $1 \le x \le 2$.

MEG 1996

10 Hannah goes to the shop to buy a loaf
of bread.
The shop is 800 m from her house.
She leaves home at 15.12 and walks to the
shop at a steady speed.
She takes 16 minutes to reach the shop and
then 5 minutes to buy a loaf of bread.
She then walks home as a steady speed arriving
at 15.48.
On a copy of this diagram draw a distance-time
graph to represent her journey.

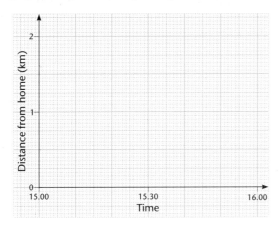

SEG 1996

8: PROPERTIES OF SHAPES

1 A, B and C are three villages on the shores
of a lake.
A is 50 km East of B and 70 km South of C.
  (a) Make an accurate scale drawing showing
  the positions of A, B and C.
  (b) A boat travels in a straight line from B to C.
  Use compasses and a ruler to construct the
  shortest distance from A to the path taken
  by the boat. What is this shortest distance?

2 (a) Make a sketch of each of these shapes.

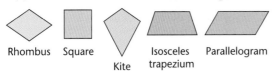

Rhombus   Square   Kite   Isosceles trapezium   Parallelogram

  (b) Mark the lines of symmetry of each shape
  on your sketch.
  (c) Say which shapes have rotational symmetry
  and write the order of rotational symmetry
  by each shape.

3 In the diagram the triangles *PQR* and *SQR* are
isosceles with *PQ = QR* and *QS = SR*.

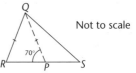

Not to scale

Angle *QPR* = 70°.
  (a) (i) Work out the size of angle *SQR* giving a
    reason for your answer.
  (ii) Work out the size of angle *SQP*.

The triangle *SQR* is reflected in the line *SR* so
that the original and reflected figures form a
quadrilateral *QSXR*, as shown.

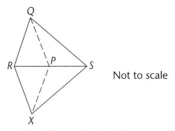

Not to scale

  (b) Which of the following correctly describes
  the quadrilateral *QSXR*?

  **square, rhombus, trapezium, rectangle,
  parallelogram, kite.**

  (c) (i) How many lines of symmetry has the
    quadrilateral *QPXR*?
  (ii) What name is given to the
    quadrilateral *QPXR*?
  (iii) Work out the size of angle *SXP*.

SEG 1995

4 (a) ABCD is a rectangle.
  The angle CAB is 32°.
  (i) What size is ∠ACD?
    Give a reason for
    your answer.
  (ii) Work out the size of
    the larger of the two angles between
    the two diagonals. Explain how you
    worked this out.

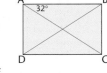

  (b) EFGH is a rhombus. The diagonals of
  the rhombus meet at X. ∠GEF = 32°.
  (i) Work out the size
    of ∠EFH. Give a
    reason for your
    answer.
  (ii) Work out the size
    of ∠EHG. Give a
    reason for your answer.

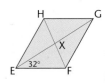

5 This design is made from a regular hexagon, a regular pentagon, a square and a triangle. The side lengths of each regular polygon are the same.
Work out the size of each angle in the triangle. Explain how you worked this out.

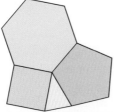

6 This is a regular octagon. O is the centre of the octagon.
(a) Work out the size of ∠x?
(b) Work out the size of ∠y?
(c) Give a reason why ∠z is equal to ∠y.
(d) What type of quadrilateral is formed by the two triangles in the diagram?
(e) What is the size of each of the four interior angles of this quadrilateral?

7 In the diagram *AB* is parallel to *ED*.
Angle *CED* = 54° and angle *BCD* = 100°.

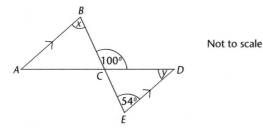

Not to scale

(a) (i) Write down the size of angle *x*.
   (ii) Find the size of angle *y*.
(b) Triangle *ABC* is similar to triangle *DEC*.
   AC:CD is 3:2.
   AB = 5.4 cm.
   Calculate the length of *DE*.

SEG 1998

8 These two triangles are similar.

 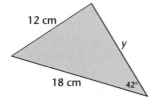

Work out the values of *x* and *y*.

9

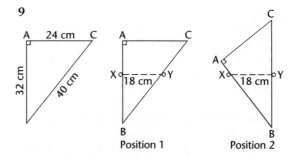

Position 1   Position 2

Triangle ABC represents the cross-section of a wedge. The wedge can be supported in various positions by two pegs X and Y on the same level and 18 cm apart.
(a) In position I, AB is perpendicular to XY. Using similar triangles, calculate the distance BX.
(b) In position II, BC is perpendicular to XY. Using similar triangles, calculate the distance BX.

CCEA 1996

10 This circle has radius *r* cm. Its centre is at O.

The length of arc PQ is *a* cm and ∠POQ = *x*°.

(a) The values of *a* and *x* are connected by one of these formulae. Which formula is the correct one?
$$a = \frac{\pi r^2 x}{180} \quad a = \frac{\pi r x}{180} \quad a = \frac{180 \times r x}{\pi} \quad a = \frac{\pi r x}{360}$$

(b) Find the length of arc PQ if the angle is 70° and the radius of the circle is 6.5 cm.
(c) Find ∠POQ if the radius of the circle and the arc length PQ are both 8 cm.

REVISION GUIDE

Read this before you start

You will be given a lot of advice about how to revise for your GCSE examinations. Much of this advice is about how to find the key facts, and how to commit them to memory. Maths is a bit different from most other subjects. In Maths examinations, being able to solve problems is probably more important than remembering facts. Of course, there are also some things you have to remember. This REVISION GUIDE will help you with both.

Remembering facts and solving problems

In this REVISION GUIDE, your GCSE syllabus has been divided into small, easy-to-remember topics. You will find the facts you have to learn for each topic. You will also find worked examples for methods of solving problems.

Practising solving problems

For each topic, there is a set of problems for you to solve. Some of these are questions from past GCSE papers. The answers are on page 289 of this book.

"So where do I start?"

The syllabus has been divided into the four major areas:

Number	15 topics
Algebra	17 topics
Shape, space and measures	22 topics
Handling data	11 topics

A list of all the topics, in all four areas, is given on page 168. The topics are listed in the order they appear in the GCSE syllabus. They are *not* in order of difficulty.

The section for each area contains the topics and, then, a miscellaneous exercise. You could look through the list of topics on page 168,

and decide which topics you need to revise. Try some of the questions, and use the notes to help you.

Warning: You will want to do some of the questions on topics that you know you understand, to give yourself confidence. However, it also important that you try some of the questions you know you cannot do. It is also tempting to look at the worked examples and think "I can do that", *without actually doing the questions*.

> **Remember:**
> **Success in a Maths exam means solving problems – so successful Maths revision means solving problems.**

"How long do I spend on each topic?"

This will depend on how confident you are about the topic. If you are 'brushing up' on something you already know, it might only take you twenty minutes to reassure yourself that you have mastered the ideas. But, if the topic is one you never really understood, it will take you longer, and you may need to talk to your teacher about it.

"When do I start revising?"

Now! Even if you are reading this in the September of Y11, you may find it helpful to look at the list of topics on page 168, and to discuss with your teacher which topics you should already know. And, if you have forgotten some topics, then you can revise them now! Or, you might plan to revise one topic per week over the next two terms.

If it is now towards the end of Spring term (the time a lot of students start their revision), then there might not be enough time to spend a long while on each topic. You will need to plan what you are going to do. Read the previous two sections again, and decide what your priorities are.

"How do I keep track of my revision programme?"

Your teacher will probably give you a copy of the REVISION ORGANISER, which contains a list of all the revision topics. There are various ways in which you can use the spaces in the REVISION ORGANISER.

- Fill in the dates when you plan to revise each topic.

- Cross out or highlight the topics you have already revised and feel confident about.

- Highlight the topics you want to come back to.

- Make notes of key points you may forget.

Your teacher might also give you a copy of the revision notes in this text book. If so, you could carry this copy around with you all the time – so that you can revise wherever you are!

"What about my coursework exam?"

Some students do coursework for their GCSE; others do a 'coursework' examination. You will need to be clear about what you are doing. If you are doing the examination, you will be asked questions which test your ability to use and apply your knowledge of Mathematics. You will need to:

- make decisions about how to tackle a problem

- write clearly about what you find out

- give reasons for your conclusions.

There is also a sheet giving criteria for assessing coursework or the coursework examination. Ask your teacher for Resource Sheet O. In many of the chapters in this book, and in *Book 1*, you will have noticed COURSEWORK OPPORTUNITIES. Tackling these will give you some idea about what to expect.

Also, you might have noticed flags like this next to some questions. This flag indicates that the question is a bit like the *Making general statements* questions you might meet in the examination.

Most importantly, talk to your teacher about your coursework examination. You will want to see coursework examinations for the last year or two, set for the particular GCSE you are taking.

"Do I need to do any other revision?"

In this REVISION GUIDE, the questions have been organised into topics for you. This is the best way of starting your revision, because then you can concentrate on the topics you are least clear about.

But, in the examination, you will have to decide for yourself what topic the question is about. This is a skill you can practise by answering the questions in the six miscellaneous exercises in this REVISION GUIDE*. But you also need to practise this skill, by doing past papers for the particular GCSE examination you are taking.

Talk to your teacher about getting hold of some past GCSE papers, and build these into the later stages of your revision programme.

*NOTE: It may be useful for you to know that there are six more miscellaneous tests in the *Teacher's Guide*. Also, half of the miscellaneous exercises and tests are to be done without a calculator, just as some GCSE papers are to be done without a calculator.

Topic	NUMBER	Page
N1	Place value and ordering whole numbers, decimals and fractions	169
N2	Rounding numbers	170
N3	Equivalence of fractions, decimals and percentages	171
N4	Negative numbers	173
N5	Multiples, factors and primes	175
N6	Powers, roots and reciprocals	176
N7	Index notation and standard form	177
N8	Arithmetic with whole numbers (without a calculator)	179
N9	The four rules of decimals	180
N10	The four rules of fractions	182
N11	Percentages	183
N12	Ratio and proportion	185
N13	Order of operations	187
N14	Efficient use of a calculator	188
N15	Estimation and approximation	189
	Miscellaneous Exercise	190

Topic	ALGEBRA	Page
A1	Algebra for functions	192
A2	Linear sequences	193
A3	Quadratic sequences	195
A4	Graphs of real-life situations	197
A5	Straight-line graphs	200
A6	Non-linear graphs	203
A7	Formulae	206
A8	Manipulating algebraic expressions	207
A9	Algebraic expressions using brackets	208
A10	Factorising	209
A11	Changing the subject of a formula	210
A12	Linear equations	211
A13	Inequalities and locating regions by lines	213
A14	Trial and improvement, including solving equations	215
A15	Quadratic equations	216
A16	Linear simultaneous equations	217
A17	Solving equations using graphs	218
	Miscellaneous Exercise	220

Topic	SHAPE, SPACE AND MEASURES	Page
S1	3D objects and their 2D representation	223
S2	Accurate construction of 2D shapes	225
S3	Congruent shapes	226
S4	Angles and lines	227

Topic	SHAPE, SPACE AND MEASURES (continued)	Page
S5	Triangles and quadrilaterals	229
S6	Polygons	231
S7	Symmetry	233
S8	Compass points and bearings	234
S9	Pythagoras' theorem	235
S10	Trigonometry	236
S11	Transformations	238
S12	Scale drawing and similarity	240
S13	Locus	242
S14	Ruler and compass constructions	243
S15	Units of measurement and conversions	244
S16	Compound measures: speed and density	245
S17	Upper and lower bounds of measures	246
S18	Area and perimeter of triangles, parallelograms and trapeziums	247
S19	Area and perimeter of circles	249
S20	Volume and surface area of cuboids	250
S21	Volume and surface area of prisms and cylinders	251
S22	Distinguish between formulae by considering dimensions	253
	Miscellaneous Exercise	254

Topic	HANDLING DATA	Page
D1	Collection and organisation of data	257
D2	Designing a questionnaire; bias	258
D3	Line graphs, bar charts, histograms and frequency polygons	259
D4	Pie charts	261
D5	Scatter diagrams and lines of best fit	263
D6	Mean, median, mode and range	265
D7	Means of frequency distributions	266
D8	Cumulative frequency, median and interquartile range	268
D9	Basic probability	270
D10	Estimating probability	271
D11	Probability of two events	273
	Miscellaneous Exercise	275

Topic	COURSE REVISION	Page
Ex 1	Non-calculator	281
Ex 2	Calculator	282
Ex 3	Non-calculator	282
Ex 4	Calculator	283
Ex 5	Non-calculator	284
Ex 6	Calculator	285

N1 PLACE VALUE AND ORDERING WHOLE NUMBERS, DECIMALS AND FRACTIONS

WHOLE NUMBERS (INTEGERS)

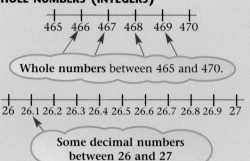

Whole numbers between 465 and 470.

Some decimal numbers between 26 and 27

And between 26.2 and 26.3 there are numbers 26.11, 26.12, 26.13, ... and so on.

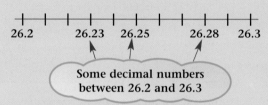

Some decimal numbers between 26.2 and 26.3

NEGATIVE NUMBERS

Negative numbers are considered to be smaller than positive numbers. So these numbers are in the correct order of size (starting with the smallest):

$$-253, -56, -8, 12, 38, 100$$

FRACTIONS

Often numbers which are *not* whole numbers are thought of as **fractions** rather than as decimals. For example, $\frac{1}{3}$ is a fraction between 0 and 1, and $5\frac{3}{4}$ is a fraction between 5 and 6.

Here are some numbers between 4 and 5.

Arranging fractions in order is harder than arranging decimals in order.

You might be able to see that:

$\frac{2}{5}$ is smaller than $\frac{3}{5}$

$\frac{1}{4}$ is smaller than $\frac{1}{3}$

but deciding whether $\frac{5}{8}$ is bigger or smaller than $\frac{2}{3}$ takes more thought (see N3).

Do not use a calculator for these questions.

1 Write down the answers to these multiplications.
   (a) 24.1×1000 (b) 150×100
   (c) $0.003\,04 \times 100$

2 Write down the answers to these divisions.
   (a) $304\,300 \div 1000$ (b) $96 \div 1000$
   (c) $0.0768 \div 100$

3 Write these numbers in order of size, starting with the smallest.

   2.7   1.98   0.085   0.09   0.1   0.003 597

4 Write these fractions in order of size, starting with the smallest.

   $\frac{1}{2}$ $\frac{1}{4}$ $\frac{1}{8}$ $\frac{3}{4}$ $\frac{3}{8}$ $\frac{5}{8}$ $\frac{7}{8}$

5 These number lines are to be marked with equally spaced numbers. Copy and complete them.

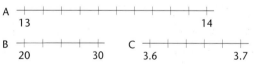

6 What number does the **?** stand for in these calculations?
   (a) $12.6 \times \textbf{?} = 1260$ (b) $\textbf{?} \times 1000 = 2.15$
   (c) $\textbf{?} \div 100 = 14.1$ (d) $\textbf{?} \div 10 = 9.85$

7 $14 \times 36 = 504$. Use this fact to write down answers for these.
   (a) 1.4×3.6 (b) $504 \div 36$
   (c) 1400×3.6 (d) $504 \div 1400$

8 $26 \times 26 \times 26 = 175\,76$. Use this fact to write down the answers for these.
   (a) $2.6 \times 2.6 \times 2.6$ (b) $175\,76 \div 26 \div 2.6$
   (c) $\dfrac{1.7576}{0.26^2}$

ROUNDING NUMBERS

Decimal places (d.p.) are counted from left to right, starting at the decimal point.

Significant figures (s.f.) are counted from the left to the right, starting at the first non-zero digit.

5.674 722 = 5.6747 (correct to 4 d.p.)

0.007 754 33 = 0.007 75 (correct to 3 s.f.)

5.674 722 = 5.675 (correct to 3 d.p.)

0.007 754 33 = 0.008 (correct to 1 s.f.)

5.674 722 = 5.67 (correct to 2 d.p.)

563 422 = 563 000 (correct to 3 s.f.)

5.674 722 = 5.7 (correct to 1 d.p.)

563 422 = 560 000 (correct to 2 s.f.)

563 422 = 600 000 (correct to 1 s.f.)

1 Round each of these numbers to 2 decimal places.
   (a) 4.366
   (b) 29.0949
   (c) 13.798
   (d) 3.5555
   (e) 9.998
   (f) –4.007
   (g) 45.003
   (h) –7.896

2 Round each of these quantities to 2 significant figures.
   (a) 174 62 people
   (b) 23.7 cm
   (c) 49.7 seconds
   (d) 464 g
   (e) 0.175 days
   (f) 183 99 million tons
   (g) 5008 miles
   (h) 0.000 387 5 g

3 It is estimated that during the summer, at a theme park, 12 600 people ride on a certain roller coaster each day. The estimate is said to be accurate to the nearest 100 people. Write down the number of people who ride on the roller coaster
   (a) correct to the nearest 1000
   (b) correct to 2 significant figures.

4 Round 4509.953 to
   (a) the nearest 10
   (b) the nearest 100
   (c) 1 significant figure
   (d) 1 decimal place

N3 EQUIVALENCE OF FRACTIONS, DECIMALS AND PERCENTAGES

EQUIVALENT FRACTIONS

These fractions are all equivalent.

$$\frac{1}{3}, \frac{2}{6}, \frac{3}{9}, \frac{4}{12}, \frac{30}{90}, \frac{250}{750}, \cdots$$

This means they all stand for the *same* number.
These fractions are all equivalent.

$$\frac{3}{4}, \frac{6}{8}, \frac{9}{12}, \frac{45}{60}, \frac{75}{100}, \cdots$$

Sometimes, you are asked to **simplify a fraction**.
This means writing an equivalent fraction with the *smallest* possible numbers.

Divide the top and bottom by the same number.

CHANGING PERCENTAGES TO FRACTIONS AND DECIMALS

$40\% = \frac{40}{100} = \frac{2}{5}$

or $40\% = 40 \div 100 = 0.4$

Remember that % means 'divide by 100'.

CHANGING FRACTIONS AND DECIMALS TO PERCENTAGES

$\frac{4}{5} = \frac{4}{5} \times 100\% = \frac{400}{5}\% = 80\%$

$0.8 = 0.8 \times 100\% = 80\%$

Multiply by 100%

EQUIVALENCE BETWEEN FRACTIONS AND DECIMALS

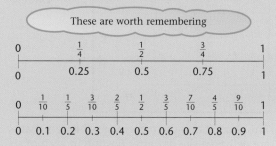

These are worth remembering

Remember that $\frac{a}{b}$ is the same as $a \div b$.

So $\frac{7}{8} = 7 \div 8 = 0.875$.

This provides the easiest way of comparing the sizes of two fractions.

$\frac{5}{8} = 5 \div 8 = 0.625$

$\frac{2}{3} = 2 \div 3 = 0.667$ (correct to 3 d.p.)

So $\frac{2}{3}$ is bigger than $\frac{5}{8}$.

To convert a decimal to a fraction, use place value, and then simplify.

$$0.6 = \frac{6}{10} = \frac{3}{5}$$

$$0.07 = \frac{7}{100}$$

$$0.375 = \frac{375}{1000} = \frac{3}{8}$$

Do not use a calculator, except for Questions 7 and 8.

1 Which fraction is the odd one out? Explain your answer.

$$\frac{5}{8} \qquad \frac{40}{64} \qquad \frac{25}{64} \qquad \frac{15}{24} \qquad \frac{25}{40}$$

2 Three students took a Science test.

Hiate scored $\frac{3}{5}$ of the total marks.

Jason scored $\frac{2}{3}$ of the total marks.

Petra scored 65%.

Who scored the highest marks?
Show all your working.

3 Copy and complete this table.

Fraction	Decimal	Percentage
$\frac{4}{5}$		
$\frac{1}{3}$		
	0.45	
	0.125	
		24%
		8%

4 The chart shows the percentage of letters that are delivered the day after posting in each of six European countries.

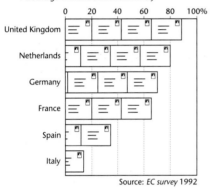

Postal reliability

Percentage of letters delivered next day

Source: *EC survey* 1992

(a) In Germany, 72% of all letters posted are delivered the next day.
Write 72% as a fraction in is simplest form.

(b) Which country has approximately $\frac{7}{20}$ of its letters delivered the next day?

(c) Forty million letters are posted every day in the United Kingdom.
Nine-tenths of these are delivered the next day.
In your head, calculate $\frac{9}{10}$ of 40 000 000.
Write down your answer.
Explain clearly how you worked out your answer.

NEAB 1994

5 Write these fractions in order of size, with the smallest first.

$\frac{2}{3}$ $\frac{7}{10}$ $\frac{3}{4}$ $\frac{11}{16}$

6 $\frac{3}{4}$ is equal to 0.75
From the list below write down **two** other equal pairs.

$\frac{2}{8}$ $\frac{5}{6}$ $\frac{3}{15}$ $\frac{4}{12}$ $\frac{9}{12}$ $\frac{18}{25}$ 0.25 20% 82%

CCEA 1998

7 (a) Change each of these fractions to a decimal, correct to 2 decimal places.

$\frac{5}{3}$ $\frac{7}{11}$ $\frac{3}{4}$ $\frac{7}{10}$ $\frac{9}{13}$ $\frac{4}{7}$ $\frac{7}{5}$ $\frac{13}{9}$

(b) List the fractions in part (a) in order of size.

8 Arrange these numbers in order of size, starting with the smallest.

$2\frac{2}{7}$ 0.227 $\frac{2}{7}$ 77% $\frac{7}{27}$ $\frac{7}{22}$ 22% 27% 2.7 $\frac{22}{7}$

NEGATIVE NUMBERS

ADDING NEGATIVE NUMBERS

$(-6) + (-3) = -9$

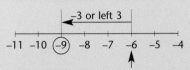

$(-6) + 8 = 2$

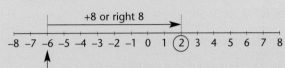

SUBTRACTING NEGATIVE NUMBERS

$33 - 27 = 6$

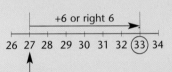

$(-6) - (+2) = -8$

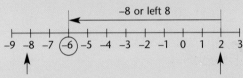

$(-3) - (-5) = 2$

MULTIPLYING AND DIVIDING NEGATIVE NUMBERS

$(-3) \times (+2) = -6$

$(+3) \times (-5) = -15$

If one sign is negative, the answer is negative.

$(-6) \div (+3) = -2$

$(+16) \div (-2) = -8$

If both signs are negative, the answer is positive.

$(-4) \times (-3) = +12$

$(-20) \div (-4) = +5$

Do not use a calculator for these questions.

1 In Birmingham, on one day last winter, the maximum temperature was recorded as 5°C. The minimum temperature was –4°C. What was the difference between the maximum and minimum temperatures?

2 Ali and Pam take part in a quiz. The rules are:

> For each correct answer +2 points
> For each wrong answer –1 point

After the first round the scores are:

Ali
–1

Pam
+2

(a) In the second round Ali gets two questions correct and two questions wrong. What is his new score?

(b) Pam is asked four questions in the second round. At the end of this round Pam's new score is –2. How many questions did she answer correctly?

NEAB 1996

3 Calculate these.
   (a) $(-3) + 5$ (b) $(-17) - 22$
   (c) $9 - 17$ (d) $16 - (-5)$
   (e) $(-14) + (-23)$ (f) $(-14) - (-23)$
   (g) $(-23) - (-14)$ (h) $(-23) + (-14)$

4 Calculate these.

(a) $3 \times (-4)$ (b) $(-6) \times (-8)$

(c) $20 \div (-5)$ (d) $(-35) \div (-7)$

(e) $(-6)^2$ (f) $(-2)^3$

(g) $\dfrac{120}{(-2) \times (-3) \times (-4)}$

(h) $(-\frac{1}{2}) \times (-\frac{1}{4})$

5 (a) Copy and complete these boxes.

(i)

(ii)

(b) Work out $\dfrac{(-1) \times (-7) \times (+8)}{-2}$

NEAB 1998

6 Copy these, replacing the squares by numbers.

(a) ☐ $\times -3 = -12$

(b) ☐ $\div 4 = -5$

(c) $-3 \times -4 \times$ ☐ $= 60$

(d) ☐ $\times$ ☐ $= -15$

(e) ☐$^3 = -27$

(f) ☐ $\div$ ☐ $= -2$

(g) ☐ $\times$ ☐ $\times$ ☐ $= -1$

7 A teacher shows her class 2 six-sided dice. On each of them are the numbers

$$-6, \quad +5, \quad -4, \quad +3, \quad -2, \quad +1.$$

The two dice are rolled.

(a) The score is obtained by **adding** the numbers on the upper faces. Calculate the score in each of the following cases:

(i)

(ii)

(b) When Natasha rolled the dice she scored +10. When Cortez rolled the dice he scored –8. By how many is Natasha's score greater than that of Cortez?

(c) The rules of the game are now changed. The score is obtained by **multiplying** the numbers on the upper faces.

Calculate the score in each of the following cases:

(i)

(ii)

NEAB 1997

MULTIPLES

If you multiply a whole number by 8, you get a **multiple** of 8.

16, 40, 64 and 160 are multiples of 8.

7, 14, 21, 28, 35 and 42 are the first six multiples of 7.

FACTORS

The **factors** of a number are those numbers that divide into it exactly.

The factors of 6 are 1, 2, 3, 6 because
$6 = 1 \times 6 = 2 \times 3$.

The factors of 20 are 1, 2, 4, 5, 10, 20 because
$20 = 1 \times 20 = 2 \times 10 = 4 \times 5$.

Prime factors are factors which are prime numbers.

$30 = 2 \times 3 \times 5$

Numbers written as the product of prime factors.

$36 = 6 \times 6$

$= 2 \times 3 \times 2 \times 3$

$= 2^2 \times 3^2$

PRIME NUMBERS

A **prime number** does not have any factors, except 1 and the number itself.

Prime numbers less than 100

2, 3, 5, 7, 11, 13, 17, 19, 23, 29, 31, 37, 41, 43, 47, 53, 59, 61, 67, 71, 73, 79, 83, 89, 97

- Apart from 2, no even number is prime (all even numbers have 2 as a factor).
- Apart from 5, no number ending in 0 or 5 is prime (it is divisible by 5).
- If the digits of a number add up to 3, that number is divisible by 3. So it is not prime, unless it is 3 itself.
- To test whether a number is prime, you only have to test whether another prime number is a factor. If 2, 3 and 5 are not factors, you need to test 7, 11 and 13. This is all you need to test for numbers up to 289 (which is 17×17).

SQUARE NUMBERS

1, 4, 9, 16, 25, ...

Do not use a calculator for these questions.

1 The National Lottery uses the numbers from 1 to 49 inclusive. To play the lottery, people have to pick six numbers.

  (a) Carlene says that she likes square numbers. What numbers might she choose?

  (b) Andrea says she will pick all prime numbers. What numbers might she pick?

  (c) Jim wants to pick only multiples of 6. What numbers might he choose?

  (d) Sharon wants to pick only factors of 48. What numbers might she choose?

  (e) Caroline wants to pick just factors of 50. Why is this not possible?

2 (a) Factorise 36, 56 and 54 into products of prime factors.

  (b) Find the highest common factor of
    (i) 36 and 56   (ii) 36 and 54
    (iii) 36, 54 and 56

3 What is the highest common factor of
  (a) 28 and 42?   (b) 280 and 420?

4 What is the lowest number that is a multiple of
  (a) 8 and 18?   (b) 7, 11 and 13?

5 In each of these, guess the number from the clues given.

  (a) I am even and I am prime.

  (b) I have exactly five factors and I am less than 50.

  (c) I am less than 40, and I am a multiple of both 3 and 4. If I was one more I would be square.

  (d) I am less than 50, and I am a square number, and I can be made by adding two other square numbers together.

6 (a) Express 540 as a product of powers of prime factors.

  (b) What is the lowest number which 540 must be multiplied by to become a square number?

WJEC 1998

POWERS, ROOTS AND RECIPROCALS

POWERS, ROOTS AND INDICES

$5^3 = 125$ means the same as $\sqrt[3]{125} = 5$
$2^5 = 32$ means the same as $\sqrt[5]{32} = 2$

$5^0 = 1$

$27^0 = 1$

$16.5^0 = 1$

Any number raised to the power of zero is equal to 1.

$x^0 = 1$

$a^m \times a^n = a^{m+n}$	$3a^4 \times 4a^5 = 12a^9$
$a^m \div a^n = a^{m-n}$	$15b^7 \div 5b^2 = 3b^5$
$a^0 = 1$	$37^0 = 1$
$a^{-m} = \dfrac{1}{a^m}$	$(0.25)^{-1} = \dfrac{1}{0.25} = 4$

RECIPROCALS

The **reciprocal** of n is $\dfrac{1}{n}$.

Number	Reciprocal
3	$\frac{1}{3}$
$\frac{1}{3}$	3
$\frac{2}{5}$	2.5
$\frac{a}{b}$	$\frac{b}{a}$

$7^{-1} = \frac{1}{7}$

$18^{-1} = \frac{1}{18}$

A negative power means '1 ÷ ...'

$5^{-2} = \frac{1}{5^2} = \frac{1}{25}$

$n^{-3} = \dfrac{1}{n^3}$

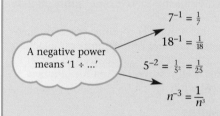

Do not use a calculator for these questions.

1 Find the value of each of these.
(a) 2^4
(b) The cube of 4
(c) $2^3 \times 5^2$
(d) 3^4
(e) $\sqrt{49}$
(f) $\sqrt[3]{125}$
(g) The cube of 6
(h) $2^3 \times 3^2$

2 Find the value of each of these.
(a) 5^4
(b) 128×4^{-3}
(c) $2^6 \div 4^3$

3 Simplify these, and write them as whole numbers or decimals.
(a) $7x^0$
(b) $(7x)^0$
(c) 4^{-1}
(d) 5^{-2}

4 Simplify these.
(a) $a^7 \div a^3$
(b) $3b^2 \times 5b^4$
(c) $2c^2 \times (2c)^2$
(d) $\dfrac{3d^2 \times 4d^3}{2d}$
(e) $4e^{-1} \times 4e$

5 Find the reciprocal of each of these numbers. Give your answer as a whole number or as a decimal.
(a) 5 (b) $\frac{1}{4}$ (c) 2 (d) $\frac{5}{8}$
(e) $\frac{2}{3}$ (f) 2.5 (g) 0.8 (h) 1.25

6 Find the value of x in each of these equations.
(a) $3^x = 9$
(b) $2^x = 32$
(c) $5 \times 2^x = 80$
(d) $4 \times 5^x = 100$
(e) $2 \times x^3 = 54$
(f) $x^3 \div 2^6 = 1$
(g) $x^x = 256$
(h) $x^3 \div 12 = 18$

Nelson GCSE Maths REVISION GUIDE: NUMBER (INTERMEDIATE)

INDEX NOTATION AND STANDARD FORM

The number 1.083×10^5 is an example of a number in **standard form**.

$1.083 \times 10^5 = 1.083 \times 10 \times 10 \times 10 \times 10 \times 10 = 108\,300$

$2.2 \times 10^{-4} = 2.2 \div 10^4 = 2.2 \div 100\,00 = 0.000\,22$

$(1.3 \times 10^3) \times (5 \times 10^{-5}) = 1.3 \times 5 \times 10^3 \times 10^{-5} = 6.5 \times 10^{-2}$

$(3.6 \times 10^{-6}) \div (3 \times 10^4) = (3.6 \div 3) \times (10^{-6} \div 10^4) = 1.2 \times 10^{-10}$

$\sqrt{4 \times 10^{-6}} = 2 \times 10^{-3}$

$(6 \times 10^3) + (7 \times 10^{-2}) = 6000 + 0.07 = 6000.07 = 6.00007 \times 10^3$

$(4 \times 10^{-3}) - (8 \times 10^{-4}) = 0.004 - 0.0008 = 0.0032 = 3.2 \times 10^{-3}$

> All these can be worked out, and the answers given in standard form, *without* using a calculator.

> You will also need to know how to *use a calculator* to do calculations in standard form, such as these.

$(4.65 \times 10^7) + (6.38 \times 10^9) = 6.43 \times 10^9$ (to 2 d.p.)

$(3.68 \times 10^3) \div (4.93 \times 10^5) = 7.46 \times 10^{-3}$ (to 2 d.p.)

Do not use a calculator for Questions 1 to 5.

1 Write these numbers in standard form.
  (a) $573\,00$
  (b) $0.009\,056$
  (c) Twenty-five million
  (d) Double 7.5×10^4

2 Write these as ordinary numbers.
  (a) 3.56×10^5
  (b) 2.08×10^{-4}
  (c) 3.768×10^6
  (d) Half of 1.6×10^{-2}

3 Calculate these. Give your answer in standard form.
  (a) $3 \times (2.3 \times 10^5)$
  (b) $(3 \times 10^2) \times (2 \times 10^3)$
  (c) $(5 \times 10^5) \times (7 \times 10^6)$
  (d) $(3 \times 10^2) \times (5 \times 10^3) \times (2 \times 10^4)$
  (e) $(4 \times 10^7)^2$
  (f) $(6.4 \times 10^8) \div 4$
  (g) $(3.6 \times 10^5) \div (1.2 \times 10^2)$
  (h) $(2.7 \times 10^6) \div (5.4 \times 10^2)$

4 Calculate these. Give your answers in standard form.
  (a) $(2.5 \times 10^3) \times (6 \times 10^5)$
  (b) $(3.6 \times 10^2) \times (2 \times 10^{-3})$
  (c) $(2.8 \times 10^7) \div (4 \times 10^5)$
  (d) $(4.8 \times 10^{-4}) \div (8 \times 10^{-7})$
  (e) $(6 \times 10^5) + (9 \times 10^3)$
  (f) $(3 \times 10^4) - (2 \times 10^2)$

5 (a) (i) Calculate the value of
$3 \times 10^{-4} \times 7 \times 10^{6}$.
Give your answer in standard form.

(ii) Give your answer to part (i) as a
product of prime numbers.

(b) Calculate the value of $(7 \times 10^{6})^{3}$.
Give your answer in standard form.

SEG 1996

6 The contents of books and newspapers can be
stored on microfilm.
ABCD is one rectangular frame of this
microfilm.

$AB = 4.5 \times 10^{-3}$ centimetres and
$BC = 6.2 \times 10^{-4}$ centimetres.

(a) Calculate the area of the rectangle
Give your answer in standard form.
Remember to state the units in
your answer.

(b) Calculate the perimeter of the rectangle.
Give your answer in standard form.
Remember to state the units in
your answer.

NEAB 1997

7 It is estimated that a water tank contains about
1.12×10^{7} drops of rain water.

By taking samples, it is further estimated that
the water contains about 5.80×10^{9} microbes.

Assuming an even distribution, give an estimate
of the number of microbes per drop of
rain water.

Give your answer in standard form, correct to
3 significant figures.

NEAB 1996

8 There are approximately 5.7×10^{7} people living
in Great Britain. On average, each person uses
20 litres of water per day.

(a) How many litres of water are used
throughout Great Britain each day?

(b) How many litres of water are used in Great
Britain each year?
Give your answers in standard form.

9

Continent	Population	Area (m²)
Europe	6.82×10^{8}	1.05×10^{10}
Asia	2.96×10^{9}	4.35×10^{10}

$$\text{Population density} = \frac{\text{Population}}{\text{Area}}$$

Which of these two continents has the larger
population density?

You **must** show all you working.

SEG 1996

10 (a) Light takes about 12 minutes and 40
seconds to reach the planet Mars from
the Sun.

Light travels at approximately 299 800
kilometres per second.

Calculate the approximate distance of the
Sun from Mars.

Give your answer in standard form correct
to 2 significant figures.

(b) The distance from the Earth to the Moon is
approximately 384 400 km.

The distance from the Earth to the Sun is
approximately 1.496×10^{8} km.

Use these approximations to express the
ratio

distance of   distance of
Earth to Moon : Earth to Sun

in the form $1 : n$

where n is a whole number.

(c) Light travels at the rate of approximately
186 000 miles per second.

Light takes 12 years to reach Earth from a
particular star.

Find the approximate distance, in miles, of
this star from the Earth.
Give your answer in standard form correct
to 3 significant figures.

NEAB 1998

N8 · ARITHMETIC WITH WHOLE NUMBERS (WITHOUT A CALCULATOR)

Quite often you can add, subtract, multiply or divide whole numbers mentally.
Sometimes, you will need to use a written method. You will want to use the one you are already familiar with.

> It is sensible to estimate the answer as a check on your working.

MULTIPLYING WHOLE NUMBERS

Here are two methods you *could* use to multiply whole numbers.

Method 1

23 × 57

	50	7
20	1000	140
3	150	21

23 × 57 = 1000 + 140 + 150 + 21 = 1311

Method 2

> Estimate:
> 20 × 60 = 1200

$$
\begin{array}{r}
23 \times 57 \\
3 \times 57 = 171 \\
20 \times 57 = 1140 \\
23 \times 57 = 1311
\end{array}
$$

DIVIDING WHOLE NUMBERS

4879 ÷ 38

> Estimate:
> 5000 ÷ 40 = 125

> It doesn't have to be 5 here.

> So the answer is 128, remainder 15, or the process can be continued.

> So the answer is 128.39... , or 128.4 correct to 1 d.p.

$$
\begin{array}{rr}
 & 4879 \\
100 \times 38 & -3800 \\
 & 1079 \\
20 \times 38 & -760 \\
 & 319 \\
5 \times 38 & -190 \\
 & 129 \\
3 \times 38 & -114 \\
128 & 15 \\
0.3 \times 38 & -11.4 \\
 & 3.6 \\
0.09 \times 38 & -3.42 \\
128.39 & 0.18 \\
\end{array}
$$

Do not use a calculator for these questions.

1 Calculate these.
   (a) 32 × 28   (b) 47 × 79   (c) 236 × 53

2 Calculate these. Give your answer as a whole number and a remainder.
   (a) 600 ÷ 23   (b) 458 ÷ 37   (c) 623 ÷ 58

3 Calculate these. Give your answer as a decimal, correct to 2 decimal places.
   (a) 300 ÷ 13   (b) 462 ÷ 31   (c) 511 ÷ 64

4 A girl goes to a shop with £2.30 to buy seven chocolate bars. After buying the chocolate bars, she has 34p left. How much is each chocolate bar?

5 A 100-litre container of wine is used to fill bottles with a capacity of 70 cl. How many bottles can be filled from the container?

6 A ball of string contains 5.5 m of string.
   (a) How many pieces of string, each 35 cm long, can be cut from this ball of string?
   (b) What is the length of the piece of string that is left over?

7 A travel company is sending 14 coaches to a holiday resort. Each coach can carry a maximum of 49 passengers. There is a total of 19 empty seats. How many people were travelling to the resort?

8 Coaches can seat 49 passengers. How many coaches are needed for 356 people?

9 When travelling abroad, a woman received 2040 Italian lire for each £1.
   (a) She changed £260 into lire. How many lire did she receive?
   (b) A pair of shoes in Italy cost 34 680 lire. How much is this in pounds?

THE FOUR RULES OF DECIMALS

Quite often, you can add, subtract, multiply or divide decimals *mentally*. Sometimes, you will need to use a *written* method. You will want to use the one you are already familiar with.

> It is sensible to estimate the answer as a check on your working.

MULTIPLYING DECIMALS

Here are two methods you *could* use to multiply decimals.

Method 1

Example 1: 4.6×8.3

> Estimate: $5 \times 8 = 40$

4×8.3	=	33.2
0.1×8.3	=	0.83
0.5×8.3	=	4.15
4.6×8.3	=	38.18

Example 2: 0.38×6.5

> Estimate: $0.4 \times 6 = 2.4$

0.1×6.5	=	0.65
0.3×6.5	=	1.95
0.01×6.5	=	0.065
0.08×6.5	=	0.52
0.38×6.5	=	2.47

Method 2

Example 1: 4.6×8.3
$46 \times 83 = 3818$ (to do this you could use one of the methods in N8) Altogether, there are two digits after the decimal point; so the same must be true in the answer.
$4.6 \times 8.3 = 38.18$

Example 2: 0.38×6.5
$38 \times 65 = 2470$
There are three digits after the decimal point.
$0.38 \times 85 = 2.470 = 2.47$
Be careful not to lose the final zero until *after* you have counted the digits.

DIVIDING DECIMALS

Here are two methods you *could* use to divide decimals.

Method 1

Example 1: $4.2 \div 0.03$

		4.2
$\underline{100} \times 0.03$	=	$\underline{-3}$
		1.2
$\underline{10} \times 0.03$	=	$\underline{-0.3}$
		0.9
$\underline{30} \times 0.03$	=	$\underline{-0.9}$
		0

So $4.2 \div 0.03 = 140$

Example 2: $46.54 \div 0.13$

		46.54
$\underline{300} \times 0.13$	=	$\underline{-39}$
		7.54
$\underline{50} \times 0.13$	=	$\underline{-6.5}$
		1.04
4×0.13	=	$\underline{-0.52}$
		0.52
4×0.13	=	$\underline{-0.52}$
		0

So $46.54 \div 0.13 = 358$

Method 2

Example 1: $4.2 \div 0.03$
Keep multiplying both numbers by 10, until the second number is a whole number.
$4.2 \div 0.03 = 42 \div 0.3 = 420 \div 3$
Then do the division.
$420 \div 3 = 140$
So, $4.2 \div 0.03 = 140$

Example 2: $46.54 \div 0.13$
$46.54 \div 0.13 = 465.4 \div 1.3 = 4654 \div 13$
$4654 \div 13 = 358$ (using whatever method you want from N8).
So, $46.54 \div 0.13 = 358$

Do not use a calculator for Questions 1 to 5.

1 Calculate these.
  (**a**) $3.45 + 8.7$
  (**b**) $21.83 + 0.171$
  (**c**) $42 - 15.98$
  (**d**) $25.031 - 2.503$

2 Calculate these.
  (**a**) 0.2×0.8
  (**b**) 0.05×460
  (**c**) $24 \div 0.2$
  (**d**) $0.9 \div 0.03$

3 Calculate these.
  (**a**) 0.02×45
  (**b**) 1.3×25
  (**c**) 4.2×5.7
  (**d**) 3.8^2

4 Calculate these, correct to 2 significant figures.
  (**a**) $5.8 \div 4$
  (**b**) $4.7 \div 6$
  (**c**) $13 \div 0.8$
  (**d**) $0.2 \div 0.7$

5 Pam, Margaret, Howard and John had a meal together.
This was the menu.

Menu	
Chef's Pate	£1.80
Soup	£1.30
Roast beef	£6.75
Salmon	£5.95
Lentil crumble	£4.75
Fresh strawberries	£1.75
Chocolate gateau	£1.95
Ice cream	£1.05

They had
  4 soups;
  2 roast beef, 1 salmon and 1 lentil crumble;
  3 fresh strawberries and 1 ice cream.
They also had a bottle of wine costing £6.50.

They agreed to share the bill equally among them.

How much did each one pay?

MEG 1998

6 This is the nutritional information shown on the side of a cereal packet. Two of the numbers are missing.

Composition		Per 100g (3½oz)	Per 30g (1oz) serving
Energy K/J		1597	479
kcal		377	113
Protein	g	9.3	
Carbohydrates	g	76.8	23.0
of which sugars	g	27.4	8.2
Fat	g	3.6	1.1
of which saturates	g	0.3	0.1
Fibre	g		1.8
Sodium	g	0.5	0.2

(a) How many grams of fibre are there in a 100 g serving of the cereal?

(b) How much protein is there in a 30 g serving of the cereal?

7 To change inches into centimetres, you multiply by 2.54.
  (a) Change 52.7 inches into centimetres.
  (b) How many inches are the same as 889 cm?

8 The diagram shows one of the bookcases in a public library.
The bookcase is 2.3 metres high.
The shelves are equally spaced.

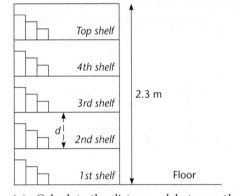

(a) Calculate the distance, d, between the shelves.
(You should ignore the thickness of the shelves.)

(b) A disabled person in a wheelchair visits the public library.

This diagram shows the maximum height she can reach from her wheelchair.

Height above ground: 158 cm

Will she be able to reach the top shelf?
Show your working clearly.

(c) A town has a population of 45 000 people.
1 in every 180 people are disabled.
How many disabled people are there in the town?

NEAB 1994

THE FOUR RULES OF FRACTIONS

ADDING AND SUBTRACTING FRACTIONS

$$\frac{1}{4} + \frac{3}{8} = \frac{2}{8} + \frac{3}{8} = \frac{5}{8}$$

> You make them the same by multiplying top and bottom of each fraction by a suitable number.

> The numbers at the bottom of each fraction must all be the same, before you can add the fractions.

> Multiply top and bottom by 3.

> Multiply top and bottom by 8.

> The same is true when you are subtracting fractions.

$$\frac{5}{8} + \frac{1}{3} = \frac{15}{24} + \frac{8}{24} = \frac{23}{24}$$

$$\frac{3}{4} - \frac{5}{16} = \frac{12}{16} - \frac{5}{16} = \frac{7}{16}$$

Example
Work out $2\frac{3}{4} + 1\frac{5}{8}$.

Either
$2\frac{3}{4} + 1\frac{5}{8}$
$= 3 + \frac{3}{4} + \frac{5}{8}$
$= 3 + \frac{6}{8} + \frac{5}{8}$
$= 3 + \frac{11}{8}$
$= 4\frac{3}{8}$

Or
$2\frac{3}{4} + 1\frac{5}{8}$
$= \frac{11}{4} + \frac{13}{8}$
$= \frac{22}{8} + \frac{13}{8}$
$= \frac{35}{8}$
$= 4\frac{3}{8}$

Example
Work out $5\frac{2}{5} - 3\frac{1}{2}$

Either
$5\frac{2}{5} - 3\frac{1}{2}$
$= 2 + \frac{2}{5} - \frac{1}{2}$
$= 2 + \frac{4}{10} - \frac{5}{10}$
$= 2 - \frac{1}{10}$
$= 1\frac{9}{10}$

Or
$5\frac{2}{5} - 3\frac{1}{2}$
$= \frac{27}{5} - \frac{7}{2}$
$= \frac{54}{10} - \frac{35}{10}$
$= \frac{19}{10}$
$= 1\frac{9}{10}$

MULTIPLYING AND DIVIDING FRACTIONS

$$\frac{1}{6} \times \frac{3}{4} = \frac{1 \times 3}{6 \times 4} = \frac{3}{24} = \frac{1}{8}$$

$$\frac{2}{3} \times \frac{3}{10} = \frac{2 \times 3}{3 \times 10} = \frac{6}{30} = \frac{1}{5}$$

> When multiplying or dividing fractions, always change mixed numbers into top-heavy fractions

> You multiply the top numbers together and the bottom numbers.

$$2\frac{2}{3} \times 4\frac{1}{2} = \frac{8}{3} \times \frac{9}{2} = \frac{8 \times 9}{3 \times 2} = 12$$

$$1\frac{3}{4} \div 2\frac{1}{3} = \frac{7}{4} \div \frac{7}{3} = \frac{7}{4} \times \frac{3}{7} = \frac{3}{4}$$

> Multiply by the reciprocal.

Do not use a calculator for the questions.

1 Calculate these.
   (a) $\frac{3}{5}$ of 225   (b) $\frac{5}{8}$ of 104
   (c) $\frac{2}{3}$ of 0.36   (d) $\frac{3}{4}$ of 2

2 At a comprehensive school on one day: half of the students had a school lunch; three-tenths of the students took sandwiches to school; and the remaining 160 students went home to lunch.
   (a) What fraction of the students stayed at school during the lunch break?
   (b) What fraction of the students went home for lunch?
   (c) How many students had a school lunch?

3 The audience at a pantomime is made up as follows: three-eighths are women; three-fifths are children; and the rest are men.
   (a) What fraction of the audience were men?
   (b) If there were 120 children in the audience, how many women were there?

4 Calculate these.
   (a) $2\frac{3}{4} + 1\frac{1}{3}$ (b) $3\frac{2}{5} + 4\frac{1}{10}$
   (c) $5 - 2\frac{3}{8}$ (d) $5\frac{1}{3} - 3\frac{3}{4}$

5 Calculate these.
   (a) $3\frac{1}{2} \times 2\frac{2}{7}$ (b) $4\frac{1}{3} \times 5$
   (c) $2\frac{2}{3} \div \frac{8}{9}$ (d) $2\frac{3}{8} \div 1\frac{1}{4}$

PERCENTAGES

WHAT DOES PERCENTAGE MEAN?

37% is the same as $\frac{37}{100}$ or 0.37

RECOGNISING SIMPLE PERCENTAGES

$1\% = \frac{1}{100}$ $10\% = \frac{1}{10}$ $20\% = \frac{1}{5}$

$25\% = \frac{1}{4}$ $33\frac{1}{3}\% = \frac{1}{3}$ $50\% = \frac{1}{2}$

$75\% = \frac{3}{4}$ $100\% = 1$

> You should know these simple percentages.

FINDING PERCENTAGES

If you can, work it out in your head!

Examples

10% of £2 = 20p   30% of £40 = £12

15% of £240 = £36   2% of £36 = 72p

Here are some tips.

- 1% means 1p in the £. So, 1% of £28 is 28p, and then you can work out 2%, 3%, etc.
- You can find 10% by dividing by 10.
- If you want 5%, halve 10%.
- If you want 15%, work out 10% and 5%, and add.
- If you want 17.5%, use 10% + 5% + 2.5%.

Examples

15% of £36 = £3.60 + £1.80 = £5.40

17.5% of £44 = £4.40 + £2.20 + £1.10 = £7.70

When you cannot work it out in your head, here is a method.

Example

37% of 16 = 37 ÷ 100 × 16 = 5.92

FINDING ONE NUMBER AS A PERCENTAGE OF ANOTHER

Example

The sale price of a coat is £70. The original price was £120. What is the percentage saving?

You save £50 out of £120. Percentage saving is

£50 ÷ £120 × 100% = 42% (to the nearest 1%)

Example

What percentage is 48 minutes of 4 hours?

> Two quantities in different units need to be put into the same unit first.

4 hours = 240 minutes ←

Percentage is 48 minutes ÷ 240 minutes × 100% = 20%.

COMPARING AMOUNTS

Example: A student scores 17 out of 25 on a Science test, and 15 out of 20 on a Maths test. At which subject did she do best?

Change both scores to a percentage:

Science: 17 ÷ 25 × 100 = 68%

Maths: 15 ÷ 20 × 100 = 75%

The student did better at Maths.

INCREASING BY A PERCENTAGE

Example: Increase £68 by 14%.

Either

First find 14 ÷ 100 × £68 = £9.52 and then add this to £68, giving

£68 + £9.52 = £77.52

Or

14% = 0.14

So, multiply by 1 + 0.14, i.e. 1.14.

£68 × 1.14 = £77.52

DECREASING BY A PERCENTAGE

Example: Decrease £68 by 14%.

Either

First find 14% of £68 (14 ÷ 100 × £68 =) £9.52 and then subtract this from £68, giving

£68 − £9.52 = £58.48

Or

Multiply by 1 − 0.14, i.e. 0.86.

£68 × 0.86 = £58.48

REPEATED PERCENTAGE INCREASE

Keep multiplying by the same amount as many times as you need.

Example: If you put £800 into a bank for four years at 7.5% **compound interest** per annum, you will end up with a total of £800 × 1.075 × 1.075 × 1.075 × 1.075, i.e. £1068.38.

REVERSE PERCENTAGES

Example: When a number is increased by 20%, it becomes 48. What is the number?

Either

The original number must be 100%.

120% = 48

10% = 4 (Divide both sides by 12)

100% = 40

Or

To increase by 20%, multiply by 1.20.

So, divide by 1.20 to reverse the process.

48 ÷ 1.20 = 40

Nelson GCSE Maths   REVISION GUIDE: NUMBER (INTERMEDIATE)

Do not use a calculator for Questions 1 to 3.

1 Calculate these.

   (a) 15% of £3   (b) 60% of £12

   (c) 10% of £7.50   (d) 2% of £300

   (e) 8% of £75   (f) 17.5% of £32

2 A bag contains 75 apples, 18 of which were found to be bad.
  What percentage of the apples were good to eat?

3 A business increases the number of people it employs by 50%. There are now 24 employees. How many employees were there before the increase?

4 These signs were displayed in a supermarket.

> Strawberries
> Were £1.20
> Now 25% off!

> Sirloin steak
> Was £7.80 per kg
> Now £5.85 per kg

> Rump steak
> Reduced from £9 per kg
> Now only £7.50 per kg

  (a) What is the new price of the strawberries?

  (b) Does sirloin steak, or rump steak, give the biggest percentage reduction?

5 In a sale, a teapot was reduced by 20% from its original price of £9.50. I bought it on the last day of the sale, when there was 30% off the sale prices.

  (a) How much did I pay for the teapot?

  (b) What percentage reduction did I get altogether?

MEG 1998

6 A car hire firm works out its charges in three parts.

    A fixed fee of £28.45

    A rate of 12.5p per mile travelled

    Value Added Tax at 17.5% added on to the total cost

  A man hires a car from this firm and travels 260 miles. How much will he have to pay?

7 This table gives information about boys and girls in a class who can, or cannot, swim.

	Boys	Girls
Can swim	8	11
Cannot swim	2	3

  (a) What percentage of the class are girls?

  (b) What percentage of the boys can swim?

  (c) What percentage of the people who can swim are girls?

8 The number of pairs of breeding herring gulls was estimated as 22 000 in 1998.
Each year, the number of breeding pairs reduces by 10%.

  (a) Estimate the number of breeding pairs of herring gulls there will be by the year 2000.

  (b) Estimate the number of breeding pairs of herring gulls left by 2005.

9 £500 is invested for 2 years at 6% per annum compound interest.

  (a) Work out the total interest earned over the 2 years.

    £250 is invested for 3 years at 7% per annum compound interest.

  (b) By what single number must £250 be multiplied to obtain the total amount at the end of the 3 years?

Edexcel 1998

10 A "Travel Saver Card" entitles the holder to 40% off the normal price of a journey.

  (a) A particular journey normally costs £28.50. How much would it cost with a Travel Saver Card?

  (b) The Travel Saver Card price for another journey is £18.60.

    What is the normal price of this journey?

SEG 1998

N12 RATIO AND PROPORTION

RATIO

Ratios are used to compare different amounts.

Toad-in-the-hole	Serves 80
Beef sausages	8 kg
Flour	2 kg
Eggs	16
Dried skimmed milk	450 g
Water	4.5 l
Seasoning	

Sausages and flour are in the ratio 4:1 (not 1:4).

Ratio of flour to skimmed milk is 2kg:450g = 2000g:450g = 40:9

PROPORTIONAL DIVISION

Example: Share £45 in the ratio 2:3:4.
You need to divide the money into (2 + 3 + 4) shares, i.e. 9 shares.
£45 ÷ 9 = £5
Each share is worth £5.
The three amounts of money are
   2 × £5 = £10
   3 × £5 = £15
   4 × £5 = £20
You can check your answer.
£10 + £15 + £20 = £45 ✔

DIRECT PROPORTION

Suppose A is **directly proportional** to B.
   If A is trebled then B is trebled.
   If A is halved then B is halved.
Direct proportion can be represented by a straight-line graph through the origin.

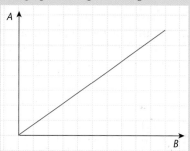

INVERSE PROPORTION

Suppose C is **inversely proportional** to D.
   If C is trebled then D is divided by 3.
   If C is halved then D is doubled.
The answer to C multiplied by D is always the same.

---

1. To make orange squash, concentrated orange is mixed with water in the ratio 2 to 5.

   (a) How much water is mixed with 50 ml of concentrated orange?

   (b) David made 840 ml of orange squash in a jug.
   How much concentrated orange did he use to make it?

   MEG 1996

2. The ratio of games won, drawn, and lost, for a football team during a season was 8:3:5.

   (a) If the team lost 15 matches, how many did they win?

   Teams are awarded three points for each match they win, one point for each match they draw and no points if they lose.

   (b) How many points did this team gain during the season?

3. The recipe below is for a cheesecake for 8 people.

Wheatmeal biscuit crumbs	160 g
Butter	50 g
Cream cheese	640 g
Caster sugar	70 g

   (a) Calculate the amount of butter required to make a cheesecake for 4 people.

   (b) Calculate the amount of caster sugar required to make a cheesecake for 12 people.

   MEG 1996

4. A large tin of dog food contains 800 g and costs 56p.
   The giant tin contains 1 kg and costs 72p.
   Which is the better value?
   Explain your answer.

5 The weights and prices of two different sizes of tomato soup are shown.

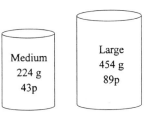

Medium
224 g
43p

Large
454 g
89p

Which size of soup gives more grams per penny?
You **must** show all your working.

SEG 1998

6 The volumes of ice cream in two tubs are in the ratio 2:3.
Write the volume of the smaller tub as a percentage of the volume of the larger tub.

7 When a metal rod is heated, its length increases in the ratio 4:5.

(a) If the rod measured 30 cm when cold, how long will it be when heated?

(b) Another rod increases its length in the ratio 5:8 when heated This rod measured 40 cm when hot. What was its length before it was heated?

8 A teacher spent time during a day either working, resting, sleeping or eating in the ratio 6:4:5:1.
How much time was spent on each of these activities?

9 The plan of a house has been drawn using a scale of 1:20.

(a) On the plan, the kitchen is 21 cm long and 16 cm wide.
What is the area of the kitchen in square metres?

(b) The actual bathroom measures 3.5 m by 2.8 m. What are the dimensions of the bathroom on the plan?

10

Two female weight lifters wish to find who is the stronger.

They decide to measure 'strength' by dividing their 'lifts' by their 'body weights'.

This table shows their lifts and their body weights.

Name	Lift	Body weight
Lorraine Costanzo	237.5 kg	90 kg
Ruthi Shafir	213 kg	67.5 kg

(a) Work out the measure of strength for Lorraine.

(b) If Ruthi had the same strength as Lorraine, what would her lift be?

(c) Who do they say is the stronger?
Show how you decide.

MEG 1995

11 y is directly proportional to the square root of x.
When $x = 25$ then $y = 15$.

(i) Work out a formula to connect x and y.

(ii) Work out the value of x when $y = 6$.

Edexcel 1995

12 The weight of a metal sphere varies directly as the cube of its radius.
The weight of a metal sphere of radius 3 cm is 1.02 kg.
Calculate the weight of a metal sphere of radius 5 cm.

NEAB 1995

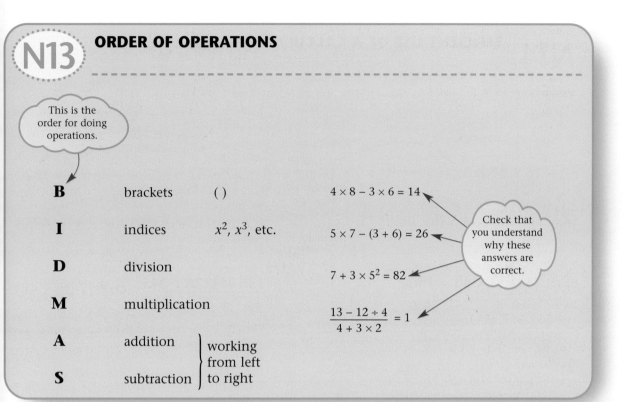

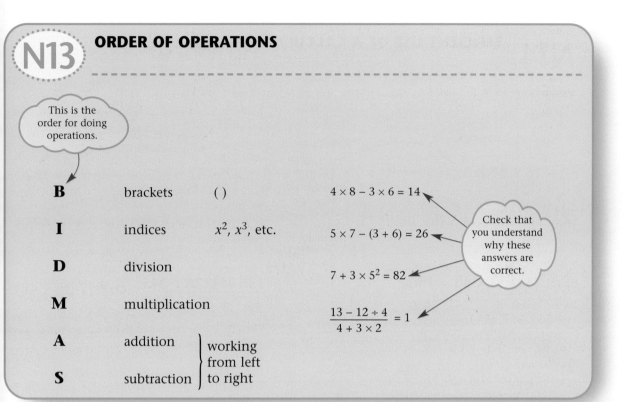

N13 ORDER OF OPERATIONS

This is the order for doing operations.

B brackets ( )

I indices x^2, x^3, etc.

D division

M multiplication

A addition ⎫ working from left to right

S subtraction ⎭

$4 \times 8 - 3 \times 6 = 14$

$5 \times 7 - (3 + 6) = 26$

$7 + 3 \times 5^2 = 82$

$\dfrac{13 - 12 \div 4}{4 + 3 \times 2} = 1$

Check that you understand why these answers are correct.

Do not use a calculator for these questions.

1 Calculate these.

(a) $\dfrac{5 + 4}{5 - 2}$

(b) $3 + 17 \times 2 + 12 \div 4$

(c) $15 - 3 \times 2 + 36 \div 9$

(d) $8 + 3 \times 4^2$

(e) $\dfrac{18 \div 3 - 5 + 3^2}{3^3 - 2^2}$

(f) $\dfrac{5 \times 4 - 4}{14 + 9 \times 2}$

2 Put brackets in these equations to make them correct.

(a) $4 \times 3 + 2 = 20$

(b) $4 \times 5 - 2 \times 2 = 24$

(c) $36 \div 3 + 2 \times 3 = 4$

(d) $36 \div 3 + 2 \times 3 = 42$

3 Signs and brackets can be inserted between the numbers 1, 2, 3, 4 and 5 in many different ways. Here are two examples.

$(1 + 2) \times 3 \div (4 + 5) = 1$

$(1 + 2 + 3 + 4) \div 5 = 2$

Make as many other numbers between 3 and 10 as you can by inserting signs and brackets between the numbers 1, 2, 3, 4 and 5.

4 The number 100 can be made by writing the digits 1 to 9 in order and inserting + and – signs. Here is one way to do it.

$123 - 45 - 67 + 89 = 100$

Find another way of making 100 by inserting + and – signs, and *without* changing the order of the digits.

N14 EFFICIENT USE OF A CALCULATOR

Learn how to use your calculator. For example, find out when brackets are essential.

$52 + 16 \times 17 = 324$

$\dfrac{2914 - 363}{47} = 54.3$ (to 3 s.f.)

$63 \times 28 - 33 \times 48 = 180$

The answers to the calculations are given. Make sure you can use your calculator to get these answers.

$47 \times 52 - (3284 - 2669) = 1829$

$4^3 + 7 \times 5^4 - 9 \times 3^2 = 4358$

$\dfrac{136 - 4326 \div 345}{427 + 326 \times 219} = 0.0017$ (to 2 s.f.)

For each of these questions, give your answer to 3 significant figures.

1 Calculate this.

$$\dfrac{9.73 + 8.23}{6.514}$$

2 Evaluate this.

$$\dfrac{7.83 \times 4.95}{0.825 - 0.378}$$

3 Work out this.

$$\sqrt{3.65^2 - 2.03^2}$$

4 Calculate this.

$$\left(\dfrac{138.97}{12.3} + \dfrac{48.7}{0.821}\right)^2$$

5 Evaluate this.

$$\sqrt{3.64^2 + 8.37^2 - 2 \times 3.64 \times 8.32 \times 0.731}$$

6 Work out this.

$$\dfrac{-8 + \sqrt{8^2 - 4 \times 3 \times 2}}{6}$$

N15 ESTIMATION AND APPROXIMATION

Making an estimate of the answer to a calculation is a way of checking that your answer is correct.

	Roughly	Using a calculator
4.15×9.89	$4 \times 10 = 40$	41.0 to 3 s.f.
$\dfrac{4.96^2 + 3.11^2}{16.89}$	$\dfrac{25 + 9}{17} = 2$	2.03 to 3 s.f.

Do not use a calculator for these questions.

1 Estimate the answer to each of the calculations.
   (a) 397×19 (b) $882 \div 28$
   (c) 3.84×0.517 (d) $0.787 \div 0.195$
   (e) $\sqrt{3.15^2 + 4.23^2}$ (f) $\dfrac{5.7}{12.2} + \dfrac{28.2}{57.6}$

2 John uses his calculator to work out
   $$\dfrac{0.39 \times 85.2}{5.8}$$

   He gets an answer of 57.3.

   Without using a calculator, use approximations to find whether John's answer is of the correct order of magnitude.
   You **must** show all your working.

   SEG 1996

3 At the bank James exchanged his £50 for Francs. He was given 425 Francs.

   Joanna has £120.
   She estimates that she will get about 900 Francs.

   Do not use a calculator.

   Use **rough estimates** to check whether her answer is about right.
   You **must** show all your working.

   SEG 1996

4 A restaurant bill for fourteen people came to a total of £312.56. Show how to estimate how much each person should pay, if they share the cost equally.

5 Samuel wrote down this calculation
   $$\dfrac{1487}{32} = \text{\#}6.5$$

   As you can see, the first figure in the answer is not clear.
   (a) Write down approximate values for 1487 and 32 and use them to estimate the answer to this calculation.
   (b) Write down the figure that is not clear.

   MEG 1996

6 Jameed is going to use his calculator to work out the value of
   $$\dfrac{1.9 \times 10^6}{502 \times \sqrt{0.95}}.$$

   He says that the answer will be approximately 4×10^4.
   (a) Write 4×10^4 as an ordinary number.
   (b) **Without using your calculator**, check Jameed's approximation.
      Show your working.
   (c) **Use your calculator** to find the value of
      $$\dfrac{1.9 \times 10^6}{502 \times \sqrt{0.95}}.$$
      Write down all the figures on the calculator display.

   MEG 1998

Nelson GCSE Maths REVISION GUIDE: NUMBER (INTERMEDIATE)

Do not use a calculator for Questions 1 to 11

1 (a) Copy and complete these calculations.
   (i) $29.6 \times ? = 29\,600$
   (ii) $0.006\,41 \times ? = 641$
   (iii) $37 \div ? = 0.37$
   (iv) $? \times 100 = 0.08$

   (b) Write down the value of these.
   (i) 2^3 (ii) 200^3
   (iii) $\sqrt[3]{8}$ (iv) $\sqrt[3]{8000}$
   (v) 0.02^3 (vi) $\sqrt[3]{0.008}$

2 (a) Write these in order of size, starting with the smallest.

   $$35\% \qquad \tfrac{2}{5} \qquad 0.04 \qquad \tfrac{8}{25}$$

   (b) Find the reciprocal of these numbers. Give each answer as a whole number or a decimal.
   (i)   5   (ii) 0.1   (iii) $\tfrac{2}{3}$ (iv) $1\tfrac{1}{4}$

3 The following were the temperatures (in °C) in four cities at midday on 1st January.

City	London	Moscow	Oslo	Sydney
Temperature	3	−8	−12	23

   (a) What was the difference in temperature between
   (i)   Oslo and Sydney,
   (ii) Oslo and Moscow?

   (b) By midday on the next day, the temperature in Moscow had risen by 2°C and the temperature in London had fallen by 5°C.
   What was the difference in temperature between Moscow and London at midday on 2nd January?

   (c) At midday on 1st February the temperature in Moscow was −2°C.
   London was 3°C warmer than Moscow.
   Oslo was 8°C colder than London.
   What was the temperature in Oslo at midday on 1st February?

   MEG 1998

4 Three friends share a cash prize of £450 in the ratio 3:5:7. How much does each receive?

5 Cheryl wishes to calculate the number of seconds in May and June.
   She multiplies $61 \times 24 \times 60 \times 60$.
   (a) What answer should she get?
   (b) Show how Cheryl could simplify the calculation in order to obtain a good mental estimate.
   You must show all the steps.

   NEAB 1997

6 Two-thirds of the members of a photography club are adults. The rest are children, and there are the same number of boys as girls. Two-fifths of the adults are women. There are 120 members in the club altogether.
   (a) How many adults are there?
   (b) How many boys are there?
   (c) How many men are there?
   (d) What fraction of the club are male?

7 A school has 1000 students registered. For each student, the school is given £2000 per annum towards the cost of running the school.
   (a) How much money does the school receive each year?
   (b) Approximately 80% of the money is spent on staff salaries.
   How much is spent on staff salaries?
   (c) Seven-eighths of the remaining money is spent on maintaining the buildings and on gas, water and electricity charges. The rest is spent on equipment for students.
   How much is spent on equipment?
   (d) The ratio of students in the school to the total population of the town is 2:25.
   What is the population of the town?

8 (a) Find the value of p when $2^p \times 3 = 48$.
   (b) Write 72 as a product of prime factors.
   (c) What is the highest common factor of 48 and 72?
   (d) What is the lowest common multiple of 48 and 72?

   SEG 1998

9 Work out these.
   (a) $3\tfrac{1}{5} + 2\tfrac{3}{10}$ (b) $7\tfrac{1}{4} - 5\tfrac{2}{3}$
   (c) $3\tfrac{1}{5} \times 1\tfrac{7}{8}$ (d) $2\tfrac{1}{4} \div \tfrac{3}{8}$

10 An electrician is working out how much to charge for a job. The materials he used cost £80, and he charges £18 per hour for his labour.

(a) He took five hours to complete the job. How much should he charge?

(b) He also has to add VAT at 17.5%. What is the total bill for the job?

11 Work out the value of each of these expressions if $s = 4 \times 10^6$ and $t = 8 \times 10^5$. Give your answers in standard form.

(a) $2t$ (b) st

(c) $s \div t$ (d) $t \div s$

(e) $s + t$ (f) $s - t$

12

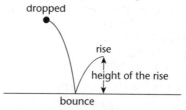

In a sale a dress costs £32.40.
The original price has been reduced by 10%.
What was the original price?

NEAB 1998

13 (a) Alex has a part-time job. His basic rate of pay is £3.70 per hour.
After he has worked 8 hours he is paid at the overtime rate.
The overtime rate is one and a half times the basic rate.

(i) Calculate the amount that Alex is paid for one hour of overtime.

(ii) Calculate Alex's total pay for a day when he worked $2\frac{3}{4}$ hours overtime after completing 8 hours at the basic rate.

Give your answer to a suitable degree of accuracy.

(b) People do not pay Income Tax on the first £3800 they earn in a year.
The remainder is taxed at 20%.

(i) Salma earned £5400 in 1997. Calculate the amount of tax that Salma paid.

(ii) Reshma paid £180 in tax in 1997. Calculate how much she earned.

MEG 1998

14 When a ball is dropped onto the floor, it bounces and then rises.
This is shown in the diagram.

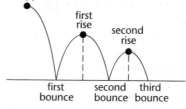

The ball rises to 80% of the height from which it was dropped.
It was dropped from a height of 3 metres.

(a) Calculate the height of the rise after the first bounce.

The ball bounces a second time.

It rises to 80% of the height of the first rise.

(b) Calculate the height of the second rise.

(c) The ball carries on bouncing in this way. Each time it rises to 80% of the last rise.

For how many bounces does it rise to a height greater than 1 metre?

NEAB 1998

15 Light travels at 186 284 miles per second.

(a) Write 186 284 in standard form.

The planet Jupiter is 483.6 million miles from the Sun.

(b) (i) Calculate how long light takes to travel from the Sun to Jupiter. Give your answer to the nearest minute.

(ii) Use approximation to check that your answer is of the right order of magnitude.
You **must** show all your working.

SEG 1998

ALGEBRA FOR FUNCTIONS

Functions are often described using algebra.

The function *add 2* can be written as

$$n \rightarrow n + 2$$

The function *divide by 2* can be written as

$$n \rightarrow \frac{n}{2}$$

The function *multiply by 3 and add 2* can be written as

$$n \rightarrow n + 2$$

The function *add 2 and multiply by 3* can be written as

$$n \rightarrow 3(n + 2)$$

The function *square the number* can be written as

$$n \rightarrow n^2$$

The function *square the number and multiply by 3* can be written as

$$n \rightarrow 3n^2$$

1 Look at at each of these rules.

$1 \rightarrow 5$	$8 \rightarrow 4$
$2 \rightarrow 8$	$5 \rightarrow 7$
$3 \rightarrow 11$	$3 \rightarrow 9$
$4 \rightarrow 14$	$6 \rightarrow 6$

What is the rule in each case? Give your answer in words, and in the form $n \rightarrow$.

2 Copy and complete each of these rules.

$n \rightarrow 4n - 2$ $n \rightarrow n^2 - n$

$1 \rightarrow ?$	$3 \rightarrow ?$
$4 \rightarrow ?$	$1 \rightarrow ?$
$-2 \rightarrow ?$	$-1 \rightarrow ?$
$? \rightarrow 10$	$? \rightarrow 2$

3 Look at this number machine.

INPUT — Multiply by 2 — Subtract 3 — OUTPUT

(a) What is the OUTPUT when the INPUT is –5?

(b) What is the OUTPUT when the INPUT is n?

WJEC 1998

4 Write these functions using n.

(a) Multiply by 4 and subtract 3

(b) Subtract 4 and multiply by 3

5 A sequence begins 1, 3, 7, 15, … .
The rule for continuing the sequence is shown.

MULTIPLY THE LAST NUMBER BY 2 AND ADD 1

(a) What is the next number in the sequence?

(b) This sequence uses the same rule.
–2, –3, –5, –9, …
What is the next number in this sequence?

SEG 1998

6 Look at this table.

L	C
2	5
3	10
4	17
5	26

Write a formula connecting L and C.

LINEAR SEQUENCES

A2

This is how to find the *n*th term of the sequence 5, 7, 9, 11, 13, ...

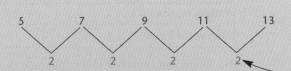

> In the table of differences for a linear sequence, the numbers in the first row of differences are constant.

The formula for this sequence begins 2*n* because the first row of differences is always 2.

The full formula is 2*n* + 3 because 5 − 2 = 3.

It is always worth checking that your formula is correct.
For example, when *n* = 4, 2*n* + 3 = 11. This agrees with the fourth term of the sequence.

---

1 Here are the first five numbers of a simple number sequence.

$$1, \quad 5, \quad 9, \quad 13, \quad 17, \ldots, \ldots,$$

(a) Write down the next two numbers in the sequence.

(b) Describe, in words, the rule to continue this sequence.

(c) Write down, in terms of *n*, the *n*th term of this sequence.

Edexcel 1998

2 Give the next two terms in each sequence, and write down a formula for the *n*th term.

(a) 6, 11, 16, 21, 26, ...

(b) 5, 8, 11, 14, 17, ...

(c) 2, 4, 6, 8, 10, ...

(d) 1, 3, 5, 7, 9, ...

3 (a) Write down the next two lines of this sequence.

$$3 \times 4 = 3 + 3^2$$
$$4 \times 5 = 4 + 4^2$$
$$5 \times 6 = 5 + 5^2$$

(b) Write out the *n*th line of the sequence.

4 (a) What are the nth terms of these sequences?

(i) $\frac{1}{2}, \frac{2}{3}, \frac{3}{4}, \frac{4}{5}, \frac{5}{6}, \ldots$

(ii) $1, \frac{1}{2}, \frac{1}{3}, \frac{1}{4}, \frac{1}{5}, \ldots$

(iii) $2, \frac{3}{2}, \frac{4}{3}, \frac{5}{4}, \frac{6}{5}, \ldots$

(iv) $1, \frac{1}{3}, \frac{1}{5}, \frac{1}{7}, \frac{1}{9}, \ldots$

(b) Look at the terms in sequences (ii) and (iii).

What is the connection between corresponding terms?

(c) What is the connection between the corresponding terms in sequences (i) and (iii)?

MEG 1995

5 The first five terms of a given sequence are

$$2, \quad 1\frac{1}{2}, \quad 1\frac{1}{3}, \quad 1\frac{1}{4}, \quad 1\frac{1}{5}$$

(a) Write down the first five terms of a new sequence of fractions whose terms are the reciprocals of the terms of the given sequence.

(b) Write down, in terms of *n*, the *n*th term of

(i) the given sequence,

(ii) the new sequence.

CCEA 1996

6 Here is a sequence of patterns.

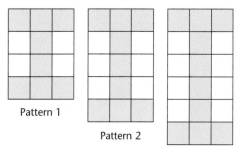

Pattern 1

Pattern 2

Pattern 3

(a) Copy and complete this table.

Pattern number, n	Number of shaded squares, s	Number of unshaded squares, u
1	8	4
2		
3		
4		
5		

(b) Write down a formula for the number shaded squares in Pattern n.

(c) Write down a formula for the number of unshaded squares in Pattern n.

(d) Write down an equation connecting the number of shaded squares, s, and the number of unshaded squares, u.

7 The three patterns below are made out of matchsticks.

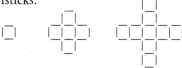

Pattern 1   Pattern 2   Pattern 3

(a) Draw the next pattern in this sequence.

(b) Copy and complete this table to show the number of matchsticks used for each pattern.

Pattern	1	2	3	4	5	6
Number of matchsticks	4	16	28			

(c) Is it possible to have a pattern in this sequence which uses 100 matchsticks?

Give a reason for your answer.

NEAB 1996

8 The diagrams show patterns made out of sticks.

Pattern number   1   2   3

(a) Draw a diagram to show pattern number 4.

The table below can be used to show the number of sticks needed for a pattern.

Pattern Number	1	2	3	4	5	6	7
Number of Sticks	3	5					

(b) Copy and complete the table.

(c) (i) Work out the number of sticks needed for pattern number 15.

(ii) Explain how you obtained your answer.

(d) Write down an formula which can be used to calculate the number of sticks, S, in terms of the pattern number, n.

Edexcel 1998

9 Here is a pattern of matchstick triangles.

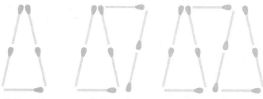

Pattern 1   Pattern 2   Pattern 3

Find a formula for the number of matches, m, in Pattern n.

10 (a) Write down the next two terms of the sequence which begins

$$\frac{1}{5}, \frac{3}{8}, \frac{5}{11}, \frac{7}{14}, \frac{9}{17}, \ldots, \ldots,$$

(b) Write down an expression, in terms of n, for the nth term of this sequence.

NEAB 1996

A3 — QUADRATIC SEQUENCES

This is how to find the nth term of the sequence 5, 7, 11, 17, 25, ...

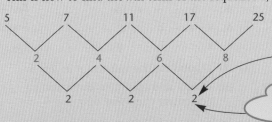

> In the table of differences for a quadratic sequence, the numbers in the second row of differences are constant.

> Remember to divide this number by 2 to find the number of n-squared in the formula.

The formula will begin with $1n^2$ (although you write just n^2). Now take the n^2 sequence away from the original sequence to work out the formula for the sequence left over.

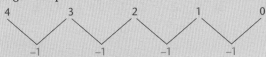

So the rest of the formula is $-n + 5$.
The full formula is $n^2 - n + 5$.

> It is always worth checking that your formula is correct. For example, when $n = 5$, $n^2 - n + 5 = 25$. This agrees with the fifth term of the sequence.

1 For each of these sequences, give the next two terms in the sequence, and the nth term.
 (a) 1, 2, 4, 7, ...
 (b) 3, 5, 9, 15, ...
 (c) 100, 99, 97, 94, ...
 (d) 5, 12, 22, 35, ...

2 Here are the first 5 numbers in sequence A.
 Sequence A 1   3   7   13   21
 Differences   2   4   __   __
 (a) (i) Copy and complete the differences between the numbers.
   (ii) Use the pattern of the differences to write down the next two numbers in sequence A.
 (b) What must be added to the 7th number in sequence A to find the 8th number?
 (c) What must be added to the 50th number in sequence A to find the 51st number?
                                    MEG 1996

3 (a) Calculate the next term in the following sequences:
   (i) 3, 10, 21, 36, ...
   (ii) 5, 14, 27, 44, ...
 (b) The two sequences in (a) have been used to form the following number pattern:

$3^2 + 4^2 = 5^2$ 3 terms
$10^2 + 11^2 + 12^2 = 13^2 + 14^2$ 5 terms
$21^2 + 22^2 + 23^2 + 24^2 = 25^2 + 26^2 + 27^2$ 7 terms
$36^2 + 37^2 + 38^2 + 39^2 + 40^2 = 41^2 + 42^2 + 43^2 + 44^2$ 9 terms

   Using your answers to (a), or otherwise, write down the next line of this number pattern.
 (c) The number of terms in each line of the number pattern form the sequence
   3, 5, 7, 9, ...
   (i) What is the 10th term of this sequence?
   (ii) Write down an expression for the nth term of this sequence.
                                    NEAB 1996

Nelson GCSE Maths: REVISION GUIDE: ALGEBRA (INTERMEDIATE)

195

4 The first three patterns in a sequence are shown below.

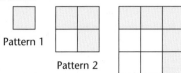

Pattern 1

Pattern 2

Pattern 3

(a) Draw the next pattern in the sequence.

(b) Copy and complete this table.

Pattern n	Number of shaded squares	Number of unshaded squares
1	1	0
2	3	1
3	5	4
4		9
5		

(c) Write down a formula, in terms of n for the number of unshaded squares in Pattern n.

(d) Write down a formula, in terms of n for the number of shaded squares in Pattern n.

5 Here are the first five numbers in a simple number sequence.

$$1, 3, 7, 13, 21, ..., ...$$

(a) Write down the next two numbers in the sequence.

(b) Describe, in words, the rule to continue this sequence.

Edexcel 1996

6 The nth term of a sequence is $3n^2$.

(a) Write the first four terms of this sequence.

(b) Use your answer to (a) to write, in terms of n, the nth term of these sequences:

(i) 5   14   29   50   ...

(ii) 4   14   30   52   ...

MEG 1998

7 Look at the number pattern below.

1	× 2	– 1	=	1	*line 1*
2	× 3	– 2	=	4	*line 2*
3	× 4	– 3	=	9	*line 3*
4	× 5	– 4	=	16	*line 4*
5	× 6	– 5	=	p	*line 5*
...	× ...	– ...	=	q	*line 6*

(a) (i) Calculate the value of p in *line 5*.

(ii) Copy and complete *line 6* and so calculate the value of q.

(b) Write down *line 20* of this number pattern.

(c) Find the nth term of each of the following sequences:

(i) 1×2, 2×3, 3×4, 4×5,   ...

(ii) 1, 4, 9, 16, ...

NEAB 1997

8 Look at the three sequences below.

Sequence p 4, 6, 8, 10, 12, ...

Sequence q 3, 8, 15, 24, 35, ...

Sequence r 5, 10, 17, ..., ..., ...

(a) The sequence r is obtained from sequences p and q as follows.

$$\sqrt{4^2 + 3^2} = 5$$

$$\sqrt{6^2 + 8^2} = 10$$

$$\sqrt{8^2 + 15^2} = 17$$

and so on.

(i) Use the numbers 10 and 24 to calculate the fourth term of sequence r.

(ii) Calculate the fifth term of sequence r.

(b) (i) Find the tenth term of sequence p.

(ii) Find the sixth term of sequence q.

NEAB 1995

9 A sequence is generated as shown

Term	1st	2nd	3rd	4th
Sequence	4	7	12	19

(a) What is the seventh number in the sequence?

(b) Another number in the sequence is 103. Which term is this?

SEG 1996

Sometimes graphs are drawn to help solve practical problems.

Here is a **conversion graph**. It is constructed using the fact that $10\,kg = 22\,lb$.

Here is a graph showing a girl's journey.

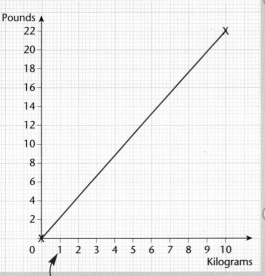

This graph can be used to convert between pounds and kilograms. It shows that 4.5kg is about 10lb. 16lb is about 7.3kg.

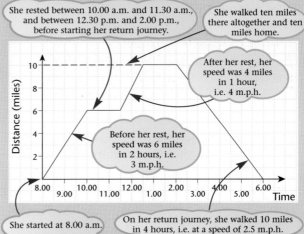

She rested between 10.00 a.m. and 11.30 a.m., and between 12.30 p.m. and 2.00 p.m., before starting her return journey.

She walked ten miles there altogether and ten miles home.

After her rest, her speed was 4 miles in 1 hour, i.e. 4 m.p.h.

Before her rest, her speed was 6 miles in 2 hours, i.e. 3 m.p.h.

She started at 8.00 a.m.

On her return journey, she walked 10 miles in 4 hours, i.e. at a speed of 2.5 m.p.h.

On a **distance–time graph**:
- speed is represented by the gradient (see A5)
- the steeper the graph, the faster the speed
- a flat bit of graph is where someone or something has stopped
- a graph sloping down represents a return journey.

---

1 The diagram shows a conversion graph between Pounds (£) and German Deutschmarks (DM).

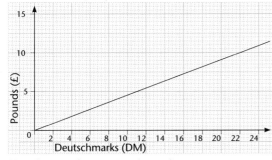

Use the graph to write down how many

(i) Deutschmarks can be exchanged for £10,

(ii) Pounds can be exchanged for 14 Deutschmarks.

Edexcel 1997

2 For each of these, decide what the two variables are, and sketch an appropriate graph.

A: Sales of ice cream depend on the weather.

B: The cost of a second hand car depends on its mileage.

C: Enjoyment of a bowl of soup depends on its temperature.

3 Sketch a graph for this story on a copy of axes like these.

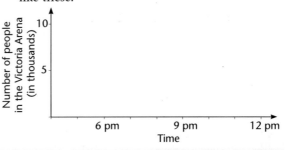

The Victoria Arena held 10 thousand people.

The Arena was empty until the doors opened at 5 p.m.

The number of people in the arena then grew steadily.

By about 7 p.m. it was half full.

There was then a rush of people. The arena filled very quickly.
It was full at 8 p.m.

The concert lasted until 11 p.m.

The arena then emptied, slowly at first, then more quickly.
It was empty by 12 p.m.

MEG 1998

4 This diagram shows three water storage tanks. The tanks are full when the tap at the base is opened.

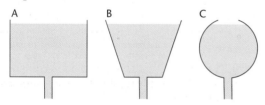

Water then flows out of each tank at a constant rate. For each tank, sketch a graph to show how the height of water varies over time.

5 A woman went on a 12 mile walk, leaving home at 12.30 p.m. She called on a friend on the way. Her daughter travelled the same route by bicycle.

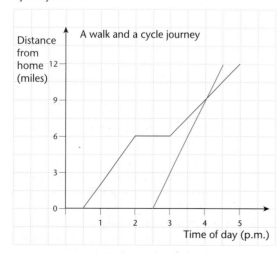

(a) Which line represents the woman's journey, the red line or the blue line?

(b) At what speed did the woman walk, before she called on her friend?

(c) How long did she spend at her friend's house?

(d) How far is it, between her house and her friend's house?

(e) At what speed did she walk, *after* she left her friend's house?

(f) At what time did she finish her walk?

(g) How long did it take her daughter to cycle 12 miles?

(h) At what speed did her daughter cycle?

(i) At what time did her daughter overtake her?

(j) How long did her daughter have to wait for her mother at the end of the journey?

6

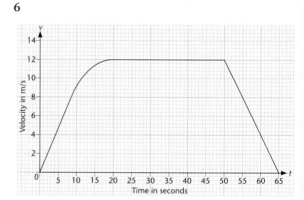

A car travels between two sets of traffic lights. The diagram is the velocity/time graph of the car.
The car leaves the first set of traffic lights.

(a) Use the graph to find the velocity of the car after 15 seconds.

(b) Describe fully the journey of the car between the two sets of traffic lights.

Edexcel 1996

7 Tracey's monthly pay, £P, is made up of a fixed basic wage plus commission on the amount of her sales, £S.

The graph shows the amounts of her sales and her corresponding monthly pay.

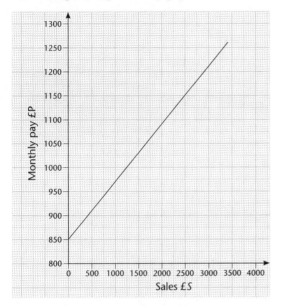

Monthly pay £P

Sales £S

Use the graph to estimate

(a) Tracey's sales when her monthly pay is £1150,

(b) her monthly pay when her sales are £1000,

(c) her fixed basic wage,

(d) her commission when her sales are £2000.

CCEA 1998

8 The distance between Southampton and London is 120 km.

A coach leaves Southampton at 0800 to travel to London.

The coach travels 60 km at an average speed of 80 kilometres per hour and then stops for 30 minutes. It then continues its journey arriving in London at 1100.

At 1115 the coach leaves London and returns to Southampton, without stopping.

It arrives in Southampton at 1230.

(a) Draw a travel graph for the journey of the coach, using axes like these.

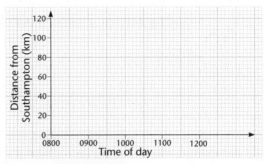

Distance from Southampton (km)

Time of day

(b) What was the average speed of the coach on the return journey?

SEG 1998

9 (a) A ball is thrown up into the air. Which of these graphs represents its motion?

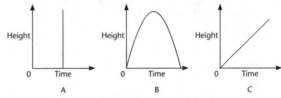

A   B   C

(b) A bath is empty. A tap is turned on. Which of these graphs shows how the bath filled up?

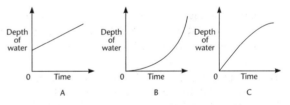

A   B   C

(c) The distance-time graph of a journey made on a bicycle is shown.

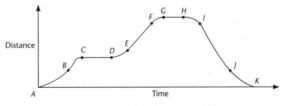

Distance

Time

(i) Between which two points is the bicycle slowing down?

(ii) Between which two points is the bicycle moving at a constant speed and travelling away from the starting point?

(iii) Between which two points is the bicycle accelerating and travelling back to the starting point?

SEG 1996

STRAIGHT-LINE GRAPHS

GRADIENTS

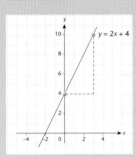

$$\text{Gradient} = \frac{\text{distance up}}{\text{distance across}}$$
$$= \frac{6}{3}$$
$$= 2$$

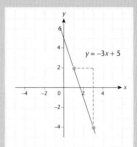

$$\text{Gradient} = \frac{\text{distance up}}{\text{distance across}}$$
$$= \frac{-6}{2}$$
$$= -3$$

EQUATIONS OF GRAPHS OF STRAIGHT LINES

$y = mx + c$ is the equation for a straight-line graph.

For example, $y = 2x + 5$, $y = -3x + 2$, $y = 3x$ and $y = \frac{1}{2}x - 1$ are all equations of straight-line graphs.

The value of m is the **gradient** of the graph.

The value of c tells you the point where the graph crosses the y-axis, sometimes called the **y-intercept**.

When the equation of the line is not in the form $y = mx + c$, it is usually easiest to work out the x and y values of some points in order to draw the line.

$y = \frac{1}{2}x - 4$ has gradient $\frac{1}{2}$ and crosses the y-axis at $(0, -4)$.

$y = -3x + 2$ has gradient -3 and crosses the y-axis at $(0, 2)$

> This graph of $2x + 3y = 6$ can be plotted by finding some points on it. The points $(3, 0)$, $(0, 2)$ and $(1.5, 1)$ all lie on the graph.

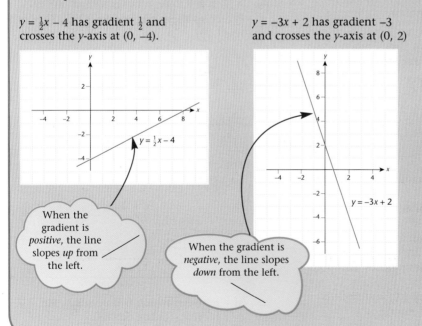

> When the gradient is *positive*, the line slopes *up* from the left.

> When the gradient is *negative*, the line slopes *down* from the left.

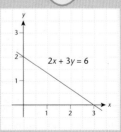

1 (a) Copy and complete this table of values for the graph of $y = 2x + 5$.

x	–3	–2	– 1	0	1	2	3
y	–1		3		7		

(b) Draw suitable axes and plot the graph.

(c) Use your graph to find

    (i)   the value of y when $x = 2.5$

    (ii) the value of x when $y = 8$

2 (a) Copy and complete this table of values for $y = 3x - 1$.

x	–2	–1	0	1	2	3
y			–1			8

(b) Draw the graph of $y = 3x - 1$ on a copy of this grid.

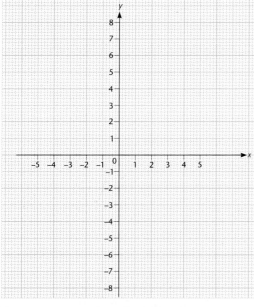

(c) Use your graph to find
    (i)   the value of x when $y = 3.5$
    (ii) the value of y when $x = -1.5$

Edexcel 1997

3 On squared paper, sketch the lines represented by these equations. Label your lines A to H.

  A: $y = -3$ B: $x = 4$

  C: $y = \frac{1}{2}x$ D: $y = -x$

  E: $y = x + 6$ F: $y = x - 2$

  G: $x + y = 8$ H: $y = 2x - 3$

4 For each of these lines, find the gradient, the y-intercept, and write down the equation of the line.

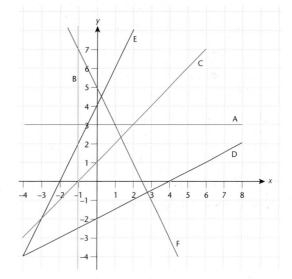

5

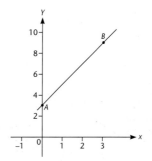

A is the point $(0, 3)$ and B is the point $(3, 9)$.

(a) Calculate the gradient of the line AB.

(b) Write down the equation of the line AB.

NEAB 1997

6 "Print-a-Word" charges £3 to design a business card and 5p for every card printed.

The cost, c pence, of x cards can be written as

c = 5x + 300.

(a) (i) Copy and complete the table of values for this equation.

x	0	50	100
c		550	

(ii) Use these values to draw the graph of c = 5x + 300, using axes like these.

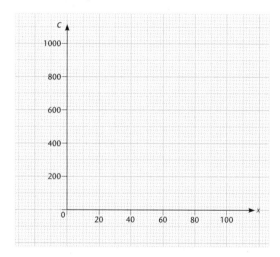

(b) Damian was charged £6.20 for some cards. How many cards did he buy?

MEG 1996

7 The table shows the largest quantity of salt, w grams, which can be dissolved in a beaker of water at temperature t°C.

t°C	10	20	25	30	40	50	60
w grams	54	58	60	62	66	70	74

(a) On a grid like this, plot the points and draw a graph to illustrate this information.

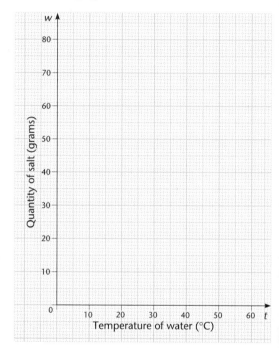

(b) Use your graph to find
   (i) the lowest temperature at which 63 g of salt will dissolve in the water.
   (ii) the largest amount of salt that will dissolve in the water at 44°C.

(c) (i) The equation of the graph is of the form

   w = at + b.

Use your graph to estimate the values of the constants a and b.
   (ii) Use the equation to calculate the largest amount of salt which will dissolve in the water at 95°C.

NEAB 1995

NON-LINEAR GRAPHS

GRAPHS INVOLVING x^2

Graphs of equations involving x^2, such as $y = x^2$, $y = 2x^2 - 1$, $y = 3 - x^2$ and $y = (x - 2)^2$ are not straight lines.
All **quadratic graphs** have the shape of a **parabola**. They all have *one* line of symmetry.

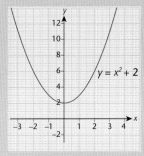

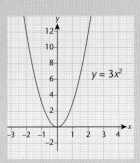

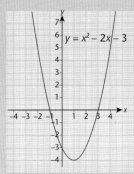

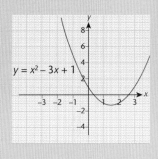

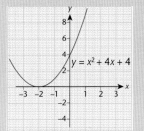

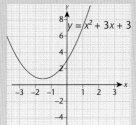

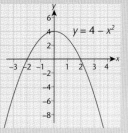

GRAPHS INVOLVING x^3

Cubic graphs are always shaped like one of these.

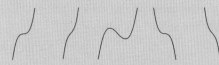

Here are two examples of cubic graphs

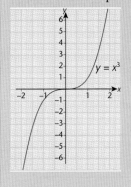

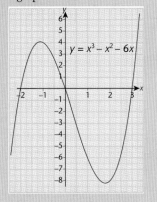

RECIPROCAL GRAPHS

These have equations like $y = \frac{6}{x}$ and $y = \frac{12}{x}$.

This is the graph of $y = \frac{1}{x}$.

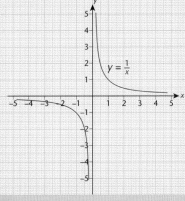

The graph has two separate branches, because when $x = 0$, it is impossible to find a value for y.

1 (a) Copy and complete these tables of values:

(i) for the equation $y = 2x$

x	−1	1	3
y			

(ii) for the equation $y = x^2$

x	−1	0	1	2	3
y					

(b) On a grid like this, draw the graphs of $y = 2x$ and $y = x^2$.

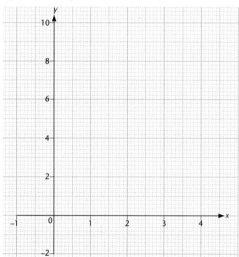

NEAB 1996

2 (a) Copy and complete this table which gives the values of $y = x^2 - 3$ for values of x ranging from −3 to 4.

x	−3	−2	−1	0	1	2	3	4
y = x² − 3	6	1			−2	1	6	13

(b) On graph paper, draw the graph of $y = x^2 - 3$ for values of x from −3 to 4.

(c) Draw the line $y = 5$ on the same graph paper and write down the coordinates of the points where your two graphs intersect.

WJEC 1998

3 (a) Copy and complete this table for the function $y = 36 - x^2$.

x	0	1	2	3	4	5	6
y				27		11	

(b) Copy this diagram onto graph paper.

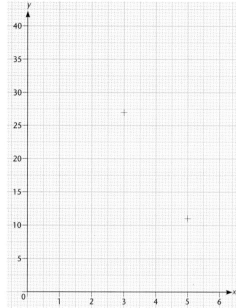

Plot the values of x and y and draw the graph of the function $y = 36 - x^2$.

(c) Use the graph, showing its use clearly, to estimate

(i) the value of y when $x = 3.6$,

(ii) the value of x when $y = 30$.

CCEA 1996

4 (a) The volume, $V \text{ cm}^3$, of box A is given by: $V = 4x$.

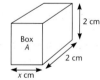

(i) Copy and complete this table by calculating values of V for the given values of x.

x	0	1.5	3
V	0		

(ii) On graph paper, draw an x-axis for $0 \le x \le 3$ and a V-axis for $0 \le V \le 20$. Draw a graph of $V = 4x$.

(b) The volume, $V\,\text{cm}^3$, of box B is given by:
$V = 2x^2.$

Box B, 2 cm, x cm, x cm

(i) Copy and complete the table by calculating values of V for the given values of x.

x	0	0.5	1	1.5	2	2.5	3
V				4.5		12.5	18

(ii) On the same set of axes, draw a graph of $V = 2x^2$.

(c) Use your graphs to find the value of x for which the volume of box A is the same as the volume of box B.

NEAB 1997

5

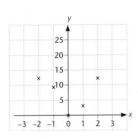

(a) Brenda was asked to draw the graph of $y = 3x^2$.
She plotted the five points shown in the diagram above.

(i) From the shape of the graph, how can you tell that one of the points is in the wrong place?

(ii) Which point did Brenda wrongly plot?

(b) Brenda was then asked to draw the graph of $y = 2x^3$.
She plotted these five points.

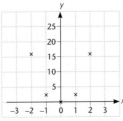

From the shape of the graph, explain the error made by Brenda.

MEG 1998

6 Here are three graphs.

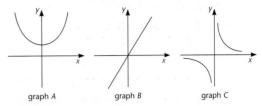

graph A   graph B   graph C

Here are four equations.

Equation (1)	$y = x^2 + 3$
Equation (2)	$y = \dfrac{1}{x}$
Equation (3)	$y = 3x$
Equation (4)	$y = x^3$

Copy and complete these statements.
Graph A represents equation ...
Graph B represents equation ...
Graph C represents equation ...

NEAB 1998

7

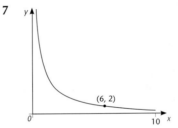

(6, 2)

The graph of a function has been sketched on the axes above for $0 < x \leq 10$.
The equation of the function is **one** of the following

$y = kx^3$ **or** $y = kx^2$ **or** $y = \dfrac{k}{x}$,

where k is a positive constant.
By choosing the appropriate equation and using the point (6, 2) which lies on the curve, calculate the value of k.

Edexcel 1996

8 On the same set of axes, sketch and label these graphs.

(a) $y = x^2 + 4$ **(b)** $y = x^2 - 3$ **(c)** $y = 2 - x^2$

9 On the same set of axes, sketch and label these graphs.

(a) $y = x^2$ **(b)** $y = 3x^2$
(c) $y = -x^2$ **(d)** $y = \frac{1}{2}x^2$

FORMULAE

THINKING WITH LETTERS

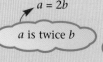 $a = 2b$

a is twice b

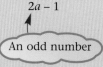 $2a - 1$

An odd number

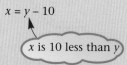 $x = y - 10$

x is 10 less than y

EVALUATING FORMULAE

Example: If the formula for the nth term of a sequence is
$2n^2 - n + 5$
then the sixth term (when $n = 6$) is $2 \times 6^2 - 6 + 5 = 72 - 6 + 5$
$= 71$

 Do not use a calculator for Questions 1 to 7

1 **(a)** Write, in symbols, the rule
"To find y, multiply k by 3 and then subtract 1"

(b) Work out the value of k when $y = 14$.

Edexcel 1996

2 The rule for how long to cook a chicken is:

Twenty minutes a pound
plus twenty minutes

For how long should a $4\frac{1}{2}$lb chicken be cooked?

3 The charge for a reception at Grey Gables is £8 per person. The manager estimates her costs using the formula: £170 + £2 per person.

(a) For a group of 75 people what would be

(i) the charge for the reception?

(ii) the estimated cost to the manager?

(iii) the profit made by Grey Gables?

(b) What is the least number of guests needed to make a profit?

4 **(a)** $T = \dfrac{\lambda x}{a}$

Find the value of T when $\lambda = 5$, $x = 7$ and $a = 10$.

(b) $I = \dfrac{PRT}{100}$

Find the value of I when $P = 45$, $R = 10$ and $T = 3$.

5 **(a)** $F = 32 + \dfrac{9C}{5}$

Find the value of F when $C = -15$.

(b) $C = \dfrac{5(F - 32)}{9}$

Find C when $F = -58$.

(c) $v = \sqrt{u^2 - 2u + 1}$
Find v when $u = -8$.

6 Find the value of $(1 - \dfrac{1}{a})(1 - b)$, when

$a = \frac{1}{3}$ and $b = -2$.

NEAB 1996

7 Find the value of $ab^2 + \dfrac{b}{a}$ when $a = \frac{4}{5}$

and $b = -3$.

NEAB 1997

8 The area, A, of a cyclic quadrilateral is given by the formula

$A = \sqrt{(S - a)(S - b)(S - c)(S - d)}$,
where a, b, c and d are the lengths of the sides of the cyclic quadrilateral and
$S = \dfrac{a + b + c + d}{2}$.

When $a = 44\,cm$, $b = 15\,cm$, $c = 27\,cm$ and $d = 30\,cm$, calculate

(a) the value of S,

(b) the value of A.

NEAB 1997

Nelson GCSE Maths · REVISION GUIDE: ALGEBRA (INTERMEDIATE)

SIMPLIFYING FORMULAE

$a + a + a = 3a$ $a \times a \times a = a^3$ $2a + 5a = 7a$ $2a \times 5a = 2 \times a \times 5 \times a = 10a^2$

$3a - 4b + 2a = 5a - 4b$ $3a \times 4b \times 2a = 24a^2b$ $3ab + 4ab = 7ab$ $3ab \times 4ab = 12a^2b^2$

$x^2 + 5x$ $x^2 \times 5x = 5x^3$ $6x^2y - 2x$ $6x^2y \div 2x = \dfrac{6x^2y}{2x} = 3xy$

These cannot be simplified.

1 Simplify these.
  (a) $2y + 3y$
  (b) $7a - 9a$
  (c) $x^2 + 2x + 3x^2 - x$
  (d) $3xy^2 + 2xy - xy^2 + xy$
  (e) $2 \times 3a$
  (f) $6x \times 2x$
  (g) $-3r \times 2r$
  (h) $2a \times b$
  (i) $3a \times 2a \times b$
  (j) $10b \div 5b$
  (k) $8xy \div 2x$
  (l) $12pq \div 3pq$

2 Simplify these.
  (a) $a \times a \times a$
  (b) $x \times x \times x \times x \times x$
  (c) $x^3 \times x \times x$
  (d) $xy \times x \times x$

3 Simplify these.
  (a) $x^5 \div x^3$
  (b) $y^2 \times y^3$
  (c) $x^5 \div x^5$
  (d) $xy^2 \div x$
  (e) $a^3b^2 \div a^2$
  (f) $a^4b^2 \div a^3b$
  (g) $3a^2 \times 2a^3$
  (h) $4ab \times 3a^2b$
  (i) $4a^5 \div 6a^7$
  (j) $9pq \div 3pq^2$

4 Collect together like terms and simplify.
  (a) $4x + 6y - 2x + y$
  (b) $3ab + 2ab - ab$
  (c) $5ab - 2c - 3ab + c$
  (d) $a - b - 7a - 5b$
  (e) $a^3 - 2a^2 + 3a^3 - a^2$
  (f) $a^2 - b^2 + 3a^2 + 2b^2$

5 (a) Write down and simplify an algebraic expression for the perimeter of this triangle.

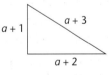

  (b) Write down and simplify an algebraic expression for the perimeter of this rectangle.

Edexcel 1998

ALGEBRAIC EXPRESSIONS USING BRACKETS

BRACKETS

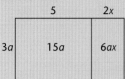

$3a(5 + 2x) = 15a + 6ax$ $2(5y + b) = 10y + 2b$

Here are some more examples.

$2(3a + 4b - 2c) = 6a + 8b - 4c$

$-6(2x - 5) = -12x + 30$

$3(6d + 1) - 2(7d - 4) = 18d + 3 - 14d + 8$
$$= 4d + 11$$

$2x(x - 3y) = 2x^2 - 6xy$

$pq(p^2 + q^2) = p^3q + pq^3$

This is how two brackets are multiplied out.
$(x + 2)(x + 3) = x^2 + 2x + 3x + 6$
$$= x^2 + 5x + 6$$

$(x - 5)^2 = (x - 5)(x - 5)$
$$= x^2 - 5x - 5x + 25$$
$$= x^2 - 10x + 25$$

$(a + b)(a - b) = a^2 + ab - ab - b^2$
$$= a^2 - b^2$$

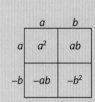

1 Rewrite these, *without* the brackets.
   (**a**) $4(x + 2)$ (**b**) $3(s - 6)$ (**c**) $2(z + a)$
   (**d**) $-3(c - 4)$ (**e**) $5(2a - b)$ (**f**) $a(2a - b)$
   (**g**) $x(3x^2 - xy)$ (**h**) $4y(2y + 3xy)$

2 Remove the brackets and simplify these.
   (**a**) $2(a + b) + 3(a - b)$
   (**b**) $3(x - y) - 2(4x - y)$
   (**c**) $3(2p - 3q) - 4(3p + 2q)$
   (**d**) $3a(2a - b) + 2(a + 5b)$

3 Remove the brackets and simplify where possible.
   (**a**) $(a + b)(c + d)$ (**b**) $(a + b)(c - d)$
   (**c**) $(a - b)(c - d)$ (**d**) $(3x + y)(a + 5b)$
   (**e**) $(8d - e)(2f - 3g)$ (**f**) $(a + b)(a + b)$
   (**g**) $(x + y)(x - y)$ (**h**) $(p - q)(p + q)$
   (**i**) $(4a + b)(4a - b)$

4 Remove the brackets and simplify these.
   (**a**) $(a + 1)(a + 3)$
   (**b**) $(b + 2)(b + 5)$
   (**c**) $(x - 2)(x + 4)$
   (**d**) $(y - 3)(y - 5)$
   (**e**) $(3 - a)(7 - a)$
   (**f**) $(3y + 1)(2y + 4)$
   (**g**) $(3a + 2)(4a + 3)$
   (**h**) $(2c - 3)(2c + 3)$
   (**i**) $(5x + 4)(5x - 4)$

5 Remove the brackets and simplify these.
   (**a**) $(x + 2)(x + 4) + (x - 1)(x - 3)$
   (**b**) $(x + 4)(x - 3) - (x - 2)(x + 6)$

6 Remove the brackets and simplify these.
   (**a**) $(a + b)^2$ (**b**) $(a - b)^2$
   (**c**) $(x + 2)^2$ (**d**) $(3x - 2y)^2$

A10 FACTORISING

COMMON FACTORS

$$4a^2 + 12a = 4a(a + 3)$$

$$10ab - 6b^2 = 2b(5a - 3)$$

DIFFERENCE OF TWO SQUARES

$$a^2 - b^2 = (a + b)(a - b)$$

$$25y^2 - 9z^2 = (5y + 3z)(5y - 3z)$$

QUADRATIC FACTORS

$$a^2 + 4a + 3 = (a + 3)(a + 1)$$

$$x^2 - x - 6 = (x - 3)(x + 2)$$

$$n^2 - 5n + 6 = (n - 2)(n - 3)$$

$$2x^2 + 5x + 2 = (2x + 1)(x + 2)$$

1 Factorise these expressions.
   (a) $3x + 3y$ (b) $5a - 5b$
   (c) $2a - 6b$ (d) $25x + 10y$
   (e) $ax - ay$ (f) $2ab - 7ac$
   (g) $6cd + 5ad$ (h) $12x - 4xy$
   (i) $6a + 3ab$ (j) $24st + 12t$

2 Factorise these expressions.
   (a) $a^2 + 4a$ (b) $x^2 - 2x$
   (c) $2b^3 - 3b^2$ (d) $6x^3 - 18x^2 - x$
   (e) $4xyz + 8xy$ (f) $x^3y^2z + x^2y^2z^2 + xy^2z^3$

3 Factorise these expressions.
   (a) $a^2 - b^2$ (b) $9x^2 - y^2$
   (c) $16a^2 - 25z^2$ (d) $p^2 - 36q^2$
   (e) $100a^2 - 49b^2$ (f) $4x^2 - y^4$

4 Factorise these expressions.
   (a) $x^2 + 6x + 8$ (b) $x^2 - 2x - 8$
   (c) $x^2 + 2x - 8$ (d) $x^2 - 12x - 13$
   (e) $x^2 + 16x + 64$ (f) $x^2 - 3x - 10$
   (g) $x^2 - 10x + 25$ (h) $x^2 + 5x - 24$
   (i) $x^2 - 10x + 16$ (j) $x^2 - 4x - 21$
   (k) $2x^2 + 7x + 3$ (l) $6x^2 - 13x - 5$

5 (a) Factorise fully
       (i) $5p - 20pt$
       (ii) $3x^2y + 9xy^2 - 15xy$

   (b) Expand and simplify
        $(2x - 3y)(4x + y)$

        NEAB 1998

6 (a) Simplify
        $$\frac{12x^5 \times 3y^3}{9x^2y}$$

   (b) Factorise completely
       (i) $9a^2b^3 + 15a^3b^2$
       (ii) $x^2 + 7x - 60$

        Edexcel 1998

Make L the subject of this equation: $s = \frac{1}{2}n(A + L)$

Double both sides:	$2s = n(A + L)$
Divide by n:	$\frac{2s}{n} = A + L$
Subtract A:	$L = \frac{2s}{n} - A$

Make c the subject of the equation:

$$a = \sqrt{c^2 - b^2}$$

Square both sides:	$a^2 = c^2 - b^2$
Add b^2:	$a^2 + b^2 = c^2$
Square root both sides:	$c = \sqrt{a^2 + b^2}$

1 Make I the subject of the formula $V = IR$.

2 Make T the subject of the formula $P = \frac{RT}{V}$.

3 Make u the subject of the formula $v^2 = u^2 + 2as$.

4 Make v the subject of the formula
$$s = \frac{(u + v)t}{2}.$$

5 Make g the subject of the formula
$$T = 2\pi\sqrt{\frac{l}{g}}.$$

6 Make r the subject of the formula $V = \pi r^2 h$.

7 Make r the subject of these formulae.
   (a) $S = 4\pi r^2$ (b) $V = \frac{4}{3}\pi r^3$

8
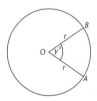

O is the centre of a circle of radius r cm.
AB is the arc of the circle of length x cm and
$\angle AOB = y^\circ$.
The length x cm of the arc AB is given by
the formula

$$x = \frac{\pi r y}{180}.$$

(a) Find the length of the arc AB when
     $\angle AOB = 80°$ and the radius is $4\frac{1}{2}$ cm.

(b) Rewrite the formula in the form $y = ...$

(c) Calculate the size of $\angle AOB$ when the radius
     is 10 cm and the length of the arc AB
     is 6 cm.

WJEC 1998

9 You are given the formula $v = u + at$.
   (a) Work out the value of v when $u = 20$,
        $a = -6$ and $t = \frac{9}{5}$.
   (b) Rearrange the formula to give t in terms of
        v, u and a.

SEG 1998

10 Trevor rears turkeys to sell at Christmas.
    He estimates that the cost, £C, of rearing each
    turkey is given by the formula
    $C = 0.1W + 0.05W^2$,
    where W kilograms is the weight of a turkey.

    (a) What is the estimated cost of rearing a 9
         kilogram turkey?

    (b) He advises his customers that they should
         cook their turkeys using the formula
         $T = 40W + 20$,
         where T minutes is the cooking time for
         each turkey.

    (i)   Re-arrange the formula to make W
          the subject.

    (ii) Anne uses this formula and cooks her
          turkey for 7 hours.

          What is the weight of the turkey
          which Anne cooks?

NEAB 1996

LINEAR EQUATIONS

SOLVING EQUATIONS BY DOING AND UNDOING

$6x + 2 = 26$
$x = 4$

$x \rightarrow \boxed{\times 6} \rightarrow \boxed{+ 2} \rightarrow 26$
$4 \leftarrow \boxed{\div 6} \leftarrow \boxed{- 2} \leftarrow 26$
$\quad\quad\quad\quad 24$

$3(x - 2) = -3$
$x = 1$

$x \rightarrow \boxed{- 2} \rightarrow \boxed{\times 3} \rightarrow -3$
$1 \leftarrow \boxed{+ 2} \leftarrow \boxed{\div 3} \leftarrow -3$
$\quad\quad\quad\quad -1$

$\dfrac{x}{6} + 5 = 10$
$x = 30$

$x \rightarrow \boxed{\div 6} \rightarrow \boxed{+ 5} \rightarrow 10$
$30 \leftarrow \boxed{\times 6} \leftarrow \boxed{- 5} \leftarrow 10$
$\quad\quad\quad\quad 5$

SOLVING EQUATIONS BY BALANCING

$3x + 7 = 5x + 3$

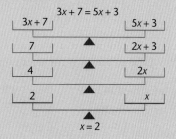

$x = 2$

FORMING AND SOLVING LINEAR EQUATIONS

A girl is y years old.
Her father is 3 times as old as she is.
Her mother is 2 years younger than her father.
The total of their ages is 103.
How old are they?

Father's age is $3y$. So, mother's age is $3y - 2$.
$y + 3y + 3y - 2 = 103$
$7y - 2 = 103$
$7y = 105$
$y = 15$
The girl is 15, the father is 45, and the mother is 43.

EQUATIONS WITH FRACTIONS

There are several ways of tackling equations with fractions. Sometimes, it is simplest to work with the fractions. At other times, it is easier to multiply through by a suitable number to clear the fractions.

$5x + 2 = \frac{3}{2}x + 16$
$\Rightarrow 5x - \frac{3}{2}x = 16 - 2$
$\Rightarrow \quad \frac{7}{2}x = 14$
$\Rightarrow \quad 7x = 28$
$\Rightarrow \quad x = 4$

$3x - \frac{1}{2}(x - 2) = 6$
$\Rightarrow \quad 3x - \frac{1}{2}x + 1 = 6$
$\Rightarrow \quad \frac{5}{2}x + 1 = 6$
$\Rightarrow \quad \frac{5}{2}x = 5$
$\Rightarrow \quad \frac{1}{2}x = 1$
$\Rightarrow \quad x = 2$

$\dfrac{x + 3}{5} = \dfrac{x - 4}{3}$
$\Rightarrow 3(x + 3) - 15 = 5(x - 4)$ (Multiply by 15)
$\Rightarrow \quad 3x + 9 - 15 = 5x - 20$
$\Rightarrow \quad 14 = 2x$
$\Rightarrow \quad x = 7$

Do not use a calculator for these questions

1 Solve these equations.
   (a) $3a + 2 = 17$ (b) $9 - 2x = 4$
   (c) $8 + 3x = 2$ (d) $1.5 - x = 1.9$
   (e) $4y + 5 = 3y + 8$ (f) $8f - 4 = 5f + 8$
   (g) $7x - 2 = 3x + 11$ (h) $8y + 3 = y - 4$

2 Solve these equations.
   (a) $3(a - 1) = 12$ (b) $6(2y - 1) = 42$
   (c) $5(2x - 3) = 50$ (d) $2(v + 5) = -4$

3 Solve these equations.
   (a) $3(2a + 1) = 2(2a + 7)$
   (b) $3(4x - 2) - 2(5x - 7) = 2$
   (c) $7(3x - 4) - 4(3 - x) = 10$
   (d) $3(2x + 7) - 2(x - 1) = 11$

4 *ABCD* is a rectangle.

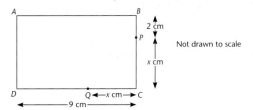

Not drawn to scale

(a) Write down the expression, in terms of *x*, for
  (i) the length of *BC*,
  (ii) the length of *DQ*.

(b) (i) Given that *BC* = *DQ*, use your answers to (a) to write down an equation in terms of *x*.

  (ii) Solve your equation to find the value of *x*.

NEAB 1997

5 A rectangular field is 3*x* metres long and 10 metres wide.

(a) What is the perimeter of the field in terms of *x*?
Write your answer as simply as possible.

The perimeter is 260 metres.

(b) (i) Use your answer to part (a) to write down an equation in *x*.
  (ii) Solve this equation.
  (iii) Write down the length of the field.

MEG 1996

6 The perimeter of this triangle is 31 cm

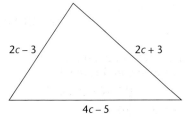

Work out the value of *c*.

Edexcel 1998

7 The length of each side of these three polygons is *x* cm.

Not drawn to scale

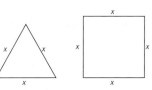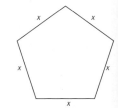

(a) What is the total length, in cm, of the sides of the pentagon?

(b) The three polygons are made from one piece of wire, 108 cm long.
  (i) Write down an equation involving *x*.
  (ii) Solve this equation to find the value of *x*.

NEAB 1996

8 *n* is a whole number.

(a) Write an expression for the next whole number bigger than *n*.

(b) These two numbers add up to 65. What are they?

9 Phil was playing games of marbles. At the start he had *x* marbles. In the first game he lost 3 of them. In the second game he won double the number he had at the start of the first game. In the third game he won 5. He finished with 23 marbles.

(a) Use the information to form an equation in *x*.

(b) Use the equation to calculate the number of marbles Phil had at the start.

CCEA 1998

10 Solve the following equation.

$$\frac{2x-3}{6} + \frac{x+2}{3} = \frac{5}{2}$$

WJEC 1998

11 Solve these equations.

(a) $\dfrac{x+1}{2} + \dfrac{x+3}{4} = \dfrac{7}{2}$ (b) $\dfrac{2x+1}{3} + \dfrac{x+3}{2} = 10$

(c) $\dfrac{4x-7}{3} - \dfrac{3x-5}{4} = -5\frac{5}{6}$

INEQUALITIES AND LOCATING REGIONS BY LINES

Inequalities use the symbols <, ≤, >, and ≥. They show the range of values for which a statement is true.

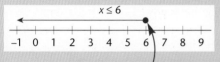

$2x - 5 \leq 7$
$\Rightarrow \quad 2x \leq 12$
$\Rightarrow \quad x \leq 6$

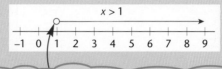

$6 - x < 5$
$\Rightarrow \quad 6 < 5 + x$
$\Rightarrow \quad 1 < x$
$\Rightarrow \quad x > 1$

Inequalities can be shown on a number line.

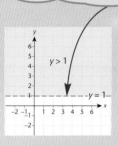

The empty circle means the end point is *not* included in the range. The filled circle means it is.

Inequalities are used to describe **regions** on a graph.

The dotted line means that the points on the boundary line are *not* included in the region. The solid line means that they are.

In this shaded region, $x \geq 0$, $y > 1$ and $x + y \leq 4$

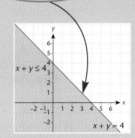

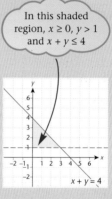

1 For each of these, list the possible integer values of x.

(a) $-3 \leq x < 5$

(b) $0 < x \leq 6$

(c) $-4 < x < 2$

(d) $-7 \leq x \leq -3$

An integer is a whole number.

2 Solve these inequalities.

(a) $x - 3 > 10$ (b) $2x + 1 \leq 7$

(c) $5x < x + 1$ (d) $4 - 2x \leq 2$

(e) $8 - 3x < 0$ (f) $\dfrac{x}{5} < -1$

3 Solve these inequalities.

(a) $x^2 < 36$ (b) $x^2 \geq 49$

(c) $3x^2 \geq 48$ (d) $5x^2 - 4 < 16$

4 Solve the following inequalities.

(a) $2 > x - 4$

(b) $2(x + 3) > 3(2 - x)$

NEAB 1997

5 For each of these inequalities, draw sketch graphs to show the region described.

(a) $3 < x < 8$ (b) $-2 < y \leq 4$

(c) $x < 5$ and $y \leq 3$ (d) $y < x$

(e) $x + y < 7$ (f) $y > x + 5$ and $y < 7$

6 The graph of $x = -1$ is shown on this grid.

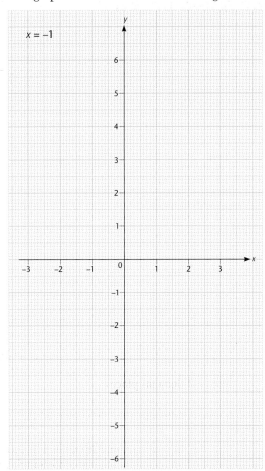

(a) Copy the grid and draw the graphs of:
(i) $y = 2$,
(ii) $y = 2x - 1$.

(b) Show clearly, on the grid, the region which is satisfied by the three inequalities $x \geq -1$, $y \leq 2$ and $y \leq 2x - 1$.

NEAB 1996

7 This graph shows the lines $y = x + 4$ and $y = 9 - x$.

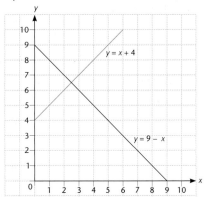

Two points, with whole number coordinates, satisfy the inequalities
$y < x + 4$,
$y < 9 - x$,
$y > 4$.
Write down the coordinates of these two points.

SEG 1996

8 (a) x is a whole number such that $-4 \leq x < 2$.
(i) Make a list of all the possible values of x.
(ii) What is the largest possible value of x^2?

(b) Every week Rucci has a test in Mathematics.

It is marked out of 20.
Rucci has always scored at least half the marks available.
She has never quite managed to score full marks.

Using x to represent Rucci's marks, write this information in the form of two inequalities.

NEAB 1995

TRIAL AND IMPROVEMENT, INCLUDING SOLVING EQUATIONS

Example: Solve $x^2 + 3x = 57$, correct to 1 decimal place.
Solutions can be found by trial and improvement, like this.

Trials	Calculation	Size
Try $x = 6$	$6^2 + 3 \times 6 = 54$	Too small
Try $x = 7$	$7^2 + 3 \times 7 = 70$	Too big
Try $x = 6.5$	$6.5^2 + 3 \times 6.5 = 61.75$	Too big
Try $x = 6.2$	$6.2^2 + 3 \times 6.2 = 57.04$	Too big
Try $x = 6.1$	$6.1^2 + 3 \times 6.1 = 55.51$	Too small

The solution is between 6.2 and 6.1, so try 6.15.

$6.15^2 + 3 \times 6.15 = 56.2725$, which is too small.
So, the solution lies between 6.15 and 6.2.
So, the solution is 6.2, correct to 1 decimal place.
The other solution is −9.2 and this would be found in the same way.

Trial and improvement can also be used to find the solutions to cubic equations. Approximate solutions can often be obtained from a graph, and a more accurate solution found using trial and improvement.

1 Use the method of trial and improvement to find a solution, to 1 decimal place, of the equation

$x^3 + x = 100$.

Show all your trials in a table like this. A first trial has been completed for you.

Trial x	$x^3 + x$	Too high/too low
5	130	too high

NEAB 1997

2 All the solutions to this equation are whole numbers.

$x^3 - 13x + 12 = 0$

One solution is negative and the other two are positive.

You may use trial and improvement.

(a) Find the smaller positive solution.

(b) Find the other positive solution.

(c) Find the negative solution.

MEG 1997

3 Use trial and improvement to find the solution to the equation $x^3 - x = 1$. Give your answer, correct to 2 decimal places.

4 A solution of the equation $x^3 - 4x = 30$ lies between 3 and 4.

Use the method of trial and improvement to find this solution correct to one decimal place.

WJEC 1998

5 (a) Copy and complete this table.

x	−4	−3	−2	−1	0	1	2	3	4
$x^3 - 6x - 2$		−11					−6		

(b) Use your table decide how many solutions there are to the equation $x^3 - 6x - 2 = 0$.

(c) Use trial and improvement to calculate each solution correct to 2 decimal places.

In Question 6, you can let the width of the rectangle be x. Then, what will the length be?

6 The perimeter of a rectangle is 28 cm and its area is 25 cm². Find the length and width of the rectangle correct to 2 decimal places.

A15 QUADRATIC EQUATIONS

Quadratic equations can sometimes be solved by factorising.

To solve:	$x^2 - 3x - 4 = 0$		To solve:	$x^2 + 5x = 0$
First factorise:	$x^2 - 3x - 4 = (x - 4)(x + 1)$		First factorise:	$x^2 + 5x = x(x + 5)$
Then:	$(x - 4)(x + 1) = 0$		Then:	$x(x + 5) = 0$

To make zero, one of the factors must be zero.

So, either $\quad x - 4 = 0 \quad$ or $\quad x + 1 = 0$
$\Rightarrow \qquad\qquad x = 4 \quad$ or $\qquad x = -1$

To make zero, one of the factors must be zero.

So, either $\quad x = 0 \quad$ or $\quad x + 5 = 0$
$\Rightarrow \qquad\qquad x = 0 \quad$ or $\qquad x = -5$

1 Solve these equations.
   (a) $(x - 3)(x - 4) = 0$
   (b) $(x + 6)(x + 5) = 0$
   (c) $(a - 7)(a + 3) = 0$
   (d) $(3x - 1)(x + 2) = 0$
   (e) $b(b + 5) = 0$

2 Solve these equations.
   (a) $x^2 - 25 = 0$ (b) $4x^2 - 81 = 0$
   (c) $16x^2 - 49 = 0$

3 Solve these equations.
   (a) $x^2 + 2x - 15 = 0$ (b) $x^2 - 7x - 8 = 0$
   (c) $x^2 - 27x + 72 = 0$ (d) $x^2 - 12x + 20 = 0$
   (e) $x^2 - 26x + 48 = 0$ (f) $x^2 - 20x + 36 = 0$

4 Solve these equations.
   (a) $x^2 - x = 2$ (b) $x^2 + 54 = 15x$
   (c) $x(x - 12) = 13$ (d) $x^2 = 4(x + 3)$
   (e) $x^2 + 8 = 9x$ (f) $2x^2 + 11x + 5 = 0$

5 When a number is subtracted from its square, the answer is 30. What could the number have been? There are two solutions.

6 A box is 4 cm high and x cm wide. It is 5 cm longer than it is wide. It has a volume of 96 cm³. Find the value of x.

7 A square floor of side x m is partially covered by a carpet 6 m wide and x m long. The area of floor not covered by the carpet is 16 m². Find x.

8 A rectangle has a perimeter of 30 cm and a width of y cm. It has an area of 50 cm².
   (a) Form a quadratic equation for y.
   (b) Solve the equation.
   (c) Why does only one solution give a sensible answer for the width of the rectangle?

9 A right-angled triangle has a hypotenuse of 13 cm. The other two sides are x and $(x + 7)$ cm long. Find the lengths of these two sides.

10

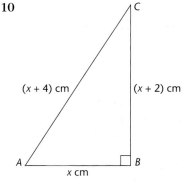

Diagram not drawn to scale

ABC is a triangle with a right angle at B.
The length of its three sides are x cm, $(x + 2)$ cm and $(x + 4)$ cm.

(a) Use Pythagoras' Theorem to show that x satisfies the equation
$x^2 - 4x - 12 = 0$.

(b) Solve the equation
$x^2 - 4x - 12 = 0$.

(c) Use your solutions in (b) to write down the lengths of the sides of the triangle.

WJEC 1998

Nelson GCSE Maths   REVISION GUIDE: ALGEBRA (INTERMEDIATE)

LINEAR SIMULTANEOUS EQUATIONS

SOLUTION BY ELIMINATION

$$3x + 2y = 8 \qquad ①$$
$$5x + 3y = 13 \qquad ②$$
$$①× 3 \quad 9x + 6y = 24 \qquad ③$$
$$②× 2 \quad 10x + 6y = 26 \qquad ④$$
$$④－③ \qquad x = 2$$
$$\text{In } ① \qquad 6 + 2y = 8$$
$$2y = 2$$
$$y = 1$$
$$\text{Check in } ② \quad 5x + 3y = 10 + 3 = 13 \ ✔$$

SOLUTION BY SUBSTITUTION

$$y = x + 8 \qquad ①$$
$$x + y = 14 \qquad ②$$

$$\text{Substitute } ① \text{ in } ② \quad x + x + 8 = 14$$
$$2x = 6$$
$$x = 3$$
$$\text{In } ① \qquad y = 3 + 8 = 11$$
$$\text{Check in } ② \qquad x + y = 3 + 11 = 14 \ ✔$$

Do not use a calculator for these questions.

1 Solve these simultaneous equations.
$$2x + y = 8$$
$$x + y = 5$$

2 Solve these simultaneous equations.
$$2x + y = -1$$
$$x + 3y = 12$$
MEG 1997

3 Solve the simultaneous equations
$$6x + 3y = 12$$
$$2x - y = -2$$
NEAB 1997

4 Solve these simultaneous equations.
(a) $4x - 3y = 9$ (b) $4x - 3y = 22$
     $3x + 2y = 11$ $x - 4y = 12$

5 Solve these simultaneous equations.
(a) $b = 2a + 4$ (b) $x = 5y - 1$
     $4a - 3b = 1$ $3x + 5y = 7$

6 The sum of two numbers is 27. Their difference is 15. Find the two numbers.

7 A fish and chips meal costs £1.50. A burger and chips meal costs £2.00. A woman buys 12 meals. She spends £20.50. Find out how many of each meal she buys.

8 Cans of beans are packed into packets or cartons. Five cans of beans can fit in a packet and 14 cans of beans can fit in a carton. A packet costs £4 and a carton costs £6. I spent £32 buying 53 cans of beans. How many packets, and how many cartons, did I buy?

9 Mrs Rogers bought 3 blouses and 2 scarfs. She paid £26. Miss Summers bought 4 blouses and 1 scarf. She paid £28. The cost of a blouse was x pounds. The cost of a scarf was y pounds.

(a) Use the information to write down two equations in x and y.

(b) Solve these equations to find the cost of one blouse.
Edexcel 1995

10 Members of a youth club can either pay a nightly fee or buy a season ticket.

When 8 members paid nightly fees and 3 members bought season tickets, the treasurer collected £50.50.

When 5 members paid nightly fees and 2 members bought season tickets, the treasurer collected £33.

Use simultaneous equations, solving them algebraically, to calculate the nightly fee and the cost of a season ticket.

Show your working.
CCEA 1998

A17 SOLVING EQUATIONS USING GRAPHS

QUADRATIC EQUATIONS

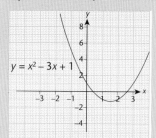
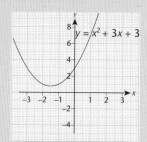
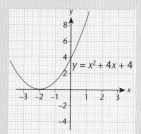

$x^2 - 3x + 1 = 0$ has two solutions. $x^2 + 3x + 3 = 0$ has no solution. $x^2 + 4x + 4 = 0$ has one solution.

Straight lines can also be drawn on quadratic graphs to solve quadratic equations.

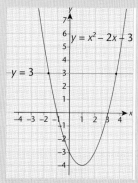
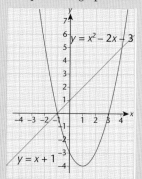

$x^2 - 2x - 3 = 3$ has
solutions $x = 3.65$ and
$x = -1.65$.

$x^2 - 2x - 3 = x + 1$ has
solutions $x = -1$ and $x = 4$.

CUBIC EQUATIONS

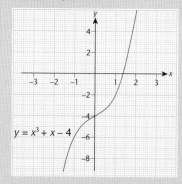
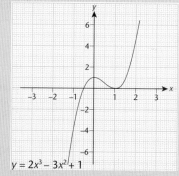
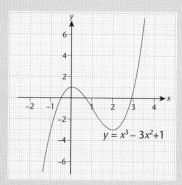

$x^3 + x - 4 = 0$ has one solution. $2x^3 + 3x^2 + 1 = 0$ has two solutions. $x^3 - 3x^2 + 1 = 0$ has three solutions.

1 Look at these graphs.

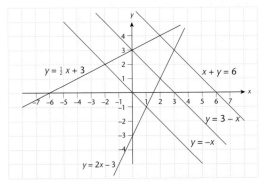

Use the graphs to solve these simultaneous equations.

(a) $y = \frac{1}{2}x + 3$
$y = -x$

(b) $x + y = 6$
$y = 2x - 3$

(c) $y = 2x - 3$
$y = 3 - x$

(d) $y = \frac{1}{2}x + 3$
$x + y = 6$

2 The line with equation $3y = -2x + 6$ is shown in this diagram.

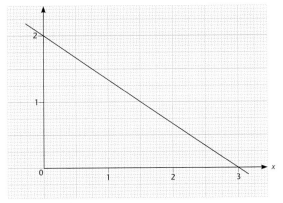

(a) Copy the diagram, and draw the graph of $y = 2x - 2$ on the same grid.

(b) Use the graphs to find the solution of the simultaneous equations

$3y = -2x + 6$
$y = 2x - 2$

A line is drawn parallel to $3y = -2x + 6$ through the point (2, 1).

(c) Find the equation of this line.

Edexcel 1998

3 Solve these simultaneous equations by drawing suitable straight lines.

$y = \frac{1}{2}x + 4$
$y = 3x - 1$

4 (a) Copy and complete the table of values for the equation

$$y = x^2 - 5.$$

x	−3	−2	−1	0	1	2	3
x^2	9						
$y = x^2 - 5$	4						

(b) Draw the graph of $y = x^2 - 5$, for values of x from −3 to 3 on axes like these.

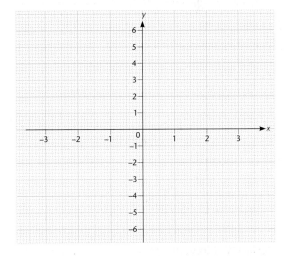

(c) Use your graph to solve the equation $x^2 - 5 = 0$.

MEG 1998

5 (a) Draw the graph of $y = x^2 - 2x - 7$ for values of x between −3 and 5.

(b) Use your graph to solve the equation $x^2 - 2x - 7 = 0$.

6 (a) Solve the equation $x^2 + 2x - 2 = 0$ by drawing a graph for values of x between −5 and 3.

(b) Use your graph to solve the equation $x^2 + 2x - 2 = 5$.

(c) Use your graph to solve the equation $x^2 + 2x - 2 = -3$.

MISCELLANEOUS EXERCISE

Do not use a calculator for Questions 1 to 11.

1 Mr McDonald is making sheep pens. He uses fences to make pens as shown in the diagram below. The pens are arranged in pairs in a row.

Number of pens	2 pens	4 pens	6 pens

Number of fences	7	12	17

(a) Draw diagrams to show the number of fences needed for

    (i)   8 pens,   (ii)   10 pens.

The table below shows the number of fences needed for different numbers of pens.

Number of pens	2	4	6	8	10	12	14	16
Number of fences	7	12	17					

(b) Copy and complete the table.

(c) Work out the number of fences needed for 30 pens.

Edexcel 1996

2 (a) Write down the nth term for each of these sequences.

    (i)   3, 5, 7, 9, 11, ...

    (ii) 2, 3, 4, 5, 6, ...

(b) (i) Form a new sequence by subtracting the sequences in part (a).

    (ii) Write down the nth term of this sequence.

    (iii) Use the nth terms from part (a) to confirm the result.

MEG 1997

3 Solve these equations.

  (a) $3x - 7 = 14$ (b) $\dfrac{4x + 8}{3} = 10$

  (c) $5(x + 6) = 2(3x + 17)$

  (d) $4(y - 4) = -12$

4 The perimeter of a rectangle is 98 m. One side is 9 m longer than the other. Form an equation, and find the length and width of the rectangle.

5 x is a whole number. Write down all the possible values of x if $-2 < x \leq 3$.

6 Solve these simultaneous equations.
$$2x + 3y = 4$$
$$3x - y = 17$$

7 This graph represents the journey of a train that travels from Shrewsbury to Hereford and then to Newport. Copy this graph.

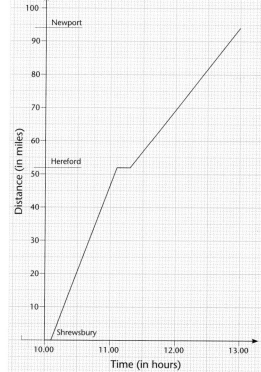

(a) What was the average speed of the train from Shrewsbury to Hereford?

(b) How long did the train wait at Hereford?

(c) The average speed of the train between Shrewsbury and Hereford is greater than its average speed between Hereford and Newport. Without calculating any average speed, explain how the graph shows this.

(d) Another train starts from Newport at 11.15 and travels non-stop to Shrewsbury at an average speed of 60 mph. Draw the graph of its journey on the same graph paper.

(e) Write down how far from Hereford the trains were when they passed each other.

WJEC 1998

8 (a) Remove the brackets and simplify these expressions.

    (i) $20(x - 3)$

    (ii) $x(x + 3)$

    (iii) $(x + 2)(x - 4)$

    (iv) $(2x + 3)(7x - 1)$

(b) Simplify these.

    (i) $5a - 4 + 8a + 3$

    (ii) $x^2 \times xy$

    (iii) $4x^2y^3 \times (3xy)^2$

    (iv) $12a^2b \div 4ab$

9 Factorise these.

    (a) $x^2 - 4x - 12$

    (b) $36a^2 - 49b^2$

    (c) $4x^3y^2 + 12x^2y - 8xy$

    (d) $2x^2 - x - 3$

10 Solve these equations by factorising.

    (a) $x^2 - 5x - 14 = 0$

    (b) $x^2 - 7x + 12 = 0$

    (c) $2x^2 + 5x - 3 = 0$

11

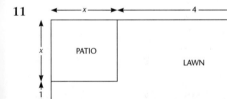

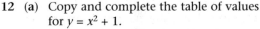

All lengths in this question are in metres.

A rectangular garden has a square patio of side x metres in one corner. The remainder of the garden is a lawn.

(a) Write down an expression, in terms of x, for the longest side of the lawn.

(b) Find an expression, in terms of x, for the perimeter of the lawn.

(c) The perimeter of the lawn is 34 metres. Find the value of x.

MEG 1998

12 (a) Copy and complete the table of values for $y = x^2 + 1$.

x	-3	-2	-1	0	1	2	3
y							

(b) Draw the graph of $y = x^2 + 1$, using axes like these.

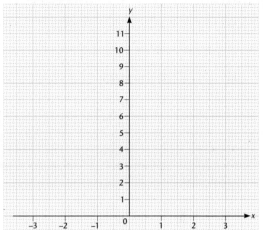

(c) By drawing a suitable line on your graph, use your graph to find the values of x when $x^2 + 1 = 9$.

Give your answers correct to **one** decimal place.

SEG 1996

13 (a) Copy the diagram and draw and label the following lines.

$$y = 2x \text{ and } x + y = 5$$

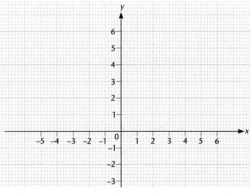

(b) Explain how to use your graph to solve the equation $2x = 5 - x$.

(c) Show clearly the single region that is satisfied by **all** of these inequalities.

    $x + y \le 5$ $y \ge 2x$ $x \ge 0$

Label this region R.

SEG 1998

Nelson GCSE Maths : REVISION GUIDE: ALGEBRA (INTERMEDIATE)

14 (a) Copy and complete this table of values of x and y for the function $y = 2x^2 + 3x$.

x	-3	-2	-1	0	1	2	3
y	9						27

(b) **(i)** Copy this graph.

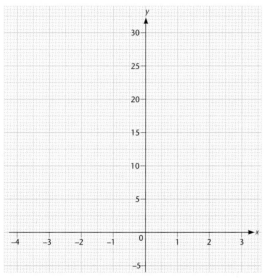

Plot the values of x and y and hence draw the graph of $y = 2x^2 + 3x$.

(ii) Using the same scales and axes, draw the graph of $y = 2x + 8$.

(c) Write down the coordinates of a point **on the graph of $y = 2x^2 + 3x$** which lies in the region defined by $y \le 2x + 8$ and $x \ge 0$.

CCEA 1998

15 (a) Write down an expression, in its simplest form, for the perimeter, P, of each of the following shapes.

(i)

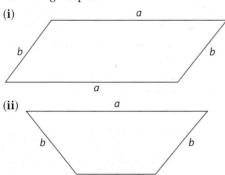

(ii)

(b) The area, A, of the trapezium below is given by the formula $A = \frac{1}{2}(a + b) h$.

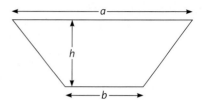

(i) Find the value of A when $h = 4$, $a = 10$ and $b = 4$.

(ii) Find an expression in terms of x, in its simplest form, for the area of the trapezium below.

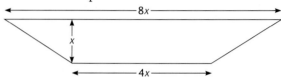

(c) A metal trough has two vertical parallel sides in the form of trapezia surmounted by rectangles. The dimensions of the trough, in metres, are shown in the diagram.

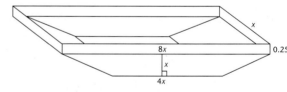

(i) Show that the volume of the trough is $6x^3 + x^2$.

The trough can hold 20 cubic metres of liquid.

(ii) Show that $3x^3 + x^2 = 10$.

(iii) Use a trial and improvement method to calculate the value of x to two decimal places. Show each stage of your working.

CCEA 1998

S1 3D OBJECTS AND THEIR 2D REPRESENTATION

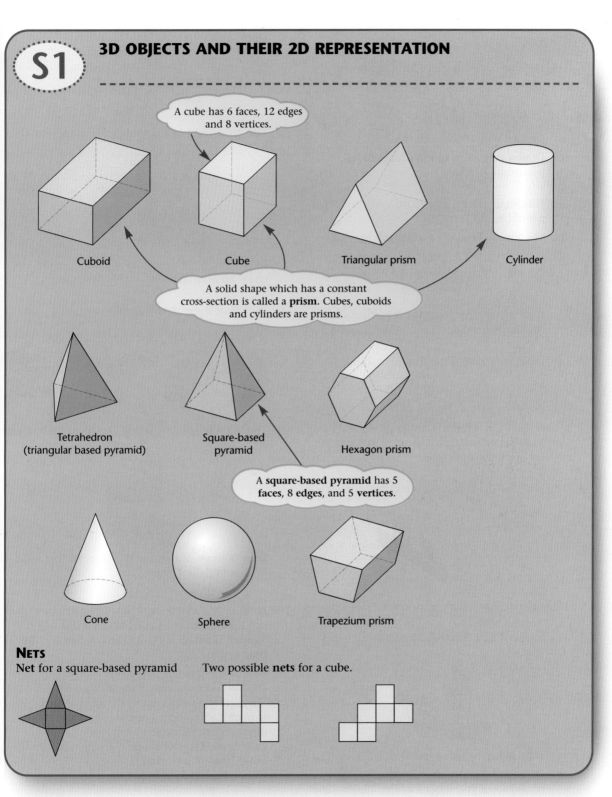

A cube has 6 faces, 12 edges and 8 vertices.

Cuboid

Cube

Triangular prism

Cylinder

A solid shape which has a constant cross-section is called a **prism**. Cubes, cuboids and cylinders are prisms.

Tetrahedron (triangular based pyramid)

Square-based pyramid

Hexagon prism

A **square-based pyramid** has 5 **faces**, 8 **edges**, and 5 **vertices**.

Cone

Sphere

Trapezium prism

NETS

Net for a square-based pyramid

Two possible **nets** for a cube.

1 This does not work as a net for a square-based pyramid.

    (**a**) Explain why it does not work.

    (**b**) Draw a correct net for a square-based pyramid.

2 (**a**) How many faces, edges and vertices does a tetrahedron have?

    (**b**) The top is sliced off a tetrahedron.

    How many faces, edges and vertices does the shape have now?

3 (**a**) Draw an accurate net for this cuboid.

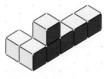

2 cm
4 cm
3 cm

    (**b**) Make an isometric drawing of this cuboid on isometric dot paper.

4 This shape is made from seven cubes. It rolls over to rest on the red face.

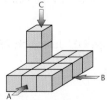

Draw the new position on isometric dot paper.

5 This shape is built from one-centimetre cubes.

C
B
A

    (**a**) How many cubes are needed?

    (**b**) On squared paper, draw exactly what you would see if you looked at the model, head on, from each of the three directions A, B and C.

6 Draw an accurate net for this prism.

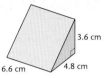

3.6 cm
6.6 cm
4.8 cm

7 This pyramid has right-angled triangles for all its faces.

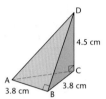

D
4.5 cm
C
A
3.8 cm
B
3.8 cm

DC = 4.5 cm, BC = 3.8 cm and AB = 3.8 cm. Draw an accurate net for this pyramid.

8 Which of these nets will fold to make a pyramid?

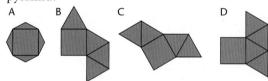

A   B   C   D

9 This picture shows the top of a solid made from six cubes.

Draw a three-dimensional picture of this solid on isometric dot paper.

10 Jasmine has a cube, a prism, a pyramid which is not a tetrahedron, a cone and a tetrahedron. She labels them A, B, C, D and E, **but not in that order**.

One of the faces of shape A is a circle.
The six faces of shape B are all squares.
The four faces of shape C are all triangles.
One of the faces of shape D is a hexagon. The other six are triangles.
Two of the faces of shape E are pentagons. The other five are rectangles.

Which shape is labelled with which letter?
WJEC 1998

S2 ACCURATE CONSTRUCTION OF 2D SHAPES

When constructing 2D shapes accurately you use a ruler, a protractor and a pair of compasses.

This is how to construct a triangle, when a side and two angles are given.

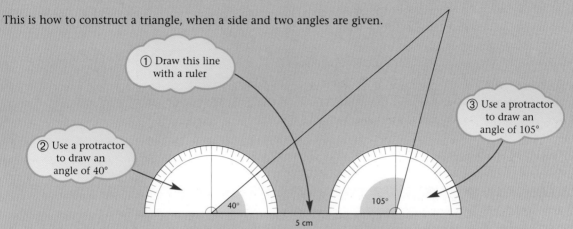

① Draw this line with a ruler

② Use a protractor to draw an angle of 40°

③ Use a protractor to draw an angle of 105°

40°   105°

5 cm

This is how to construct a triangle, when three sides are given.

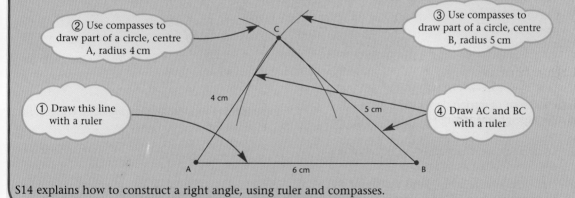

② Use compasses to draw part of a circle, centre A, radius 4 cm

③ Use compasses to draw part of a circle, centre B, radius 5 cm

① Draw this line with a ruler

④ Draw AC and BC with a ruler

4 cm   5 cm

A   6 cm   B

S14 explains how to construct a right angle, using ruler and compasses.

1 Draw triangle XYZ in which XY = 9 cm, XZ = 5 cm and YZ = 7 cm.
Measure ∠YZX.

2 Draw triangle ABC in which AB = 6.8 cm, BC = 4.6 cm and AC = 7.4 cm.
Measure ∠CBA.

3 Draw triangle PQR in which QR = 6 cm, QP = 7 cm and ∠PQR = 68°.
Measure PR.

4 Draw triangle LMN in which LM = 8.4 cm, ∠LMN = 56° and ∠MLN = 32°.
Measure LN.

5 Draw triangle DEF in which EF = 5.4 cm, ∠DEF = 94° and ∠EDF = 31°.
Measure DF.

6 Draw quadrilateral ABCD in which AB = BC = 4.5 cm, ∠ABC = 90°, AD = 8.7 cm and ∠BCD = 110°.
Measure ∠ADC.

Nelson GCSE Maths · REVISION GUIDE: SHAPE, SPACE AND MEASURES (INTERMEDIATE)

S3 CONGRUENT SHAPES

Two shapes are **congruent** if one fits exactly on the other (after turning over if necessary).

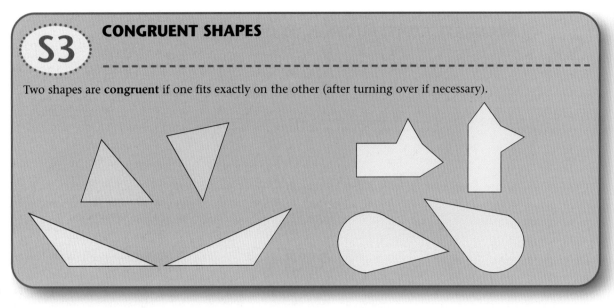

1 Draw a 4 cm-by-2 cm rectangle. Draw one line on the rectangle which cuts it into two congruent rectangles.

2 Draw a 4 cm-by-2 cm rectangle. Draw one line on the rectangle which cuts it into two congruent triangles.

3 Draw a sketch of a triangle which can be cut into two congruent triangles.

4 (a) Draw a square. Draw lines on it to cut it into four congruent triangles.

(b) Draw the square again. Find a *different* way of cutting it into four congruent triangles.

5

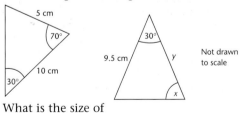

Match up three pairs of congruent shapes above.

CCEA 1996

6 These triangles are congruent.

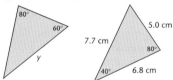

Find y.

7 Explain why these triangles *cannot* be congruent.

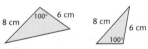

8 These triangles are congruent.

What is the size of
(a) x?   (b) y?

NEAB 1998

9 These triangles are congruent. Find x.

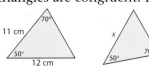

ANGLES AND LINES

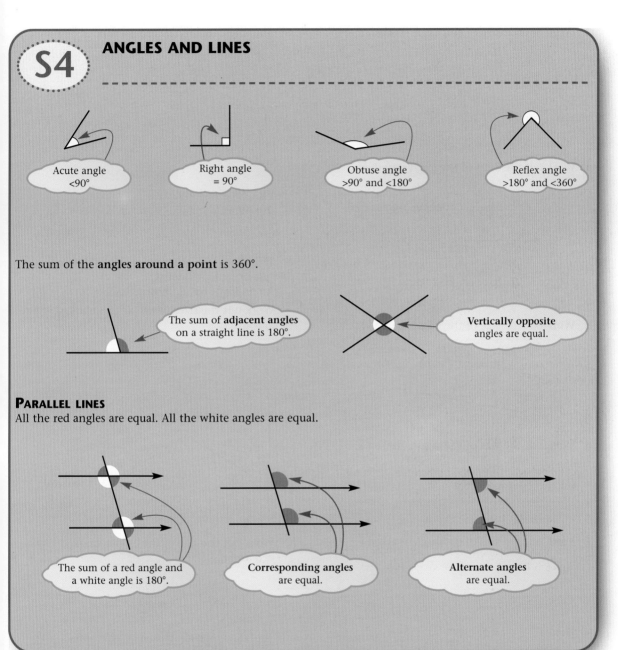

Acute angle
<90°

Right angle
= 90°

Obtuse angle
>90° and <180°

Reflex angle
>180° and <360°

The sum of the **angles around a point** is 360°.

The sum of **adjacent angles** on a straight line is 180°.

Vertically opposite angles are equal.

PARALLEL LINES
All the red angles are equal. All the white angles are equal.

The sum of a red angle and a white angle is 180°.

Corresponding angles are equal.

Alternate angles are equal.

Nelson GCSE Maths   REVISION GUIDE: SHAPE, SPACE AND MEASURES (INTERMEDIATE)

1 Work out the sizes of the angles marked *a* and *b*.

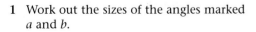

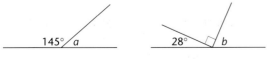

2 Work out the sizes of the angles marked *c* and *d*.

3 Work out the size of the angle marked *e*.

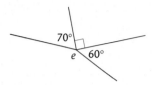

4 Work out the sizes of the angles marked *g* and *h*.

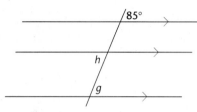

5 Work out the size of the angle marked *j*.

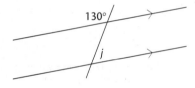

6 Work out the size of the angle marked *x*.

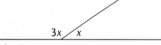

7 Work out the size of the angle marked *y*.

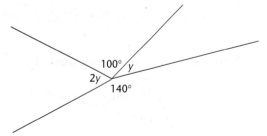

8 The lines *AB* and *CD* are parallel

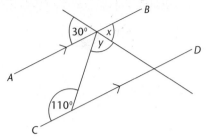

Not to scale

(a) Work out angle *x*.

(b) Work out angle *y*.

SEG 1996

9 This shape has three pairs of parallel lines and one line of symmetry.
An angle of 60° is shown.

Work out the sizes of the angles marked *a*, *b* and *c*.

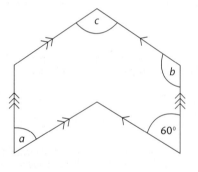

Not drawn to scale

NEAB 1998

10 Work out the size of the angles marked *p*, *q* and *r*.

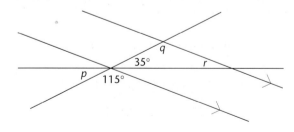

S5 TRIANGLES AND QUADRILATERALS

TRIANGLES

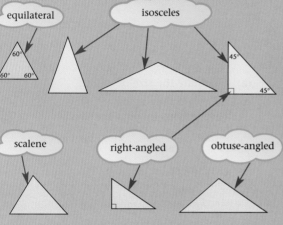

QUADRILATERALS

A quadrilateral has four sides.
Here are some special quadrilaterals.

Shape		Diagonals always			
		same length	cross at right angles	cross at mid-points	bisect angles of quad
Square Regular quadrilateral; all angles right-angles and all sides equal		YES	YES	YES	YES
Rectangle All angles right-angles		YES	NO	YES	NO
Rhombus All sides equal		NO	YES	YES	YES
Parallelogram Opposite sides parallel		NO	NO	YES	NO
Kite Two pairs of adjacent sides equal		NO	YES	NO	NO
Trapezium One pair of opposite sides parallel		NO	NO	NO	NO
Isosceles trapezium Trapezium with non-parallel sides equal		YES	NO	NO	NO

The sum of the interior angles of a triangle is 180°.
$x + y + z = 180°$

The sum of the interior angles of a quadrilateral is 360°.
$p + q + r + s = 360°$

Exterior angle theorem
This angle is equal to $x + y$

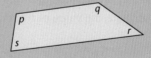

---

1 Work out the size of the angle marked p.

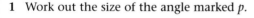

3 Work out the size of the angle marked w.

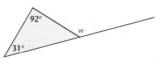

2 Work out the size of the angles marked x and y.

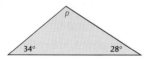

4 Work out the size of the angle marked d.

Nelson GCSE Maths   REVISION GUIDE: SHAPE, SPACE AND MEASURES (INTERMEDIATE)

5 Work out the size of the angles marked *e* and *f*.

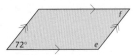

6 Look at this diagram.

(a) Calculate the value of *u*.
Give reasons for your answer.

(b) Calculate the value of *v*.
Give reasons for your answer.

7 Look at this diagram.

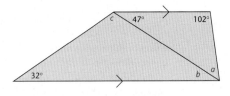

(a) Calculate the value of *a*.

(b) Calculate the value of *b* and *c*.

8 The diagram shows the side view of an ironing board standing on a horizontal floor.

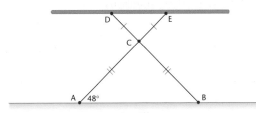

Calculate the size of ∠EDC.
Give reasons for your answer.

9 This diagram shows a kite.

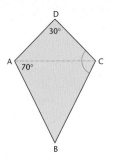

(a) Calculate the size of ∠ABC.

(b) Calculate the size of ∠BCD.
Give reasons for your answers.

10 ABCD is a rectangle.

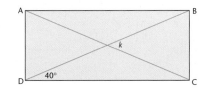

Work out the size of the angle marked *k*.

11 Copy this diagram onto squared paper.

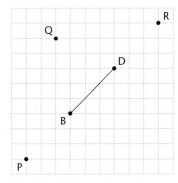

(a) BD is a diagonal of the square ABCD.
Draw the square on squared paper and mark points A and C.

(b) When completed, what type of quadrilateral is APCR?

(c) What type of quadrilateral is APCD?

(d) On your diagram, mark the point S for which PQRS is a parallelogram.

CCEA 1998

S6 POLYGONS

Polygon names	Number of sides
Triangle	3
Quadrilateral	4
Pentagon	5
Hexagon	6
Heptagon	7
Octagon	8
Nonagon	9
Decagon	10
Dodecagon	12

A **regular polygon** has all its sides equal *and* all its angles equal.

The **sum of the angles of a polygon** can be found by dividing the polygon into triangles.

A hexagon can be divided into four triangles.

The sum of the angles of a **hexagon** is 4 × 180°, i.e. 720°.

INTERIOR AND EXTERIOR ANGLES

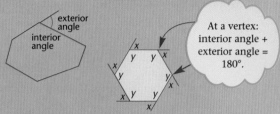

exterior angle

interior angle

At a vertex: interior angle + exterior angle = 180°.

The exterior angles of a polygon add up to 360°.
In a **regular polygon** with *n* sides all the **exterior angles** are equal, and are found by dividing 360 by *n*.
Example: A regular pentagon has five sides.

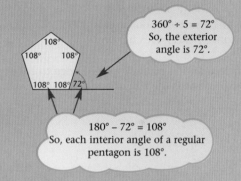

360° ÷ 5 = 72°
So, the exterior angle is 72°.

180° − 72° = 108°
So, each interior angle of a regular pentagon is 108°.

Do not use a calculator for these questions.

1 This diagram shows a regular pentagon drawn in a circle.

(a) What is the size of angle *x*?

(b) What is the size of angle *y*?

(c) How do you use your answer to part (b) to work out the size of an interior angle of the pentagon?

2 (a) Name these polygons.

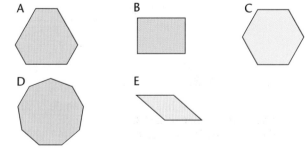

(b) State which of the polygons are regular.

(c) State which of the polygons have all their angles equal.

Nelson GCSE Maths   REVISION GUIDE: SHAPE, SPACE AND MEASURES (INTERMEDIATE)

3 Work out the angle sum for polygon A in Question 2.

4 Work out the size of each interior angle for polygon D in Question 2.

5 (a) Work out the angle sum for this polygon.

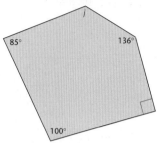

(b) Work out the size of angle *j*.

6 The angle sum of a polygon is 900°. How many sides does it have?

7 Two regular octagons are placed edge to edge as shown. What is the size of angle *w*?

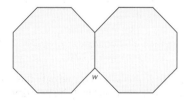

8 A regular decagon, an equilateral triangle and a square are fitted together as shown.

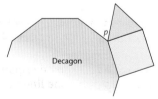

Work out the size of angle *p*.

9 A regular polygon has each exterior angle equal to 20°. How many sides does it have?

10 *ABCDEF* is a regular hexagon.

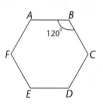

(a) Show how you can calculate that angle *ABC* is 120°.

Squares are placed on each side of the hexagon.

The polygon *OPQRSTUVWXYZ* is formed by joining the outer corners of the squares, as shown in the diagram.

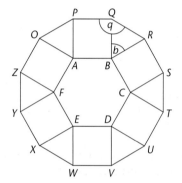

(b) (i) Calculate the size of angle *QBR* (*b* in the diagram).

Show your method clearly.

(ii) Calculate the size of angle *PQR* (*q* in the diagram).

(c) What type of triangle is *QBR*?

NEAB 1998

SYMMETRY

S7

- -

LINE SYMMETRY

The dotted lines are lines of symmetry.

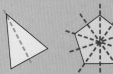 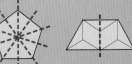

ROTATIONAL SYMMETRY

The **order** of rotational symmetry of a shape is the number of ways it can be fitted into its outline by rotating it.

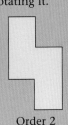 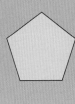

Order 2   Order 5   Order 3

1 Draw a square and mark on it all its lines of symmetry.
Write down the order of rotational symmetry of a square.

2 Draw a shape with rotational symmetry of order 3 and three lines of symmetry.

3 Here are some diagrams.

A
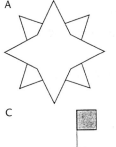

C
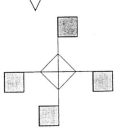

B

D
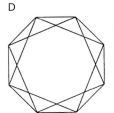

Write the order of rotational symmetry that each one has.
If it has no rotational symmetry write 'none'.

MEG 1998

4 Add one line to each of the figures to give them rotational symmetry.

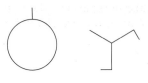

MEG 1996

5 (a) Draw a quadrilateral which has rotational symmetry of order 2, but *no* lines of symmetry.

(b) Draw a quadrilateral which has exactly two lines of symmetry.

6 Draw a simple shape which has rotational symmetry of order 4, but *no* lines of symmetry.

7 (a) Draw this shape. Add one square to it to make a shape with one line of symmetry.

(b) Draw the shape again. This t...
square to make a shape wit...
symmetry, but rotational sy...
order 2.

Nelson GC...

Nelson GCSE Maths · REVISION GUIDE: SHAPE, SPACE AND MEASURES (II

COMPASS POINTS AND BEARINGS

A bearing is an angle measured clockwise from North. A bearing can be any angle between 0° and 360°.

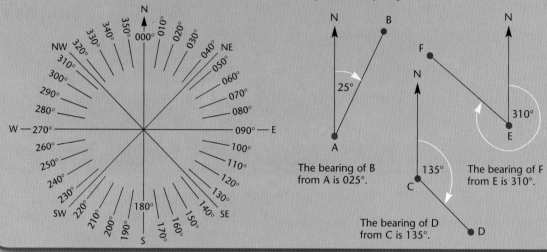

The bearing of B from A is 025°.

The bearing of D from C is 135°.

The bearing of F from E is 310°.

1 Give three figure bearings for
   (a) E (b) NE (c) SW (d) W

2 I am heading in the direction 040°.
   (a) If I turn 60° clockwise, what is my new bearing?
   (b) If I turn 60° anticlockwise instead, what is my new bearing?

3 In this diagram, the bearing of A from B is 310°.

   What is the size of the angle marked y?

4 Look at this diagram.

   Calculate the bearing of
   (a) A from B (b) C from D (c) E from F

5 During the survey of a town the positions of the church (C), the town hall (H) and the library (L) are marked by points on a map. The distances between them are shown on the following diagram.

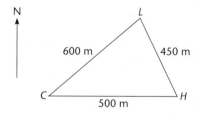

   (a) Using a cm square grid, draw an accurate scale drawing of triangle CHL, using a scale of 1 cm to represent 50 m.

   (b) The position of the police station is to be marked by the letter P on the map. The bearing of P from C is 042° (N42°E). The bearing of P from H is 300° (N60°W).

   By drawing suitable lines, mark the position of P on your diagram.

   WJEC 1998

S9   PYTHAGORAS' THEOREM

Area of square A + Area of square B
= Area of square C
or
$a^2 + b^2 = c^2$

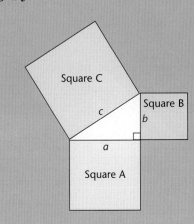

Square C

Square B

c

b

a

Square A

Example 1
$c^2 = 5^2 + 12^2$
$\quad = 25 + 144$
$\quad = 169$
$\quad c = \sqrt{169}$
$\quad = 13$

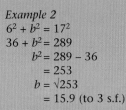

Example 2
$6^2 + b^2 = 17^2$
$36 + b^2 = 289$
$\quad b^2 = 289 - 36$
$\quad\quad = 253$
$\quad\quad b = \sqrt{253}$
$\quad\quad = 15.9$ (to 3 s.f.)

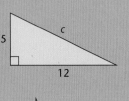

5

c

12

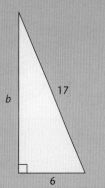

17

b

6

Nelson GCSE Maths · REVISION GUIDE: SHAPE, SPACE AND MEASURES (IN

1   Calculate the lengths of the sides marked p and q in these diagrams.

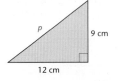

p

9 cm

12 cm

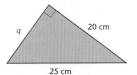

q

20 cm

25 cm

2   Work out the length of JK in this diagram, correct to 2 significant figures.

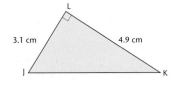

L

3.1 cm

4.9 cm

J

K

3   Calculate the length of RQ in this diagram, correct to 2 significant figures.

R

6.4 cm

P   4.8 cm   Q

4   A ship sails 28 km east, and then 52 km north. What is its direct distance from the start?

5   Calculate the distance between points A(4, –1) and B(–1, 3), correct to 2 significant figures.

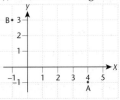

6   Calculate the distance between the points (–2, 5) and (10, 10).

7   A ladder, 4.2 m long, is leant against a vertical wall. The foot of the ladder is 1.1 m away from the bottom of the wall.

4.2 m

←1.1 m→

Find, by calculation, whether it will re~~~
windowsill that is 3.8 m up the

Nelson G~~

8   Find the length, correct to 3 s.f.,
diagonal of a square with side of

S10 TRIGONOMETRY

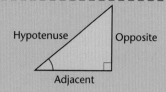

Hypotenuse Opposite

Adjacent

THE TRIGONOMETRIC FORMULAE

$$\sin x = \frac{\text{opp}}{\text{hyp}}$$

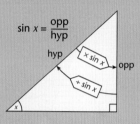

$$\cos x = \frac{\text{adj}}{\text{hyp}}$$

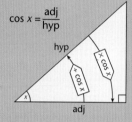

$$\tan x = \frac{\text{opp}}{\text{adj}}$$

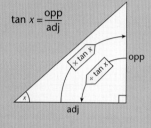

Examples

Find the side labelled *a* in this triangle.

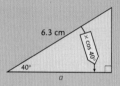

$$a = 6.3\,\text{cm} \times \cos 40°$$
$$= 4.8\,\text{cm}$$

Find the side labelled *b* in this triangle.

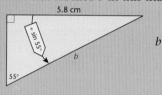

$$b = 5.8\,\text{cm} \div \sin 55°$$
$$= 7.1\,\text{cm}$$

Find the angle marked *x* in this triangle.

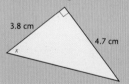

$$\tan x = \frac{\text{opp}}{\text{adj}}$$
$$= \frac{4.7}{3.8}$$
$$= 1.237$$
$$x = 51°$$

Angle of elevation

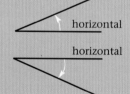

horizontal

Angle of depression

horizontal

Do not use a calculator for Question 4.

1 Calculate *p* and *q*, correct to 3 s.f.

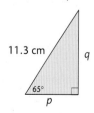

11.3 cm   *q*

65°

p

2 Calculate *a* and *b*, correct to 2 s.f.

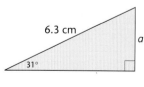

6.3 cm   *a*

31°

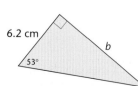

6.2 cm   *b*

53°

3 Calculate angles x and y, to the nearest degree.

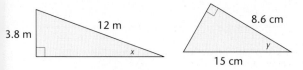

4 Look at this diagram.

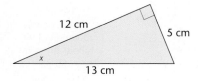

Write down the exact fraction for

(a) $\tan x$ (b) $\sin x$

5 Calculate m and n, correct to 2 s.f.

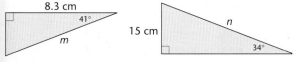

6 A ship sails 16 km from U to V on a bearing of 058°.

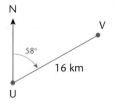

How far east of U is the ship then? Give your answer correct to 2 s.f.

7 Q is 11 km north and 24 km east of P.

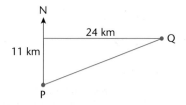

Work out the bearing of Q from P.

8 A 4.2 m long ladder is placed against a wall so that it reaches 3.9 m up the wall. For safety reasons, the angle between the ladder and the ground should be between 70° and 80°.

Work out whether the ladder is safely placed.

9

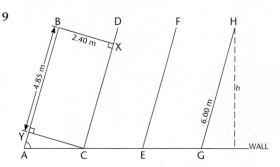

In the diagram, AB, CD, EF, GH, ... represent parallel lines running out from the boundary wall of a car park to mark off individual parking spaces.
Each parking space provides a rectangular parking area, such as CXBY which is 4.85 m long and 2.40 m wide.
The parallel lines are each 6.00 m long and are equally spaced along the wall.

Calculate, correct to 1 decimal place,

(a) the size of angle YAC,

(b) h, the distance of H from the wall of the car park.

CCEA 1998

10 A, B and C are three communication satellites orbiting the Earth on a circular path. They are equal distances from each other. The radius of the Earth is approximately 6400 km.

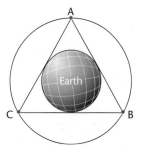

Calculate the radius of the orbit.

TRANSFORMATIONS

Transforming shapes means changing them in some way. The shape you start with is called the **object**; the result of changing the shape is called the **image.**

Reflections need a mirror line. Every point on the object is the same distance from the mirror as the corresponding point on the image.

Rotations need a centre, an angle of rotation and a direction of rotation.

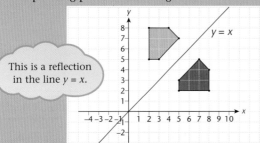

This is a reflection in the line $y = x$.

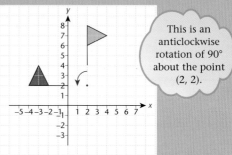

This is an anticlockwise rotation of 90° about the point (2, 2).

Translation is a sliding movement. **Vectors** are used to describe translations.

Enlargements need a scale factor and a centre of the enlargement. Even if the object becomes smaller, it is still called an enlargement.

This is a translation by the vector $\begin{pmatrix} 1 \\ -3 \end{pmatrix}$.

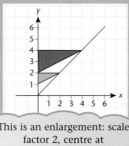

This is an enlargement: scale factor 2, centre at the origin

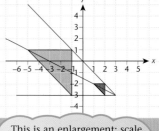

This is an enlargement: scale factor 0.25, centre at (3, –3)

1 (a) Copy this diagram.

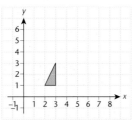

 (b) Draw the image of the shape when it is reflected in the line $y = x$.

 (c) Draw the image of the same shape when it is reflected in $x = 5$.

2 (a) Copy this diagram.

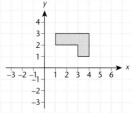

 (b) Draw the image of the shape when it is rotated 90° clockwise about the point (1, 0).

3 Look at this diagram.

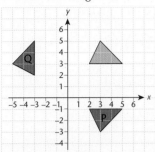

(a) Triangle P is a reflection of the blue triangle. What is the equation of the mirror line?

(b) Describe, fully, the transformation that maps the blue triangle on to triangle Q.

4 In a translation, the point (1, 7) moves to (–3, 4). What is the vector for the translation?

5 In a translation, the point (2, 1) moves to (7, 3). To what point does (–2, 7) move in this translation?

6 (a) Copy and complete this diagram to show the reflection of the shape in the line AB.

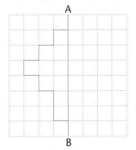

(b) Copy and complete this diagram to show the enlargement of the rectangle by a scale factor of 2 with centre of enlargement C.

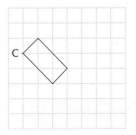

(c) Copy and complete this diagram to show the new position of the triangle after a quarter turn clockwise about D.

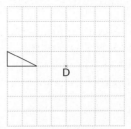

CCEA 1996

7

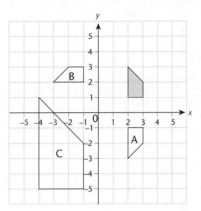

Describe fully a single transformation that would map the shaded shape on to

(a) shape *A*,　　(b) shape *B*,

(c) shape *C*.

NEAB 1997

8 Draw axes with *x* and *y* from 0 to 9. Draw triangle PQR with P at (2, 1), Q at (4, 1) and R at (4, 4).

(a) Enlarge triangle PQR by scale factor 2, using (0, 0) as centre. Label the image P′Q′R′.

(b) Now enlarge P′Q′R′ by scale factor $\frac{1}{2}$, using (6, 0) as centre. Label the image P″Q″R″.

(c) What is the vector of the translation that shifts triangle PQR to P″Q″R″?

9 An enlargement has centre (2, 0) and P has coordinates (8, 2).

(a) If the image of P is (14, 4), what is the scale factor?

(b) If the scale factor is $\frac{1}{2}$, what are the coordinates of P's image?

Nelson GCSE Maths REVISION GUIDE: SHAPE, SPACE AND MEASURES (INTERMEDIATE)

SCALE DRAWING AND SIMILARITY

S12

SCALES

Scales are used on maps and plans. You need to be able to read maps and plans, using their scales.
You also need to be able to draw them.

On a plan, the scale might be, for example,
2 cm to represent 1 m (which is 1:50),
or 1 cm to represent 2 m (which is 1:200).

On a map, the scale might be, for example,
1 cm to represent 3 km (which is 1:300 000),
or 4 cm to represent 1 km (which is 1:25 000).

SIMILARITY

In Mathematics, two shapes are **similar** if they are the same shape; they can be a different size.

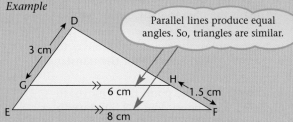

If two shapes are similar their sides are in the same ratio.
This result can be used to calculate missing lengths.
Example

Parallel lines produce equal angles. So, triangles are similar.

The lengths in triangle DEF are $\frac{8}{6}$ times those in triangle DGH.
So, length of DE = $\frac{8}{6} \times 3$ cm = 4 cm
So, GE is 4 cm – 3 cm = 1 cm, which is $\frac{1}{3}$ of GD.
Hence, FH is $\frac{1}{3}$ of DH. So, DH is 3 × 1.5 cm, i.e. 4.5 cm.

Two similar rectangles

Two similar triangles

---

1 This shape is enlarged by a scale factor of 3.

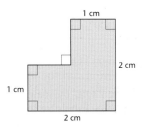

Draw and label a sketch of the enlarged shape.
What is its perimeter?

2 Doll's house furniture is constructed to a scale of one-twelfth. Calculate, to the nearest millimetre, the measurements needed for a scale model of a rug that is 75 cm by 200 cm.

3 A rectangular room is 4.8 m by 2.6 m, with a door and a window as shown.

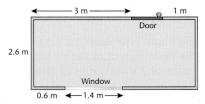

Make an accurate scale drawing of this room, using a scale of 2 cm to 1 m.

4 A distance of 5 cm on a map represents a distance of 200 km in real life.
What is the scale of the map in the form 1:*n*?

5 Look at this map of a walk on the Isle of Wight.

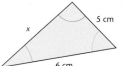

© Crown copyright

(a) Use the scale to *estimate* the length of the walk in miles.

(b) Measure the scale line to the 1 km mark, and work out the scale in the form 1:*n*.

6 A map has a scale of 1:250 000.
The distance between a farmhouse and the post office is 1.2 cm on the map.
What is the real distance?

7 A scale model of a double-decker bus is 6 cm high. The real bus is 3.6 m high.
What scale was used for making the model?

8 In these similar triangles, the equal angles are marked in the same way.

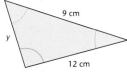

Calculate the lengths marked with letters.

9 Calculate the lengths marked *p* and *q* in this diagram.

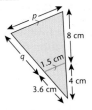

10 Look at this diagram.

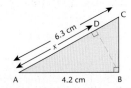

(a) Explain why triangles ABC and ADB are similar.

(b) Calculate the length of AD.

11

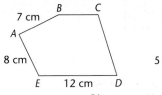

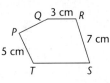

Diagrams not to scale

The diagram above shows two **similar** figures *ABCDE* and *PQRST*.
AB = 7 cm, *DE* = 12 cm, *EA* = 8cm, *QR* = 3 cm, *RS* = 7 cm and *TP* = 5 cm.

(a) Calculate the length of *TS*.

(b) Calculate the length of *CD*.

WJEC 1998

12

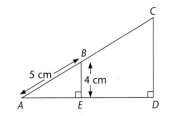

Diagram NOT accurately drawn

AB : *AC* = 1 : 3

(i) Work out the length of *CD*.

(ii) Work out the length of *BC*.

Edexcel 1998

The **locus** of a point that is always a constant distance away from a fixed point is a **circle**.

This is the locus of a point that is always a constant distance from a line of fixed length.

The locus of a point which is equidistant from two fixed points A and B is the **perpendicular bisector** of the line joining A and B.

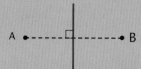

The locus of a point which is equidistant from two fixed lines is made up of both **angle bisectors** of the two lines.

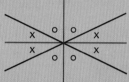

S14 explains how to construct perpendicular bisectors and angle bisectors, using a compass.

1 Mark two points, X and Y, 8 cm apart.

   (a) Draw the locus of points that are 6 cm from Y.

   (b) Draw the locus of points that are equidistant from X and Y.

   (c) Shade the region where the points are less than 6 cm from Y, and are nearer to X than Y.

2 A new tree is being put in this garden.

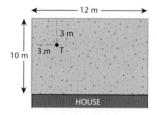

   It must follow these three rules.

   A: It must be at least 4 m from the house.

   B: It must be at least 2 m from the other three edges of the garden.

   C: It must be more than 4 m from an existing tree(T).

Draw the garden to a scale of 2 cm to 1 m, and the boundaries, for rules A, B and C.
Shade the region where the tree may be put.

3

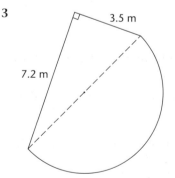

The diagram shows a penguin pool at a zoo. It consists of a right-angled triangle and a semi-circle of diameter 8m.

A safety fence is put up around the pool. The fence is always 2 m from the pool. Draw accurately the position of the fence on a scale diagram using a scale of 1 cm to 1 m.

SEG 1998

RULER AND COMPASS CONSTRUCTIONS

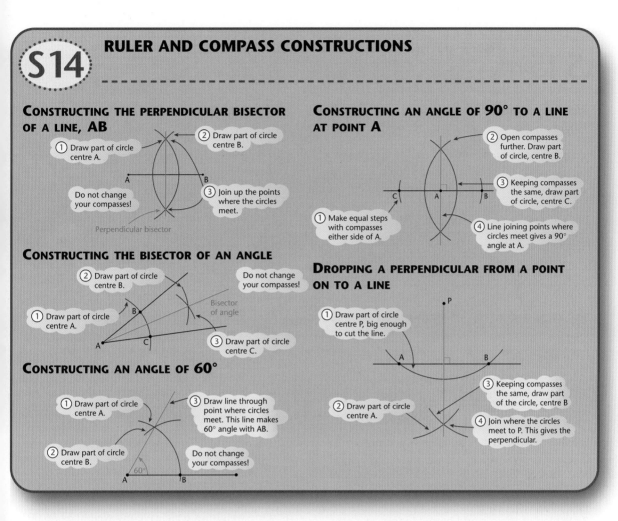

CONSTRUCTING THE PERPENDICULAR BISECTOR OF A LINE, AB

① Draw part of circle centre A.

② Draw part of circle centre B.

Do not change your compasses!

③ Join up the points where the circles meet.

Perpendicular bisector

CONSTRUCTING THE BISECTOR OF AN ANGLE

② Draw part of circle centre B.

Do not change your compasses!

① Draw part of circle centre A.

Bisector of angle

③ Draw part of circle centre C.

CONSTRUCTING AN ANGLE OF 60°

① Draw part of circle centre A.

③ Draw line through point where circles meet. This line makes 60° angle with AB.

② Draw part of circle centre B.

Do not change your compasses!

60°

CONSTRUCTING AN ANGLE OF 90° TO A LINE AT POINT A

② Open compasses further. Draw part of circle, centre B.

③ Keeping compasses the same, draw part of circle, centre C.

① Make equal steps with compasses either side of A.

④ Line joining points where circles meet gives a 90° angle at A.

DROPPING A PERPENDICULAR FROM A POINT ON TO A LINE

•P

① Draw part of circle centre P, big enough to cut the line.

② Draw part of circle centre A.

③ Keeping compasses the same, draw part of the circle, centre B

④ Join where the circles meet to P. This gives the perpendicular.

**Use only a ruler and compasses for these questions.
Do not use a protractor.**

1 Mark two points, A and B, 8 cm apart. Construct the perpendicular bisector of AB.

2 Construct an equilateral triangle, PQR, with each side of length 6 cm.

Construct the bisector of ∠PQR.

3 Construct this triangle.

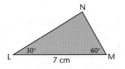

Measure the length of LN.

4 Starting from a line AB, 7 cm long, construct a square ABCD.

5 (a) Construct this triangle accurately.

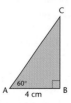

(b) Construct a perpendicular from B on to AC. Measure the length of this perpendicular.

S15   UNITS OF MEASUREMENT AND CONVERSIONS

METRIC MEASURES

Length

1 km	=	1000 m		
1 m	=	100 cm	=	1000 mm
1 cm	=	10 mm		

Mass or weight

1 tonne	=	1000 kg
1 kg	=	1000 g

Capacity or volume

1 litre	=	1000 ml	=	1000 cm³
1 m³	=	1000 litres		
1 cm³	=	1 ml		

IMPERIAL MEASURES

Length

1 mile	=	1760 yards		
1 yard	=	3 feet	=	36 inches
1 foot	=	12 inches		

Mass or weight

1 pound (lb)	=	16 ounces (oz)

Capacity or volume

1 gallon	=	8 pints

RELATIONSHIP BETWEEN METRIC AND IMPERIAL UNITS

Length
1 mile is about 1.6 km
1 foot is about 30 cm
1 metre is a bit more than a yard

Mass or weight
1 kilogram is about 2.2 lb
1 ounce is about 30 g

Capacity or volume
1 litre is about $1\frac{3}{4}$ pints
1 gallon is about 4.5 litres

Also remember: 1 cm³ of water weighs 1 g.

---

1   Which of these could be the volume of a mug?
2 pints, $\frac{1}{2}$ pint or 10 pints?

2   Which of these could be the length of a car?
35 inches, 4 feet or 4 yards?

3   This sign would be seen outside a French town, warning of a 50 km per hour speed limit.

Is 30 m.p.h. slower, or faster, than this?
Show your working.

4   My car holds 6 gallons of petrol when full.
If I fill it with petrol costing 52.3p per litre, approximately how much will it cost?

5   How much longer than 1 yard is 1 metre?
Give your estimate in inches.

6   One weighing scale gave my weight as 56.00 kg.
Another gave it as 58.20 kg.
What was the difference in weight in pounds?

7   A recipe needs half a pint of yoghurt. How many millilitres is this? Give your answer to the nearest 10 ml.

8   Iron has a density of 7900 kg /m³.
What is this in
  (a) kg /cm³?   (b) g /cm³?

9   A spacecraft is travelling at 12.4 km per second.
Write this speed in
  (a) km per minute   (b) metres per second

10 One litre of water weighs one kilogram.
  (a) What does 450 ml of water weigh?
  (b) What is the volume of 87 g of water?

S16 COMPOUND MEASURES: SPEED AND DENSITY

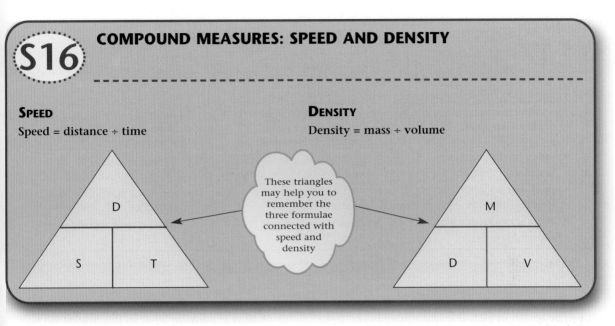

SPEED

Speed = distance ÷ time

DENSITY

Density = mass ÷ volume

These triangles may help you to remember the three formulae connected with speed and density

Do not use a calculator for Questions 1 and 2.

1 A train travels 150 miles in two hours.
   What is its average speed?

2 An aeroplane's average speed is 360 m.p.h.
   How far will it travel in

   (a) two hours?

   (b) twenty minutes?

   (c) three hours and ten minutes?

3 A car travels two miles in four minutes.

   (a) What is its average speed in miles
        per minute?

   (b) What is its average speed in miles per hour?

4 A cyclist worked out her average speed for a
   journey as 18 km per hour.
   Her journey took $2\frac{1}{2}$ hours.

   (a) How long was her journey?

   (b) How far would she travel in 15 minutes at
        the same average speed?

5 A bus travels on average at 10 m.p.h.

   (a) How many minutes would a two-mile
        journey take?

   (b) How far would a bus travel in 45 minutes?

6 Iron has a density of $7900 \, \text{kg}/\text{m}^3$.
   What is the mass of $0.8 \, \text{m}^3$ of iron?

7 The average density of the planet Mercury is
   $5400 \, \text{kg}/\text{m}^3$ and its mass is $3.3 \times 10^{23} \, \text{kg}$.
   What is the planet's volume?

8 The weight of 0.5 litres of hydrogen is 0.045 g.
   What is the density of hydrogen?

9 The density of mercury is $13.6 \, \text{g}/\text{cm}^3$.
   Find how much a 5-ml teaspoon of
   mercury weighs.

10 A piece of cork has a density of $0.25 \, \text{g}/\text{cm}^3$.
    Find the volume of a piece of cork
    weighing 3.5 g.

S17 UPPER AND LOWER BOUNDS OF MEASURES

Something might be measured as 19 cm to the nearest centimetre. This means that
- the upper bound for its length is 19.5 cm, and
- the lower bound for its length is 18.5 cm.

Another way of writing this is 19 cm ± 0.5 cm.

Something might be measured as 18.3 cm to the nearest millimetre. This means that
- the upper bound for its length is 18.35 cm, and
- the lower bound for its length is 18.25 cm.

Another way of writing this is 18.3 cm ± 0.05 cm.

Something might be measured as 85 g to the nearest 5 grams. This means that
- the upper bound for its mass (weight) is 87.5 g, and
- the lower bound for its mass is 82.5 g.

Another way of writing this is 85 g ± 2.5 g.

1 The length of each side of a square is 12 cm, to the nearest centimetre.

(a) What is the smallest that each side of the square could be?

(b) What is the smallest the perimeter could be?

2 The population of a town is estimated to be 26 800, to the nearest 100.

(a) What is the smallest that the population could be?

(b) What is the largest that the population could be?

The town covers an area of 130 km², to the nearest 10 km².

(c) What is the smallest value that this area could be?

3 The attendance at a football match was estimated as 12 000, to the nearest 1000. What are the upper and lower bounds for this number?

4 A car is travelling at a speed of 66 m.p.h., measured to the nearest 2 m.p.h. What is the greatest that the speed could be?

5 A time is given as 5.6 s, to the nearest 0.1 s. What are the largest and smallest possible values for this time?

6 The winning time for a 100-m race was given as 10.34 s to the nearest 0.01 s. What was the longest that this time could have been?

7 A long jumper won with a jump of 6.99 m to the nearest 0.01 m. What was the shortest that this jump could have been?

8 Stephanie ran 100 metres. The distance was correct to the nearest metre.

(a) Write down the shortest distance Stephanie could have run.

Stephanie's time for the run was 14.9 seconds. Her time was correct to the nearest tenth of a second.

(b) Write down

(i) her shortest possible time for the run,

(ii) her longest possible time for the run.

Edexcel 1995

AREA AND PERIMETER OF TRIANGLES, PARALLELOGRAMS AND TRAPEZIUMS

AREA OF A TRIANGLE

All these triangles have the same area, because they have the same base and height.

Area = $\frac{1}{2} \times 3\,\text{cm} \times 2\,\text{cm} = 3\,\text{cm}^2$

The area of any triangle is $\frac{1}{2} \times$ **base** $\times$ **height**.

The height must always be measured at right angles to the base. The base may be in any orientation.

Area = $\frac{1}{2} \times 5\,\text{cm} \times 4\,\text{cm} = 10\,\text{cm}^2$

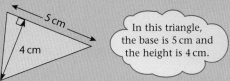

In this triangle, the base is 5 cm and the height is 4 cm.

AREA OF A PARALLELOGRAM

All these parallelograms have the same area, because they have the same base and height.

Area = $3\,\text{cm} \times 2\,\text{cm} = 6\,\text{cm}^2$

The area of any parallelogram is **base** $\times$ **height**.

AREA OF A TRAPEZIUM

Area of trapezium is half the sum of the parallel sides × height.

$A = \frac{1}{2}(a + b)h$

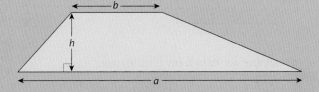

PERIMETER

The **perimeter** of a shape is the distance around its boundary.

1 Calculate the areas of these triangles.

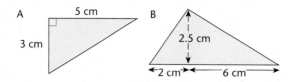

2 Find the area of this parallelogram.

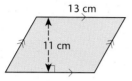

3 Find the area of this trapezium.

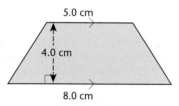

4 Calculate the area of this shape.

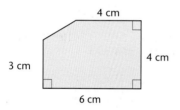

5 These four shapes are drawn on centimetre-squared dot paper. Find their areas.

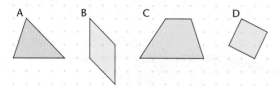

6 This is the side view of a model house.

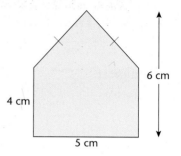

Calculate the area of the end of the model house.

7 The area of a square is 36 cm². Calculate its perimeter.

8 Calculate the area of this sign.

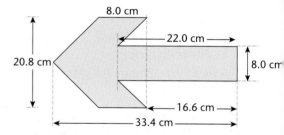

9 The perimeter of a rectangle is 40 cm. The width is 8 cm.

   (a) Work out the length of the rectangle.

   (b) Work out the area of the rectangle.

   (c) A different rectangle with a perimeter of 40 cm has a bigger area. Find a possible width and length for this rectangle.

10 Find the area of an equilateral triangle with side length 8 cm.

Nelson GCSE Maths   REVISION GUIDE: SHAPE, SPACE AND MEASURES   (INTERMEDIATE)

S19   AREA AND PERIMETER OF CIRCLES

These words are used for circles.

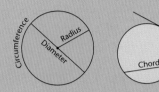

The perimeter of a circle is called its **circumference**.

Circumference of a circle = π × diameter
$$= \pi d$$
$$= 2\pi r$$

When estimating you can use 3 for π.

Area of a circle = π × radius × radius
$$= \pi r^2$$

π is about 3.14. Use this value or the π button on your calculator.

Do not use a calculator for Questions 9 and 10.

1 A circle has a radius of 4.2 cm.
   (a) Find the circumference of the circle to 2 significant figures.
   (b) Find the area of the circle to 2 significant figures.

2 A circle has a circumference of 28.4 cm. Find its diameter to 3 significant figures.

3 The wheel on a child's bicycle rotates 12 times as it moves along 10 m.
   Find the diameter of the wheel, to the nearest centimetre.

4 This window is made from a semicircle and a rectangle.
   (a) Find the area of the window.
   (b) Find the perimeter of the window.

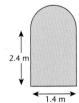

2.4 m

1.4 m

5 The inside lane of a race track consists of two straights, 110 m long, and two semicircles (as shown).

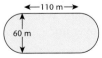

←110 m→

60 m

Does a 400 m race need *more* than, or *less* than, one lap of this track?

6 A circular piece of diameter 4.4 cm is cut from a circular disc of radius 4.4 cm as shown. Find the area left (shaded).

4.4 m

7 A disc of radius 2.36 cm is fitted on to a square of side 4.72 cm as shown.

Find the shaded area.

8 This oil drum has a diameter of 82 cm. It is being rolled along the ground.

How far is it rolled before the word OIL is the same way up again?

9 A circle has a diameter of 5 cm. Find its circumference and area in terms of π.

10 The area inside a circle is 36π cm². Find the radius of the circle.

VOLUME AND SURFACE AREA OF CUBOIDS

S20

VOLUME OF A CUBOID

The volume of a cuboid is
length × width × height

SURFACE AREA OF A CUBOID

To find the surface area of a cuboid, find the areas
of the six rectangular faces, and add them.

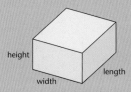

X Do not use a calculator for Questions 1, 4 and 5.

1 (a) Find the volume of this cuboid.

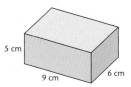

5 cm
9 cm
6 cm

(b) Find its surface area.

2 This cuboid has a square base.
Its volume is 252 cm³.

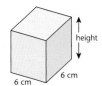

height
6 cm
6 cm

Find its height.

3 The volume of a cuboid is 168 cm³.
Its length is 7 cm and its height is 4 cm.
Find its width.

4 A rectangular pool measures 10 m by 16 m.
The volume of water in the pool is 208 m³.
Find the depth of the water.

5 How many cuboids, 2 cm by 3 cm by 5 cm,
would fit in a cuboid box 12 cm by 8 cm by
10 cm? Describe how they would fit in.

6 160 litres of liquid are poured into this tank.

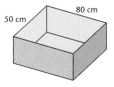

50 cm
80 cm

1 litre = 1000 cm³

(a) How deep will the liquid be?

(b) The tank is 75 cm deep.
Would it hold 320 litres?

7 A cuboid has two square ends with edge length
7 cm. Its surface area is 238 cm².
Find the volume of the cuboid.

8 (a) A cube is made from 729 one-centimetre
cubes.

(i) What is the length of an edge of
this cube?

(ii) What is the surface area of this cube?

(b) An identical cube, made from 729 one-
centimetre cubes is broken up. All the small
cubes are placed in contact with a table top
and then arranged into a large square. The
first cube (made from 729 cubes) is placed
on this square. What fraction of the square
does it cover up?

VOLUME AND SURFACE AREA OF PRISMS AND CYLINDERS

S21

VOLUME OF A PRISM

Volume of a prism
= area of base × height

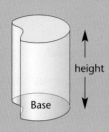

height

Base

VOLUME OF A CYLINDER

A **cylinder** is a prism with a circular cross-section.
Volume of a cylinder
= area of circular base × height
= $\pi r^2 h$

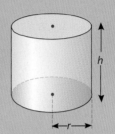

h

r

SURFACE AREA OF A CYLINDER

Curved surface area of a cylinder
= circumference of circular end × h
= π × diameter × h
= $2\pi rh$

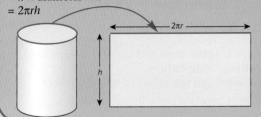

$2\pi r$

h

If the cylinder has a base, you need to add πr^2 for the area
of the base.
If it has both ends closed, you need to add another πr^2.
So, the total surface area of a closed (or solid) cylinder
= $2\pi rh + 2\pi r^2$.

Nelson GCSE Maths   REVISION GUIDE: SHAPE, SPACE AND MEASURES (INTERMEDIATE)

---

1 Calculate the volume of this prism.

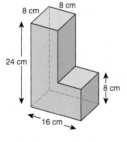

8 cm

8 cm

24 cm

8 cm

16 cm

2 Calculate the volume of this prism.

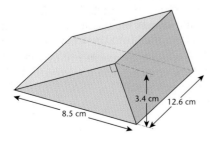

3.4 cm   12.6 cm

8.5 cm

3 This cylindrical can has a diameter of 7.4 cm
and a height of 11.6 cm.

7.4 cm

FINAN's
**Baked
Beans**
in tomato
sauce

11.6 cm

(a) Calculate the volume of the can.

(b) This label goes round the can with an
overlap of 1 cm.

1 cm

FINAN's
**Baked
Beans**
in tomato
sauce

Ingredients: Beans,
Tomato Juice, Emulsifier,
Ascorbic Acid (E301)(E40)

FINAN's
**Baked
Beans**
in tomato
sauce

OVERLAP

What are the dimensions of the label?

4 **(a)** Find the volume of this wedge.

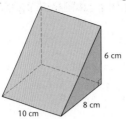

6 cm

8 cm

10 cm

(b) Find the surface area of the wedge.

5 The shape of this package is a trapezium prism. Find its volume.

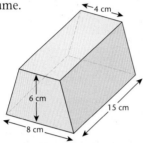

4 cm

6 cm

15 cm

8 cm

6 This swimming pool has a cross-section area in the shape of a trapezium.
The water is 1 m deep at the shallow end and 1.8 m deep at the deep end.

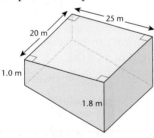

25 m

20 m

1.0 m

1.8 m

(a) Find the cross-section area of the water.

(b) Find the volume of water in the pool
    (i)   in m^3 **(ii)**   in litres

7 This trough has a trapezium for its cross-section.

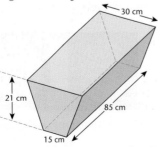

30 cm

21 cm

85 cm

15 cm

Find its capacity, correct to 2 s.f.

8 Two litres of liquid are poured into a cylindrical container which has a diameter of 12.4 cm. How deep is the liquid?

9

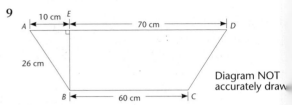

10 cm E

A   70 cm   D

26 cm

Diagram NOT
accurately drawn

B   60 cm   C

In triangle *ABE*, *AB* = 26 cm, *AE* = 10 cm and angle *AEB* = 90°.

(a) Calculate the length of *BE*.

(b) Calculate the area of the trapezium *ABCD*.

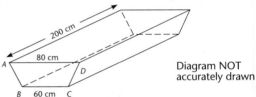

200 cm

80 cm

A

D

Diagram NOT
accurately drawn

B   60 cm C

ABCD is the cross section of a trough used in a village competition.
The trough is a prism of length 200 cm.

(c) Calculate the volume of the trough.

Cylindrical containers are also used in the competition.
Each cylindrical container has radius 10 cm and height 80 cm.

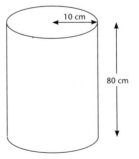

10 cm

80 cm

(d) Calculate the volume of one cylindrical container.

In the competition the cylinders are filled with water and emptied into the trough.

(e) What is the least number of cylinders that must be emptied into the trough so that the trough is full?

Edexcel 1996

S22 DISTINGUISH BETWEEN FORMULAE BY CONSIDERING DIMENSIONS

LENGTH

In formulae for **length**, each term consists of just one length.

- $2(l + w)$ = perimeter of a rectangle
- $2\pi r$ = circumference of a circle
- $\dfrac{2A}{h}$ = base of a triangle given its area and height

AREA

In formulae for **area**, each term consists of two lengths multiplied together.

- lw = area of a rectangle
- πr^2 = area of a circle
- $2\pi rh + 2\pi r^2$ = surface area of a cylinder
- $\dfrac{V}{h}$ = cross-section of a prism, given its volume and height

VOLUME

In formulae for **volume**, each term consists of three lengths multiplied together.

- lwh = volume of a cuboid
- $\pi r^2 h$ = volume of a cylinder
- Ah = volume of a prism, given its cross-sectional area and length

---

r = radius A = area V = volume
h = height
l = length
w = width

---

1 From this set of formulae, pick those which could be

   (a) for an area   (b) for a length

   $$a + 2c$$
   $$\pi d \qquad \dfrac{ab}{2} \qquad r\sqrt{p^2 + q^2}$$
   $$\pi(a + b) \qquad \pi ab$$

2 Why is the formula $4\pi r^2 + \pi r^3$ neither a volume nor an area?

3 Pick the formulae which could be for volume.

   $$a(b + c)$$
   $$2ab + d \qquad 4p^2q \qquad xy\sqrt{u^2 + v^2}$$

4 Here are some expressions.

$\pi r^2 l$	$2\pi r^2$	$4\pi r^3$	$abrl$	$\dfrac{abl}{r}$	$3(a^2 + b^2)r$	πrl

   The letters r, l, a and b represent lengths. π, 2, 3 and 4 are numbers that have no dimensions.

   Three of the expressions represent volumes. Which are they?

   Edexcel 1998

5 A factory uses wire to make frames for plant covers as shown in the diagram. Each frame has width W, depth D and uprights of height H.

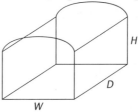

Diagram not to scale

One of these formulae may be used to estimate L, the total length of wire required for each frame.

$$L = 5W + 4D + 4H$$
$$L = 5W + 4DH$$
$$L = 5W(4D + 4H)$$
$$L = 5WDH$$

   (a) Explain why the formula $L = 5WDH$ cannot be used to estimate the total length of wire required.

   (b) State, with a reason, which of the above formulae may be used to estimate the total length of wire required.

   WJEC 1998

1 Draw triangle LMN in which LM is 5.6 cm, MN is 7.3 cm and LN is 8.4 cm.
Measure angle LMN.

2 This is a net of a 3–D shape.

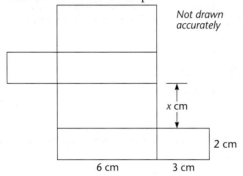

Not drawn accurately

x cm

2 cm

6 cm   3 cm

(a) (i) What is the value of *x*?
    (ii) Calculate the perimeter of this net.
    (iii) Calculate the area of this net.

(b) What is the name of the 3–D shape?

(c) Calculate the total length of all the edges of this 3–D shape.

CCEA 1998

3 (a) Write down the size of the angle marked *x* in **each** of the following diagrams.

(i)   (ii)

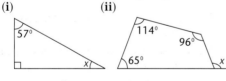

(b)

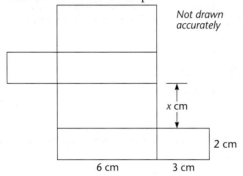

The above diagram shows a regular pentagon *ABCDE*, a diagonal *EC* and a line *DF* which is parallel to *EC*.

(i) Calculate the size of ∠EDC.

(ii) Calculate the size of ∠ECD.

(iii) Calculate the size of ∠CDF.

WJEC 1998

4 These triangles are congruent.

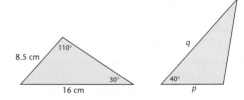

8.5 cm 110°

30°

16 cm

q

40°

p

Find the lengths marked *p* and *q*.

5 Diagram NOT accurately drawn

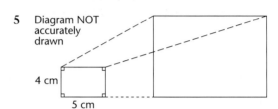

4 cm

5 cm

The diagram represents two photographs.

(a) Work out the area of the small photograph. State the units of your answer.

The photograph is to be enlarged by scale factor 3.

(b) Write down the measurements of the enlarged photograph.

(c) How many times bigger is the area of the enlarged photograph than the area of the small photograph?

Edexcel 1998

6

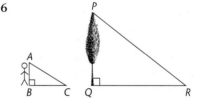

P

A

B C Q   R

The diagram shows Mr Hall and a tree with their shadows cast by the sun at 12 noon.

The triangles *ABC* and *PQR* are similar.

Mr Hall knows he is 180 cm tall.

He measures his own shadow, *BC*, as 75 cm. He measures the tree's shadow, *QR*, as 220 cm.

Calculate the height, *PQ*, of the tree.

NEAB 1996

7 The weight of a packet of oatcakes is given as 300 g to the nearest 10 g. What is the smallest that it could weigh?

8 **(a)** Chris is 13 cm taller than Steven.
Their heights add up to 307 cm.
How tall is Steven?

Sarah is 122 cm tall.

(b) **(i)** Sarah's height has been given to
the nearest centimetre.
What is the minimum height she
could be?

(ii) Estimate Sarah's height in feet.
Give your answer to the nearest foot.

SEG 1998

9

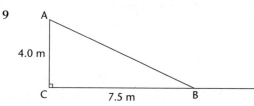

In the diagram, AB represents a gangway
leading up to the deck of a ship.

B, the lower end of the gangway, rests on the
horizontal dockside. At high tide the upper end,
A, is 4.0 m vertically above C, a point on the
edge of the dockside. B is then 7.5 m from C.

(a) Calculate the length of the gangway.

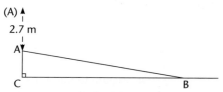

Several hours later, as the tide has fallen and
some cargo has been taken on board ship, the
upper end of the gangway has dropped a
distance of 2.7 m.

(b) Calculate how far B has moved across
the dockside.

CCEA 1998

10 This diagram shows a design for a window in
the shape of a semicircle above a rectangle.

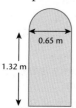

What area of glass is needed for it?

11 In the following expressions, *a* and *b* both
represent lengths.

$$3a + 3b \qquad a^2b^2 \qquad \frac{a+b}{b} \qquad a^2b$$

$$ab \qquad ab + b \qquad a^3b \qquad a^3b^3$$

By considering the dimensions of each
expression, write down one which could
represent

(a) a perimeter,

(b) an area,

(c) a volume.

MEG 1998

12 This diagram shows the cross-section, *ABCDEF*,
of a metal block.

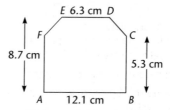

Diagram not drawn to scale

AB and ED are parallel, with
AB = 12.1 cm and ED = 6.3 cm.
AF and BC are perpendicular to AB and are
each 5.3 cm.
The perpendicular distance between ED and AB
is 8.7 cm.

(a) Calculate the area of cross-section of the
metal block.

(b) The metal block is 10.5 cm long and
weighs 2500 g.

Calculate the density of the block, giving
your answer in g/cm³.

WJEC 1998

13 Yasmin has a loop of string. The distance round the loop is 20 cm.

She loops the string over a drawing pin at A. With a pencil P in the loop as shown, keeping the string taut, she traces out the path of P on a piece of paper.

(a) Describe the path.

Next she loops the string over two drawing pins, A and B, 8cm apart.

(b) This is one position, with the pencil at P and $PA = PB$.

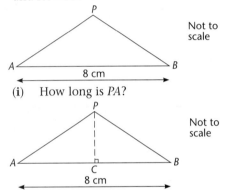

Not to scale

8 cm

(i) How long is PA?

Not to scale

8 cm

(ii) Calculate PC, the perpendicular distance of P from AB.

(c) This is another position.

(i) **Sketch** the locus of P as the pencil moves, with the string kept taut.

(ii) Mark the positions of A and B and show the main dimensions.

MEG 1996

14 The cylinder is 20 cm high and holds 1000 cm³ of water.

20 cm

Not to scale

Find the radius of the cylinder.

SEG 1998

15

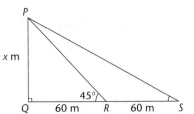

x m

45°

Q   60 m   R   60 m   S

A boat is anchored at point P. Point P is x metres from the beach, QS.
Raja walks along the edge of the beach for 60 m from point Q to a point R.
Angle QRP is 45°.

(a) Write down the value of x.

Raja walks for another 60 m along the beach to the point S. QS is a straight line.

(b) **Calculate** the size of angle QSP. Give your answer to the nearest degree.

London 1996

16 The sketch map shows the positions of Poolbridge (P), Rosegrove (R) and Beacon Point (B).

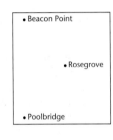

• Beacon Point

• Rosegrove

• Poolbridge

Beacon Point is 10 km due North of Poolbridge.

Rosegrove is 7 km from Poolbridge on a bearing of 056°.

(a) (i) Construct triangle PBR using a scale of 1 cm to represent 1 km.

(ii) Use your diagram to find the distance of Rosegrove from Beacon Point.

(iii) Use your diagram to find the bearing of Rosegrove from Beacon Point.

(b) A town, Seton (S), is 3.5 km due West of Beacon Point.

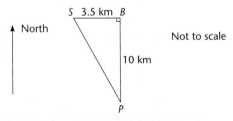

S 3.5 km B

North

Not to scale

10 km

P

(i) Calculate the distance from Poolbridge to Seton.

(ii) Calculate the bearing of Seton from Poolbridge.

MEG 1998

D1 COLLECTION AND ORGANISATION OF DATA

A **statistical investigation** has four stages:

Questioning → Data collection → Analysis → Interpretation

Hypothesis: an idea that underlies the questions asked in a statistical investigation

Different types of data
- Qualitative – e.g. hair colour
- Discrete (counting) – e.g. the number of children in a family
- Continuous (measuring) – e.g. height in centimetres

---

1 Jane does a survey about vehicles passing her school.
She wants to know about the types of vehicles and their colours.
Design a suitable observation sheet to record this information.
Fill in your observation sheet as if you had carried out this survey.
You should invent suitable data for 25 vehicles.
NEAB 1998

2 Which of these are examples of discrete data?
Which are examples of continuous data?

A: Millimetres of rainfall

B: Shoe size

C: Temperature of classroom

D: Price of unleaded fuel

E: Weight of animals at zoo

F: Age of pets taken to vet

3 Which of these collections of information are qualitative data?

A: Favourite soap

B: Number of children in a family

C: The television programmes watched yesterday

D: Money spent on food items

E: Age of mothers when they have the first baby

F: Favourite subject at school

4 The table shows the number of people working different shifts at a factory.

Sex	Age (years)	Shift		
		Morning	Afternoon	Evening
Men	Under 30	6	8	9
	30 and over	7	12	17
Women	Under 30	8	11	18
	30 and over	6	15	23

John thinks that the proportion of people aged 30 years and over who work the evening shift is greater than the proportion of people who are under 30 years of age who work the evening shift.
Is he correct?

You **must** show all your working.
SEG 1996

D2 DESIGNING A QUESTIONNAIRE; BIAS

DESIGNING QUESTIONNAIRES

Questions need to be

- clear and unambiguous
- free from bias
- easy to answer and analyse
- not too open ended

You don't like Maths, do you?

> A biased question

How much television do you watch?

> Too vague

CHOOSING A SAMPLE

Choose a fair cross-section of people and not just a particular group who might all have the same ideas.

OBSERVATION SHEETS

These are for collecting data rather than asking questions.
Example
How many vehicles of different types pass the school in the lunch hour?

---

1 In a survey, some 16-year-old students were asked:

   How long did you spend doing your homework last night?

   Design an observation sheet to collect this data.

2 Howard is doing a survey about shops opening on a Sunday.

   Two of his questions are

   Question 1   How old are you?

   Question 2   Everybody deserves to have a day off work to spend relaxing with their families, and going out. So shops shouldn't open on a Sunday, don't you agree?

   (a) Explain why each question is not a good one for this questionnaire.

   (b) Write a suitable question for Howard to ask to replace his question 2.

   NEAB 1997

3 Design a survey on 'favourite subjects at school'.

   (a) Write three questions for each student to answer.

   (b) Describe how you could choose a fair sample which would avoid bias.

4 In a survey, Jason uses the following questionnaire to test the hypothesis "more boys than girls like sport".

Which sex are you?   Male ☐   Female ☐
Which ONE of these sports do you like best?
Football Cricket Netball Basketball Hockey Rugby
☐ ☐ ☐ ☐ ☐ ☐
None of these ☐

   (a) Explain why this questionnaire is not suitable for his survey.

   (b) One evening he gives the questionnaire to all the people in the local gymnasium. Give **two** reasons why this is unlikely to be a suitable group of people to survey.

   WJEC 1998

A **bar chart** can be used to represent qualitative data or discrete data.

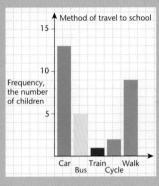

A **histogram** can be used to represent continuous data.

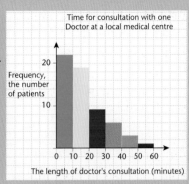

A **frequency polygon** can be used for continuous data. It can be obtained by joining up the mid-points of tops of bars on a histogram.

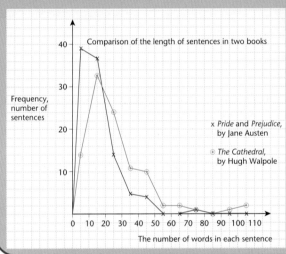

Line graph

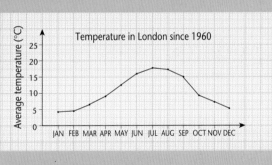

Nelson GCSE Maths REVISION GUIDE: HANDLING DATA (INTERMEDIATE)

1 A shoe size survey is carried out in Y8.

Class 8S		shoe sizes		
6	9	10	7	4
9	3	7	5	8
4	6	6	4	11
5	5	8	6	5
5	7	3	6	6
8	5			

Class 8J		shoe sizes		
5	8	5	7	7
7	4	8	6	6
7	6	4	8	8
8	11	10	5	9
10	7	3	9	6
5	7	6	3	

(a) Draw a bar chart for the results from class 8S.

(b) Use another chart, with the same axis labels, to show the results from class 8J.

(c) Comment on the distribution of shoe sizes in the two classes.

2 The height of each member of a class is measured and given in this table.

Height, h cm	$145 \leq h < 150$	$150 \leq h < 155$	$155 \leq h < 160$
Frequency	1	1	3

Height, h cm	$160 \leq h < 165$	$165 \leq h < 170$	$170 \leq h < 175$
Frequency	5	7	9

Height, h cm	$175 \leq h < 180$	$180 \leq h < 190$	
Frequency	3	1	

Display the data as a histogram.

3 Fred grows potatoes in his garden.
Last year he tested a new fertiliser, *MEGACROP*.

Half the potato plants were given the fertiliser and half not.
Here are the results.
Potatoes grown **without** *MEGACROP*.

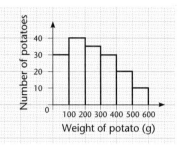

(**a**) What is the total number of potatoes?

Potatoes grown **with** *MEGACROP*.

Weight of potato (*x* grams)	Frequency
$0 \leq x < 100$	2
$100 \leq x < 200$	12
$200 \leq x < 300$	37
$300 \leq x < 400$	23
$400 \leq x < 500$	5
$500 \leq x < 600$	1

(**b**) Draw a frequency diagram for the potatoes grown with *MEGACROP*, using axes like these.

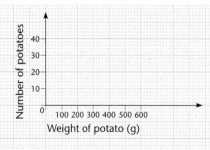

MEG 1996

4 (**a**) The age of each employee of the Buywell supermarket chain at the start of 1990 was recorded. The ages were grouped into intervals of ten years and the percentage of employees in each interval was calculated. The set of data is represented by this histogram.

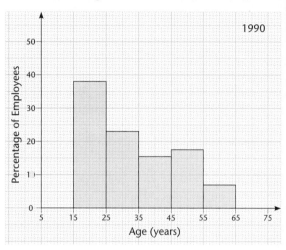

Copy the diagram on to graph paper and draw a frequency polygon for the 1990 data.

(**b**) The table shows similar data recorded at the start of 1995.

On another set of axes, drawn to the same scale, draw a frequency polygon to represent this set of data.

Age *a* (years)	Percentage of employees (frequency)
$15 \leq a < 25$	9.0
$25 \leq a < 35$	14.5
$35 \leq a < 45$	22.5
$45 \leq a < 55$	31.0
$55 \leq a < 65$	23.0

(**c**) In 1993, in a statement to the press, the personnel manager said, "It is our policy to give jobs to older applicants; they have more patience and are more polite than many young people today."

(**i**) By comparing the two frequency polygons, state whether or not this policy seems to have been put into practice.

(**ii**) Give reasons for your answer to (i).

CCEA 1996

D4 PIE CHARTS

This information can be put into a **pie chart**.

Type of transport	Number of children	Size of angle in pie chart
Car	13	13 × 12° = 156°
Bus	5	5 × 12° = 60°
Train	1	1 × 12° = 12°
Cycle	2	2 × 12° = 24°
Walk	9	9 × 12° = 108°
Total	30	360°

There are 30 students altogether. So, each student is represented by 360° ÷ 30 = 12°

How do you get to school?

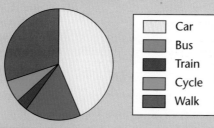

- Car
- Bus
- Train
- Cycle
- Walk

1 A survey of holiday destinations was carried out in a supermarket.

Holiday	Europe	America	Asia	Australia	Other	Total
Frequency	115	45	15	5		200

(a) 200 people were asked altogether. How many people are there in the category 'Other'?

(b) A pie chart is to be made of this data. Copy and complete this table, showing each angle needed.

	Frequency	Angle
Europe	115	207°
America	45	
Asia	15	
Australia	5	
Other		
Total	200	

(c) Draw a labelled pie chart to illustrate the results of this survey.

2 A group of 45 teachers and 90 accountants were asked which newspaper they usually bought.

	Teachers	Accountants
The Guardian	18	10
The Independent	11	12
The Times	2	10
The Financial Times	0	·51
The Mirror	5	2
Daily Mail	7	3
Other	2	2
Total	45	90

(a) Draw two pie charts: one for the teachers and one for the accountants.

(b) By comparing the pie charts, make two statements about the newspapers bought by the two groups of people.

3 The times devoted to different types of television programme on one channel in a period of 20 hours is shown on this pie chart.

Number of hours and type of programme on one TV channel

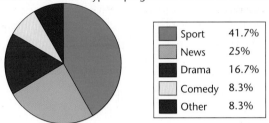

	Sport	41.7%
	News	25%
	Drama	16.7%
	Comedy	8.3%
	Other	8.3%

(a) Calculate the number of hours spent on each type.

(b) Draw a bar chart to show this information.

4 A newspaper is surveyed for its coverage of different types of article.

	Coverage in pages
Sport	7
News	20
Fashion	6
Adverts	21
General	6

(a) Calculate the angles needed to draw a pie chart of this survey.

(b) Draw a pie chart.

5 (a) The pie chart shows the nutritional content of **white** bread.

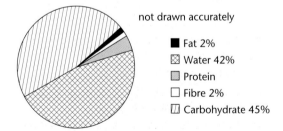

not drawn accurately

■	Fat 2%
⊠	Water 42%
▨	Protein
□	Fibre 2%
▨	Carbohydrate 45%

(i) What percentage of the nutritional content is protein?

(ii) What size of angle should represent carbohydrate in an accurate diagram?

(b) The nutritional content of **wholemeal** bread may be represented in a pie chart using the following angles:

Fat	11°
Water	151°
Protein	36°
Fibre	
Carbohydrate	137°

(i) What size of angle represents fibre?

(ii) What percentage of the total nutritional content of **wholemeal** bread is carbohydrate?

(c) Draw a pie chart showing the nutritional content of **wholemeal** bread.

(d) A diet that is high in fibre and low in carbohydrate is said to be good for people who are watching their weight. Compare the content of each of the 2 kinds of bread and decide which kind of bread these people should eat. Give **two** reasons for your answer.

CCEA 1998

6 The pie chart shows information from a survey about the holiday destinations of a number of people.

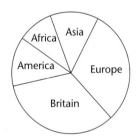

(a) (i) Which holiday destination is the mode?

(ii) America is the holiday destination of 24 people.
How many people go to Africa?

In another survey it was found that America is the holiday destination of 21 people out of 180 people asked.

(b) What percentage of all the people asked in these two surveys gave America as their holiday destination?

SEG 1998

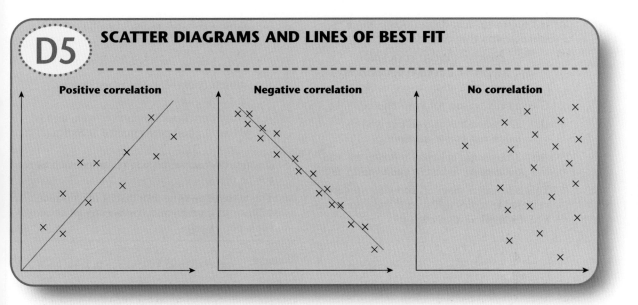

Positive correlation   **Negative correlation**   **No correlation**

1   This table shows pairs of test results gained by students, in Geography and History.

Geog.	Hist.
58	30
54	31
61	33
37	24
30	24
43	31
65	34
51	30
27	20
48	28

Geog.	Hist.
41	27
37	26
44	35
54	33
43	27
56	29
56	33
36	27
66	37
34	23

The Geography test was out of 70, and the History test out of 40.

(a) Plot the results on a scatter diagram.

(b) A student obtained 60 marks in the Geography test, but was absent for the History test. Estimate the History mark for this student.

(c) Comment on this statement.

     Students who are poor at Geography are good at History.

2   This table shows the price and age of some second-hand cars.

Age	Price
2	3500
3	2400
1	5450
4	2000
5	1750
2	3050
3	3000
6	1500
2	3750
3	3950

(a) Plot the points on a scatter diagram and describe the correlation.

(b) Draw a line of best fit.

(c) Estimate the cost of a second-hand car which is $3\frac{1}{2}$ years old.

(d) A second-hand car costs £3250. What age would you expect it to be?

3 **(a)** For each pair of variables below, state whether you think there would be:

> **positive** (direct) correlation
> or **negative** (inverse) correlation
> or **no** correlation.

Give a brief reason for your choice.

(i) *The amount of rain falling* and *the number of people outdoors.*

(ii) *The amount of apples a person ate* and *the person's results in mathematics tests.*

This is a scatter diagram showing students' percentage scores in Paper 1 and Paper 2 of a Mathematics examination.

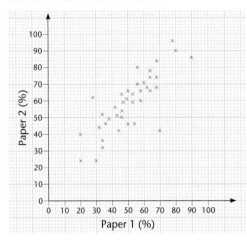

(b) What type of correlation does the diagram show?

Student A scored 43% on Paper 1, but did not take Paper 2.

(c) Use the scatter diagram to estimate the percentage the student might have scored on Paper 2.

Edexcel 1996

4 This scatter diagram shows the results of an analysis of the performance of seven cricketers.

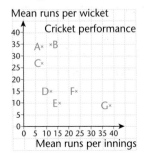

(a) What evidence is there to support this statement?

Good bowlers are poor batsmen.

(b) Which cricketer is the worst bowler in the group?

(c) Which cricketer bowls very well, and is giving a good performance at batting?

5 Information about oil was recorded each year for 12 years.

The table shows the amount of oil produced (in billions of barrels) and the average price of oil (in £ per barrel).

Amount of oil produced (billions of barrels)	7.0	11.4	10.8	11.3	9.6	8.2	7.7	10.9	8.0	9.9	9.2	9.4
Average price of oil (£ per barrel)	34	13	19	12	23	33	30	12.5	28.5	13.5	26.5	15.5

(a) Draw a scatter graph to show the information in the table. Use axes like these.

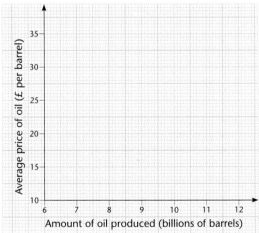

(b) Describe the correlation between the average price of oil and the amount of oil produced.

(c) Draw a line of best fit on the scatter graph.

In another year the amount of oil produced was 10.4 billion barrels.

(d) Use your line of best fit to estimate the average price of oil per barrel in that year.

Edexcel 1997

D6   MEAN, MEDIAN, MODE AND RANGE

MEAN

> Add all the items of data together.

> Divide by the number of items.

MODE OR MODAL CLASS

> Pick the item of data or group of data occurring most frequently

> Mean, median and mode are all measures of average.

MEDIAN

> List all the items in order of size.

> Pick out the item in the middle of the list.

RANGE

> Work out the difference between the largest and smallest items of data.

> Range tells you how spread out the data is.

---

1 Twelve students were asked to measure the width of their right hands. The results are in centimetres.

| 6.4 | 7.2 | 5.8 | 6.2 | 5.6 | 5.7 | 5.8 | 6.3 | 5.3 | 5.4 | 7.1 | 6.9 |

For this data, find the

(**a**) mean   (**b**) median   (**c**) range

2 A company marks its bags of crisps 'Average contents 25g'. A customer protection group surveys this company's crisps by weighing 25 bags. Here are the results.

27	25	25	24	25	24	22	26	26	25
29	25	25	27	27	23	24	25	23	24
26	25	24	27	23					

Investigate and comment on the truth of the company's statement 'Average contents 25g'.

3 This table shows the results for an English test. The marks are out of 70.

| 10 | 15 | 18 | 29 | 33 | 35 | 35 | 37 | 38 | 44 |
| 48 | 51 | 54 | 54 | 56 | 56 | 58 | 61 | 65 | 66 |

(**a**) Find the median mark of the test.

(**b**) Calculate the mean mark of the test.

4 The following is a list of marks obtained by 10 students in an end of term examination.

$$95, 45, 42, 48, 10, 38, 90, 45, 47, 50$$

(**a**) What is the median mark?

(**b**) What is the modal mark?
In the class examination above the mean mark of the 10 students is 51.

(**c**) Which of the 3 averages – mean, median or mode – least reflects the typical performance of a student in the class above? Give a reason for your answer.
CCEA 1998

5 A class took a test. The mean mark of the 20 boys in the class was 17.4. The mean mark of the 10 girls in the class was 13.8.

(**a**) Calculate the mean mark for the whole class.

5 pupils in another class took the test. Their marks, written in order, were 1, 2, 3, 4 and x.
The mean of these 5 marks is equal to twice the median of these 5 marks.

(**b**) Calculate the value of x.
Edexcel 1998

D7 MEANS OF FREQUENCY DISTRIBUTIONS

MEAN OF A FREQUENCY DISTRIBUTION

Example: Find the mean number of children in the families of this Y10 class.

Number of children	1	2	3	4	5
Frequency	6	12	4	2	1

This means that there are four families with 3 children.

Number of children	Frequency of children	Total number
1	6	6 × 1 = 6
2	12	12 × 2 = 24
3	4	4 × 3 = 12
4	2	2 × 4 = 8
5	1	1 × 5 = 5
Total	25	55

55 ÷ 25 = 2.2
So, the mean number of children is 2.2 children.

MEAN OF GROUPED FREQUENCY DISTRIBUTION

Example: Find the mean hand span of students in this Y10 class.

Hand span (*h*cm)	Frequency	Middle value	Frequency × middle value
$16 \leq h < 17$	3	16.5	3 × 16.5 = 49.5
$17 \leq h < 18$	2	17.5	2 × 17.5 = 35
$18 \leq h < 19$	1	18.5	1 × 18.5 = 18.5
$19 \leq h < 20$	4	19.5	4 × 19.5 = 78
$20 \leq h < 21$	4	20.5	4 × 20.5 = 82
$21 \leq h < 22$	2	21.5	2 × 21.5 = 43
$22 \leq h < 23$	4	22.5	4 × 22.5 = 90
$23 \leq h < 24$	2	23.5	2 × 23.5 = 47
Total	22		443

The mean hand span is 443 cm ÷ 22 = 20.1 cm (to 1 d.p.)

---

1 Students in a Y11 class are asked how many holidays they have spent in a foreign country.

Number of holidays	0	1	2	3	4	5
Frequency	1	3	5	10	8	3

Calculate these statistics.

(a) Mean   (b) Mode

(c) Median   (d) Range

2 From this data, calculate the mean number of people in a car.

Number of people in the car	1	2	3	4	5
Number of cars	34	36	21	12	5

3 A survey was carried out to find out how much time was needed by a group of pupils to complete homework set on a particular Monday evening. The results are shown in the table below.

Time, *t* hours spent on homework	Number of pupils
0	3
$0 < t \leq 1$	14
$1 < t \leq 2$	17
$2 < t \leq 3$	5
$3 < t \leq 4$	1

Calculate an estimate for the mean time spent on homework by the pupils in the group.

Edexcel 1997

4 The first 500 words of a book were examined to find the number of letters in each word.

(a) Calculate the mean number of letters in a word.

(b) Work out the median number of letters in a word.

Number of letters in each word	Number of words
1	25
2	24
3	44
4	76
5	109
6	93
7	78
8	42
9	5
10	2
11	2

(c) Another five books are analysed in a similar way.

	Median	Range
Book 1	5	7
Book 2	4	12
Book 3	7	14
Book 4	6	12
Book 5	5	13

Explain why these statements might be true.

A: Book 1 is easier to read than Book 5, because the range is smaller.

B: Book 2 is easier to read than Book 4, because the median is smaller.

5 One afternoon a survey was taken of 100 customers at a supermarket.

The time they spent queuing at the checkout was recorded.

The results are shown below.

Time, t minutes	Number of customers
$0 < t \le 5$	18
$5 < t \le 10$	42
$10 < t \le 15$	30
$15 < t \le 20$	8
$20 < t \le 25$	2

(a) Calculate an estimate of the mean time these customers had to queue.

(b) On another occasion this mean time was 12.5 minutes.
Give a reason why the mean time might have changed.

NEAB 1997

6 50 children take part in a sponsored spell to raise money for 'Comic Relief'.

They are given 40 words to learn and are then tested on them.

The results are shown in the table below.

Correct spellings	Frequency
1 to 10	1
11 to 20	7
21 to 30	26
31 to 40	16

(a) Calculate the estimate of the mean number of spellings each child got correct.

(b) For each word a child spells correctly they receive 5p from their sponsor.
Altogether £592 was raised by this sponsored spell.
No person sponsored more than one child.
Use your answer to (a) to estimate the total number of people who sponsored the children.

NEAB 1996

Nelson GCSE Maths REVISION GUIDE: HANDLING DATA (INTERMEDIATE)

D8 CUMULATIVE FREQUENCY, MEDIAN AND INTERQUARTILE RANGE

MEDIAN AND QUARTILES FOR SMALL DATA SETS

These are the marks obtained by 13 students in a test.

14, 12, 22, 34, 23, 61, 49, 27, 31, 43, 27, 33, 62

List the marks in order of size.

12, 14, **22**, **23**, 27, 27, **31**, 33, 34, **43**, **49**, 61, 62

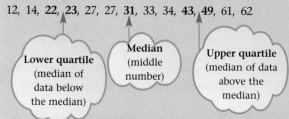

Lower quartile (median of data below the median)

Median (middle number)

Upper quartile (median of data above the median)

Interquartile range = upper quartile – lower quartile
= 46 – 22.5
= 23.5

This measures how spread out the results are.

Use the upper bound of the class interval and the cumulative frequency for plotting points. So, plot (20,4), (30, 37), (40, 97), (50, 138) and (30, 22)

MEDIAN AND QUARTILES FOR LARGE DATA SETS: CUMULATIVE FREQUENCY

These are the ages of people in a sports club.

Age (years)	Frequency	Cumulative frequency
$10 \leq y < 20$	4	4
$20 \leq y < 30$	33	37
$30 \leq y < 40$	60	97
$40 \leq y < 50$	41	138
$50 \leq y < 60$	22	160
Total	160	

To work out the numbers in this column: add up the frequencies as you go along e.g 4 + 33 = 37.

These should be the same.

Median is 37 years.

Lower quartile   Upper quartile

Interquartile range is 46 – 31 = 15 years.

---

1   Two types of leaves were collected and their lengths measured.
The results are shown by the cumulative frequency curves.

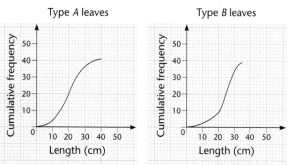

Type A leaves

Type B leaves

Length (cm)

(a)   How many type A leaves were collected?

(b)   (i)   Find the inter-quartile range for the type B leaves.

  (ii)   The inter-quartile range for the type A leaves was 12 cm.
What does this show about the length of the type A leaves compared with the type B leaves?

(c)   How many type A leaves were longer than the longest type B leaf?

SEG 1995

2 A secretary conducted a survey of the weights of 500 letters posted one week.

Weight in grams (w)	Frequency
$0 \leq w < 10$	52
$10 \leq w < 20$	157
$20 \leq w < 30$	125
$30 \leq w < 40$	71
$40 \leq w < 50$	51
$50 \leq w < 60$	44

(a) Construct a cumulative frequency table.

(b) Draw a cumulative frequency graph.

(c) Find the median weight of the letters.

(d) How many letters weighed more than 45 grams?

3 The table gives the weights of 35 students.

(a) Draw a cumulative frequency graph.

(b) From your graph, estimate the median weight of the students.

(c) Estimate the interquartile range for the weights given.

Weight (w kg)	Frequency
$40 \leq w < 45$	1
$45 \leq w < 50$	1
$50 \leq w < 55$	2
$55 \leq w < 60$	15
$60 \leq w < 65$	12
$65 \leq w < 70$	2
$70 \leq w < 75$	2

4 The table below shows a grouped frequency distribution of the ages, in complete years, of the 80 people taking part in a carnival in 1997.

Age in years	0 to 29	30 to 39	40 to 49	50 to 59	60 to 69	70 to 89
Frequency	2	18	27	18	12	3

(a) Complete this cumulative frequency table.

Age (less than)	30	40	50	60	70	90
Cumulative frequency						

(b) On graph paper, draw a cumulative frequency diagram to show these results.

(c) Copy this table which shows the median, lower quartile, upper quartile and inter-quartile range for the ages of the people taking part in the carnival for the years 1995 to 1996.

Use your graph to complete the table for 1997.

Year	Median	Lower quartile	Upper quartile	Inter-quartile range
1995	60	50	75	25
1996	52	46	60	15
1997				

(d) One year the local newspaper stated: **"Twenty-five percent of the people taking part in the carnival this year are aged 60 or more."** Which of the three years was it? Give a reason for your answer.

WJEC 1998

5 Claire did a survey on students' part time weekly earnings.

Some of her results are shown in the table.

Number of students	**59**
Lowest earnings	£5
Highest earnings	£37
Median	£15
Lower quartile	£12
Upper quartile	£21

Use this information to draw a possible cumulative frequency curve, using axes like these.

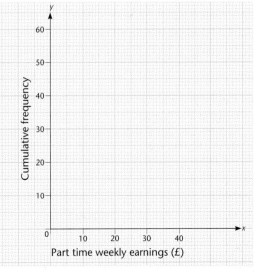

(b) Find the inter-quartile range.

(c) How many students' weekly earnings were more than £20?

SEG 1996

CALCULATING PROBABILITY FOR EQUALLY LIKELY OUTCOMES

Equally likely outcomes are when all the outcomes have the same chance of happening. To calculate the probability, list all the equally likely outcomes and find how many times the event you want occurs in the list.

$$\text{Probability} = \frac{\text{number of times the event occurs}}{\text{total number of outcomes}}$$

PROBABILITY LINE

Impossible	Evens	Certain
0	$\frac{1}{2}$	1

Example: If a dice is thrown, there are six outcomes: 1, 2, 3, 4, 5, 6.
If the event you want is to throw an even number, this occurs three times in the list: 2, 4, 6.
So, the probability of throwing an even number is $\frac{3}{6} = \frac{1}{2}$.

---

1   The probability of an event happening is 0.4. What is the probability of it *not* happening?

2   What is the probability of
   (a) drawing a King from a complete pack of playing cards?
   (b) drawing a red ball from a bag containing 5 red and 35 blue balls?
   (c) throwing a number greater than 2 with a dice numbered 1 to 6?
   (d) winning the first prize in a raffle if you have bought 5 tickets out of the two hundred tickets sold?
   (e) picking an odd numbered card from a pack numbered 1 to 12?
   (f) drawing a picture card (Jack, Queen or King) from a complete pack of playing cards?

3   Five people stand in a line. One of them is picked at random. What is the probability that the person picked is at one end of the line?

4   Twenty discs, marked with the numbers 1 to 20, are placed in a bag. One of them is drawn at random. What is the probability of
   (a) drawing a number less than 6?
   (b) drawing a multiple of 5?
   (c) drawing an even number?

5   The letters of the word MATHEMATICS are written on cards, and the cards are shuffled. One of the cards is drawn at random. What is the probability that the card contains
   (a) the letter E?
   (b) the letter A?
   (c) one of the letters in the word EXAMINATION?

   Drawing a card at random means each card is equally likely to be drawn.

6   A bag contains red, blue and yellow counters. One counter is drawn at random. The probability of it being red is 0.25. The probability of it being either red or blue is 0.36.
   (a) Calculate the probability that it is yellow.
   (b) Calculate the probability that it is blue.
   (c) If the bag contains 200 counters altogether, calculate the number of each colour.

7   The weather at Budmouth is recorded as either sunny or wet or cloudy.
   In winter, the probability that the weather is sunny is 0.15, the probability that it is wet is 0.4.
   (a) What is the probability that the weather is cloudy?
   In summer, the weather is equally likely to be sunny or wet.
   The probability that it is cloudy is 0.5.
   (b) What is the probability that the weather is sunny?

MEG 1995

Nelson GCSE Maths   REVISION GUIDE: HANDLING DATA   (INTERMEDIATE)

ESTIMATING PROBABILITY

Probability can sometimes be estimated from the results of an experiment.

$$\text{Probability} = \frac{\text{number of times the event occurs}}{\text{number of times the experiment takes place}}$$

This is also called **relative frequency**.

Example: If 40 drawing pins are dropped on to a table, and 26 of them land point up, the probability of the drawing pin landing point up is estimated to be $\frac{26}{40}$ (or 0.65 or 65%).

1

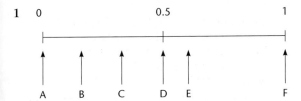

Six events are given below.
Select a letter on the probability scale above which best shows the probability of each of these events happening:

(**i**)   throwing a 6 on a fair die,

(**ii**) a new born baby being a boy,

(**iii**) selecting a month with 31 days from the calendar,

(**iv**) February will have 31 days next year,

(**v**)   there will be 30 days in June,

(**vi**) selecting a chocolate sweet from a bag containing one mint, one chocolate and one jelly sweet.

CCEA 1998

2   In a factory, 400 components are checked as they come off the production line, and 35 are found to be faulty. On another occasion, a component is selected at random. Estimate the probability that this component is *not* faulty.

3   Two pupils are doing a survey on the makes of cars passing their school.
The results so far are shown below.

Ford	136
Vauxhall	35
Renault	18
Nissan	41
Rover	17
Other makes	22

Using this data, answer true or false to the following statements, giving a reason for your answer.

(**a**)   The probability that the next car will be a Ford is roughly $\frac{1}{2}$.

(**b**)   The probability that the next car will be a Rolls-Royce is zero.

(**c**)   The probability that the next car will be a Renault is $\frac{1}{6}$.

MEG 1998

4   David goes shopping every Friday evening at a supermarket.
The supermarket has 10 check-outs.
Each week as he finished shopping, David noted the number of trolleys waiting at each check-out.
He did this for ten weeks.
His results are in this table.

Number of trolleys	0	1	2	3	4	5
Frequency	5	15	36	19	22	3

Nelson GCSE Maths   REVISION GUIDE: HANDLING DATA (INTERMEDIATE)

(a) The next week, when he has finished shopping, David goes to the nearest check-out.
What is the probability that

  (i) there is no trolley waiting,

  (ii) there are more than 3 trolleys waiting?

(b) Another week David went to a different supermarket with 10 check-outs.
He found only 1 of the check-outs had more than 3 trolleys waiting.
He said
"At this supermarket the probability of the nearest check-out having more than 3 trolleys waiting is lower".
Comment on his statement.

MEG 1998

5 (a) A teacher wants to know the relative frequency of left-handed pupils in the school.
To do this, twenty pupils were told to ask five other pupils each whether they were left-handed.
The teacher gathered all the data together and worked out the ralative frequency of left-handed pupils.
Give **two** reasons why this method may not give a reliable result

(b) Elizabeth throws five dice at a time and counts the number of times that two sixes appear. Here are her cumulative results.

Number of throws	10	20	30	40	50
Number of times two sixes occur	2	4	5	6	8
Relative frequency of two sixes occurring	0.2				

  (i) Copy the table and complete the relative frequencies.

  (ii) From your table, what is the best estimate of the probability of two sixes occurring when five dice are thrown? Give your reason.

---

6 Gemma carries out a series of tests with a coin which she believes is biased. In each test she tosses the coin ten times and records the number of heads obtained. She repeats the test ten times. Her results are as follows.

Test	1st	2nd	3rd	4th	5th	6th	7th	8th	9th	10th
Number of Heads		1	6	8	10	4	7	6	7	6

(a) Copy and complete this table.

After Test	1	2	3	4	5	6	7	8	9	10
Total Number of Tosses	10	20	30	40	50	60	70	80	90	100
Total number of heads	8	9	15	23	33	37				
Relative Frequency of Number of Heads as a Fraction	$\frac{8}{10}$	$\frac{9}{20}$	$\frac{15}{30}$	$\frac{23}{40}$	$\frac{33}{50}$					
Relative Frequency of Number of Heads as a Decimal	0.8	0.45	0.5	0.575						

(b) Copy and complete this graph of "Relative Frequency" against "Total Number of Tosses".

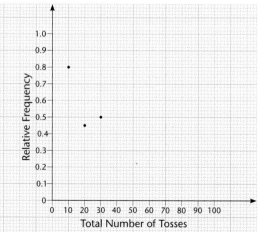

(c) Write down an estimate of the probability of obtaining a head when the coin is tossed once.

WJEC 1998

PROBABILITY OF TWO EVENTS

Example: A bag contains two red cubes, one blue cube and one yellow cube. One cube is drawn and then replaced. Another cube is drawn.

TABLE OF OUTCOMES

Second draw

		R	R	B	Y
First draw	R	RR	RR	RB	RY
	R	RR	RR	RB	RY
	B	BR	BR	BB	BY
	Y	YR	YR	YB	YY

So, the probability of drawing a red followed by a blue is $\frac{2}{16} = \frac{1}{8}$

The probability of drawing one red and one yellow is $\frac{4}{16} = \frac{1}{4}$

TREE DIAGRAM

First draw	Second draw	Outcome	Probability
R	R	RR	$\frac{2}{4} \times \frac{2}{4} = \frac{4}{16}$
	B	RB	$\frac{2}{4} \times \frac{1}{4} = \frac{2}{16}$
	Y	RY	$\frac{2}{4} \times \frac{1}{4} = \frac{2}{16}$
B	R	BR	$\frac{1}{4} \times \frac{2}{4} = \frac{2}{16}$
	B	BB	$\frac{1}{4} \times \frac{1}{4} = \frac{1}{16}$
	Y	BY	$\frac{1}{4} \times \frac{1}{4} = \frac{1}{16}$
Y	R	YR	$\frac{1}{4} \times \frac{2}{4} = \frac{2}{16}$
	B	YB	$\frac{1}{4} \times \frac{1}{4} = \frac{1}{16}$
	Y	YY	$\frac{1}{4} \times \frac{1}{4} = \frac{1}{16}$

So, the probability of drawing a red followed by a blue is $\frac{2}{16} = \frac{1}{8}$

The probability of drawing one red and one yellow is $\frac{2}{16} + \frac{2}{16} = \frac{4}{16} = \frac{1}{4}$

---

1 Three girls run a race.
They are called Ann, Bala and Carol.

(a) Copy this table, and write down all the different orders in which they could finish. You will not need to use every line of the table.

(b) Explain why the table cannot be used to work out the probability that Ann wins.

The probability that Ann comes first is 0.52.
The probability that she comes second is 0.31.

(c) Work out the probability that she comes third.

1st	2nd	3rd

MEG 1998

2   Two dice are thrown together. One has four sides with the letters A, B, C, and D, and the other has six sides numbered from 1 to 6.

(a) Copy and complete this table to show all the possible outcomes.

+	1	2	3	4	5	6
A	A1	A2				
B	B1					
C						
D						

(b) What is the probability that you throw letter A and number 3?

(c) What is the probability that the letter is B?

(d) What is the probability that the number is greater than 4?

(e) What is the probability that the letter is either C or D, and the number is 2?

3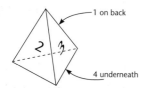
1 on back
4 underneath

A die is in the form of a regular tetrahedron with its faces marked red 1, 2, 3 and 4. The "score" is the number on the face on which the die lands.

(a) Find the probability that when this die is thrown the score is a number which is
   (i)   odd,
   (ii) prime,
   (iii) odd but not prime.

Two such tetrahedral dice, one coloured red and one coloured blue, are thrown and their scores noted.

(b) By drawing a table or otherwise, list all the possible pairs of outcomes.

(c) Find the probability
   (i)   that the sum of the two scores is 5,
   (ii) that the product of the two scores is a multiple of 4,
   (iii) that the difference between the two scores is 1.

CCEA 1998

4   Two dice are thrown and the result is obtained by adding the two numbers shown. Two sets of dice are available.

Set A: one dice has 4 faces numbered 1 to 4; the other has 8 faces, numbered 1 to 8.

Set B: both dice have 6 faces numbered from 1 to 6.

(a) Copy and complete these tables to show the possible results for each set of dice.

Set A

+	1	2	3	4	5	6	7	8
1								
2								
3								
4								

Set B

+	1	2	3	4	5	6
1						
2						
3						
4						
5						
6						

(b) In an experiment with one of the sets of dice, these results were obtained.

Dice score	Frequency
2	15
3	25
4	44
5	54
6	68
7	87
8	66
9	54
10	43
11	30
12	14

Calculate the relative frequency for each score.

(c) Which set of dice were being used? Give reasons for your answer.

5 Two counters are drawn at random from a bag containing three red, five blue and ten yellow counters. The first counter is replaced, before the second is selected.

(a) Copy and complete this tree diagram to show all the possible outcomes.

First counter	Second counter	Outcome	Probability

Red $\frac{3}{18}$ Red   Red Red $\frac{3}{18} \times \frac{3}{18} = \frac{9}{324}$

$\frac{3}{18}$ Red — Blue

Yellow

$\frac{3}{18}$

Blue

Yellow

(b) What is the probability that two blue counters will be drawn?

(c) What is the probability that one red and one yellow counter will be drawn?

(d) What is the probability that two counters of the *same* colour will be drawn?

(e) What is the probability that two counters of *different* colours will be drawn?

6 Boxes P and Q each contain five numbered balls. The balls in each box are numbered as shown.

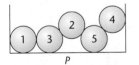

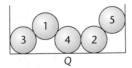

A ball is taken from each box at random.

(a) What is the probability that both balls are numbered 2?

(b) What is the probability that both balls have the same number?

(c) What is the probability that the number on the ball from box P is greater than the number on the ball from box Q?

SEG 1998

7 Lauren and Yasmina each try to score a goal. They each have one attempt.
The probability that Lauren will score a goal is 0.85.
The probability that Yasmina will score a goal is 0.6.

(a) Work out the probability that **both** Lauren **and** Yasmina will score a goal.

(b) Work out the probability that Lauren **will** score a goal **and** Yasmina **will not** score a goal.

Edexcel 1998

8 Russell and Jane are twins.
They take their driving tests.
The probability that Russell will pass is estimated to be 0.6.
The probability that Jane will pass is estimated to by 0.85.

Calculate the probability that only one of the twins passes the driving test.

NEAB 1998

MISCELLANEOUS EXERCISE

1 Martin bought a packet of mixed flower seeds. The seeds produce flowers that are Red or Blue or White or Yellow.
The probability of a flower seed producing a flower of a particular colour is:

Colour	Red	Blue	White	Yellow
Probability	0.6	0.15		0.15

(a) Write down the most common colour of a flower.

Martin chooses a flower seed at random from the packet.

(b) (i) Work out the probability that the flower produced will be White.

(ii) Write down the probability that the flower produced will be Orange.

Edexcel 1998

2 The table below shows the scores of six pupils in Paper 1 and Paper 2 of a mathematics examination.

Score in Paper 1	20	32	15	6	25	16
Score in Paper 2	14	21	11	4	15	13

(a) On graph paper with axes like these, draw a scatter diagram to show these scores.

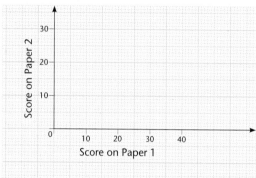

(b) Calculate the mean score of these six pupils in Paper 1.

(c) The mean score of these pupils in Paper 2 is 13. Draw a line of best fit on your scatter diagram.

(d) Judith scored 10 on Paper 1. She was absent for Paper 2. Estimate her score for Paper 2.

WJEC 1998

3 The table shows the time spent on homework in one week by the students in classes 9A, 9B and 9C.

Time spent (to nearest hour)	Number of students		
	9A	9B	9C
1	1	0	1
2	4	5	0
3	4	6	2
4	5	5	1
5	1	0	0
6	3	2	4
7	0	0	6
8	0	2	3
9	2	0	1
10	0	0	2
Total	20	20	20

(a) Write down the class which had the highest mean time.

(b) Which class had the lowest modal time?

(c) Which class's times were less spread out than the others?

(d) What was the modal time for all 60 students?

(e) What was the median time for class 9C?

SEG 1996

4 Shara collected data on the colour of different vehicles passing her home.
The table shows the results of her survey.

		Type of Vehicle				
		Car	Van	Lorry	Bus	Total
Colour of vehicle	Red	15	2	3	5	25
	Blue	9	3	2	0	14
	White	9	4	1	0	14
	Green	2	2	2	1	7
	Total	35	11	8	6	60

(a) Which colour of vehicle is the mode?

(b) Draw a pie chart to show the proportion of each type of vehicle.
Label your pie chart clearly.

SEG 1996

5 A bag contains 4 red beads and 3 blue beads.
A second bag contains 2 red beads and 8 blue beads.
Jahal takes one bead at random from each bag.

(a) Copy and complete this probability tree diagram.

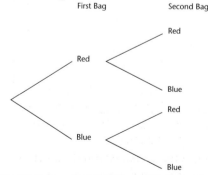

(b) Find the probability that Jahal takes
(i) two red beads,
(ii) one bead of each colour.

WJEC 1998

Nelson GCSE Maths REVISION GUIDE: HANDLING DATA (IINTERMEDIATE)

6 Medical scientists sometimes need to test anti-bacterial drugs. They use microscopes to view colonies of bacteria. Each colony shows up as a black spot. The scientists count the number of colonies in each square of a grid.

Here is a grid showing 25 squares and some colonies. This is sample 1.

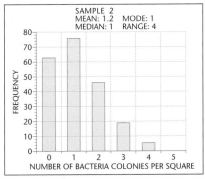

(a) Copy and complete this frequency table to show the number of colonies per square.

Number of colonies per square	Tally	Frequency
0		
1		
2		
3		
4		

(b) Calculate the mean number of colonies per square. Show your working.

(c) What is the modal number of colonies per square?

(d) Some modern microscopes count the colonies automatically. The print-out shows the results as a bar chart. It also shows the mean, mode, median and range.

Here is the print-out for Sample 2.

SAMPLE 2
MEAN: 1.2   MODE: 1
MEDIAN: 1   RANGE: 4

FREQUENCY vs NUMBER OF BACTERIA COLONIES PER SQUARE

(i) State one similarity between the two samples.

(ii) State one difference between the two samples.

MEG 1998

7 A survey was carried out in Mathstown High School to find out how long it takes the pupils to travel to school.

The results of the survey are shown in the table.

Time, t minutes, to travel to school	Number of pupils in Year 9	Number of pupils in Year 10	Number of pupils in Year 11
$0 < t \le 10$	23	15	14
$10 < t \le 20$	16	14	12
$20 < t \le 30$	9	17	19
$30 < t \le 40$	4	1	5
Totals	52	47	50

(a) (i) Use the information in the table to write down the year group which takes the longest time to travel to school.

(ii) Give a reason for your answer.

Two Year 9 pupils were absent when the survey was carried out. It takes them 26 minutes and 30 minutes to travel to school.

(b) Copy and complete this table so that it includes the times of these two pupils.

Time, t minutes, to travel to school	Number of pupils in Year 9
$0 < t \le 10$	23
$10 < t \le 20$	
$20 < t \le 30$	
$30 < t \le 40$	
Totals	54

The names of all the **Year 10** pupils in the survey are put into a bag. All the names are different. The headteacher picks one out without looking.

(c) Write down the probability that the headteacher will pick the pupil who takes over 30 minutes to travel to school.

The names of all the **Year 11** pupils in the survey are now put into another bag. All the names are different. The headteacher picks one out without looking.

(d) Write down the probability that the headteacher will pick a pupil who takes over 30 minutes to travel to school.

(e) Write down the modal interval for **Year 11** pupils.

(f) Work out an estimate for the mean time taken for **Year 11** pupils to travel to school.

Edexcel 1995

8 Julia did a survey about diet.
She thought that most young people have a healthier diet than adults.

(a) She wrote the following question for the questionnaire.
"Do you agree that young people have a healthier diet than adults?"
Give **two** reasons why this is **not** a suitable question.

Julia asked some people how many packets of crisps they ate last week.

The results were as follows.

Under 18 years old

Number of Packets	Number of people (Frequency)
0	0
1	0
2	0
3	4
4	7
5	0
6	1
7	0
8	4
Total	16

18 years and over

Number of Packets	Number of people (Frequency)
0	4
1	0
2	4
3	6
4	2
5	1
6	0
7	3
8	0
Total	20

(b) Which age group has the wider range of numbers of packets?
Give the value of this range.

(c) Which age group has the larger mode?
Give the value of this mode.

(d) Julia thought that young people eat fewer crisps than adults. The mean for the 18 years and over group is 3.0.
Calculate the mean number of packets per person, for the under 18 years old age group, to decide whether she was correct.
Explain your answer.

(e) Julia chooses one person at random from the whole group.
What is the probability that this person is under 18 years of age?

(f) (i) Julia chooses one person at random from the under 18 years old age group.
What is the probability that this person ate four packets of crisps?

(ii) Julia starts again and now chooses one person at random from each group.
What is the probability that these two people ate three packets of crisps each?

SEG 1995

9 This table shows the results of a survey at a small building merchants. It shows the weekly wage in pounds, and the age in years, for the nine employees.

Age (in years)	Weekly wage (£)
21	164
22	205
25	125
28	210
36	167
39	660
43	143
55	805
57	564

(a) Calculate the mean age of these employees.

(b) Calculate the mean weekly wage of these employees.

(c) Draw a scatter diagram of wage against age for the nine employees.

(d) On the scatter diagram, plot the point which represents the mean age and the mean weekly wage.

(e) Make two comments about this data.

10 Two fair spinners are used for a game. The scores from each spinner are added together.

For example: The total score from these two spinners is 4 + 5 = 9

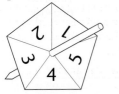 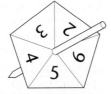

(a) Copy and complete this table to show all the possible totals for the two spinners.

	1	2	3	4	5
2	3	4			
3	4	5			
4					
5					
6					

(b) What is the probability of scoring
   (i) a total of 3?
   (ii) a total of more than 8?

(c) Tom played the game 500 times and kept a record of how many times he scored a total of 7.

He recorded his results in this table.

Number of spins	Total number of 7s	Relative frequency
first 50	13	0.26
first 100	23	0.23
first 150	27	
first 200	38	
first 500	105	

   (i) Complete the table by calculating the relative frequencies for 150 spins, 200 spins and 500 spins.

   (ii) Which of these relative frequency results gives the best estimate of the probability of scoring a total of 7? Give a reason for your answer.

NEAB 1998

11 The cumulative frequency graph gives information about the heights of 120 students.

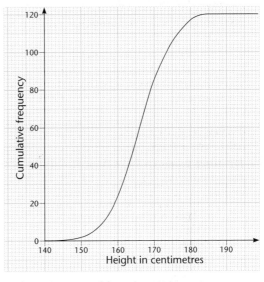

(a) Estimate the median height.
(b) Estimate the inter-quartile range.
(c) Estimate the number of students whose height was over 172 cm.
(d) What is the probability of a student chosen at random having a height between 160 cm and 170 cm?

MEG 1996

12 The probability that a washing machine will break down in the first 5 years of use is 0.27. The probability that a television will break down in the first 5 years of use is 0.17. Mr. Khan buys a washing machine and a television on the same day.

(a) Calculate the probability that, in the five years after that day, the television will NOT break down.

(b) Calculate the probability that, in the five years after that day, both the washing machine and the television will break down.

Edexcel 1998

Nelson GCSE Maths   REVISION GUIDE: HANDLING DATA (IINTERMEDIATE)

13 A radar detector has measured the speeds of 81 cars on a motorway.

Speed (s m.p.h.)	Frequency
$50 \leq s < 55$	2
$55 \leq s < 60$	8
$60 \leq s < 65$	11
$65 \leq s < 70$	34
$70 \leq s < 75$	21
$75 \leq s < 80$	5

A further nine cars have their speeds (in m.p.h.) measured as 63, 75, 66, 77, 54, 79, 75, 65, and 68.

(a) Copy the frequency table, amending it to include the further nine cars.

(b) Calculate the mean speed of the 90 cars.

(c) Draw up a table to show the cumulative frequencies.

(d) Use your table to draw a cumulative frequency graph for the data.

(e) From your graph, estimate
 (i) the median speed for the 90 cars
 (ii) the interquartile range for the speeds
 (iii) the probability that the next car whose speed is measured will be travelling at speed greater than 70 m.p.h.

14 A survey is made of all 120 houses on an estate. The floor area, in m², of each house is recorded. The results are shown in the cumulative frequency table.

Floor area (x) in M²	Cumulative freqency
$0 < x \leq 100$	4
$0 < x \leq 150$	20
$0 < x \leq 200$	49
$0 < x \leq 250$	97
$0 < x \leq 300$	114
$0 < x \leq 350$	118
$0 < x \leq 400$	120

(a) On a grid like this, draw a cumulative frequency graph for the table.

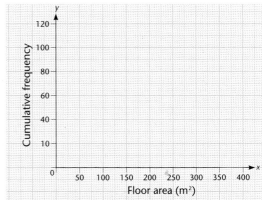

(b) Use your cumulative frequency graph to estimate the inter-quartile range of the floor areas of the houses.

The houses on the estate with the greatest floor areas are called luxury houses. 10% of the houses are luxury houses.

(c) Use your graph to estimate the minimum floor area for a luxury house.

Edexcel 1997

COURSE REVISION EXERCISES

1 Put these numbers in order of size, smallest first.
60.4   6.532   0.657

2 A family packet of Crunchy Crispies weighs
500 g and costs £1.20.

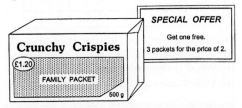

(a) Crunchy Crispies contain nuts and cornflakes.
The nuts and cornflakes are mixed by weight
in the ratio 1:3.
What is the weight of the nuts in each
family packet?
(b) Sally gets three family packets of Crunchy
Crispies at the special offer price.
What is the cost per kilogram of these
Crunchy Crispies?
(c) The contents of each family packet is given
to the nearest 10 g.
What is the minimum weight of one of
these packets?

SEG 1996

3 (a) The mass of an electron is
0.000 000 000 000 000 000 000 000 000 91 g.
Express this mass in standard form.
(b) The 1971 census recorded 48.8 million
people in England and Wales, living in
16.5 million households.
Estimate the mean number of people per
household.

4 In prime factors, $9801 = 11^2 \times a^4$.
(a) Find the value of a.
(b) 9801 is a square number. Show how to use
its factors to find its square root.

5 (a) Complete this sentence for this rectangle:
The length is ... times the width.

(b) The perimeter is 40 cm.
(i) Write an equation for x.
(ii) Use your equation to find the length
and the width.

(c) A similar rectangle has an area of 48 cm².

(i) Write an equation for x in this case.
(ii) Use your equation to find the length
and the width.

6 (a) In a survey, some 14-year-olds are going to
be asked this question.

How long did you spend watching
television last weekend?

Design an observation sheet suitable for
collecting their answers.

(b) Here are the results of a survey of thirty 16-
year-olds about which television channel
they had watched most during the previous
week.

BBC1	BBC2	ITV	CH4
9	1	15	5

Draw a pie chart to illustrate this data.

7 For the formula $d = 3a - 15$
(a) find d when $a = 2$
(b) make a the subject of the formula

8 (a) Simplify these.
(i) $a^3 \times a^4$ (ii) $t^5 \div t^2$
(b) (i) Simplify $4x + 3 - x$.
(ii) Multiply out $3(2b - 4)$.
(iii) Find the missing numbers in
$?(2p + ?) = 10p + 35$.

9 Draw graphs to find where the lines
$3x + 2y = 12$ and $2y = x - 6$ intersect.

10

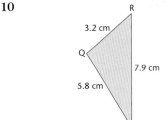

(a) Two triangles, congruent to PQR, are put
together to form a kite.
Using ruler and compasses, make an
accurate drawing to show this.

(b) Construct the perpendicular from Q to PR
using ruler and compasses only.
Measure this height

(c) Use the height found in part (b) to calculate
the area of the kite.

(d) In a sketch, show how kites must be placed
so that they tessellate.

1 Put these numbers in order of size, with the smallest first.

1.3   -0.6   -1.2   -1.7   0.72

2 Fill in these boxes.
   (a) ☐ × ☐ = −12   (b) ☐ × ☐ × ☐ = −36
   (c) ☐ ÷ ☐ = −6

3 Work out these.
   (a) $\frac{3}{4} \times \frac{2}{3} + \frac{1}{5}$ (b) $\frac{2}{5} \div \frac{1}{10}$

4 The speed of light is 3×10^8 m/s^1. The Earth is about 149 million kilometres from the Sun. How long does it take light to come from the Sun to the Earth?

5 Josie bought a mountain bike costing £565 in January 1993.
   By January 1994 the value had depreciated by 20%.
   By January 1995 it had depreciated by 15% of the January 1994 value.
   She sold the bike at the January 1995 value.
   (a) What was the selling price of the bike?
   (b) Express her loss as a percentage of the cost price of the bike.

   CCEA 1996

6 Solve these.
   (a) $4(x - 3) = 28$ (b) $2x + 6 < 28$
   (c) $(x + 4)(x - 7) = 0$

7 (a) List all the possible outcomes when a fair coin and a fair dice are tossed together.
   (b) What is the probability of a head with an even number?
   (c) What is the probability of a tail with a score of five or more?

8 Use trial and improvement to find, correct to 1 d.p., the solution of $x^2 - 5x = 8$ that is close to 6.

9 This diagram shows the shape of the inside of a garage.

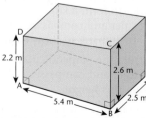

   (a) Make a scale drawing of ABCD, using a scale of 1cm to represent 0.5 m.
   Measure ∠ADC.

   (b) Use trigonometry to calculate the angle between the vertical CB and the sloping edge CD.
   (c) Find the capacity of the garage.

10 Students in a class found out how many uncles each of them had.

Number of uncles	0	1	2	3	4	5
Frequency	15	9	3	8	3	2

   (a) What is the modal number of uncles?
   (b) What is the median number of uncles?
   (c) What is the mean number of uncles?
   (d) Which average best represents this data?

1 (a) Work out $2000 \div 0.04$.
   (b) Estimate, to 1 s.f., $\frac{0.83}{0.0241} \times \frac{57.1}{2.9}$.

2 A 500-g pack of cereal has been made 12% taller for a special offer '15% extra free'.
   (a) What is the new amount in the packet?
   (b) The taller packet is 28 cm tall. How tall is the usual packet?

3 Calculate these, and give your answer in standard form.
   (a) $(2.5 \times 10^{13}) \times (3 \times 10^5)$
   (b) $(4.5 \times 10^8) \div (1.5 \times 10^4)$

4 (a) The winning jump in a triple jump competition was measured as 14.93 m, to the nearest 0.01 m. What is the shortest distance the jump could have been?
   (b) The jump of the competitor coming second was given as 14.92 m to the nearest 0.01 m. Was the awarding of places correct?

5 (a) Solve this.
   $2x + 5 = 3x + 1$
   (b) Solve these simultaneous equations.
   $2x + 3y = 18$
   $3x + y = 13$
   (c) Find the whole numbers for which $x^2 < 9$.

6 Use the formula $r = \frac{s}{10} - 14$ to find the value of
   (a) r, when $s = 95$ (b) s, when $r = -4$

7 (a) Simplify these.
   (i) $(5t)^3$
   (ii) $\frac{w^8 \times w^5}{w^4}$
   (b) (i) Simplify $8 - 2(p + 1)$.
   (ii) Multiply out $2t(3t + 2)$.

8 Jenny cycles to school each day.
The graph shows her journey from home to school.
On the way she stops to talk to her friends.

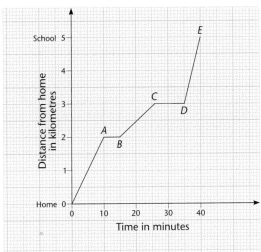

(a) How many times does she stop to talk to her friends?
(b) (i) How far does she travel in the first stage from home to A?
(ii) What is her average speed over the first ten minutes?
Give your answer in kilometres per hour.
(c) On which stage of the journey is her average speed the fastest?

NEAB 1998

9 (a) The direct distance between Niton church and The Pepper Pot on a map is 5.0 cm. The scale on the map is 1:25 000. What is the real distance? Give your answer in kilometres.
(b) On the map, the Hoy monument is 9.0 cm away from the church on a bearing of 333°. The bearing of The Pepper Pot from the church is 294°.
Draw an accurate diagram of what the map shows for Niton Church, The Pepper Pot and the Hoy monument.
(c) From your diagram, find the bearing of the Pepper Pot from the Hoy monument.
(d) Part of the walk from the church to these two places goes up a steep path. It rises 45 m for about 300 m. What is the gradient of the path?

10 This table shows the heights of seedling fir trees.

Height(cm)	20–25	25–30	30–35	35–40	40–45	45–50	50–55	55–60	Total
Number	3	17	24	30	22	23	11	5	135

(a) Draw a cumulative frequency diagram for this data.
(b) Find an estimate of the median height from your graph.
(c) From your graph, find the interquartile range.
(d) What percentage of the seedlings were 48 cm, or more, tall?
(e) Another type of seedling had a median height of 42 cm, and an interquartile range of 10 cm by the same age. Which type would be better to choose to make a hedge?

EXERCISE 4

1 (a) In a class of 32 students, 24 of them have passed their Bronze certificate for rock climbing. What percentage of the class is this?
(b) In another class of 30 students, four-fifths have passed. How many is that?

2 (a) (i) Calculate the value of 3^4.
(ii) Give the fraction that is 3^{-2}.
(iii) Write $\frac{1}{27}$ as a power of 3.
(b) $72 = 2^3 \times 3^2$
(i) Write 972 as the product of its prime factors.
(ii) What is the highest common factor of 72 and 972?

3 The average distance from the Sun of the asteroid, Juno, is 247 800 000 miles.
(a) Write this distance in standard form.
(b) The orbit round the Sun is roughly circular. Find the distance Juno travels in one orbit. Give your answer in standard form, correct to 3 s.f.

4 Complete these boxes.
(a) $\boxed{} \div \boxed{} = 0$
(b) $\boxed{} + \boxed{} = 0$
(c) $\boxed{} \times \boxed{} = 0$

5 (a) Write down the next two numbers in these sequences.
(i) 3, 6, 9, 12, ..., ...
(ii) 2, 5, 8, 11, ..., ...
(iii) 3, 7, 11, 15, ..., ...
(b) Find an expression for the nth number in each sequence.

(c) The number 99 is in the first and third sequences, but not in the second. What is its position in the first sequence? What is its position in the third sequence? Why is it *not* in the second sequence?

6 (a) Multiply out $3x(2x + 5)$.
  (b) Use the formula $v = u + at$ to work out v, given $u = 5$, $a = 3$, and $t = 10$.
  (c) Make t the subject of this formula: $v = u + at$.

7 (a) Complete this table of values for $y = x^2 + 5$.

x	-2	-1	0	1	2
y		6			

  (b) Draw the graph of $y = x^2 + 5$ for values of x between -2 and 2. Use 1 cm for 1 unit on each axis.
  (c) From your graph, find when $x^2 + 5 = 7$.

8 Calculate the height of this kite above the ground.

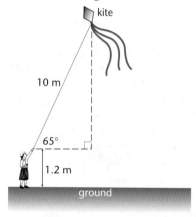

9 Calculate the size of angles p and q. Give reasons for your answers.

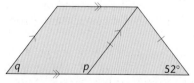

10 In a bag, there are 12 coloured beads: 5 are red and the rest are white. One bead is taken out, at random, and its colour noted. Then it is replaced. This is then repeated.
  (a) Draw a tree diagram, showing the outcomes and probabilities for this situation.
  (b) What is the probability that the first bead is red and the second is white?
  (c) What is the probability that the two beads are the *same* colour?

EXERCISE 5

1 One night at a school concert the audience is made up as follows:

> $\frac{1}{4}$ are men, $\frac{3}{5}$ are women, and the rest are children.

  (a) (i) What percentage of the audience are women?
     (ii) What fraction of the audience are children?

  (b) The next night the audience is made up in the following ratio:

> men : women : children = 2 : 4 : 3.

There are 270 people in the audience. Calculate the number of men.

NEAB 1997

2 (a) Write the number that is halfway between 5 million and 5 600 000.
  (b) Write these numbers in standard form.
     (i) 35 000 000   (ii) 0.000 634

3 (a) Write down the cube root of 125.
  (b) Use your answer to part (a) to work out the cube roots of
     (i) 0.125   (ii) 125 000

4 (a) Joanne wants to work out $58 \times 12 \div 143$ on her calculator. She starts by making an estimate **without using her calculator**. Write down a calculation that Joanne could use to make her estimate.
  (b) All six faces of this cuboid are to be painted. There is enough paint to cover 5 m².

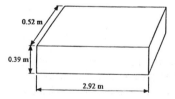

Covers 5 m²

Not to scale

Estimate whether there is enough paint. Show all your working clearly.

SEG 1996

5 Here are some instructions.

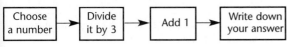

Choose a number → Divide it by 3 → Add 1 → Write down your answer

(a) If you start with 27, what is your answer?
(b) If the answer is 19, what was the chosen number?
(c) If the chosen number is c, write an expression for the answer.

6 (a) A mistake has been made in this table for a straight-line graph. Find the mistake, and work out the correct value.

x	−2	−1	0	1	2
y	−5	−4	1	4	7

(b) Find the gradient of the line.
(c) Find the equation of the line.

7 (a) Simplify these.

(i) $\dfrac{a^2 \times a^7}{a^5}$

(ii) $3(2x - 1) - 2x$
(iii) $2t \times (5t)^2$

(b) Factorise and solve the equation $x^2 - x - 12 = 0$.

8 (a) Copy this diagram.

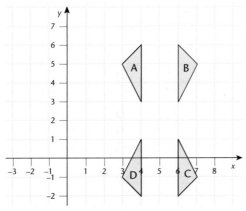

(i) Draw in the mirror line needed for reflecting shape A on to shape B.
(ii) Draw in the mirror line needed for reflecting shape B on to shape C.

(b) What are the equations of the mirror lines drawn in part (a)?
(c) Describe completely the transformation which maps shape B on to shape D.
(d) Translate shape A by $\binom{-5}{0}$. Label the image E. What are the coordinates of the three corners of the image triangle?

(e) What transformation maps shape B to shape E?
(f) What further transformations are needed to complete this pattern?

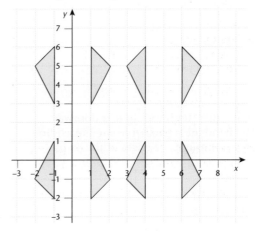

9 (a) What size is each exterior angle of a regular decagon?
(b) An octagon has interior angles x, $3x$, $1.5x$, $2x$, $1.5x$, $2x$, $4x$ and x. Find the size of the two smallest angles.

10 A bag contains 20 cubes. Jenny has conducted an experiment in which one cube was taken at random each time. These are her results.

Colour	Blue	Yellow	Purple
Frequency	205	94	201

(a) Estimate the number of blue cubes in the bag. Give reasons for your estimate.
(b) If the experiment had been carried out 200 times, how many times might you expect the yellow cube to appear?

EXERCISE 6

1 To make 10 litres of a shade of green paint, 6 litres of yellow are mixed with 4 litres of blue.
(a) How much yellow paint is needed, if you want 15 litres of this green paint?
(b) How much blue is needed, if you are using 21 litres of yellow?

2 A 12% deposit is paid when ordering a sofa. The amount paid for the deposit is £84. What is the full price of the sofa?

3 The Jurassic period lasted from 204 million years ago to 130 million years ago. Write how long this was, in standard form.

4 This model is made from six cubes. It is rolled over to rest on its shaded face. Draw the new position on isometric dot paper.

5 Four equal steps lead up to a doorway. The handrail is parallel to the dotted line drawn through the edges of the steps.

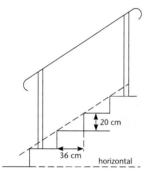

(a) Calculate, to the nearest degree, the angle which the handrail makes with the horizontal.

On one side of the steps is a ramp for wheelchair access.

The ramp makes an angle of 4.5° with the horizontal.

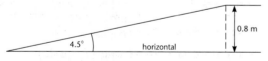

(b) Calculate the length of the ramp, correct to 3 significant figures.

CCEA 1996

6 Here are some patterns made with sticks.

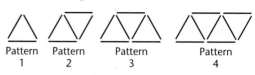

Pattern 1   Pattern 2   Pattern 3   Pattern 4

(a) How many sticks are used in Pattern 8?
(b) How many sticks are used in Pattern 20?
(c) Find a formula for the number of sticks, s, used to make Pattern n.
(d) If 75 sticks have been used, which pattern is it?

7 (a) Simplify these.
    (i) $5(2x + 4) - 3x$
    (ii) $2y^2 \times (3y)^3$
(b) Solve these simultaneous equations.
$$2x + 5y = 21$$
$$3x - 2y = -16$$

8 In this square-based pyramid, each of the triangular faces are right-angled triangles.

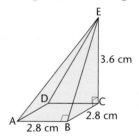

(a) Draw a net for the pyramid. Measure lengths BE and AE.
(b) Use Pythagoras' rule to check the length of BE by calculation.
(c) Calculate the surface area of the pyramid.

9 (a) Factorise $x^2 + 2x - 15$.
(b) Hence, solve the equation $x^2 + 2x - 15 = 0$.

10 A small factory has 200 employees, and the yearly wages are as shown in this table.

Wage (£)	6000–8400	8400–10800	10800–13200	18000	24000	36000	60000
Number	112	35	15	24	9	4	1

(a) Calculate the mean wage.
(b) State the mode.
(c) In which group does the median lie?
(d) Which form of average would you use if you were
    (i) a union official bargaining for a pay rise?
    (ii) the managing director?

SELECTED ANSWERS

1 FURTHER METHODS OF COMPUTATION

EXERCISE 15   P13

1 (a) 30 times   (b) 8.3×10^5 square miles
  (c) 3.275×10^7 square miles.

2 (a) 100 people/square kilometre
  (b) 3240 people/square kilometre
  (c) 5.76×10^7 people

3 (a) Heka   (b) 4 times greater
  (c) 1430 light years   (d) 4×10^{14} km

4 3.9×10^{13} km

5 (a) 5.9×10^{21} tons   (b) 2.4×10^{19} tons

6 2.8×10^2 m

EXERCISE 16   P15

1 (a) Yes   (b) £1 = 9.2fr
  (c) 460fr   (d) £45

2 (a) £5   (b) £13
  (c) No: if you double the francs you do not
      double the £ because of the £3 handling
      charge

3 No, because of the tax allowance: if she doubles
  her earnings she does not double her tax

4 (b) Yes: the graph is approximately a straight
      line passing through (0, 0)

5 No

6 220 people

7 £53.20

8 £22.50

9 37.5 miles

10 £129.90

EXERCISE 17   P18

1 (a) 2, 80, 1.2, 120
  (c) Because speed × time is a constant (= 120)

2 (a) 36 hours
  (b) 12 hours

3 (a)

4	5	6	12	11
30	24	20	10	10

(b) The number of books is *not* inversely
    proportional to the cost of each book
    because you do not always obtain the
    same product. This can be seen by looking
    at the case when the books cost £11 each.
    You can only buy 10 books; it is not
    possible to buy part of a book.

4 (a) Graph B   (b) Graph A

3 ALGEBRAIC MANIPULATION

EXERCISE 1   P41

1 720

2 24

3 27

4 (a) 3.87   (b) 2.51

5 (a) 9.76   (b) 4.33

6 (a) 1   (b) 2

7 (a) 3   (b) 18

8 (a) 4   (b) –1.5

9 (a) 16   (b) 14

10 (a) $\frac{2}{3}$ (b) $3\frac{1}{3}$

11 (a) 10   (b) 40

12 (a) 13.5   (b) 2

4 STATISTICS AND PROBABILITY

EXERCISE 5   P56

1 (a) 60–64%   (b) 58%   (c) 56%

2 (a) 0–14 days (b) 10 days (c) 14 days

3 31 years

4 95 minutes

EXERCISE 7   P60

1 Median: 63°F

  IQR = 67° – 59° = 8°F

2 (a) Median is about 0.8 miles
  (b) Range is 7.5 miles – 0 miles = 7.5 miles
      IQR = 1.3 miles – 0.5 mile = 0.8 mile
  (c) 0.6 or $\frac{3}{5}$
  (d) 120 students

(e) 75 students

3 (a) About 62%   (b) D
   (c) About 65%–85%   (d) 0.25

4 (a) A: 2.2 hours; B: 2.1 hours
   (b) A: 2.7 hours –1.7 hours = 1 hour
        B: 2.3 hours –1.8 hours = 0.5 hour
   (c) Batteries have a similar average life; type B
        is more consistent, perhaps

5 (a) Cumulative frequency figures are:
        37, 57, 92, 132, 173, 197, 212, 221, 224
   (c) 7 months
   (d) IQR = $6\frac{1}{2}$ months
   (e) $\frac{27}{224}$ = 0.12

6 (b) Median is 137 pupils; IQR is about 83
   (c) 10 schools
   (d) 225 pupils

7

	Median	IQR
Males	£13 500	£7000
Females	£9000	£6000

Wages of females have a similar spread to
those of males but are considerably less

EXERCISE 10   P68

1 (a) 0.85   (b) 0.68   (c) 0.29

2 (a) $\frac{7}{16}$ (b) $\frac{3}{16}$ (c) $\frac{13}{16}$

3 (a) 0.4   (b) 0.28   (c) 0.24

4 (a) $\frac{1}{6}$ (b) $\frac{3}{4}$ (c) $\frac{2}{9}$ (d) $\frac{1}{6}$

5 (a) $\frac{1}{4}$ (b) $\frac{1}{4}$ (c) $\frac{1}{8}$ (d) $\frac{3}{8}$
   (e) $\frac{1}{2}$

6 (a) (i) 0.4225   (ii) 0.455
   (b) (i) $0.35^2 = 0.043$ (ii) $1 - 0.65^2 = 0.73$

7 (a) $\frac{2}{25}$ (b) $\frac{3}{25}$

8 $\frac{5}{96}$

6 MEASURES REVISITED

EXERCISE 3   P88

1 (a) 400 cm³   (b) 0.75 g/cm³

2 (a) 290 cm³   (b) 0.43 g/cm³

3 0.92 g/cm³

4 (a) 2270 cm³   (b) 0.20 g/cm³

5 0.33 g/cm³

6 1.4 g/cm³

7 0.59 g/cm³

8 (b) 1000 g
   (c) Golden syrup, jam, lemon curd
   (d) Highest: golden syrup (1.3 g/cm³);
        lowest: cocoa (0.47 g/cm³)
   (e) About 165 ml
   (f) About 140 ml

9 140 ml

10 720 ml

11 1 kg

12 2.6 cm³

13 550 g

14 8.1 cm

15 10.2 cm

EXERCISE 7   PAGE 97

1 North 68 km, East 134 km

2 South 61 km, East 22 km

3 236°

4 125°

5 (a) 90°   (b) 20 km

6 (a) 90°   (b) 9.9 km

7 (a) 90°   (b) 053°

8 (a) 90°   (b) 60°
   (c) 5.2 km   (d) 6 km

9 (a) 90°   (b) 68°   (c) 157°

10 (a) 86 km   (b) 29 km   (c) 90 km

EXERCISE 8   PAGE 98

1 A: 5.4 cm²   B: 3.9 cm²   C: 3.1 cm²

2 A: 5.2 cm²   B: 4.8 cm²   C: 7.5 cm²

3 A: 13.6 cm² B: 14.3 cm² C: 6.9 cm²

4 44 cm²

5 (a) 19.7 cm² (b) 18.1 cm² (c) 17.7 cm²

6 11.5 cm

ANSWERS TO REVISION GUIDE EXERCISES

N1: PLACE VALUE AND ORDERING WHOLE NUMBERS, DECIMALS AND FRACTIONS

1 (a) 24 100 (b) 15 000 (c) 0.304

2 (a) 304.3 (b) 0.096 (c) 0.000 768

3 0.003 597, 0.085, 0.09, 0.1, 1.98, 2.7

4 $\frac{1}{8}, \frac{1}{4}, \frac{3}{8}, \frac{1}{2}, \frac{5}{8}, \frac{3}{4}, \frac{7}{8}$

5 A: 13.1, 13.2, 13.3, 13.4, 13.5, 13.6, 13.7, 13.8, 13.9

   B: 22.5, 25, 27.5

   C: 3.62, 3.64, 3.66, 3.68

6 (a) 100 (b) 0.002 15 (c) 1410 (d) 98.5

7 (a) 5.04 (b) 14 (c) 5040 (d) 0.36

8 (a) 17.576 (b) 260 (c) 26

N2: ROUNDING NUMBERS

1 (a) 4.37 (b) 29.09 (c) 13.80
   (d) 3.56 (e) 10.00 (f) −4.01
   (g) 45.00 (h) −7.90

2 (a) 18 000 (b) 24 cm (c) 50 seconds
   (d) 460 g (e) 0.18 days
   (f) 18 000 million tons
   (g) 5000 miles (h) 0.000 39 g

3 (a) 13 000 (b) 13 000

4 (a) 4510 (b) 4500
   (c) 5000 (d) 4510.0

N3: EQUIVALENCE OF FRACTIONS, DECIMALS AND PERCENTAGES

1 $\frac{25}{64}$; rest all equal to $\frac{5}{8}$

2 Hiate: 60%; Jason: 66.7%; Petra: 65%
   Jason scored the highest

3

Fraction	Decimal	Percentage
$\frac{4}{5}$	0.8	80%
$\frac{1}{3}$	0.$\dot{3}$	$33\frac{1}{3}$%
$\frac{9}{20}$	0.45	45%
$\frac{1}{8}$	0.125	12.5%
$\frac{6}{25}$	0.24	24%
$\frac{2}{25}$	0.08	8%

4 (a) $\frac{18}{25}$ (b) Spain (c) 36 000 000

5 $\frac{2}{3}, \frac{11}{16}, \frac{7}{10}, \frac{3}{4}$

6 $\frac{2}{8}$ = 0.25, $\frac{3}{15}$ = 20%

7 (a) 0.75, 0.57, 0.64, 1.40, 1.67, 0.70, 0.69, 1.44
   (b) $\frac{4}{7}, \frac{7}{11}, \frac{9}{13}, \frac{7}{10}, \frac{3}{4}, \frac{7}{5}, \frac{13}{9}, \frac{5}{3}$

8 22%, 0.227, $\frac{7}{27}$, 27%, $\frac{2}{7}, \frac{7}{22}$, 77%, $2\frac{2}{7}$, 2.7, $\frac{22}{7}$

N4: NEGATIVE NUMBERS

1 9°C

2 (a) 1 (b) None

3 (a) 2 (b) −39 (c) −8 (d) 21
   (e) −37 (f) 9 (g) −9 (h) −37

4 (a) −12 (b) 48 (c) −4 (d) 5
   (e) 36 (f) −8 (g) −5 (h) $\frac{1}{8}$

5 (a) (i) Many possibilities
       (ii) Many possibilities
   (b) −28

6 (a) 4 (b) −20 (c) 5
   (d) E.g. 5, −3 (e) −3 (f) E.g. −8, 4
   (g) E.g. 1, 1, −1

7 (a) (i) −6 (ii) 3
   (b) 18
   (c) (i) −18 (ii) 8

N5: MULTIPLES, FACTORS AND PRIMES

1 (a) Any six from 1, 4, 9, 16, 25, 36, 49
   (b) Any six from 2, 3, 5, 7, 11, 13, 17, 19, 23, 29, 31, 37, 41, 43, 47
   (c) Any six from 6, 12, 18, 24, 30, 36, 42, 48
   (d) Any six from 1, 2, 3, 4, 6, 8, 12, 16, 24, 48
   (e) Only five of the factors of 50 are less than 50 (1, 2, 5, 10, 25)

2 (a) $36 = 2^2 \times 3^2$, $56 = 2^3 \times 7$, $54 = 2 \times 3^3$
   (b) 4 (c) 18 (d) 2

3 (a) 14 (b) 140

4 (a) 72 (b) 1001

5 (a) 2 (b) 16 (c) 24 (d) 25

N6: POWERS, ROOTS AND RECIPROCALS

1 (a) 16   (b) 64   (c) 200   (d) 81
   (e) 7   (f) 5   (g) 216   (h) 72

2 (a) 625   (b) 2   (c) 1

3 (a) 7   (b) 1   (c) 0.25   (d) 0.04

4 (a) a^4 (b) $15b^6$ (c) $8c^4$ (d) $6d^4$ (e) 16

5 (a) 0.2   (b) 4   (c) 0.5   (d) 1.6
   (e) 1.5   (f) 0.4   (g) 1.25   (h) 0.8

6 (a) 2   (b) 5   (c) 4   (d) 2
   (e) 3   (f) 4   (g) 4   (h) 6

N7: INDEX NOTATION AND STANDARD FORM

1 (a) 5.73×10^4 (b) 9.056×10^{-3}
   (c) 2.5×10^7 (d) 1.5×10^5

2 (a) 356 000   (b) 0.000 208
   (c) 3 768 000   (d) 0.008

3 (a) 6.9×10^5 (b) 6×10^5
   (c) 3.5×10^{12} (d) 3×10^{10}
   (e) 1.6×10^{15} (f) 1.6×10^8
   (g) 3×10^3 (h) 5×10^3

4 (a) 1.5×10^9 (b) 7.2×10^{-1}
   (c) 7×10^1 (d) 6×10^2
   (e) 6.09×10^5 (f) 2.98×10^4

5 (a) (i) 2.1×10^3 (ii) $2^2 \times 3 \times 5^2 \times 7$
   (b) 3.43×10^{20}

6 (a) $2.79 \times 10^{-6}\,\text{cm}^2$ (b) $1.024 \times 10^{-2}\,\text{cm}$

7 5.18×10^2

8 (a) 1.1×10^9 litres of water
   (b) 4.2×10^{11} litres of water

9 Europe: 0.65; Asia: 0.68; so, Asia has the larger population density

10 (a) $2.3 \times 10^8\,\text{km}$ (b) 1:389
   (c) 7.04×10^{13} miles

N8: ARITHMETIC WITH WHOLE NUMBERS (WITHOUT A CALCULATOR)

1 (a) 896   (b) 3713   (c) 12 508

2 (a) 26 r 2   (b) 12 r 14   (c) 10 r 43

3 (a) 23.08   (b) 14.90   (c) 7.98

4 28p

5 142 bottles

6 (a) 15 pieces   (b) 25 cm

7 667 people

8 8 coaches

9 (a) 530 400 lire   (b) £17

N9: THE FOUR RULES OF DECIMALS

1 (a) 12.15   (b) 22.001
   (c) 26.02   (d) 22.528

2 (a) 0.16   (b) 23   (c) 120   (d) 30

3 (a) 0.9   (b) 32.5   (c) 23.94   (d) 14.44

4 (a) 1.45   (b) 0.78   (c) 16.25   (d) 0.29

5 £10.55

6 (a) 6 g   (b) 2.8 g

7 (a) 133.9 cm   (b) 350 inches

8 (a) $d = 46$ cm
   (b) She cannot reach the top shelf
   (c) 250 disabled people

N10: THE FOUR RULES OF FRACTIONS

1 (a) 135   (b) 65   (c) 0.24   (d) $1\frac{1}{2}$

2 (a) $\frac{4}{5}$ (b) $\frac{1}{5}$ (c) 400 students

3 (a) $\frac{1}{40}$ (b) 75 women

4 (a) $4\frac{1}{12}$ (b) $7\frac{1}{2}$ (c) $2\frac{5}{8}$ (d) $1\frac{7}{12}$

5 (a) 8   (b) $21\frac{2}{3}$ (c) 3   (d) $1\frac{9}{10}$

N11: PERCENTAGES

1 (a) 45p   (b) £7.20   (c) 75p   (d) £6
   (e) £6   (f) £5.60

2 76%

3 16 employees

4 (a) 90p
   (b) Sirloin steak 25%; rump steak 17%; so, sirloin steak has the biggest percentage reduction

5 (a) £5.32   (b) 44%

6 £71.62

7 (a) 58%   (b) 80%   (c) 58%

8 (a) 17 820 pairs   (b) 10 522 pairs

9 (a) £61.80   (b) $1.07^3 = 1.225\,043$

10 (a) £17.10   (b) £31

N12: RATIO AND PROPORTION

1 (a) 125 ml water
 (b) 240 ml concentrated orange

2 (a) 24 matches (b) 81 points

3 (a) 25 g butter (b) 105 g caster sugar

4 The large tin is better value (14.3 g per penny compared with 13.9 g per penny)

5 Medium: 5.2 g per penny; large: 5.1 g per penny

6 66.7%

7 (a) 37.5 cm (b) 25 cm

8 9 hours working, 6 hours resting, 7.5 hours sleeping, 1.5 hours eating

9 (a) 13.44 m^2 (b) 17.5 cm by 14 cm

10 (a) 2.64 (b) 178 kg
 (c) Ruthi, because lifts 213 kg rather than 178 kg (or 213 ÷ 67.5 = 3.16 > 2.64)

11 (i) $y = 3\sqrt{x}$ (ii) $x = 4$

12 4.72 kg

N13: ORDER OF OPERATIONS

1 (a) 3 (b) 40 (c) 13 (d) 56 (e) 5 (f) $\frac{1}{2}$

2 (a) $4 \times (3 + 2)$ (b) $4 \times (5 - 2) \times 2$
 (c) $36 \div (3 + 2 \times 3)$ (d) $(36 \div 3 + 2) \times 3$

3 $1 - 2 + 3 - 4 + 5 = 3$, $1 - 2 \times 3 + 4 + 5 = 4$,
 $1 \times 2 \times 3 + 4 - 5 = 5$, $1 - 2 + 3 \times 4 - 5 = 6$,
 $1 + 2 + 3 - 4 + 5 = 7$, $1 \times 2 - 3 + 4 + 5 = 8$,
 $1 \times 2 \times (3 + 4) - 5 = 9$, $(1 + 2) \div 3 + 4 + 5 = 10$

N14: EFFICIENT USE OF A CALCULATOR

1 2.76 2 86.7

3 3.03 4 4990

5 6.25 6 −0.279

N15: ESTIMATION AND APPROXIMATION

Answers to this exercise may vary.

1 (a) 8000 (b) 30 (c) 2
 (d) 4 (e) 5 (f) 1

2 No, answer is about 6

3 No, she should get just over 80 francs for every £10 – more like 1000 francs

4 About £20

5 (a) 1500 ÷ 30 = 50 (b) 46.5

6 (a) 40 000
 (b) $\dfrac{2 \times 10^6}{500 \times \sqrt{1}} = \dfrac{200\,0000}{500} = \dfrac{20\,000}{5} = 4000$
 So Jameed is wrong.
 (c) 3883.185 (or more accurate figures)

MISCELLANEOUS EXERCISE

1 (a) (i) 1000 (ii) 100 000
  (iii) 100 (iv) 0.002 15
  (v) 0.0008
 (b) (i) 8 (ii) 8000 000
  (iii) 2 (iv) 20
  (v) 0.000 008 (vi) 0.2

2 (a) 0.04, $\frac{8}{25}$, 35%, $\frac{2}{5}$
 (b) (i) 0.2 (ii) 10 (iii) 1.5 (iv) 0.8

3 (a) (i) (±)35°C (ii) (±)4°C
 (b) (±)4°C
 (c) −7°C

4 £90, £150 and £210

5 (a) 5270 400 seconds
 (b) E.g. 60 × 20 × 60 × 60 = 4320 000

6 (a) 80 adults (b) 20 boys
 (c) 48 men (d) $\frac{17}{40}$

7 (a) £2000 000 (b) £1600 000
 (c) £50 000 (d) 12 500

8 (a) p = 4 (b) $72 = 2^3 \times 3^2$
 (c) 24 (d) 144

9 (a) $5\frac{1}{2}$ (b) $1\frac{7}{12}$ (c) 6 (d) 6

10 (a) £170 (b) £199.75

11 (a) 1.6×10^6 (b) 3.2×10^{12}
  (c) 5 or 5×10^0 (d) 2×10^{-1}
  (e) 4.8×10^6 (f) 3.2×10^6

12 £36

13 (a) (i) £5.55 (ii) £44.86 or £44.87
 (b) (i) £320 (ii) £4700

14 (a) 2.4 m (b) 1.92 m
 (c) 4 bounces

15 (a) 1.86284×10^5
   (b) (i) 43 minutes
      (ii) 500 million seconds ÷ 200 000 =
         2500 seconds = 40 minutes

A1: ALGEBRA FOR FUNCTIONS

1 Multiply by 3 and add 2; $n \rightarrow 3n + 2$
   Subtract from 12; $n \rightarrow 12 - n$

2 $1 \rightarrow 2, 4 \rightarrow 14, -2 \rightarrow -10, 3 \rightarrow 10$
   $3 \rightarrow 6, 1 \rightarrow 0, -1 \rightarrow 2, 2 \rightarrow 2$

3 (a) -13 (b) $2n - 3$

4 (a) $n \rightarrow 4n - 3$ (b) $n \rightarrow 3(n - 4)$

5 (a) 31   (b) -17

6 $C = L^2 + 1$

A2: LINEAR SEQUENCES

1 (a) 21, 25   (b) Add on four
   (c) $4(n - 1) + 1$ or $4n - 3$

2 (a) 31, 36; $5n + 1$ (b) 20, 23; $3n + 2$
   (c) 12, 14; $2n$ (d) 11, 13; $2n - 1$

3 (a) $6 \times 7 = 6 + 6^2; 7 \times 8 = 7 + 7^2$
   (b) $n(n + 1) = n + n^2$

4 (a) (i) $\dfrac{n}{n + 1}$ (ii) $\dfrac{1}{n}$

   (iii) $\dfrac{n + 1}{n}$ (iv) $\dfrac{1}{2n - 1}$

   (b) (iii) term is $n + 1$ times the (ii) term
   (c) One is the reciprocal of the other

5 (a) $\frac{1}{2}, \frac{2}{3}, \frac{3}{4}, \frac{4}{5}, \frac{5}{6}$
   (b) (i) $1\frac{1}{n}$ or $\dfrac{n + 1}{n}$ (ii) $\dfrac{n}{n + 1}$

6 (a)

Pattern number, n	Number of shaded squares, s	Number of unshaded squares, u
1	8	4
2	9	6
3	10	8
4	11	10
5	12	12

   (b) $s = 7 + n$
   (c) $u = 2(n + 1)$
   (d) $u = 2s - 12$

7 (b) 40, 52, 64
   (c) Yes; 9th term is 100; nth is $12n - 8$;
      square continues: 76, 88, 100

8 (b) Missing numbers are 7, 9, 11, 13, 15
   (c) (i) 31 sticks
      (ii) Multiply pattern number by 2 and add 1
   (d) $S = 2n + 1$

9 $m = 3n + 2$

10 (a) $\frac{11}{20}, \frac{13}{23}$ (b) $\dfrac{2n - 1}{3n + 2}$

A3: QUADRATIC SEQUENCES

1 (a) 11, 16, $\frac{1}{2}n^2 - \frac{1}{2}n + 1$
   (b) 23, 33, $n^2 - n + 3$
   (c) 90, 85, $100 + \frac{1}{2}n - \frac{1}{2}n^2$
   (d) 51, 70, $\frac{1}{2}(3n^2 + 5n + 2)$

2 (a) (i) 6, 8   (ii) 31, 43
   (b) 14   (c) 100

3 (a) (i) 55   (ii) 65
   (b) $55^2 + 56^2 + 57^2 + 58^2 + 59^2 + 60^2 =$
      $61^2 + 62^2 + 63^2 + 64^2 + 65^2$
   (c) (i) 21   (ii) $2n + 1$

4 (b)

Pattern n	Number of shaded squares	Number of unshaded squares
1	1	0
2	3	1
3	5	4
4	7	9
5	9	16

   (c) Number of unshaded squares = $(n - 1)^2$
   (d) Number of shaded squares = $2n - 1$

5 (a) 31, 43
   (b) Add on two more each time: 2, 4, 6, 8, ...

6 (a) 3, 12, 27, 48
   (b) (i) $3n^2 + 2$ (ii) $3n^2 + n$

7 (a) (i) $p = 25$ (ii) $6 \times 7 - 6 = 36; q = 36$
   (b) $20 \times 21 - 20 = 400$
   (c) (i) $n(n + 1)$ (ii) n^2

8 (a) (i) 26   (ii) 37
   (b) (i) 22   (ii) 48

9 (a) 52   (b) 10th

A4: GRAPHS OF REAL-LIFE SITUATIONS

1 **(i)** 22 DM   **(ii)** £6.50

2

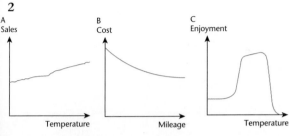

A Sales / Temperature

B Cost / Mileage

C Enjoyment / Temperature

3

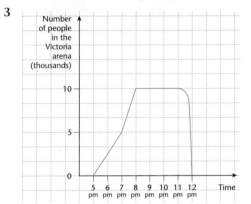

4

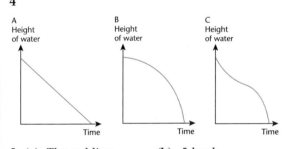

A Height of water / Time

B Height of water / Time

C Height of water / Time

5 **(a)** The red line   **(b)** 5 k.p.h.
  (c) 1 hour   **(d)** 10 km
  (e) 10 k.p.h.   **(f)** 5 p.m.
  (g) 2 hours   **(h)** 10 k.p.h.
  (i) 4 p.m.   **(j)** Half an hour

6 **(a)** $11.5 \, \text{m s}^{-1}$

  (b) The car gradually accelerates until it is travelling at $12 \, \text{m s}^{-1}$ after 20 secs; it continues at this speed until it has been travelling for 50 secs; it then brakes and decelerates for 15 secs until it is stationary

7 **(a)** £2500   **(b)** £970
  (c) £850   **(d)** £240

8 **(a)**

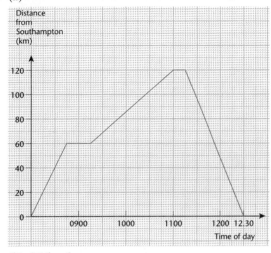

(b) 96 k.p.h.

9 **(a)** B   **(b)** C
  (c) **(i)** B, C or F, G, or J, K (or possibly I, J)
      (ii) E, F   **(iii)** H, I

A5: STRAIGHT-LINE GRAPHS

1 **(a)**

x	–3	–2	–1	0	1	2	3
y	–1	1	3	5	7	9	11

  (c) **(i)** $y = 10$ **(ii)** $x = 1.5$

2 **(a)**

x	–2	–1	0	1	2	3
y	–7	–4	–1	2	5	8

  (c) **(i)** $x = 1.5$ **(ii)** $y = -5.5$

3

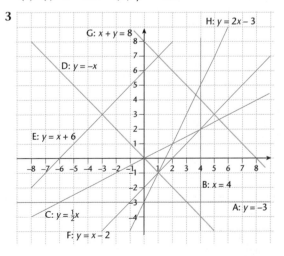

Nelson GCSE Maths ANSWERS TO REVISION GUIDE EXERCISES (INTERMEDIATE)

4

Line	Gradient	Intercept	Equation
A	0	3	$y = 3$
B	∞	$x = -1$	$x = -1$
C	1	1	$y = x + 1$
D	$\frac{1}{2}$	-2	$y = \frac{1}{2}x - 2$
E	2	4	$y = 2x + 4$
F	-2	5	$y = -2x + 5$

5 (a) 2   **(b)** $y = 2x + 3$

6 (a) (i)

x	0	50	100
c	300	550	800

    (b) 64 cards

7 (b) (i) 32.5°   **(ii)** 68 g
    (c) (i) $a = 0.4$, $b = 50$
       (ii) 88 g

A6: NON-LINEAR GRAPHS

1 (a) (i)

x	-1	1	3
y	-2	2	6

    (ii)

x	-1	0	1	2	3
y	1	0	1	4	9

2 (a)

x	-3	-2	-1	0	1	2	3	4
$y = x^2 - 3$	6	1	-2	-3	-2	1	6	13

    (c) $(-2.8, 5)(2.8, 5)$

3 (a) Missing values for y are 36, 35, 32, 20, 0
    (c) (i) $y = 23$ **(ii)** $x = 2.4$ (or 2.5)

4 (a) (i)

x	0	1.5	3
V	0	6	12

    (b) (i)

x	0	0.5	1	1.5	2	2.5	3
V	0	0.5	2	4.5	8	12.5	18

    (c) $x = 2\,\text{cm}$

5 (a) (i) Because the graph should be
        symmetrical about the y-axis
     (ii) Point plotted for $x = -1$ is incorrect
    (b) The y values should be negative when x is
       negative

6 A represents $y = x^2 + 3$; B represents $y = 3x$;
   C represents $y = \dfrac{1}{x}$

7 $y = \dfrac{12}{x}$

8

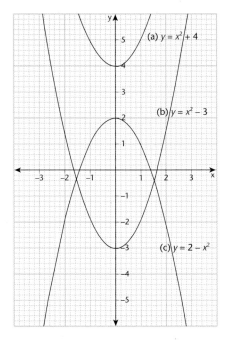

9

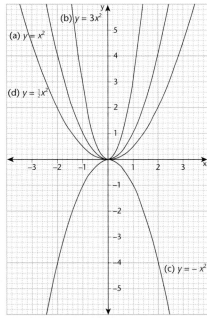

A7: FORMULAE

1 (a) $y = 3k - 1$ **(b)** $k = 5$

2 110 minutes or 1 hour and 50 minutes

3 (a) (i) £600   **(ii)** £320   **(iii)** £280
    (b) 29 guests

Nelson GCSE Maths · ANSWERS TO REVISION GUIDE EXERCISES (IINTERMEDIATE)

4 (a) $T = 3.5$ (b) $I = 13.5$

5 (a) $F = 5°F$ (b) $C = -50°C$ (c) $v = 9$

6 (a) -6

7 (a) $3\frac{9}{20}$

8 (a) $S = 58\,cm$ (b) $A = 723\,cm^2$

A8: MANIPULATING ALGEBRAIC EXPRESSIONS

1 (a) $5y$ (b) $-2a$ (c) $4x^2 + x$
   (d) $2xy^2 + 3xy$ (e) $6a$ (f) $12x^2$
   (g) $-6r^2$ (h) $2ab$ (i) $6a^2b$
   (j) 2 (k) $4y$ (l) 4

2 (a) a^3 (b) x^4 (c) x^5 (d) x^3y

3 (a) x^2 (b) y^5 (c) 1 (d) y^2
   (e) ab^2 (f) ab (g) $6a^5$ (h) $12a^3b^2$
   (i) $\dfrac{2}{3a^2}$ (j) $\dfrac{3}{q}$

4 (a) $2x + 7y$ (b) $4ab$ (c) $2ab - c$
   (d) $-6a - 6b$ (e) $4a^3 - 3a^2$ (f) $4a^2 + b^2$

5 (a) $3a + 6$ (b) $10b + 4$

A9: ALGEBRAIC EXPRESSIONS USING BRACKETS

1 (a) $4x + 8$ (b) $3s - 18$ (c) $2z + 2a$
   (d) $-3c + 12$ (e) $10a - 5b$ (f) $2a^2 - ab$
   (g) $3x^3 - x^2y$ (h) $8y^2 + 12xy^2$

2 (a) $5a - b$ (b) $-5x - y$
   (c) $-6p - 17q$ (d) $6a^2 - 3ab + 2a + 10b$

3 (a) $ac + bc + ad + bd$ (b) $ac + bc - ad - bd$
   (c) $ac - bc - ad + bd$
   (d) $3ax + ay + 15bx + 5by$
   (e) $16df - 2ef - 24dg + 3eg$
   (f) $a^2 + 2ab + b^2$ (g) $x^2 - y^2$
   (h) $p^2 - q^2$ (i) $16a^2 - b^2$

4 (a) $a^2 + 4a + 3$ (b) $b^2 + 7b + 10$
   (c) $x^2 + 2x - 8$ (d) $y^2 - 8y + 15$
   (e) $a^2 - 10a + 21$ (f) $6y^2 + 14y + 4$
   (g) $12a^2 + 17a + 6$ (h) $24c^2 - 8$
   (i) $15x^2 - 16$

5 (a) $2x^2 + 2x + 11$ (b) $-3x$

6 (a) $a^2 + 2ab + b^2$ (b) $a^2 - 2ab + b^2$
   (c) $x^2 + 4x + 4$ (d) $9x^2 - 12xy + 4y^2$

A10: FACTORISING

1 (a) $3(x + y)$ (b) $5(a - b)$ (c) $2(a - 3b)$
   (d) $5(5x + 2y)$ (e) $a(x - y)$ (f) $a(2b - 7c)$
   (g) $d(6c + 5a)$ (h) $4x(3 - y)$ (i) $3a(2 + b)$
   (j) $12t(2s + 1)$

2 (a) $a(a + 4)$ (b) $x(x - 2)$
   (c) $b^2(2b - 3)$ (d) $x(6x^2 - 18x - 1)$
   (e) $4xy(z + 2)$ (f) $xy^2z(x^2 + xz + z^2)$

3 (a) $(a + b)(a - b)$ (b) $(3x + y)(3x - y)$
   (c) $(4a + 5z)(4a - 5z)$ (d) $(p + 6q)(p - 6q)$
   (e) $(10a + 7b)(10a - 7b)$ (f) $(2x + y^2)(2x - y^2)$

4 (a) $(x + 2)(x + 4)$ (b) $(x - 4)(x + 2)$
   (c) $(x + 4)(x - 2)$ (d) $(x - 13)(x + 1)$
   (e) $(x + 8)(x + 8)$ (f) $(x - 5)(x + 2)$
   (g) $(x - 5)(x - 5)$ (h) $(x - 3)(x + 8)$
   (i) $(x - 8)(x - 2)$ (j) $(x - 7)(x + 3)$
   (k) $(2x + 1)(x + 3)$ (l) $(3x + 1)(2x - 5)$

5 (a) (i) $5p(1 - 4t)$ (ii) $3xy(x + 3y - 5)$
   (b) $8x^2 - 10xy - 3y^2$

6 (a) $4x^3y^2$
   (b) (i) $3a^2b^2(3b + 5a)$ (ii) $(x + 12)(x - 5)$

A11: CHANGING THE SUBJECT OF A FORMULA

1 $I = \dfrac{V}{R}$

2 $T = \dfrac{PV}{R}$

3 $u = \sqrt{v^2 - 2as}$

4 $v = \dfrac{2s}{t} - u$

5 $g = \dfrac{4\pi^2 l}{T^2}$

6 $r = \sqrt{\dfrac{V}{\pi h}}$

7 (a) $r = \sqrt{\dfrac{S}{4\pi}}$ (b) $r = \sqrt[3]{\dfrac{3V}{4\pi}}$

8 (a) $6.3\,cm$ (b) $y = 180\frac{x}{\pi r}$ (c) $34.4°$

9 (a) $v = 9.2$ (b) $t = \dfrac{v - u}{a}$

10 (a) £4.95
   (b) (i) $W = \dfrac{T - 20}{40}$ (ii) $10\,kg$

A12: LINEAR EQUATIONS

1 (a) $a = 5$ (b) $x = 2\frac{1}{2}$ (c) $x = -2$
   (d) $x = -0.4$ (e) $y = 3$ (f) $f = 4$
   (g) $x = 3\frac{1}{4}$ (h) $y = -1$

2 (a) $a = 5$ (b) $y = 4$ (c) $x = 6\frac{1}{2}$
   (d) $v = -7$

3 (a) $a = 5\frac{1}{2}$ (b) $x = -3$ (c) $x = 2$
   (d) $y = -3$

4 (a) (i) $x + 2$ (ii) $9 - x$
   (b) (i) $x + 2 = 9 - x$ (ii) $x = 3\frac{1}{2}$

5 (a) $6x + 20$
   (b) (i) $6x + 20 = 260$
       (ii) $x = 40\,\text{m}$
       (iii) 120 m long

6 $c = 4.5\,\text{cm}$

7 (a) $5x$
   (b) (i) $12x = 108$ (ii) $x = 9\,\text{cm}$

8 (a) $n + 1$ (b) 32 and 33

9 (a) $x - 3 + 2x + 5 = 23$ (b) 7 marbles

10 $x = 3\frac{1}{2}$

11 (a) $x = 3$ (b) $x = 7$ (c) $x = 17$

A13: INEQUALITIES AND LOCATING REGIONS BY LINES

1 (a) $-3, -2, -1, 0, 1, 2, 3, 4$ (b) $1, 2, 3, 4, 5, 6$
   (c) $-3, -2, -1, 0, 1$ (d) $-7, -6, -5, -4, -3$

2 (a) $x > 13$ (b) $x \le 3$ (c) $x < \frac{1}{4}$ (d) $x \ge 1$
   (e) $x > 2\frac{2}{3}$ (f) $x < -5$

3 (a) $-6 < x < 6$ (b) $x \ge 7$ and $x \le -7$
   (c) $x \ge 4, x \le -4$ (d) $-2 < x < 2$

4 (a) $x < 6$ (b) $x > 0$

5 Here the unwanted region has been shaded

(a)   (b)

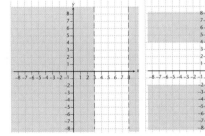

(c)   (d)

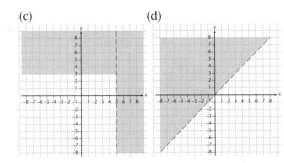

(e)   (f)

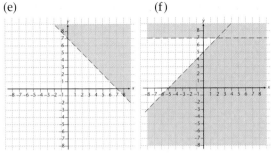

6 The unwanted region has been shaded.

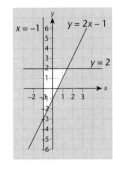

7 $(2, 5), (3, 5)$

8 (a) (i) $-4, -3, -2, -1, 0, 1$ (ii) 16
   (b) $10 \le x < 20$

A14: TRIAL AND IMPROVEMENT, INCLUDING SOLVING EQUATIONS

1 $x = 4.6$

2 (a) $x = 1$ (b) $x = 3$ (c) $x = -4$

3 $x = 1.32$

4 $x = 3.5$

5 (a)

x	-4	-3	-2	-1	0	1	2	3	4
$x^3 - 6x - 2$	-42	-11	2	3	-2	-7	-6	7	38

   (b) Three solutions, because $x^3 - 6x - 2$ changes sign three times
   (c) $x = -2.26, x = -0.34,$ or $x = 2.60$

6 2.10 cm

A15: QUADRATIC EQUATIONS

1 (a) $x = 3$ or $x = 4$ (b) $x = -6$ or $x = -5$
   (c) $a = 7$ or $a = -3$ (d) $x = \frac{1}{3}$ or $x = -2$
   (e) $b = 0$ or $b = -5$

2 (a) $x = 5$ or $x = -5$ (b) $x = \pm 4\frac{1}{2}$
   (c) $x = \pm 1\frac{3}{4}$

3 **(a)** $x = -5$ or $x = 3$ **(b)** $x = 8$ or $x = -1$

  (c) $x = 3$ or $x = 24$ **(d)** $x = 10$ or $x = 2$

  (e) $x = 2$ or $x = 24$ **(f)** $x = 2$ or $x = 18$

4 **(a)** $x = 2$ or $x = -1$ **(b)** $x = 6$ or $x = -6$

  (c) $x = 13$ or $x = -1$ **(d)** $x = 6$ or $x = -2$

  (e) $x = 1$ or $x = 8$ **(f)** $x = -\frac{1}{2}$ or $x = -5$

5 6 or –5

6 3 cm (from the equation $4x(x + 5) = 96$, which simplifies to $x^2 + 5x - 24 = 0$)

7 8 m (from the equation $x^2 - 6x = 16$)

8 **(a)** $y(15 - y) = 50$ **(b)** $y = 5$ or $y = 10$

  (c) Width is usually taken to mean the shorter side (rectangle is 10 cm by 5 cm)

9 5 cm and 12 cm
  From the equation $x^2 + (x + 7)^2 = 13^2$ which simplifies to $x^2 + 7x - 60 = 0$

10 **(a)** $(x + 4)^2 = x^2 + (x + 2)^2$ which simplifies to the equation given

  (b) $x = 6$ or $x = -2$

  (c) Sides are: 6 cm, 8 cm and 10 cm

A16: LINEAR SIMULTANEOUS EQUATIONS

1 $x = 3,\ y = 2$

2 $x = -3,\ y = 5$

3 $x = \frac{1}{2},\ y = 3$

4 **(a)** $x = 3,\ y = 1$ **(b)** $x = 4,\ y = -2$

5 **(a)** $a = -6\frac{1}{2},\ b = -9$ **(b)** $x = 1\frac{1}{2},\ y = \frac{1}{2}$

6 6 and 21

7 5 burger and chips, 7 fish and chips

8 5 packets and 2 cartons

9 **(a)** $3x + 2y = 26,\ 4x + y = 28$
  (b) A blouse costs £6

10 Nightly fee £2; season ticket £11.50

A17: SOLVING EQUATIONS USING GRAPHS

1 **(a)** $x = -2,\ y = 2$ **(b)** $x = 3,\ y = 3$
  (c) $x = 2,\ y = 1$ **(d)** $x = 2,\ y = 4$

2 **(b)** $x = 1\frac{1}{2},\ y = 1$ **(c)** $3y = -2x + 7$

3 $x = 2,\ y = 5$

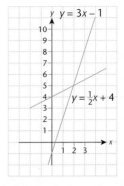

4 **(a)** $y = 4, -1, -4, -5, -4, -1, 4$
  (c) x between 2.2 and 2.3; or between –2.3 and –2.2

5 **(a)**

x	–3	–2	–1	0	1	2	3	4	5
y	8	1	–4	–7	–8	–7	–4	1	8

  (b) $x = -1.8$ or $x = 3.8$

6 **(a)**

x	–5	–4	–3	–2	–1	0	1	2	3
y	13	6	1	–2	–3	–2	1	6	13

  $x = -2.7$ or $x = 0.7$
  (b) $x = -3.8$ or $x = 1.8$
  (c) $x = -1$

MISCELLANEOUS EXERCISE

1 **(a)** **(i)** 8 pens   **(ii)**   10 pens

22   27

  (b)

Number of pens	2	4	6	8	10	12	14	16
Number of fences	7	12	17	22	27	32	37	42

  (c) 77 fences

2 **(a)** **(i)** $2n + 1$ **(ii)** $n + 1$
  (b) **(i)** 1, 2, 3, 4, 5, ...   **(ii)** n
    (iii) $2n + 1 - (n + 1) = n$

3 **(a)** $x = 7$ **(b)** $x = 5\frac{1}{2}$ **(c)** $x = -4$ **(d)** $y = 1$

4 20 m by 29 m

5 –1, 0, 1, 2, 3

6 $x = 5,\ y = -2$

7 **(a)** 52 m.p.h.   **(b)** 12 minutes
   (c) The gradient is steeper **(e)** 12 miles

8 **(a)** **(i)** $20x - 60$ **(ii)** $x^2 + 3x$
      (iii) $x^2 - 2x - 8$ **(iv)** $14x^2 + 19x - 3$
  (b) **(i)** $13a - 1$ **(ii)** x^3y
      (iii) $36x^4y^5$ **(iv)** $3a$

9 **(a)** $(x - 6)(x + 2)$ **(b)** $(6a - 7b)(6a + 7b)$
  (c) $4xy(x^2y + 3x - 2)$ **(d)** $(2x - 3)(x + 1)$

10 **(a)** $x = -2$ or $x = 7$ **(b)** $x = 3$ or $x = 4$
  (c) $x = \frac{1}{2}$ or $x = -3$

11 **(a)** $x + 4$ **(b)** $4x + 10$
  (c) $x = 6$

12 **(a)** y: 10, 5, 2, 1, 2, 5, 10
  (c) Draw $y = 9$; $x = -2.8$ or $x = 2.8$

13 **(a) and (c)**

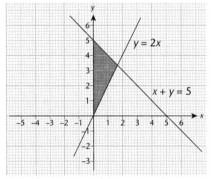

  (b) Find point where lines cross at $x = 1\frac{2}{3}$ or
    $x = 1.7$

14 **(a)** 2, –1, 0, 5, 14

  (b)

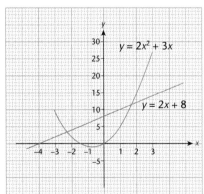

  (c) $x = 1$, $y = 5$ or $x = -2$, $y = 2$, or any other
    point on dotted part of graph

15 **(a)** **(i)** $p = 2a + 2b$ **(ii)** $p = a + 3b$
  (b) **(i)** $A = 28$ **(ii)** $A = 6x^2$
  (c) **(i)** Volume of lower part $= 6x^2 \times x = 6x^3$
       Volume of upper part $= 8x \times x \times 0.25$
       $= 2x^2$

     (ii) $6x^3 + 2x^2 = 20$ and, so, $3x^3 + x^2 = 10$
     (iii) 1.39

S1: 3D OBJECTS AND THEIR 2D REPRESENTATION

2 **(a)** $F = 4$, $E = 6$, $V = 4$
  (b) $F = 5$, $E = 9$, $V = 6$

3 **(a)** E.g.

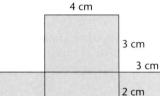

4

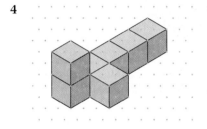

5 **(a)** 13 cubes
  (b)

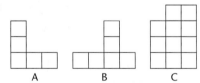

     A   B   C

6 E.g.

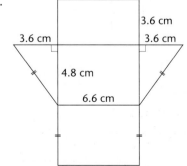

7 E.g.

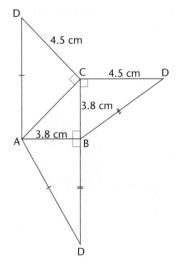

8 C

9

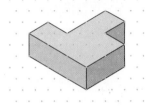

10 The cube is B; the prism is E; the pyramid is D; the cone is A; the tetrahedron is C

S2: ACCURATE CONSTRUCTION OF 2D SHAPES

1 96°   **2** 78°

3 7.3 cm   **4** 7.0 cm

5 10.5 cm   **6** 42°

S3: CONGRUENT SHAPES

1

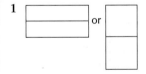

2

3 Any isosceles triangle

4 (a) and (b)

 or

5 A–H, C–E, D–F

6 $y = 7.7$ cm

7 The 8 cm is opposite the 100° in the 2nd, but adjacent in the 1st, and the triangle is not isosceles

8 (a) $x = 70°$ (b) $y = 10$ cm

9 $x = 12$ cm

S4: ANGLES AND LINES

1 $a = 35°$; $b = 62°$ **2** $c = 160°$; $d = 20°$

3 $e = 140°$ **4** $g = 85°$; $h = 85°$

5 $j = 50°$ **6** $x = 45°$

7 $y = 40°$ **8** $x = 30°$; $y = 80°$

9 $a = 60°$; $b = 120°$; $c = 120°$

10 $p = 35°$; $q = 115°$; $r = 30°$

S5: TRIANGLES AND QUADRILATERALS

1 $p = 118°$ **2** $x = 76°$; $y = 128°$

3 $w = 123°$ **4** $d = 56°$

5 $e = 108°$; $f = 72°$ **6** $u = 68°$; $v = 44°$

7 $a = 31°$; $b = 47°$; $c = 101°$

8 48°, by finding angles in the isosceles triangles; this then proves that AB is parallel to DE.

9 (a) 40°   (b) 145°

10 $k = 80°$

11 (a) and (d)

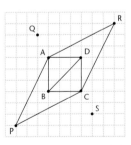

(b) Rhombus   (c) Kite

S6: POLYGONS

1 (a) $x = 72°$ (b) $y = 54°$ (c) $2 \times 54° = 108°$

2 (a) A hexagon, B rectangle or oblong, C hexagon, D nonagon, E rhombus

(b) C and D are regular

(c) A, B, C, D have equal angles

3   720°

4   140°

5   (a) 540°   (b) $j = 129°$

6   7 sides

7   $w = 90°$

8   $p = 66°$

9   18 sides

10 (a) E.g. exterior angle = 360° ÷ 6 = 60°;
        180° − 60° = 120° or two 60° angles in
        equilateral triangles
    (b) (i)   360° − 90° − 90° − 120° = 60°
         (ii   90° + 60° = 150°
    (c) Equilateral

S7: SYMMETRY

1   Order is 4

2   E.g. equilateral triangle

3   A: 4   B: 2   C: None   D: 8

4

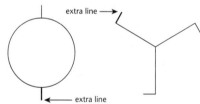

extra line →

← extra line

5   (a) Parallelogram
    (b) Rectangle or rhombus

6   E.g.

7   (a)   (b)

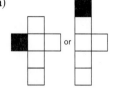   or

S8: COMPASS POINTS AND BEARINGS

1   (a) 090°   (b) 045°   (c) 225°   (d) 270°

2   (a) 100°   (b) 340°

3   $y = 130°$

4   (a) 242°   (b) 118°   (c) 117°

5

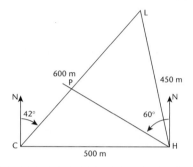

S9: PYTHAGORAS' THEOREM

1   $p = 15\,cm$, $q = 15\,cm$ 2   5.8 cm

3   4.2 cm   4   59 km

5   6.4 units   6   13 units

7   4.1 m; yes   8   14.1 cm

S10: TRIGONOMETRY

1   $p = 4.78\,cm$, $q = 10.2\,cm$

2   $a = 3.2\,cm$, $b = 8.2\,cm$

3   $x = 18°$, $y = 55°$

4   (a) $\frac{5}{12}$ (b) $\frac{5}{13}$

5   $m = 11\,cm$, $n = 27\,cm$

6   14 km

7   065°

8   68° so not safe

9   (a) 64.4°   (b) $h = 5.4\,m$

10 12 800 km

S11: TRANSFORMATIONS

1

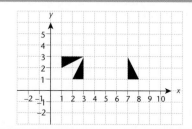

2

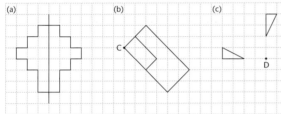

3 (a) $y = 1$
   (b) Rotation 90° anticlockwise about origin

4 $\begin{pmatrix} -4 \\ -3 \end{pmatrix}$

5 (3, 9)

6

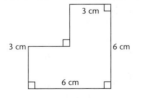

7 (a) Reflection in x-axis
   (b) Rotation 90° anticlockwise about origin
   (c) Enlargement, scale factor 3, centre (5, 4)

8 (a) P′(4, 2), Q′(8, 2), R′(8, 8)
   (b) P″(5, 1), Q″(7, 1), R″(7, 4)
   (c) $\begin{pmatrix} 3 \\ 0 \end{pmatrix}$

9 (a) 2   (b) (5, 1)

S12: SCALE DRAWING AND SIMILARITY

1 Perimeter is 24 cm

2 6.3 cm by 16.7 cm

3 Check: 9.6 cm by 5.2 cm, door 1.6 cm and 6 cm from top LH corner, window 2.8 cm and 1.2 cm from bottom LH corner

4 1:4 000 000

5 (a) About 8 miles   (b) About 1:60 000

6 3 km

7 $\frac{1}{60}$ th

8 $x = 8$ cm, $y = 7.5$ cm

9 $p = 4.5$ cm, $q = 7.2$ cm

10 (a) They have 90° and angle A in common
    (b) AD = 2.8 cm

11 (a) 7.5 cm   (b) 11.2 cm

12 (i) 12 cm   (ii) 10 cm

S13: LOCUS

1 (a) Circle centre Y, radius 6 cm
   (b) Perpendicular bisector of XY

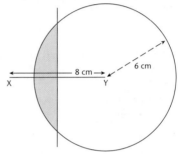

2

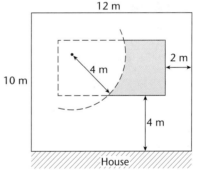

3

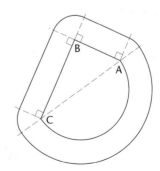

S14: RULER AND COMPASS CONSTRUCTIONS

3 6 cm to 6.1 cm   5 3.4 cm to 3.5 cm

S15: UNITS OF MEASUREMENT AND CONVERSIONS

1 $\frac{1}{2}$ pint

2 4 yards

3 Slower (31.25 m.p.h)

4 Just over £14

5 4 inches

6 4.84 lb

7 290 ml

8 (a) 7.9×10^{-3} kg/cm^3 (b) 7.9 g/cm

9 (a) 744 km per min   (b) 12 400 m/s

10 (a) 0.45 kg or 450 g   (b) 0.087 litres or 870 ml

S16: COMPOUND MEASURES: SPEED AND DENSITY

1 75 m.p.h.

2 (a) 720 m   (b) 120 m   (c) 1140 m

3 (a) 0.5 miles per min   (b) 30 m.p.h.

4 (a) 45 km   (b) 4.5 km

5 (a) 12 min   (b) 7.5 miles

6 6320 kg

7 6.1×10^{19} m^3

8 0.000 09 g/cm^3

9 68 g

10 14 cm^3

S17: UPPER AND LOWER BOUNDS OF MEASURES

1 (a) 11.5 cm   (b) 46 cm

2 (a) 26 750   (b) 26 849   (c) 125 cm^2

3 11 500 and 12 499

4 68 m.p.h.

5 5.55 s and 5.65 s

6 10.345 s

7 6.985 m

8 (a) 99.5 m
   (b) (i) 14.85 secs   (ii) 14.95 secs

S18: AREAS AND PERIMETERS OF TRIANGLES, PARALLELOGRAMS AND TRAPEZIUMS

1 7.5 cm^2, 10 cm^2 2 143 cm^2

3 26 cm^2 4 23 cm^2

5 A: 6 cm^2 B: 6 cm^2 C: 10.5 cm^2 D: 5 cm^2

6 25 cm^2

7 24 cm

8 356 cm^2

9 (a) 12 cm   (b) 96 cm^2
   (c) Use values closer in size, e.g. 9 by 11

10 27.7 cm^2

S19: AREA AND PERIMETER OF CIRCLES

1 (a) 26 cm   (b) 55 cm^2

2 9.04 cm

3 27 cm

4 (a) 4.1 m^2 to 2 s.f.   (b) 8.4 m to 2 s.f.

5 Perimeter is 408 m; race needs less than 1 lap

6 45.6 m^2 or 46 m^2

7 4.78 cm^2

8 257.6 cm or 258 cm

9 $C = 5\pi$, $A = 6.25\pi$

10 6 cm

S20: VOLUME AND SURFACE AREA OF CUBOIDS

1 (a) 270 m^3 (b) 258 m^2

2 7 cm

3 6 cm

4 1.3 m

5 32 cuboids, with the 5 cm along the 10 cm, the
   3 cm along the 12 cm and the 2 cm along the
   8 cm

6 (a) 40 cm   (b) No

7 245 cm^3

8 (a) 9 cm   (b) 486 cm^2 (c) $\frac{1}{9}$

S21: VOLUME AND SURFACE AREA OF PRISMS AND CYLINDERS

1 $2048\,\text{cm}^3$

2 $182.07\,\text{cm}^3$ or $180\,\text{cm}^3$

3 (a) $498.9\,\text{cm}^3$ or $499\,\text{cm}^3$ or $500\,\text{cm}^3$
    (b) 11.6 cm by 24.2 cm

4 (a) $240\,\text{cm}^3$ (b) $288\,\text{cm}^2$

5 $540\,\text{cm}^3$

6 (a) $35\,\text{m}^2$
    (b) (i) $700\,\text{m}^3$ (ii) 700 000 litres

7 $40\,000\,\text{cm}^3$

8 16 cm

9 (a) 24 cm   (b) $1560\,\text{cm}^2$
    (c) $312\,000\,\text{cm}^3$ (d) $25\,100\,\text{cm}^3$
    (e) 13 cylinders

S22: DISTINGUISH BETWEEN FORMULAE BY CONSIDERING DIMENSIONS

1 (a) πab, $r\sqrt{p^2 + q^2}$, $\dfrac{ab}{2}$ (b) πd, $a + 2c$, $\pi(a + b)$

2 $4\pi r^2$ contains two lengths; $4\pi r^3$ contains three lengths

3 $4p^2q$, xy, $\sqrt{u^2 + v^2}$

4 $\pi r^2 l$, $4\pi r^3$, $3(a^2 + b^2)r$

5 (a) It is a formula for volume (contains three lengths)
    (b) $L = 5W + 4D + H$ (only formula with one length in each term)

MISCELLANEOUS EXERCISE

1 80°

2 (a) (i) $x = 3\,\text{cm}$ (ii) 44 cm   (iii) $72\,\text{cm}^2$
    (b) Cuboid
    (c) 44 cm

3 (a) (i) $x = 33°$ (ii) $x = 95°$
    (b) (i) 108°   (ii) 36°   (iii) 36°

4 $p = 8.5\,\text{cm}$; $q = 16\,\text{cm}$

5 (a) $20\,\text{cm}^2$ (b) 12 cm by 15 cm
    (c) 9 times

6 528 cm, or 530 cm more sensibly

7 295 g

8 (a) 147 cm
    (b) (i) 121.5 cm (ii) 4 feet

9 (a) 8.5 m   (b) 0.9 m

10 $1.02\,\text{m}^2$

11 (a) $3a + 3b$ (b) ab (c) a^2b

12 (a) $95.4\,\text{cm}^2$ (b) $2.50\,\text{g/cm}^3$

13 (a) Circle: radius 10 cm, centre A
    (b) (i) 6 cm   (ii) 4.5 cm
    (c)

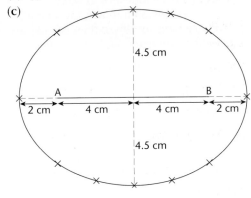

14 4.0 cm

15 (a) $x = 60$ (b) 27°

16 (a) (i)

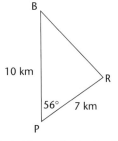

    (ii) 8.4 km (±0.1 km)   (iii) 136° (±2°)
    (b) (i) 10.6 km   (ii) 341°

D1: COLLECTION AND ORGANISATION OF DATA

1 E.g.

Type of vehicle	Colour					Total
	Red	Navy/Black	Cream	Green	Other	
Car	IIII	III	I	II	IIII	14
Lorry	I	I	I		I	4
Van	I	II	I			4
Bicycle	II					2
Motorbike		I				1
Totals	8	7	3	2	5	25

2 Continuous: (**a**), (**c**), (**e**) and (**f**)
Discrete: (**b**), (**d**)

3 A, C, F

4 $\frac{27}{60}$ = 45% of under 30s work evening shift.

$\frac{40}{80}$ = 50% of over 30s work evening shift; so,
John is right

D2: DESIGNING A QUESTIONNAIRE; BIAS

1 Show clear categories such as $0 < t \le 30$
minutes, $30 < t \le 60$ minutes, etc. and a
reasonable range of times; there should also be
a place for tally marks and the frequency

2 (**a**) Question 1: not relevant

Question 2: biased; invites people to agree

(**b**) E.g. Do you think shops should stay open
on Sunday? YES/NO

3 (**a**) There are many possible answers

(**b**) Age and gender should be taken into
account in the sample; a balance is
required. And do not just ask your friends

4 (**a**) You are asked only to pick your *favourite*
sport and so it does not *indicate how much*
you like sport

(**b**) (**i**) E.g. People keen on sport will go to the
gym

(**ii**) E.g. People at the gym may only like
the sport they do there, so, for example,
excludes those who like football

D3: LINE GRAPHS, BAR CHARTS, HISTOGRAMS AND FREQUENCY POLYGONS

1 (**a**) and (**b**)

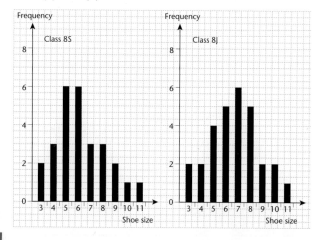

(**c**) Answers like: 8S has more pupils with shoe
size less than size 6 than 8J

2

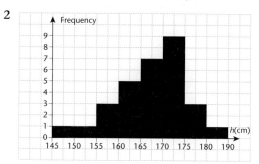

3 (**a**) 165 potatoes

(**b**) Bar chart or frequency polygon is acceptable

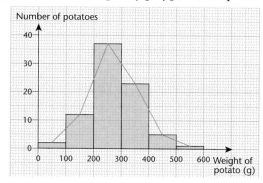

4 (**a**) For 1990:

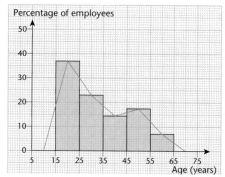

(**b**) For 1995:

(c) (i) Yes
   (ii) E.g. in 1990, mode is 15–25 age group;
        in 1995, mode is 45–55

D4: PIE CHARTS

1 (a) 20 people in 'Other'
   (b)

	Frequency	Angle
Europe	115	207°
America	45	81°
Asia	15	27°
Australia	5	9°
Other	20	36°
Total	200	360°

   (c)

Holiday destinations
of 200 people

- Europe
- America
- Asia
- Australia
- Other

2 (a)

Teachers' papers

Accountants' papers

The Guardian (144°)
The Independent (88°)
The Times (16°)
The Financial Times (0°)
The Mirror (40°)
Daily Mail (56°)
Other (16°)

The Guardian (40°)
The Independent (48°)
The Times (40°)
The Financial Times (204°)
The Mirror (8°)
Daily Mail (12°)
Other (8°)

   (b) Statements like:
       The Guardian is the most popular paper
       with teachers, *The Financial Times* with
       accountants
       A larger proportion of teachers than
       accountants buy *The Guardian*

3 (a) Sport: 8.3 hours; News: 5 hours; Drama:
       3.3 hours; Comedy: 1.7 hours; Other 1.7
       hours

(b)

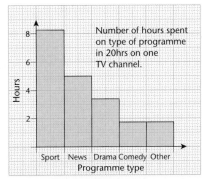

Number of hours spent
on type of programme
in 20hrs on one
TV channel.

4 (a) and (b)

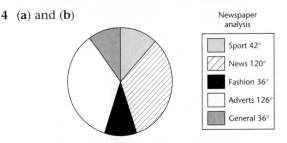

Newspaper
analysis

- Sport 42°
- News 120°
- Fashion 36°
- Adverts 126°
- General 36°

5 (a) (i) 9%   (ii) 162°
   (b) (i) 25°   (ii) 38%
   (d) Wholemeal: only 38% carbohydrate,
       compared with 45% in white bread; and
       7% fibre compared with 2% in white bread

6 (a) (i) Britain   (ii) 17 people
   (b) 180 people in both surveys; $\frac{45}{360}$ = 12.5%

D5: SCATTER DIAGRAMS AND LINES OF BEST FIT

1 (a)

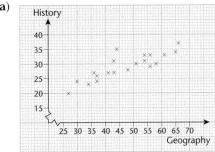

   (b) About 33 marks
   (c) There is evidence for positive correlation
       between the marks for the Geography and
       History tests and, so, the statement is false

Nelson GCSE Maths   ANSWERS TO REVISION GUIDE EXERCISES (INTERMEDIATE)

2 (a) Negative (inverse) correlation

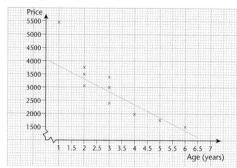

(c) About £2600

(d) Just over 2 years

3 (a) (i) Negative; more people stay in when it rains
    (ii) No correlation; nothing to do with each other!

(b) Positive

(c) About 50% to 54%

4 (a) No; there is evidence of negative correlation, which means that good bowlers are good batsmen

(b) B

(c) G

5 (a) and (c)

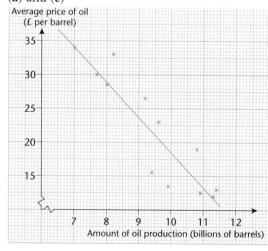

(b) Negative

(d) About £17

D6: MEAN, MEDIAN, MODE AND RANGE

1 (a) 6.1 cm   (b) 6.0 cm   (c) 1.9 cm

2 Calculation of any of the averages results in 25 g; the statement is true

3 (a) 46 marks (b) 43 marks

4 (a) 46 marks   (b) 45 marks
    (c) Mean, because 8 out of 10 scored less than the mean

5 (a) $486 \div 30 = 16.2$ marks
    (b) Median is 3, and so marks must add to 30 to give mean of 6; $x = 20$

D7: MEANS OF FREQUENCY DISTRIBUTIONS

1 (a) 3   (b) 3   (c) 3   (d) 5

2 (a) 2.2 people

3 48.5 hours $\div 40 = 1.2$; 1.2 hours

4 (a) 5.16 letters   (b) 5 letters
    (c) A: The medians of the two books are the same
        The range is larger in Book 5 so there are some longer words in Book 5
        These long words might cause difficulty
        B: The range is the same for both books
        The median for Book 2 is smaller than that of Book 4
        Book 2 is probably easier to read than Book 4 because it has more short words

5 (a) $920 \div 100 = 9.2$; 9.2 minutes
    (b) More people in supermarket; fewer checkouts operating; people buying more

6 (a) 27
    (b) About 440 people

D8: CUMULATIVE FREQUENCY, MEDIAN AND INTERQUARTILE RANGE

1 (a) 41 type A leaves
    (b) (i) $29 \text{ cm} - 21 \text{ cm} = 8 \text{ cm}$
        (ii) Type A leaves vary more in length than type B leaves
    (c) Longest type B is 35 cm. Two type A leaves are longer

2 (a)

Weight in grams	Frequency	Cumulative frequency
$0 < w < 10$	52	52
$10 \le w < 20$	157	209
$20 \le w < 30$	125	334
$30 \le w < 40$	71	405
$40 \le w < 50$	51	456
$50 \le w < 60$	44	500

(b)

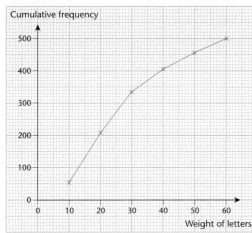

(c) About 24 g

(d) About 70 letters

3 (a)

Upper bound	Cumulative frequency
45	1
50	2
55	4
60	19
65	31
70	33
75	35

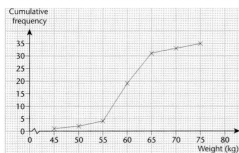

(b) About 59 kg

(d) About 63 kg − 57 kg = 6 kg

4 (a) Cumulative frequencies: 2, 20, 47, 65, 77, 80

(b)

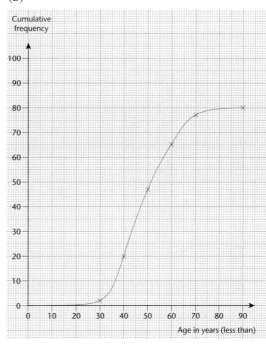

(c) 1997: median 47; LQ 40; UQ 56; IQR 17

(d) 1996; upper quartile gives age at which 25% of people are older

5 (a)

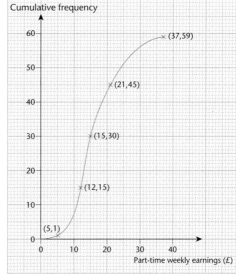

(b) £9

(c) About 16 students

Nelson GCSE Maths   ANSWERS TO REVISION GUIDE EXERCISES (INTERMEDIATE)

D9: BASIC PROBABILITY

1 0.6

2 (a) $\frac{1}{13}$　　　(b) $\frac{1}{8}$　　　(c) $\frac{2}{3}$

　　(d) $\frac{5}{200} = \frac{1}{40}$　(e) $\frac{6}{12} = \frac{1}{2}$　(f) $\frac{3}{13}$

3 $\frac{2}{5}$

4 (a) $\frac{1}{4}$　　　(b) $\frac{1}{5}$　　　(c) $\frac{1}{2}$

5 (a) $\frac{1}{11}$　　　(b) $\frac{2}{11}$　　　(c) $\frac{8}{11}$

6 (a) 0.64　　(b) 0.11
　　(c) 50 red, 22 blue, 128 yellow

7 (a) 0.45　　(b) 0.25

D10: ESTIMATING PROBABILITY

1 (i) B　　　(ii) D　　　(iii) E　　　(iv) A
　　(v) F　　　(vi) C

2 91%

3 (a) True; $\frac{136}{269}$ is about $\frac{1}{2}$
　　(b) False; Rolls Royce could have appeared in 'Other makes'
　　(c) False; $\frac{18}{269}$ is a lot less than $\frac{1}{6}$

4 (a) (i) 0.05　　(ii) 0.25
　　(b) True on the evidence; 0.1 compared to 0.25, but not comparing similar amounts of data; more evidence is needed from second supermarket

5 (a) Not a random sample (may ask friends all the same age)
　　　Same person may be asked twice
　　(b) (i) 0.2, 0.17, 0.15, 0.16
　　　　(ii) 0.16 – from largest amount of data

6 (a)

Total no. of heads	8	9	15	23	33	37	44	50	57	63
Rel. freq. fractions	$\frac{8}{10}$	$\frac{9}{20}$	$\frac{15}{30}$	$\frac{23}{40}$	$\frac{33}{50}$	$\frac{37}{60}$	$\frac{44}{70}$	$\frac{50}{80}$	$\frac{57}{90}$	$\frac{63}{100}$
Rel. freq. decimals	0.8	0.45	0.5	0.575	0.66	0.617	0.629	0.625	0.633	0.63

(b)

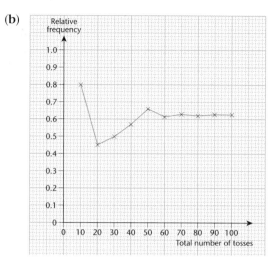

(c) 0.63

D11: PROBABILITY OF TWO EVENTS

1 (a) There are six different possible orders
　　(b) Because the six outcomes may not all be equally likely
　　(c) 0.17

2 (b) $\frac{1}{24}$　　(c) $\frac{1}{4}$　　(d) $\frac{1}{3}$　　(e) $\frac{1}{12}$

3 (a) (i) $\frac{1}{2}$　　(ii) $\frac{1}{2}$　　(iii) $\frac{1}{4}$
　　(b) There are 16 pairs of outcomes
　　(c) (i) $\frac{4}{16} = \frac{1}{4}$　(ii) $\frac{8}{16} = \frac{1}{2}$　(iii) $\frac{6}{16} = \frac{3}{8}$

4 (a)

Set A

+	1	2	3	4	5	6	7	8
1	2	3	4	5	6	7	8	9
2	3	4	5	6	7	8	9	10
3	4	5	6	7	8	9	10	11
4	5	6	7	8	9	10	11	12

Set B

+	1	2	3	4	5	6
1	2	3	4	5	6	7
2	3	4	5	6	7	8
3	4	5	6	7	8	9
4	5	6	7	8	9	10
5	6	7	8	9	10	11
6	7	8	9	10	11	12

(b) Relative frequency: 0.03, 0.05, 0.088, 0.108, 0.136, 0.174, 0.132, 0.108, 0.086, 0.06, 0.028

(c) Set B: The relative frequency is largest for score 7; Table for Set A shows that the probability for scores of 5,6,7,8 and 9 are the same; Table for Set B shows the largest probability is for score 7

5 (a)

First counter	Second counter	Outcome		Probability
	Red	Red Red		$\frac{3}{18} \times \frac{3}{18} = \frac{9}{324}$
Red	Blue	Red Blue		$\frac{3}{18} \times \frac{5}{18} = \frac{15}{324}$
	Yellow	Red Yellow		$\frac{3}{18} \times \frac{10}{18} = \frac{30}{324}$
	Red	Blue Red		$\frac{5}{18} \times \frac{3}{18} = \frac{15}{324}$
Blue	Blue	Blue Blue		$\frac{5}{18} \times \frac{5}{18} = \frac{25}{324}$
	Yellow	Blue Yellow		$\frac{5}{18} \times \frac{10}{18} = \frac{50}{324}$
	Red	Yellow Red		$\frac{10}{18} \times \frac{3}{18} = \frac{30}{324}$
Yellow	Blue	Yellow Blue		$\frac{10}{18} \times \frac{5}{18} = \frac{50}{324}$
	Yellow	Yellow Yellow		$\frac{10}{18} \times \frac{10}{18} = \frac{100}{324}$

(b) $\frac{5}{18} \times \frac{5}{18} = \frac{25}{324}$

(c) $\frac{3}{18} \times \frac{10}{18} + \frac{10}{18} \times \frac{3}{18} = \frac{60}{324} = \frac{5}{27}$

(d) $\frac{9}{324} + \frac{25}{324} + \frac{100}{324} = \frac{134}{324} = \frac{67}{162}$

(e) $\frac{95}{162}$

6 (a) $\frac{1}{5} \times \frac{1}{5} = \frac{1}{25}$

(b) $\frac{1}{25} + \frac{1}{25} + \frac{1}{25} + \frac{1}{25} + \frac{1}{25} = \frac{5}{25} = \frac{1}{5}$

(c) $\frac{10}{25} = \frac{2}{5}$

7 (a) $0.85 \times 0.6 = 0.51$ (b) $0.85 \times 0.4 = 0.34$

8 $0.6 \times 0.15 + 0.4 \times 0.85 = 0.43$

MISCELLANEOUS EXERCISE

1 (a) Red

(b) (i) 0.1   (ii) 0

2 (a)

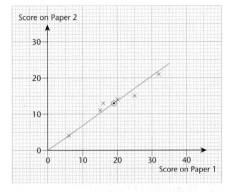

(b) 19

(c) Line of best fit should go through mean (19, 13) and the origin

(d) 7

3 (a) Class 9C (by inspection of table)

(b) Class 9B

(c) Class 9B

(d) 3 hours (12 students)

(e) 7 hours

4 (a) Red

(b)

Type	Car	Van	Lorry	Bus	Total
Number	35	11	8	6	60
Angle for pie chart	210°	66°	48°	36°	360°

5 (a)

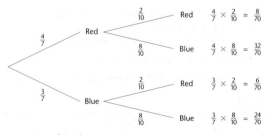

(b) (i) $\frac{8}{70} = \frac{4}{35}$

(ii) $\frac{32}{70} + \frac{6}{70} = \frac{38}{70} = \frac{19}{35}$

6 (a)

Number of colonies	0	1	2	3	4
Frequency	7	10	5	2	1

(b) $\dfrac{7 \times 0 + 10 \times 1 + 5 \times 2 + 2 \times 3 + 1 \times 4}{25} = 1.2$

(c) 1

(d) (i) Means, modes, ranges and medians are the same

(ii) Second sample is much bigger than 25

7 (a) (i) Y11

(ii) In Y11, nearly half have a journey of over 20 minutes
In Y10, it is less than half and, in Y9, only one quarter

(b) Frequencies are 23, 16, 11, 4

(c) $\frac{1}{47}$

(d) $\frac{5}{50} = \frac{1}{10}$

(e) $20 < t \le 30$

(f) $\dfrac{14 \times 5 + 12 \times 15 + 19 \times 25 + 5 \times 35}{50} = \frac{900}{50} = 18$

18 minutes

8 (a) The question is biased and leads people to agree with the statement in the question
The question is vague: e.g. 'young people' and 'healthier diet' are not defined

(b) Age group: 18 years and over
Range: 7 packets

(c) Age group: Under 18 years old
Mode is 4 packets

(d) $\dfrac{3 \times 4 + 4 \times 7 + 6 \times 1 + 8 \times 4}{16} = \frac{78}{16} = 4.9$

4.9 packets; Julia is wrong; under-18-year-olds have a significantly higher mean

(e) $\frac{16}{36} = \frac{4}{9}$

(f) (i) $\frac{7}{16}$

(ii) $\frac{4}{16} \times \frac{6}{20} = \frac{3}{40}$

9 (a) 36 years **(b)** £338

(c) and (d)

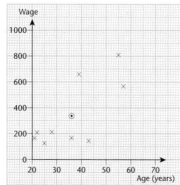

(e) The mean is not representative
There are 5 people with comparatively low wages where age makes little difference
There are 3 people earning a lot more, of whom two are significantly older than anyone else
So, although at first glance there is some indication of positive correlation between wages and ages there is not any strong evidence for it

10 (a)

	1	2	3	4	5
2	3	4	5	6	7
3	4	5	6	7	8
4	5	6	7	8	9
5	6	7	8	9	10
6	7	8	9	10	11

(b) (i) $\frac{1}{25}$ **(ii)** $\frac{6}{25}$

(c) (i) 0.18, 0.19, 0.21

(ii) 0.21 gives the best estimate, because it is calculated from most data (from table, the probability is $\frac{5}{25} = 0.2$)

11 (a) 166 cm

(b) 171 cm − 162 cm = 9 cm

(c) 26 students

(d) $\dfrac{86 - 24}{120} = \frac{62}{120} = 0.52$

12 (a) 0.83   **(b)** 0.0459

13 (a) Frequencies are: 3, 8, 12, 37, 21, 9

(b) 68 m.p.h. (to nearest m.p.h.)

(c)

	Frequency	Cumulative frequency
$50 < s < 55$	3	3
$55 \le s < 60$	8	11
$60 \le s < 65$	12	23
$65 \le s < 70$	37	60
$70 \le s < 75$	21	81
$75 \le s < 80$	9	90

(d)

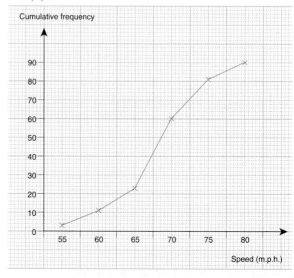

(e) (i) About 68 m.p.h

(ii) About 7 m.p.h

14 (a)

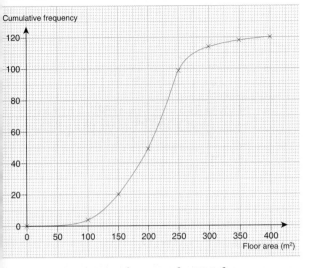

(b) About 240 m² – 170 m² = 70 m²

(c) About 270 m² (read off at 108)

COURSE REVISION EXERCISE 1

1 0.657, 6.532, 60.4

2 (a) 125 g   (b) £1.60 per kg
   (c) 495 g

3 (a) 9.1 × 10⁻²⁸ g
   (b) Three people per household

4 (a) a = 3
   (b) 9801 = (11 × 3²) × (11 × 3²)
       so √9801 = 11 × 3² = 99

5 (a) Three
   (b) (i) 8x = 40   (ii) 5 cm by 15 cm
   (c) (i) 48 = 3x² (ii) 4 cm and 12 cm

6 (a) Answers must contain at least three
       options to categorise and/or sort data
   (b) Angles needed: 108°, 12°, 180°, 60°

7 (a) d = –9   (b) a = $\frac{d}{3}$ + 5

8 (a) (i) a⁷   (ii) t³
   (b) (i) 3x + 3
       (ii) 6b – 12
       (iii) 5(2p + 7) = 10p + 35

9 (4.5, –0.75)

10 (b) 1.95 cm to 2.05 cm
   (c) 15.4 cm² to 16.2 cm² dep on (b)

COURSE REVISION EXERCISE 2

1 –1.7, –1.2, –0.6, 0.72, 1.3

3 (a) $\frac{7}{10}$ (b) 4

4 8 minutes 17 seconds

5 (a) £384.20 (b) 32%

6 (a) x = 10   (b) x < 11   (c) x = –4, or x = 7

7 (a) H1, H2, H3, H4, H5, H6, T1, T2, T3, T4,
       T5, T6
   (b) $\frac{3}{12}$ = $\frac{1}{4}$
   (c) $\frac{2}{12}$ = $\frac{1}{6}$

8 6.3

9 (a) AD = 4.4 cm; AB = 10.8 cm; BC = 5.2 cm;
       ∠ADC: 94° to 95°
   (b) 86°
   (c) 32.4 m³

10 (a) 0 uncles   (b) 1 uncle
   (c) 1.525 uncles
   (d) Any answer, as long as a sensible reason
       is given

COURSE REVISION EXERCISE 3

1 (a) 50 000   (b) 800

2 (a) 575 kg   (b) 25 cm

3 (a) 7.5 × 10¹⁸   (b) 3 × 10⁴

4 (a) 14.925 m
   (b) Yes, but could have just about been a tie
       (14.925 and 19.924 999)

5 (a) x = 4
   (b) x = 3, y = 4
   (c) –2, –1, 0, 1, 2

6 (a) r = –4.5   (b) s = 100

7 (a) (i) 125t³   (ii) w⁹
   (b) (i) 6 – 2p   (ii) 6t² + 4t

8 (a) 2 times
   (b) (i) 2 km   (ii) 12 k.p.h.
   (c) DE (steepest)

9 (a) 1.25 km
   (c) 184° to 186°
   (d) 0.15

10 (a)

Up to this height (cm)	25	30	35	40	45	50	55	60
Cumulative frequency	3	20	44	74	96	119	130	135

(b) 39 cm   (c) 16 cm   (d) 18% to 19%

(e) Second type is more consistent in height

COURSE REVISION EXERCISE 4

1 (a) 75%   (b) 24 students

2 (a) (i) 81   (ii) $\frac{1}{9}$ (iii) 3^{-3}

(b) (i) $2^2 \times 3^5$ (ii) $2^2 \times 3^2 = 36$

3 (a) 2.478×10^8 miles

(b) 1.56×10^9 miles

4 (a) Of form $0 \div a$ (b) Any of form $a + -a$

(c) One at least is 0

5 (a) (i) 15, 18   (ii) 14, 17   (iii) 19, 23

(b) (i) $3n$ (ii) $3n - 1$ (iii) $4n - 1$

(c) 33rd and 25th; 99 is a multiple of 3 whereas $3n - 1$ is one less

6 (a) $6x^2 + 15x$ (b) $v = 35$ (c) $t = \dfrac{v - u}{a}$

7 (a)

x	-2	-1	0	1	2
y	9	6	5	6	9

(b) Some non-integer values are needed for a good curve

(c) $x = -1.4$ and $x = 1.4$

8 10.3 m

9 $p = 128°$; $q = 52°$

10 (b) $\frac{35}{144}$ (c) $\frac{37}{72}$

COURSE REVISION EXERCISE 5

1 (a) (i) 60%   (ii) $\frac{3}{20}$

(b) 60 men

2 (a) 5 300 000

(b) (i) 3.5×10^7 (ii) 6.34×10^{-4}

3 (a) 5

(b) (i) 0.5   (ii) 50

4 (a) $60 \times 10 \div 150 = 4$

(b) SA > 5 m^2, so, no

5 (a) 10   (b) 54   (c) $\frac{c}{3} + 1$

6 (a) $(-1, -4)$ does not fit; $(-1, -2)$ would

(b) Gradient 3

(c) $y = 3x + 1$

7 (a) (i) a^4 (ii) $4x - 3$ (iii) $50t^3$

(b) $(x - 4)(x + 3) = 0$, so $x = -3$ or $x = 4$

8 (b) $x = 5$, $y = 2$

(c) Half turn about (5, 2)

(d) $(-1, 3)$, $(-1, 6)$, $(-2, 5)$

(e) Reflect in $x = 2.5$

(f) Many possibilities: e.g. reflect E in y-axis; then reflect E and its image in $y = 2$

9 (a) 36°   (b) 67.5°

10 (a) 8 blue cubes

(b) 37 or 38 times

COURSE REVISION EXERCISE 6

1 (a) 9 litres   (b) 14 litres

2 £700

3 7.4×10^7 years

4

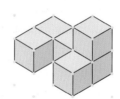

5 (a) 29°   (b) 10.2 metres

6 (a) 17 sticks   (b) 41 sticks

(c) $s = 2n + 1$ (d) Pattern 37

7 (a) (i) $7x + 20$ (ii) $54y^5$

(b) $x = -2$; $y = 5$

8 (a) BE is 4.6 cm; AE is 5.4 cm

(b) 4.6 cm

(c) 31 cm^2

9 (a) $(x + 5)(x - 3)$

(b) $x = -5$ or $x = 3$

10 (a) £10 872

(b) £6000 to £8400

(c) £6000 to £8400

(d) (i) Mode or median

(ii) Mean

INDEX

accurate drawing 225, 243
adding
  fractions 5, 19, 182
  negative numbers 173
adjacent angles on
  a straight line 227
alternate angles 227
angle(s)
  adjacent 227
  alternate 227
  around a point 227
  bisectors 243
  corresponding 227
  exterior 231
  exterior angle property
    of a triangle 43, 229
  in a semicircle 152, 154
  interior 231
  of depression 236
  of elevation 236
  on a straight line 227
  sum of the angles of a
    polygon 231
  vertically opposite 227
area
  of a circle 249
  of a parallelogram 247
  of a triangle 247
  of a trapezium 92, 101, 247
  see also surface area

balancing, solving
  equations by 211
bar chart 259
bearings 95, 101, 234
bisector
  angle 243
  perpendicular 243
bounds, upper and
  lower 90, 100, 246
brackets
  one 43, 208
  two 45, 49, 208
calculator, use of 4, 188

capacity 244
changing the subject
  of a formula 41, 49, 210
circle(s)
  arc 149, 154
  area 249
  chord 149, 154, 249
  circumference 249
  locus of a point 242
  tangent 149, 154, 249
circumference of a circle 249
comparing amounts, as
  percentages 183
congruence, congruent shapes
  35, 226
conversion graphs 197
correlation 63, 72, 263
corresponding angles 227
cosine (cos) 97, 101, 236
cuboid, surface area of 250
cumulative frequency
  diagrams 59, 71, 268
cylinder
  surface area 251
  volume 87, 251

data
  different types of 257
  representing data
    259, 261, 263
decimals
  changing decimals
    to percentages 171
  changing percentages
    to decimals 171
  decimal places 170
  dividing 180
  equivalence between
    fractions and decimals 171
  multiplying 2, 180
  ordering 169
  recurring 7, 19
density 87, 100, 245
diagonals of quadrilaterals 229

depression, angle of 236
differences, table of 193, 195
dimensions of
  formulae 84, 100, 253
direct proportion 15, 20, 185
dividing
  fractions 5, 19, 182
  negative numbers 173
division, proportional 185

edges 223
elevation, angle of 236
enlargements 32, 40, 238
equally likely outcomes 66, 270
equations
  of graphs of straight
    lines 200
  linear equations, forming
    and solving 74, 211
  linear equations with
    fractions 74, 82, 211
  quadratic equations
    79, 83, 216
  simultaneous equations
    75, 83, 104, 128, 217
  solving by balancing 211
  solving by doing and
    undoing 211
  using graphs 102, 130, 218
  using trial and improvement
    114, 215
estimating
  calculations 4, 18, 189
  means of grouped
    frequency distribution 266
  probability using
    experimental results 271
evaluating formulae 206
experimental results,
  estimating probability 271
exterior angles 231
exterior angle property
  of a triangle 229

faces 223
factorising
  common factors 44, 49, 209
  difference of two
    squares 47, 49, 209
  quadratic expressions
    48, 49, 209
  to solve quadratic
    equations 79, 83, 216
see also factorising
factors 175
formulae
  constructing 192, 206
  distinguishing by
    dimensions 84, 100, 253
  evaluating 206
  finding formulae for
    sequences 193, 195
  rearranging 41, 49, 210
  simplifying 207, 208
fractions
  adding 5, 19, 182
  changing to percentages 171
  dividing 5, 19, 182
  equivalence between fractions
    and decimals 7, 19, 171
  multiplying 5, 19, 182
  subtracting 5, 19, 182
frequency distribution
  mean of 266
  grouped, mean of 266
frequency polygon 259
functions 192

gradient 211
graphs
  gradient 211
  involving $1/x$ 110, 129, 203
  involving x^2 106, 128, 203
  involving x^3 109, 129, 203
  practical uses of 124, 131, 197
  straight line 104, 121, 200
  to solve equations
    102, 104, 114, 128, 130, 218
  $y = mx + c$ 200

histogram 259
hypotenuse 236

hypothesis 50, 65, 257

Imperial measures 244
increasing
  by a percentage 183
  repeated increase 183
indices, index notation 9, 20
inequalities 118, 131
interior angles 231
interquartile range 57, 71, 268
inverse operations 211
inverse proportion 17, 20, 185
isometric drawing 224

kite 229

length 244
line symmetry 136, 233
linear equations 74, 82, 211
locus, loci 242
long multiplication and
  division, strategies for 3, 179

maps and map scales 240
mass 244
mean
  of a frequency distribution
    54, 266
  of grouped frequency
    distribution 55, 70, 266
measures
  Imperial 244
  metric 244
  relationship between metric
    and Imperial units 244
  upper and lower bounds of
    90, 100, 246
median 54, 57, 70, 71, 265, 268
mental calculations 179
metric measures 245
mode, modal class 54, 70, 265
multiples 175
multiplying
  decimals 180
  expressions (one
    bracket) 43, 208
  expressions (two
    brackets) 45, 49, 208

fractions 5, 19, 182
  mentally 179
  negative numbers 173
negative numbers 173
nets 223

observation sheet 50, 258
operations, order of 187

parallel lines 227
parallelogram 229
  area 247
percentages 172
  finding one number as a
    percentage of another
    3, 86, 100, 171
perpendicular 132, 243
pie chart 261
place value 1
polygons
  exterior angles 145, 154, 231
  frequency polygon 259
  interior angles 145, 231
  regular polygon 145, 154, 231
  sum of the angles
    of a polygon 145, 154, 231
powers 9, 20, 176
prime factors 175
prime numbers 175
prism
  triangular prism 223
  volume of a prism 251
probability
  calculating using equally likely
    outcomes 66, 270
  estimating using experimental
    results 271
  of more than one event
    66, 72, 273
  probability line 270
  relative frequency 271
  sample space diagrams
    66, 72, 273
  tree diagrams 68, 72, 273
proportion
  direct 15, 20, 185
  inverse 17, 20, 185

proportional division 185
pyramid 223
Pythagoras' theorem
142, 154, 235
Pythagorean triads 144

quadratic equations 79, 83, 216
quadrilateral 135, 229
quartiles, upper and
lower 57, 71, 268
questionnaire design 50, 258

range 265
ratio 185, 240
reciprocal 8, 19
recurring decimals 7, 19
reflections 21, 39, 238
regions 121, 131
regular polygon 231
relative frequency 271
representing data 259, 261, 263
right-angled triangle
142, 229, 235, 236
roots 9, 20, 176
rotational symmetry 135, 233
rotations 26, 40, 238
rounding 170
ruler-and-compass
constructions 132, 243

sampling 52, 258
sample space diagram 66, 72, 273

scale drawing 240
scales, in maps 240
scatter diagrams 63, 72, 263
sequences, finding formulae for
linear 193
quadratic 195
semicircle, angle in a 152, 154
shapes, solid 223
significant figures 170
similarity 35, 137, 154, 240
simplifying formulae 207
simultaneous equations
75, 83, 104, 128, 217
sine (sin) 97, 101, 236
solid shapes 223
speed 124, 197, 245
square numbers 175
square roots 235
square-based pyramid 223
standard form 11, 20
statistical investigation 257
straight lines, equations of 201
subject, changing the 41, 49
substituting in formulae 206
subtracting
fractions 5, 19, 182
negative numbers 173
surface area
of a cuboid 250
of a cylinder 251
of a prism 251
symmetry 136, 233

table of differences 193, 195
tangent (tan) 97, 101, 236
tangent of a circle 149, 154, 249
tetrahedron 223
transformations 21, 31, 39, 238
combining 37
translation 29, 40, 238
trapezium 92, 101, 229, 247
travel graphs 124, 131, 197
tree diagram 68, 72, 273
trial and improvement 114, 215
triangle
area 247
exterior angle property
142, 229
right-angled 142, 229, 235, 236
triangular prism 223
trigonometry 97, 101, 236
two-way tables 53

units, relationship between
metric and Imperial units 244

vectors 29, 40, 238
vertex, vertices 223
vertically opposite angles 227
volume
of a cuboid 88, 250
of a cylinder 87, 251
of a prism 251

weight 244